THE ROOTS
OF
HUMAN BEHAVIOR

THE ROOTS
OF
HUMAN BEHAVIOR

AN INTRODUCTION TO THE PSYCHOBIOLOGY
OF EARLY DEVELOPMENT

MYRON A. HOFER

Albert Einstein College of Medicine

W. H. FREEMAN AND COMPANY
San Francisco

Project Editor: Pearl C. Vapnek
Copyeditor: Julie Segedy
Designer: Sharon Helen Smith
Production Coordinator: Linda Jupiter
Illustration Coordinator: Audre W. Loverde
Compositor: Graphic Typesetting Service
Printer and Binder: The Maple-Vail Book Manufacturing Group

Figures 4-1, 4-2, 5-1, 5-2, 5-3, and 10-1 are from the book *A Child Is Born* by Lennart Nilsson. English translation copyright © 1966, 1977 by Dell Publishing Co., Inc. Originally published in Swedish under the title *Et Barn Blir Till* by Albert Bonniers Förlag. Copyright © 1965 by Albert Bonniers Förlag, Stockholm. Revised edition copyright © 1976 by Lennart Nilsson, Mirjam Furuhjelm, Axel Ingelman-Sundberg, Claes Wirsén. Used by permission of Delacorte Press/Seymour Lawrence.

Library of Congress Cataloging in Publication Data

Hofer, Myron A   1931–
   The roots of human behavior.

   (A Series of books in psychology)
   Includes bibliographies and index.
   1. Psychology, Physiological.   2. Human behavior.
3. Child psychology.   4. Psychobiology.   I. Title.
[DNLM: 1. Behavior.   2. Child development.   3. Human
development.   4. Psychophysiology.   WL 103 H697r]
QP360.H63   152   80-28377
ISBN 0-7167-1277-6
ISBN 0-7167-1278-4 (pbk.)

Printed in the United States of America

9 8 7 6 5 4 3 2 1

To Lynne

Contents

Preface ix

INTRODUCTION 1

Biology and Psychology 1

Levels of Biological Organization 2

Biology as History 4

Behavior as a Subject for Biological Study 5

PART I   THE NATURE OF BEHAVIOR 7

    1   Evolution 9

*The Expression of Genetic Potential
    Through Environmental Interactions 10*

Evolution of the Brain 12

*Neoteny and Other Parallels
    Between Evolution and Development 14*

*The Evolutionary Basis
    for the Goal-Directed Nature of Behavior 17*

*The Implications of Altruistic Behavior
    for the Evolution of Social Relationships 19*

    2   Basic Properties of Behavior 25

Activity 25

Receptivity 31

Integration 34

    3   The Organization of Behavior 41

The Behavior of a Single-Celled Organism 42

The Units of Behavior 46

Elementary Forms of Learning 49

Hierarchy in Brain and Behavior 52

States of Arousal, Motivation, and Emotion 54

Adaptive Behavior 60

Consciousness 67

PART II   FROM CELL TO PSYCHE 75

4   The Sperm and the Egg 77

Origins and Life History 77

The Great Sperm Lottery 79

The Behavior of Sperm 82

Female Selection Mechanisms 83

5   Prenatal Behavior 87

The Embryonic Period: Before 7 Weeks 88

The Early Fetal Period: 6–16 Weeks 90

A Functional Role for Early Fetal Behavior? 93

The First Discontinuity: 17–22 Weeks 97

*The Origins of State Organization and Rhythms
in Behavior: 24–32 Weeks 100*

*The Origins of Posture, Integrated Behavior,
and Facial Expression: 32–36 Weeks 105*

6   The Newborn 110

Birth 110

*The Organization of Sleep–Wake States
and Behavior 112*

Sensation and Response 117

Disappearing Behaviors 120

Affective Behaviors and States 123

Nursing 125

Individuality 127

7 From Biology to Psychology 131

Problem Solving 132

Imitation 136

The Acquisition of Mind 138

PART III INTERACTIONS AND ENVIRONMENTS 143

8 The Early History of the Neuron 147

Migration and Outgrowth 147

*The Role of Function in the Formation
of Nerve Networks 151*

*Interactions Shaping the Nature
of the Neuron 153*

9 Processes Modifying Brain Organization 157

Stimulation 157

Hormones 164

Nutrition 169

*Sensorimotor Interaction
with the Environment 172*

10 The Intrauterine Environment 179

Prenatal Maternal Experience 180

*The (Transuterine) Inheritance
of Acquired Characteristics 183*

*Pathways from the Outside World:
Sensory Influences 184*

The Placental Route 187

11 The Parent–Infant Relationship 193

Development of the Relationship 194

Developmental Impact of the Relationship 205

Regulation of Development 212

PART IV THE EMERGENCE OF THE CHILD 235

12 The Forces of Rapid Change 237

Early Learning and Cognition 239

*Infantile Amnesia and the Construction
    of Memories 243*

States of Arousal, Motivation, and Emotion 246

Neurobiological Maturation 250

Stages, Discontinuities, and Constraints 255

13 The Origins of Language 260

From Sounds to Speech 261

*Critical Periods and the Role
    of Experience 262*

Song Development in Birds as a Model 265

14 Play: The Cradle of Adult Behavior 272

Special Characteristics 272

Role in Development 273

Regulation 277

15 Early Sexual, Aggressive, and Parenting Behavior 281

Incomplete Differentiation of the Categories 282

Precursors of Adult Behaviors 282

Behavioral Differences Between the Sexes 286

SUMMARY AND PERSPECTIVE 299

*Basic Questions and a Framework
    for Answering Them 299*

Major Themes 301

A Developmental Perspective on Mind 306

Glossary 311
Index 325

Preface

The goal of this book is to provide a coherent view of the biological foundations of human behavior in early development, from the time the germ cells originate to the emergence of complex behavior in children. This early period spans levels of organization from the single motile cell to the emergent property of consciousness and contains within it the transition from biological to psychological realms. Although the focus of the book is on the human, principles learned from the study of other animals are used to illuminate those many areas for which we have no human data.

The first section presents a brief but comprehensive analysis of the biological nature and organization of behavior, drawing particularly on recent advances in evolutionary theory (including sociobiology), ethology, and the neurosciences. This understanding is then applied, in the second section, to the extensive series of changes in behavior as they unfold during human development from sperm and egg to newborn infant. The third section explores how behavior is shaped by interactions between the developing organism and its environments. The fourth section describes the continuing interplay of biological forces in the emergence of learning, memory, language, play, aggression, and sexual behavior.

I have written this book for people interested in learning about the new biology of behavior development, a field emerging under the name *developmental psychobiology*. Although a recent course in general biology would be helpful to the reader, it should not be necessary. A glossary is provided at the end of the book to give definitions of terms that may be unfamiliar or that are used with particular meanings. For those who want to go deeper into certain areas, I have included a list of further readings at the end of each chapter.

Some of the most important and difficult conceptual relationships in human behavior are raised with great clarity in early development: the relationship of biology to psychology, the nature of the interactions by which genetic and environmental influences shape behavior, the transitions between levels of organization in the causation of behavior, and the relevance of research on simpler animal systems to complex human behavior. One of the reasons for writing this book now is that new discoveries from several different disciplines have made it possible to create a framework for dealing with these perplexing issues. Thus, although the problems are far from solved, this book presents an orderly approach to their understanding. Bringing examples of well-studied behaviors in simpler animals together with descriptions of the behaviors of very early forms of human development serves to create a bridge between animal and human realms. By beginning with the transition between molecular and cellular levels and then tracing each subsequent step in the hierarchy of behavior organization, we gain a clarifying perspective on the relationship between inferences made in biological terms and inferred psychological processes. Developmental interactions that shape future behavior are introduced with relatively simple neurobiological examples, which are then used as models for understanding more complex behavioral interactions between organism and environment. An analysis of the actual processes involved undercuts the perennial gene-environment confusion. Throughout, the approach is that of natural history, but interwoven with experimental evidence on questions of *how* and *why*. Because this book crosses several different academic disciplines and many areas of research, I have selected only a few examples from the work of current investigators and have not dealt with the contributions of many great scientists of the past. Without these people, none of what follows would be possible, but a much longer and different kind of book would have been required to include them.

Knowledge about early developmental processes is basic to an understanding of mental health problems because so many of these conditions can be traced to disorders of development and because an understanding of the individual patient's life history is so useful in finding ways to help. Thus, the application of most of the information and ideas in this book will be relatively straightforward, but will be different for one reader than for another, depending on individual interests and approaches. I hope that implications of a more speculative sort will also be aroused, since study of our early origins should help us find new approaches to the unsolved problems of later years.

There are a number of people who have played vital roles in the genesis of this book. My children, Tim, Nina, and Andrew, undoubtedly inspired my interest in early development some years ago by their individual, sometimes baffling, and altogether wonderful progress through its various stages. My wife, Lynne, made the writing of the book bearable for us both through her humor, loving support, and perceptive questions. The sabbatical leave granted by Montefiore Hospital and Albert Einstein College of Medicine gave me the time necessary to develop my thoughts and integrate a great deal of information from different areas. The National Institute of Mental Health, through a Research Scientist Award and project grant support, has fostered the laboratory and field research that generated many of the questions and ideas that appear in the following chapters. I am especially indebted to my teachers and in particular to Herbert Weiner, who, through his example, collaboration, and long-standing friendship, opened my eyes to so many new ideas and areas of knowledge. Harold G. Wolff, Lawrence E. Hinkle, John W. Mason, Morton F. Reiser, and Ethel Tobach were crucial influences at turning points in my career that led to the interests reflected in this book. I owe a great deal to my colleagues and friends, in particular to Carl Wolff, Peter Penick, Daniel Stern, Howard Roffwarg, Sigurd Ackerman, William Grossman, Thomas Anders, Russell Gardner, Pauline Jirik-Babb, Phyllis Ackman, Stephen Brake, and Harry Shair. They have shaped my thinking over the years by the generous sharing of their thoughts and the generally tactful criticism of mine.

Richard Thompson, Peter Marler, Gilbert Gottlieb, Daniel Stern, and Lewis Lipsitt reviewed parts or all of the manuscript and gave specific suggestions for improvement, for which I am extremely grateful.

I would like to thank Norma Tan, who helped with library research and typed most of the first draft; Barbara Tuttle, Mildred Pleasant, and Roberta Wiener, who typed subsequent revisions; and Susan Brunelli, who proofread the final product. W. Hayward Rogers, of W. H. Freeman and Company, shepherded the book along during its early stages with enthusiasm and thoughtfulness. Julie Segedy made copyediting almost painless, and Pearl Vapnek has been a most helpful editor.

January 1981   Myron A. Hofer

THE ROOTS
OF
HUMAN BEHAVIOR

Introduction

Although human behavior is usually viewed in psychological terms, its origins are biological—not only on an evolutionary time scale, but during the early development of each of us. Somewhere in the transition from fetus to child, psychological concepts come to dominate our thinking about behavior, while the relative role of biological determinants becomes increasingly difficult to weigh and eventually the subject of heated controversy.

In this book I try to convey an understanding of behavior as a biological phenomenon and take a view of biology that encompasses behavior as a natural bridge to psychology. In order to explore basic questions about behavior and development, I have chosen examples that move across biological levels from molecules to the whole organism and across species from the bacterium to the human. These examples are used to clarify our thinking about human behavior and to point toward new concepts and hypotheses rather than to answer questions about human nature. By concentrating on early development, I can illustrate how biological events and forces shape behavior and thus provide the foundation on which human psychology is built. And by following human development forward into childhood, I will show how and when we are forced to move from biological to psychological concepts in order to deal with the increasingly complex aspects of behavior. The aim of this book is to show how some of the new findings and concepts in the biology of behavior development tend toward an eventual integration of the two fields.

BIOLOGY AND PSYCHOLOGY

The division of human behavior development into biological and psychological phases is, of course, not a natural one. In nature the two are on a continuum, as are physics and chemistry and biology. But we have a great deal more trouble thinking of biology and psychology as being on a single continuum. This difficulty goes back to our language, which developed in an era of deep religious belief and therefore draws a clear distinction between the spiritual and the physical. The word *psyche* means breath in Greek, the breath of life that was thought to endow the body (*soma*) with activity. The spirit or mind has continued to be sharply distinguished in our language from the body and its physical processes. The available words thus tend to imprison us in a series of mutually exclusive conceptual categories: psyche–soma, soul–body, mental–physical, psychological–biological.

A middle ground can be found between biology and psychology in the study of behavior, which is at once a physical event and a manifestation of inferred mental processes. Some kinds of behavior can be understood in terms of the functioning of biochemical processes within cells, whereas other kinds of behavior cannot. More complex kinds of behavior force us to infer processes such as "imitation," "associative learning," "social attachment," and so forth, which we call psychological processes. In the past decade or two, the study of behavior has begun to narrow the gap between the realms of biology and psychology. Behavioral phenomena such as learning and memory in simple organisms are beginning to be understandable in terms of biological processes within nerve cells, while psychological concepts such as "choice" and "discrimination" are being used by biologists to organize and describe behavior at the level of systems of cells, and even in the single-celled bacterium. An understanding of evolutionary processes and of self-regulating biological systems has given us a way to conceive of purpose in nature without resorting to inferred cosmic or psychic force.

But it is not clear how far this process of integration can be extended. The phenomenon of consciousness and the world of inner experience may be separated from biological processes by more than a semantic gap. Not only do we use different vocabulary in speaking of inner experience, but the "behavior" of thoughts, images, and memories seems to obey a different set of rules than does overt behavior. Furthermore, we have no satisfactory idea of how the inner experiences that characterize consciousness derive from the biological processes of brain function. The essence of the problem of consciousness is beyond either psychology or biology at present; even the philosophers have trouble with it.

LEVELS OF BIOLOGICAL ORGANIZATION

Implied in the idea that we can trace the origins of our behavior back to the germ cells of our parents is the concept of levels of biological organization. In the way that the behavior of nations is to be understood in part on the basis of the behavior of individual people, so the behavior of cells may be understood in part on the basis of the behavior of molecules acting in chemical processes within the cell. The concepts and words we use to describe the behavior of individual people in a society are different from those we use to deal with international politics, yet we can see the ways in which the level of the individual is related to the level of nations. New concepts are necessary at each level to deal with the fact that the component parts are organized to interact and so create new behaviors to be understood. For example, we can learn everything there is to know about the way in which the muscles of the heart cause it to act as a pump, but this will not be sufficient to explain its behavior during exercise or congestive heart failure. For the heart is part of a higher level of organization—the organism—and is regulated, along with blood-vessel diameter and fluid volume, according to principles of regulation at this level.

Thus, in the biology of behavior we have four main levels to deal with: the molecule, the cell, the organ, and the organism. Studies in the past few years at the level of the individual nerve cell and of the chemical processes within cells have been helpful in giving us an understanding of behavior at the organismic level; I will be moving back and forth across these levels throughout most of this book. The problem in moving from one level to another, however, is that the processes are different at each level. But the higher-level processes are built up out of processes at the next lower level of organization. We are familiar with the idea that the whole is not *identical* to the *sum* of its parts, but the whole should be *explicable* in terms of the *organization* of its parts. That is what we try to do when we move from one level of organization to the next in order to get a better understanding of behavior. For example, it is illuminating to discover that when a person flinches from contact with a hot stove, a sensory cell in the brain relays its message to the motor cell by releasing molecules that act as chemical messengers. These in turn are bound to specific receptors on the membrane of the motor cell across a short space, the *synaptic cleft*. This example involves all four levels of organization. The behavior of the cell membrane, for example, can be understood in terms of the behavior of the complex protein and lipid molecules of which it is composed. This approach works fairly well until we reach the level of more complex behaviors. Whereas a simple reflex act can be understood in terms of the workings of an organized assemblage of cells, a child sorting novel objects into categories cannot. When confronted with complex behaviors, we have to state that they cannot be understood in terms of known processes and then go on to invent imaginary processes that can help in ordering the evidence, in making predictions, and in clarifying our thinking. This is how we arrive at psychological concepts. But we must not lose sight of the fact that these inferred processes do not describe actual events in the brain. What is responsible for the many schools of thought in the field of psychology is that different people derive these inferred processes from very different sources. Biologists work with the processes they know and understand, and many psychologists also use biological processes as conceptual building blocks. Some psychologists use other models and metaphors. However, the two most comprehensive current human psychological theories were invented by men who began as biologists: Freud and Piaget. There is much biological thinking in both their theories, and they both acknowledge an indebtedness to their biological training. It seems likely that future advances in psychology will be based on the new advances in the biology of behavior that have taken place in recent years.

The inferring of psychological processes and the ordering of our thinking and observation along these lines is not, of course, unique to psychology. All scientists do this as a step toward further study and as a means of exploration. Therefore, the methods of the biologist and the psychologist are not really different, and there is hope that a common language will slowly develop and a conceptual integration become possible. For the present, we can come closest to this goal in dealing with the simpler behaviors of early development.

BIOLOGY AS HISTORY

We are all familiar with the forces of historical change in human affairs, but it is not so generally appreciated that history is an essential element in biology. There are two great forces that give biology its historical quality: development and evolution. This book is concerned primarily with development. History is a good analogy for the processes of development because historical processes are known to involve complex interactions over time and cannot be reduced to simple notions of cause and effect. Likewise, behavior develops neither by the action of genes nor experience alone. Development is the history of how the organism interacts with its environment and is thereby changed so that its next interaction differs. Genes act only at the molecular level. Development, however, goes on at all levels of organization, and it is interesting to follow how the nerve cell interacts with its environment as it moves and grows its long interweaving extensions to form the brain (Chapter 8).

The second way in which the historical nature of biology has implications for the understanding of behavior is in the evolutionary relationship between the human primate and other animals. Information about the behavior of other species can never be used to *settle* questions about human behavior. But historically we are closely related to other species, and we share their problems, even if we do not always share their solutions. For example, by learning how other mammals solve the problem of reproduction and the raising of young, we have not answered these questions about the behaviors in humans. But we will have learned about new processes that may provide a partial understanding of the human situation and new concepts that allow us to reorder our thinking about human behavior. The useful products of any research are ideas and methods. Whether ideas gained from studying rats are useful in understanding the behavior of mice or men can only be settled by testing them out. So basic research in one species generates new questions, new ideas, and new methods for research in other species, including our own.

The beauty of animal behavior lies in the unity of nature. Evolution has been a conservative force, using the same biological processes again and again. Thus, for example, our brain is not a new creation, but uses the plan for the brain of the reptile and the brain of a primitive mammal as a foundation upon which is added—like an additional level of a building—the large, integrating system of our cerebral cortex. The nerve cells of marine invertebrates and of humans are of the same design; they even use the same chemicals for neurotransmitters. This unity in the basic design for nervous systems throughout nature makes it likely that what we learn from animal behavior will be useful in some way toward understanding human behavior.

BEHAVIOR AS A SUBJECT
FOR BIOLOGICAL STUDY

It is as difficult to find a beginning and an end to a behavioral event as a historical one. The flow of behavior is continuous, and each act depends on preceding events and leaves consequences for the future. However, biological studies at the cellular level have recently given us evidence for two basic units of behavior: the reflex act and the fixed-action pattern. Descriptive studies under natural conditions have helped to develop methods for distinguishing larger behavioral sequences made up of these units according to the *form* or spatiotemporal characteristics of the actions involved and according to the *consequences* of the sequence of actions. Some behaviors resemble each other in formal characteristics but may have widely different consequences, depending on the context in which they occur: for example, raising one's arm in greeting, in anger, or in sleep. Conversely, behaviors may be very different in appearance, timing, and pattern, yet result in the same consequence, as in courtship.

Behavior can be described in both these ways, but its essence in *biological* terms lies in how it is organized to serve the adaptive purposes of the organism. Specific behaviors evolved in animals to allow them to adapt better to their environment, both living and nonliving. This principle allows us to classify behaviors and forms the basis for our understanding of the *organization* of behavior (Chapter 3).

Until recently, behavior has been left out of many introductory biology courses and textbooks, and is still left out of nearly all textbooks on embryology, even though the behavior of embryos is a general phenomenon across animal species. Why has behavior been neglected by biologists, despite their commitment to the concept of adaptation to the environment and the obvious primary role of behavior in facilitating this adaptation? The reasons for these omissions go back to the issues discussed above: the compartmentalization forced on us by our language and by our academic traditions, the difficulties in classifying and ordering observations of behavior, and finally, our vast ignorance of the workings of the nervous system.

On the other hand, biology has been relatively neglected by human psychologists because it was viewed as rigid, mechanical, and not "dynamic" enough to deal with the ever-changing nature of behavior. Also, the nature of known biological processes seemed to remove the self from control of its own behavior—a frightening idea. Recently our understanding of biological processes has grown enormously, and new concepts have arisen that are flexible and interesting enough to be applied successfully, at least to simple behaviors. It is still impossible to fit the existing language and concepts of biology to more complex behaviors or to the realm of inner experience. But in the earliest phases of human development, a coherent story can be told and the data from experimental studies on simpler animals can be reasonably applied to illuminate the origins of our own behavior.

Part I
THE NATURE
OF BEHAVIOR

Since it is only by comparing that we can judge, since our knowledge rests entirely on the relations that things have with others that are similar or different, and since, if there were no animals, the nature of man would be even more incomprehensible, after considering man in and of himself, shouldn't we employ the comparative method? Isn't it necessary to examine the nature of animals, compare their structures, study the animal kingdom in general, in order to . . . arrive at the capital science of which man himself is the object?—George Louis Buffon, Histoire Naturelle de L'Homme, *1749*

This appeal for a comparative method in the study of human nature antedated Darwin by a century and is yet to be fulfilled. But we are in a much stronger position now in our search for a biological perspective on human behavior. This section of the book begins with the role of evolutionary processes in shaping the form of our behavior and providing its function or purpose in ways that are common to humans and other animals. Theories on the evolution of behavior have advanced recently to the point where they can deal with altruistic behavior and some other complex human activities previously thought to have been created by human culture. Sociobiology, the discipline that arose around these theories, has generated much resistance and controversy. When new knowledge about the developmental determinants of the expression of genetic potential is integrated with evolutionary theory, much of this controversy will eventually subside.

The *ultimate* origins of our behavior are evolutionary, but the more *immediate* determinants are to be understood in terms of the basic properties and organization of behavior, as they can be discerned across a wide spectrum of the natural world. By looking at levels of biological organization, ranging from enzymes to consciousness, we

7

can distill certain central themes that may give us a firmer grasp on the nature of behavior than if we simply look at ourselves. The second chapter in this section outlines the basic properties of behavior: activity, receptivity, and integration. The third chapter considers the units and processes that express these properties and how they are organized to work together in the production of adaptive behavior. Although consciousness remains essentially mysterious, a certain perspective can be gained from viewing it as an outgrowth of the increasingly complex organization of behavior across the phylogenetic scale.

1
Evolution

It is still extraordinarily difficult for us to accept the fact that our behavior and even our minds are the products of biological evolution. Darwin himself shrank back at first from the full implication of his theory for human behavior in the *Origin of Species* (1859): "I must premise that I have nothing to do with the origin of the primary mental powers . . . only with the diversities of instinct and of the other mental qualities of animals within the same class" (p. 234). He was in conflict within himself on this issue and afraid of the social consequences of his own philosophical materialism. In addition to the issue of the spiritual and special "mental qualities" of humans, he struggled with another problem: where to draw the line between behaviors that seemed to be acquired only through experience, which he called "habits," and those that were acquired through inheritance, which he termed "instincts." Darwin wrote: "An action which we ourselves should require experience in order to perform, when performed by an animal, more especially by a very young one without any experience . . . is usually said to be instinctive" (p. 234).

These quotations suggest two possible reservations in the application of Darwin's theory of evolution to human nature: first, that humans are endowed with qualities of mind that transcend the biological processes of evolution and, second, that human behavior is fundamentally different from animal behavior—being learned, rather than inherited. From Darwin's early notebooks, written 20 years before the publication of the *Origin of Species*, and from his later works, it is clear that he did not himself subscribe to these reservations. But his initial caution in expressing himself publicly was apparently well founded, for these reservations are still with us today and provide much of the heat for the current controversy over sociobiology (the extension of evolutionary principles to the understanding of the social behavior of humans and other animals).

THE EXPRESSION OF GENETIC POTENTIAL
THROUGH ENVIRONMENTAL INTERACTIONS

An important source of argument both in Darwin's time and today is the mistaken view that behavior is divisible into two distinct categories: those behaviors that have been acquired by experience and those that have been inherited. This approach leads to sterile controversy over which behaviors in which species belong in each of these two categories. Endless arguments ensue over which human behaviors are "innate" and which "acquired" or, to phrase it differently, which are "genetically determined" and which are "products of the environment."

It is difficult to understand why this mistake persists, despite all we have learned in the last 120 years about the biological processes of genetics and development. It is abundantly clear that *all* behavior has a genetic basis that can, however, be expressed only through interaction with the environment during development. This is as true for structural development as it is for behavior, the difference being that environmental influences are far less obvious in the development of structure than of behavior. For instance, it is not generally appreciated that the amount of dark fur on the feet and nose of Siamese cats depends on the ambient temperature in which they are raised as kittens, the skin on the extremities being normally cooler than other skin areas. The expression of this genetic predisposition depends on the temperature of the skin during a critical period of postnatal development. Raised in an incubator, Siamese cats turn out uniformly light, and if in an icebox, uniformly dark. In another example (1), American lobsters grown in smooth-bottomed tanks during certain larval stages were found to grow up with two cutter claws instead of one crusher and one cutter claw. The presence of crushed oyster shells or small rocks during that period enables the genes for the crusher claw to express themselves.

These are two examples of environmental interaction in structural development at the level of the whole organism. Many other examples have been studied at the level of the cells and of the molecular mechanisms within the individual cell. Genes consist of segments of a complex molecule, DNA, within the nucleus of the cell; they function like a mold to make smaller molecules, RNA, by a process known as *transcription*. These "messenger" and "transfer" RNA molecules then act to organize the assembly of protein molecules by structures within the cell known as "ribosomes." Thus the gene's action is simply to provide a template for the manufacture of proteins within the cell. Obviously there are a large number of steps that must intervene between the action of the gene and the final structure of the organ; even more steps between the gene and a function such as behavior. At each of these steps, environmental interactions take place that are critical in determining the final shape of the organ or behavior. Even at the first step, the action of neighboring genes plays a role, so that one gene can be turned on or off by a second, regulator gene. Best estimates are that less than 10 percent of the genes in a typical mammalian cell are actually used in the course of the individual's life, so that one's genetic endowment has a vast unexpressed potential. It is the degree of constancy of the environment from the level of cells to cultures that allows the influence of the genes to become apparent.

Thus, genes do not in themselves determine either structure or behavior. Their influence is detectable only in the form of *differences* between individuals in a given structure or behavior, when environmental interactions are identical for both individuals. If the individuals are raised in a new environment, the genetic difference may not express itself in the same way, and no difference or a difference in another direction or quality may result.

When we deal with the development of behavior, the role of environmental interaction is a great deal more obvious than it is for structure, and is not limited to the kinds of environmental interactions that Darwin saw as producing "habits" and that we call learning. Many other kinds of interactions occur, at all levels of biological organization—from the whole child down to the cell and its molecular mechanisms—and at all stages of development—from old age back to the sperm and the egg. These interactions constitute the processes by which genetic potential is expressed and by which environmental influences are exerted. We are only beginning to understand some of these developmental processes, and already it is clear that they exist in extraordinary variety. Only in working out the individual processes in each case can we say something meaningful about the relative contribution of gene and environment to the development of a behavior. For a gene may exert its effect, for example, by increasing the susceptibility of an individual child to certain aspects of its relationship with its mother. With a different sort of mothering, an entirely different behavior may emerge. Is this a case of predominant genetic or environmental determination? Ginsberg has shown that the susceptibility to certain environmental influences is, in fact, a trait that can have a genetic basis, with some strains of mice being environmentally buffered or "stable," and others, environmentally "labile."

The neural systems necessary for learning, memory, imitation, and even for the more complex functions of language and thought were made possible by natural selection working upon genetic variation and taking place within the environment in which we evolved. It is in this sense that all behavior has a genetic basis, even if the genes have "chosen" to delegate much of the work to environmental interaction, to social relationships, and even to experiences that are part of an enduring culture. This fact enables us to look to the processes of evolution for answers to basic questions about the ultimate causes or origins of our behavior.

EVOLUTION OF THE BRAIN

Evidence for the descent of humans from a common ancestor that we share with the modern-day apes is, of course, based on fossilized remains of skeletons and dates back about 15 million years. Beyond this, the ancestor that we have in common with all primates lived 70 million years ago, and the one that we share with all mammals and reptiles lived more than 300 million years ago. Over all this time and through all the evolutionary changes, the basic skeleton and body plan was retained, as was the general overall plan of the nervous system, with the major part of its central mass lying protected within the bony case of the skull and vertebral column. It is not too surprising, then, to find the basic plan of the reptile brain within the human brain today. Natural selection is a conservative process and creates change by adding features and by minor revision rather than by major redesign.

What has happened, apparently, is that evolution has added enormously to the basic reptilian brain so that the most recently evolved mammals have the highest ratio of brain size to body size. Furthermore, this relative increase in mass has not been distributed equally throughout the brain. Almost all the added mass has been to the structures that are on top of, or in front of, the rest of the nervous system: the limbic system and the neocortex in particular. (One exception is the olfactory bulb, which also is positioned at the top end of the nervous system, but has progressed the least in size in the most recently evolved primates.) The layering of new brain on top of old brain, as you can see in Figure 1–1, is possible because all the neural machinery for basic life-sustaining behaviors is present in the basal brain areas, whose plan we share with modern-day reptiles and which has probably remained relatively unchanged since the days of our common ancestor.

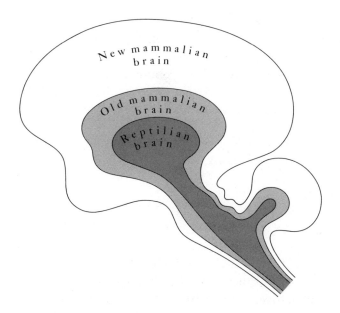

FIGURE 1-1
The hierarchical organization of the three basic brain types, which in evolution of the mammalian brain became a part of our inheritance. (After P. D. MacLean, "The Triune Brain, Emotion and Scientific Bias." In F. O. Schmitt, Ed., *The Neurosciences: Second Study Program*. New York: Rockefeller University Press, 1970.)

Thus, evolution has superimposed a hierarchy of more sophisticated control systems on top of the basic neural machinery for living. The first addition is the area of our brain that mediates our emotions, the *limbic system*, and is referred to by MacLean (1970) as the "old mammalian brain," while the more recent addition, the "new brain," contributes the possibility of language, reason, and the higher mental faculties. MacLean has dubbed this arrangement of ours the "triune brain," and likens it to a single chassis with three drivers. Pursuing his analogy, he suggests that a patient lying on a psychoanalyst's couch brings into treatment, in addition to himself, two others: an anteater and a crocodile.

A serious implication of how our nervous system seems to have evolved is that we share many of the neural mechanisms for behavior with other mammals, with birds, and even with reptiles, whose nervous systems have not changed as much as ours since the time of our common ancestors. It is this similarity in the general plan of nervous systems that allows us to generalize at all from studies on other animals to human behavior.

Although I have emphasized the overall similarity that forms the basis for the relevance of animal studies to human behavior, the differences should also be recognized. Other animals have also evolved appreciably since the days of our common ancestors millions of years ago. Considering the distance that evolution has put between species, we must be careful how we use information about the biology of behavior in other species to interpret our own behavior. Specific examples of such a comparative approach to the understanding of behavior will appear throughout this book.

NEOTENY AND OTHER PARALLELS
BETWEEN EVOLUTION AND DEVELOPMENT

The question of the essential differences between humans and other primates has been argued vociferously for more than a century. How did we come to diverge so far from other primates in the course of our evolution? There is general agreement that the size and special capacities of our brain have given us a number of competitive advantages to account for our present dominance over other living beings. We did not simply acquire a large cranium as a feature added onto a typical primate frame; we evolved, for example, smaller facial features (particularly in the jaws), a skull mounted directly on top of our backbone, unrotated great toes, and much reduced body hair. These and some other features distinguish us most clearly from our genetically close relatives among the great apes. But these are not simply a "laundry list" of features; there is a unifying theme that applies to all of these critical differences: they are found in other primates during their infancy. That is, a human adult resembles most closely a chimpanzee that has not grown up (see Figure 1–2). The word "neoteny" is used to convey the notion of holding onto features of infancy. Such a proposition is strengthened by the fact that humans have a very slow schedule of development compared to other primates. Human babies do not close the bones of the skull fully until adulthood, and many of our systems continue to grow for years after they have ceased in other primates. This general retardation of development seems to have resulted in a reduction of the final extent of developmental change in certain physical features. For example, the skulls of juvenile and adult orangutans are grossly different in shape, whereas the changes are much less pronounced between the human infant and adult skulls (see again Figure 1–2).

(b)

(a)

FIGURE 1-2
Infant and adult chimpanzees, showing how much more closely the infant (*a*) resembles a human being than the adult chimpanzee (*b*). (From A. Naef, "Uber die Urformen der Anthropomorphen," *Naturwissenschaften*, 14:445–452, 1926.)

The potential usefulness of such physical characteristics is not difficult to surmise. A long period of immaturity allows the maximal amount of time for the individual to adapt both physically and behaviorally to a changing environment, since immature organs are far more malleable than fully mature ones. The retention of the infant's large cranium and its high frontal vault have facilitated the expansion of the human neocortex upon the basic mammalian plan as described above. The human brain, greatly enlarged in size and slow in maturing, is thus doubly suited to developing sophisticated behavioral capacities on the basis of its lengthy experience.

The beauty of this theory is that it requires only a few key genetic mutations in order to accomplish a great deal of structural and functional change during recent evolutionary time. Genetic information for a whole new set of structures need not be provided, only an alteration in the regulation of *rates* of development. For example, the chimpanzee and the human are identical in more than 99 percent of their genetic material (2), but are far from identical in appearance, behavior, or mental capacities. This apparent paradox can best be explained by the theory that, although we are identical in structural genes, a few key "regulator" genes account for the differences by their capacity to alter the timing of development and thus to displace stages of development in certain organ systems.

Phylogenetic history is filled with examples of new species created by the process of displacement within developmental schedules. The juvenile stage of an ancestor shellfish or reptile may be displaced forward in the developmental sequence of the descendants, as we have described above for several features of the human primate. This is known as *paedomorphosis*. In an even greater number of cases the reverse seems to have occurred: the adult stages of the ancestors seem to have shifted progressively to earlier developmental stages of the descendents. This accelerated schedule results in the early development of a present-day individual repeating or "recapitulating" the adult stages of its evolutionary forebears. Recognition of this second form of displacement gave rise to the phrase that still bewilders high-school biology students: "ontogeny recapitulates phylogeny."

The concept of recapitulation dazzled biologists of the late nineteenth and early twentieth centuries, since it placed the adult human so literally at the peak of a heartening progressive trend in evolution. The concept of recapitulation was also extremely useful to psychologists of the early part of this century. For Freud: ". . . those whom we describe as savages . . . must have a pecular interest for us, if we are right in seeing in [them] a well-preserved picture of the early stages of our own development" (3). And for Jung: "The child lives in a prerational world, the world of men who existed before us. Our roots lie in that world and every child grows from those roots. Maturity bears him away from his roots and immaturity binds him to them" (4).

We now know that the parallel between infant and savage minds is far from perfect and that differences between civilized and uncivilized adults is largely cultural. We also know that evolution can work through a retardation of development, resulting in neoteny, as well as through the acceleration that underlies recapitulation.

Many examples of both forms of "evolution-by-displacement" can be found in the fossil record, and human evolution has no doubt been made possible by an interweaving of displacements involving both acceleration and retardation. The modern synthesis of this evidence has been set forth by Gould (1977b). The concept of *mosaic evolution* allows that organs evolve in different ways to meet varying selection pressures. The schedules for the development of different organs each have a genetically programmed clock regulating the size, shape, and functioning of the organ relative to the age of the individual throughout development. Genetic change need act only to accelerate or retard the clock in one or another organ in order to produce enormous diversity of species. This "heterochrony" in development underlies the parallel between the development of the individual and the evolution of the species, between ontogeny and phylogeny.

THE EVOLUTIONARY BASIS
FOR THE GOAL-DIRECTED NATURE OF BEHAVIOR

Natural selection has favored the survival of an incredibly wide variety of species. In animals, behavior has evolved because it has added significantly to the capacity of animals to adapt to their environments. It is behavior that determines the position of species in the food chain, and it is the complexity and adaptability of our behavior that have put us at the top of this food chain in so many different environments over the surface of the earth. In Darwin's words: "It will be universally admitted that instincts are as important as corporeal structure for the welfare of each species . . . . I can see no difficulty in natural selection preserving and continually accumulating variations of instinct to any extent that may be profitable" (p. 236).

Many breeding experiments have shown that the capacity for learning—and even the particular capacity for learning *certain* behaviors—can be selectively increased across generations and inherited by offspring. This does not mean that "it is all in the genes," for nothing will be learned if specific learning experience is not given, and even the potential may not be expressed if the early rearing environment is altered beyond a certain point. For example, rats can be selectively bred for learning a certain type of maze so that after several generations, subgroups of "maze bright" and "maze dull" rats are produced that are much further apart on this characteristic than their ancestors in the first generation of selection. Yet if representatives of both these different subgroups are raised alone in single cages with little environmental stimulation, the difference in performance between the two groups is almost entirely abolished, both groups performing in the "dull" range (5).

Evolution, like selective breeding, depends on the existence of variation between individuals, for without variability, natural selection could not operate. Furthermore, the variation between individuals must reflect differences in genetic characteristics for the selection to result in changes that are transmitted across generations. The success of animal breeding techniques based on behavior of adults (for example, in the creation of various types of hunting dogs and pets) demonstrates how much naturally occurring variation between individuals in this species indeed has a genetic basis. The reason that sexual reproduction is so widely present in nature is that it allows a new recombination of genes with each generation. And since the particular combination itself determines whether a gene is expressed (e.g., dominant) or stored (e.g., recessive) or modified (e.g., polygenic), this recombination results in a high degree of genetically-based variation in behavior for selection pressures to work upon.

If the environment is so important in genetic expression, a good deal of the existing variation between individuals must be the result of individual differences in environment at some level and phase of development. This has also been demonstrated by Ginsberg's studies on highly inbred strains of mice that have become virtually identical twins in genetic terms. In some strains there was considerable individual variability in behavioral and structural characteristics, and selection for such characteristics by selective breeding had none of the effects previously described for normally heterogeneous genetic populations. This is because the variation between individuals was due to the action of slight variations in environment during development.

Thus, in behavior as in structure, the same adult form may be the result primarily of genetic or environmental variation, and variations in adult form are likely to reflect major differences in genetic makeup, environmental experience, or both, as is most often the case.

For a genetically based variation in behavior to spread in a population, the behavior trait must increase the number of its genes represented in the next generation, at the expense of genes for other traits. A behavior trait can do this not only by (1) increasing the likelihood of an individual surviving to a reproductive age, but also by (2) increasing the reproductive capacity of the individual, and by (3) increasing the survival and reproductive capacity of relatives who share the same genes. There are many behavioral tactics by which each of these three strategic aims can be furthered. Indeed, the great variety of behaviors encountered in every species is a testimony to this fact. The selection of traits that have been successful in reaching these goals has given to behavior its goal-directed and purposeful nature. This characteristic is an important organizing principle for behavior and greatly helps in describing, classifying, and conceptualizing the processes by which behavior is mediated (see Chapter 3).

The "purposes" of behaviors can only be understood in terms of the environments in which the organism was living during the period when the behaviors were selected. Thus, the selection of a set of genes implies a prediction about the environment of the future and its demands. If the prediction is highly specific, the behavior can be rigidly programmed by the genes, but the organism will be suited only to relatively stable environments, as is found in the insects and invertebrates. If the prediction is to allow for a variety of possibilities and even for experiences never before encountered, then a great deal of susceptibility to shaping by environmental interaction must be made possible by the genes. This is the case for humans, other primates, and many species of highly adaptable mammals. In these species, different behavioral traits are unveiled by rearing in different environments, and the interaction of genetic predisposition and the experiences of the individual during development are most interesting.

Among the highly adaptable mammals, in addition to the opportunity for the shaping of behavior by the environment, evolution has selected individuals that are capable of a number of alternative, competing tactics for solving environmental challenges. This evolutionary trend has given us not only flexibility but also conflict: for most situations, we have more than one behavioral response available. In the absence of smooth processes of choice, we are prone to hesitation, alternation, and blocking of behavioral expression.

Thus, in summary, the genes that have been selected for us in the process of evolution are a series of hedged bets as to environments that may be encountered and the behavioral strategies that will be required to deal with them. The information is essentially historical—what has worked in the past—and contains numerous options that are the result of numerous different kinds of selection pressures at work during our long evolutionary history. The flexibility available in a system such as I have just described is enormous and reveals the phrase "biological determinism" to reflect a lack of understanding of how evolution has created human behavior. Not only does our genetic makeup contain hidden potential that awaits new environments to be expressed, but the behavioral capacities that we are predisposed to acquire also allow us different behavioral options at any moment in time.

THE IMPLICATIONS OF ALTRUISTIC BEHAVIOR FOR THE EVOLUTION OF SOCIAL RELATIONSHIPS

Until 15 years ago, the widespread presence of altruistic behavior could not be explained according to the principles of biological evolution. In fact, it was held as an example of the importance of culture in determining behavior and of the unique nature of humans. The discovery of an increasing number of examples of altruistic behavior in an ever-widening range of mammals and birds has gradually destroyed both the notion that altruistic behavior is unique to humans and that it is a special creation of civilization like the parliamentary system of government.

How then can a behavior be selected during evolution that may actually reduce an individual's chance of survival and interfere with its own reproductive success? The key lies in the last of the three major strategies of the genes given above: by increasing the survival and/or reproductive capacity of *relatives who share the same genes*. Of course genes do not have strategies, and people do not behave altruistically out of a careful calculation of the odds favoring the perpetuation of their genes. Rather, the genes that predispose to altruistic traits are preserved and spread within a population because individuals with identical genes have behaved so as to increase the probability of those genes surviving and replicating themselves. This principle implies that altruistic acts should occur most frequently between individuals that are closely related and thus most likely to share genes from common descent. It is believed that this principle accounts for the origin of the cooperative and aid-giving behavior that characterizes social organization in animals and humans. Such genes will spread within a community, even if the animal cannot distinguish degrees of relatedness, so long as members of the community can be distinguished from others and so long as the community is small enough to carry a high percentage of closely related individuals.

As J. B. S. Haldane, the great English biologist, once stated, "I would gladly lay down my life for two brothers or eight cousins." Hamilton extended this idea into a mathematical model for the "genetical evolution of social behavior," which first appeared in 1964 and provided the foundation for the new discipline of sociobiology. The relationship that he developed was between the frequency of the genetic basis for a behavioral trait in a population, the degree of genetic relationship between individuals, and the cost–benefit ratio of the behavior to each individual. He showed that a gene for a certain altruistic behavior will increase in a population if the coefficient of relationship between the actor and the recipient of the behavior is greater than the cost–benefit ratio. The cost and benefit in this equation are stated in terms of the likelihood of genes identical to the actors being preserved as a result of the behavior. This theory of "kin selection" thus predicts that a given altruistic behavior will be more frequently observed, the closer the genetic relationship between participants. For example, parents share half of their genes with their children, siblings have a 50 percent likelihood of sharing a given gene, half-brothers or half-sisters a 25 percent chance, and so forth. In certain insect societies, individuals may be identical genetically, and indeed this is where altruistic acts are the most widespread and compelling. Worker bees, for example, regularly sacrifice themselves in suicidal but lethal attacks on intruders.

Observations of behavior in social mammals, including humans, tend to follow the rules of kin selection if one takes into account the degree to which a human or an animal can accurately determine its genetic relatedness to another. This is at best an estimate and is most accurate between a mother and her offspring, less accurate between siblings or between a father and his offspring, for obvious reasons. Thus, the true genetic relatedness between brothers must be diluted by chance of error, in estimating the likelihood of altruistic behavior between siblings, and the same is true between fathers and offspring. Similarly, the age of the participants must be taken into account in coming to the cost–benefit estimates. This last point allows us to understand the greater degree of altruism exhibited by mothers toward offspring, than vice versa. For the potential benefit depends on the likelihood of the act perpetuating representative genes in the *next* generation, and this is far greater in an act by a mother toward her offspring than if the offspring acts altruistically toward its mother. The predominance of altruistic acts by mothers toward their offspring among mammals and birds is to be understood as a result of this kind of genetic selection process, and forms the basis for many parental influences on development that we will be considering later on.

Another form of altruistic behavior, reciprocal altruism, also may have a genetic basis, and certainly provides the "glue" for many social activities: as Dawkins puts it, "You scratch my back, I'll ride on yours" (p. 179). This behavioral strategy is one that apes and other higher mammals, in addition to humans, have evolved. The development of this behavior seems to depend on early social experience and may require opportunity for imitation and learning. It is the *predisposition* to learn this complex behavior that has evolved through genetic mechanisms.

It is important to note that the selection pressures favoring altruistic behavior come into conflict with selection pressures favoring "selfish" behaviors, which maximize survival of the individual. This kind of conflict is similar to that which exists between selection for reproductive success and for survival of the individual. For example, male animals and men may expend great energy and risk their lives in order to enhance their access to females.

Out of the three strategies of the genes comes a vast array of behavioral tendencies that are in conflict with each other. These goal-directed behavior traits can be considered as "games" and analyzed according to mathematical game theory. This theory allows us to understand more thoroughly and predict the relative frequency of various behavioral traits in populations under a variety of environmental "rules." It can be shown that individuals that are limited to one behavioral "game" in all situations can only exist as a small minority in any population and that the optimal strategy for an individual is to vary its initial game plans within a certain range. Out of this game-theory analysis of evolutionary selection pressures comes an understanding of the origins of the many different social behaviors potentially available to each individual and of the characteristic behavior patterns that distinguish individuals from each other.

Thus, through kin selection and the application of game theory to population genetics, the existence and nature of a great many complex social behaviors can be explained on the basis of biological evolution. Equally convincing explanations are possible using cultural evolution and social learning theory. It seems most likely that there is a "meshing" between the two kinds of evolutionary processes, with the older, biological form setting the stage and providing a predisposition for the development of many of the themes of human cultures.

SUMMARY

The implications of evolution for behavior have been extremely difficult for us to reconcile with our own vision of ourselves as unique, and are hotly debated even today. The source of much of this heat lies in the false dichotomy drawn so often between innate and acquired behaviors, and in mistakenly equating innate with animal, and acquired with human behavior. The concept of genetic potential, the nature of environmental interaction, and knowledge about the process of genetic expression through this interaction, has cut through sterile arguments about "nature" versus "nurture."

The human brain has evolved through a process of addition at the top while retaining the features of reptile and primitive mammal brains virtually intact underneath. This forms a structural basis for the many similarities between human behavior and that of other vertebrates.

The question of how we have diverged so far in appearance and higher mental capacity from our nearest primate relatives can be answered by the concept of *neoteny* (the persistence of infantile features into adulthood) and by new information on genes that regulate rates of development.

Evolution has been the main force responsible for giving behavior its goal-directed character and for allowing us to use the concept of purpose in attempting to understand how behavior is organized. The information stored in the genes has thus come to be historical information as to which characteristics have worked best in the past. Even the potential for the shaping of behavior by the environment in which the individual grows up has been selected because this characteristic increases the likelihood of that individual getting its genes more widely distributed in the next generation.

There are three ways in which behavior traits are selected by evolution: (1) by increasing individual survival to reproductive age; (2) by increasing the reproductive capacity of the individual; and (3) by increasing either or both these elements in other individuals that carry the same genes (usually close kin). The organization of behavior is ultimately to be understood, then, in terms of its enabling the individual to achieve one or another of these purposes. An unraveling of the mystery of altruistic behavior has been made possible through a realization of the implications of the third of these, "kin selection." In fact, a new view of all behavior, based on the strategies of the genes, has become known as *sociobiology*, a field with great potential whose limits and precise contributions have yet to be adequately tested.

The three major strategies of the genes give rise to a bewildering array of potential behaviors, each more or less useful depending on the environment or the likely response of other people.

If we accept the proposition that inner experience is in part a reflection of behavioral response potential, then the inner conflict that is characteristic of so much of human experience must be the legacy of these competing selection pressures. Similarly, the origin of the psychological processes that organize and mediate between these conflicting response tendencies must also lie in the long period of evolution we have undergone as an intensely social species.

Evolutionary explanations deal with the *ultimate* causation of behavior but do not tell us much about the here and the now—the *proximate* causes of behavior. The process of early development forms the bridge between our ancient past and the demands of the present. Only by knowing about development can we understand how the legacies of evolution become translated into the people we are.

FURTHER READING

Brown, J. L. *The Evolution of Behavior.* New York: Norton, 1975.
Darwin, C. *The Expression of the Emotions in Man and Animals.* 1872. Reprinted by University of Chicago Press, 1965.
Darwin, C. *The Origin of Species.* 1859. Reprinted by Penguin Books, 1968.
Dawkins, R. *The Selfish Gene.* New York: Oxford University Press, 1976.
Ginsberg, B. E. Genetic parameters in behavioral research. In J. Hirsch (Ed.), *Behavior-Genetic Analysis.* New York: McGraw-Hill, 1967. Pp. 135–153.
Gould, S. J. *Ever Since Darwin.* New York: Norton, 1977a.
Gould, S. J. *Ontogeny and Phylogeny.* Cambridge, Mass.: Harvard University Press, 1977b.
Hamilton, W. D. The genetical evolution of social behaviour. *Journal of Theoretical Biology,* 7:1–52, 1964.
MacLean, P. D. The triune brain, emotion and scientific bias. In F. O. Schmitt (Ed.), *The Neurosciences: Second Study Program.* New York: Rockefeller University Press, 1970. Pp. 336–349.
McClearn, G. E., and DeFries, J. C. *Introduction to Behavioral Genetics.* San Francisco: W. H. Freeman and Company, 1973.
Wilson, E. O. *Sociobiology.* Cambridge, Mass.: Belknap Press of Harvard University Press, 1975.

REFERENCES CITED

1. Lang, F., Govind, C. K., and Costello, W. J. Experimental transformation of muscle fiber properties in lobster. *Science,* 201:1037–1039, 1978.
2. King, M. C., and Wilson, A. C. Evolution at two levels in humans and chimpanzees. *Science,* 188:107–116, 1975.
3. Freud, S. Totem and taboo. In *Standard Edition of the Complete Psychological Works.* London: Hogarth Press, 1953. P. 1.
4. Jung, C. G. *Psychology and Education.* Princeton, N.J.: Princeton University Press, 1954. P. 151.
5. Cooper, R. M., and Zubek, J. P. Effects of enriched and restricted early environments on the learning ability of bright and dull rats. *Canadian Journal of Psychology,* 12:159–164, 1958.

2

Basic Properties
of Behavior

Behavior is not like other aspects of biological systems because it does not have the permanent structure of skeleton, blood, cell membranes, or molecules. In this book I will be dealing mainly with human behavior, with the actions and reactions of the whole person. But behavior, in the dictionary sense of "a course of action," also occurs at the level of organs (e.g., muscles), cells (e.g., nerve impulses), and molecules (e.g., chemical reactions). Moreover, there is a continuity between these levels of biological organization because nature, in the form of evolution, did not discard the actions of molecules in producing the behavior of organisms. Rather the processes of chemical reactions have been used as basic building blocks for the behavior of individual cells of the nervous system (neurons), and the properties of these neurons, in turn, have been used as building blocks for the behavior of the individual person. The basic nature of behavior can thus best be understood in terms of this continuity, and I will sketch this out as I consider the three basic properties of behavior: activity, receptivity, and integration.

ACTIVITY

Source

The essential characteristic of behavior is action, but what is the *source* of this tendency to behave? Stimulation can elicit, guide, and even prevent behavior; it can organize and shape behavior, but it is not the driving force. We talk about the "tendency" and we feel the "urge" to eat or mate or sleep, but such drive concepts, however useful they may be, beg the question of what drives the drives—what the original source of behavior is.

In attempting to answer this question, we can go back to the level of the single, isolated muscle or nerve cell and point to its tendency to contract or fire spontaneously. In most animals, only cardiac muscle contracts spontaneously under normal conditions, but by a change in any muscle's chemical environment, it can be made to contract. This is the basis for how nerve impulses initiate and control muscular movement. Many types of nerve cells periodically generate sudden bursts of electrochemical change called "action potentials," and do so without any change in their environment (see Figure 2–1). This spontaneous activity of nerve cells can be seen in cell groups in the whole brain even during sleep and in isolated sections of brain kept in cultures where the environment of the cell can be held absolutely constant. This property of muscle and nerve cells is of particular interest for understanding the early development of behavior because all animal species begin to move very early in their development, while they are protected from stimulation by the egg or womb and long before this behavior has any obvious usefulness. Our search for understanding this "anticipatory" behavior is described in Chapter 5.

We can go further than this in our understanding of why behavior occurs. To trace the generation of neural and muscular activity back to certain cell types tells us that we are endowed with certain engines set to run in a way that will cause behavior. But it does not tell us how the engines run. This is a matter for cell biology, and involves interactions between a number of structures within the cell. At this level of biological organization, we may again use the word *behavior*, but apply it to units within the cell such as ribosomes and membrane channels or to molecules such as messenger RNA and enzymes. The generation of the nerve impulse or "action potential" and the muscle contraction are gradually becoming understood on the basis of the behavior of molecules, large molecules that can, for example, change their shape, thus shortening or lengthening a muscle cell, or attach to a cell membrane and open or close a channel to the passage of the charged ions that are the basis for electrical activity (see Figure 2–1).

The spontaneous activity of nerve and muscle cells is thus the result of the behavior of molecules within the cell, molecules that are participating in chemical reactions. The origin of behavior is therefore to be found in the forces accounting for spontaneous chemical reactions. A newspaper turns slowly brown in the bottom of the closet, a process identical to a very slow burning. Heat is given off, and the newspaper slowly turns into carbon dioxide and water by spontaneously combining with oxygen in the air. Two forces are recognized to be at work in turning this newspaper to dust: the tendency of organized matter—molecules—to decay toward states of lower heat energy *(enthalpy)* and the tendency to disintegrate toward states of greater disorder *(entropy)*. These are the fundamental forces that drive spontaneous chemical

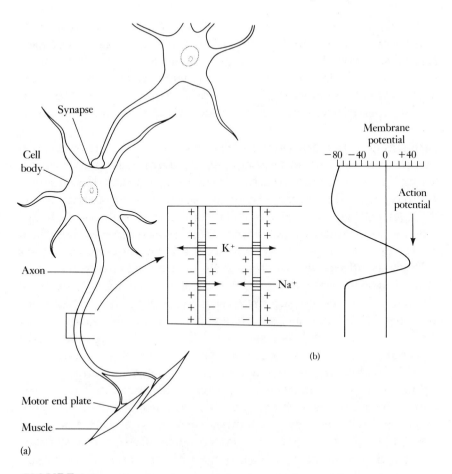

FIGURE 2-1

(*a*) A neuron and its connection with muscle and another nerve cell. (*b*) The flow of sodium ions (Na⁺) and potassium ions (K⁺) through channels in the axon membrane that propagates the nerve impulse or "action potential." (Function at synapse is illustrated in Figure 2-4.) (After C. F. Stevens, "The Neuron," *Scientific American*, 241:55–65, 1979. Copyright © 1979 by Scientific American, Inc. All rights reserved.)

reactions toward *equilibrium*, the final state of minimal energy and maximal disorder. The redeeming short-term virtue of this downward trend is that, in the process of these forms of decay and disintegration, free energy is released. Vast amounts of energy are available in the atomic and molecular binding forces of matter, and life processes have evolved that harness this energy to construct the organized systems with which we are all familiar. Many of these systems, or organisms, move about and behave in the sense of the word we are using here.

Thus, the moving force behind behavior, the force behind spontaneity, can be traced back to the basic forces of spontaneous chemical reactions. Beyond this we cannot go, and the reader may feel that we have gone too far already in this search for the cause behind the cause. Yet it is well to describe the many steps along the way, for it gives us a clearer perspective on the basic nature of behavior and its dynamic quality.

In addition, this brief journey has crossed several layers of organization, from the level of the behaving organism, through the organ, the cell, and the chemical reaction, to end in the organization of atoms and molecules. The characteristics of molecules are necessary for us to understand chemical reactions, but they are not sufficient in themselves for a complete understanding of chemical reactions. For when molecules interact, they behave in ways that are different from their behavior as individuals. Similarly, cells, organs, and organisms behave differently when interacting with each other than when considered separately. The special patterns and rules governing these interactions are what make these levels of biological organization different. Yet there are many tantalizing similarities between the organization of chemical reactions within a cell and the organization of the reactions of an individual within its environment, as will be described in the following sections: the tendency to move in certain directions, the utilization and production of energy, the presence of equilibrium conditions and the tendency to maintain them, the use of feedback control, and the ability to alter function in response to changed conditions. These activities are carried out through different means by an organism and a cell-free chemical system in a test tube. But certain principles are common to both levels of function, and the behavior of the whole organism is built upon the behavior of its chemical, cellular, and organ systems.

Rhythm

If the essential characteristic of behavior is action, then the dimension of time is surely crucial. For unlike the structures of nature, behavior is essentially evanescent, and its timing is the key to its effectiveness. A simple act like a muscle contraction can occur over a period of hours or even days in some smooth muscles, or it can twitch so fast that the eye misses it. Furthermore, it can increase and decrease slowly or rapidly. Finally, and perhaps most important, it can occur repeatedly and with a random or patterned set of intervals, a *rhythm*. If an act will tend to occur because of chemical forces, what determines the pattern of its occurrence? Insofar as behavior can be said to have form and to possess distinctive qualities, its timing is essential to these characteristics.

In order for timing to occur, a behavior must be able to be turned off as well as on. Spontaneous chemical reactions turn themselves off when end products accumulate in sufficient concentration to create a state of equilibrium with reactants. But when this occurs, renewed reaction must await the formation of new reactants. The evolution of enzymes provided a more precise and quicker means of turning chemical reactions on and off.

Chemical reactions in nature often cannot proceed rapidly because the first step involves the formation of an intermediate molecular form of even higher energy state than the potential reactants. Enzymes reduce the energy state of the intermediate form and eliminate this barrier to spontaneous reaction. Special molecules, including some of the products of the reaction, can then bind to sites on the enzyme, alter its shape, and thus prevent its interaction with the intermediate forms. This *feedback* of the results of a chemical reaction upon its enabling enzyme can turn off the reaction well before an equilibrium state is reached. With time, dissociation of the feedback molecules from the enzyme reaches a critical point when the enzyme regains its shape and turns the reaction on again. A repetitive pattern of reactivity can thus be established through the operation of feedback processes in a relatively simple chemical system. The timing of each phase of this cycle can vary with the individual reactions and enzymes involved, endowing each system with a distinctive rhythm. Thus, single-celled organisms have numerous rhythmic functions based on "biological clocks" powered by such chemical processes.

Spontaneously active neurons and muscles each have a characteristic rhythmic discharge by which they can be identified, like the personal signature of a drummer. The cycles that occur are of many lengths in different neurons, from fractions of a second to about as long as a day, the so-called *circadian rhythm*. The origin of the electrical activity of the neuron has been traced to the cell membrane, which maintains an electrical potential difference between the outside and the inside of the cell by pumping positively charged sodium ions out of the cell (see Figure 2–1). The action of enzymes within the cell results in changes in the shape of the large protein molecules that compose the membrane and are thought to open channels for such ions, thus allowing a change in the membrane potential. Nerve cell membranes are specialized so that where this change reaches a certain point, a sudden marked switch in membrane potential is triggered. This wave of sudden electrical change spreads down the long axonal process of the nerve as the action potential or nerve impulse. Thus, the chemical processes within the cell trigger the nerve impulse, which is the unit of its activity. It is not known exactly how the distinctive rhythms of some nerve cells are produced, but it is reasonable to suppose that they are based on feedback systems such as the one described above for chemical reactions facilitated by enzymes. Individual differences in the chemical composition of the membranes, the enzymes within the cells, and the reactants utilized seem to form the basis for the individual differences in rhythmicity found among cells.

Thus, we have some understanding of the origin of patterned activity within the nervous system, based on the properties of biochemical systems within each cell. If we attached muscles to such cells, the system would move, or at least twitch repeatedly and even rhythmically. Assemblies of such cells are capable of generating much more complex rhythms, which underlie the transition between sleep and wakefulness as well as many other rhythmic functions.

Coordination

One of the qualities that is lacking in our system so far is *coordination* of activity in one part with activity in another. Without sequence and coordination, activity cannot propel the organism in any direction. In order to have such coordination, some means must be found for cells to communicate so that the discharge of one cell can become a signal affecting the activity of the next. The action potential that spreads down a nerve fiber can stimulate a muscle or a gland or another nerve cell with which it makes a synaptic connection. It does so by altering the membrane function of the structure to which it is connected. Two kinds of membrane changes are possible as a result: one that excites discharge in a silent cell and another that inhibits discharge in an active cell.

Stent has worked out how a simple arrangement of five cells produces the wavelike, swimming movement of the leech, based simply on the fact that excitation of one cell can lead to inhibition of firing in the next (see Figure 2–2). All five cells have the same property and the same effect on each other.

This example illustrates how simple properties of a system of connected neurons can generate a rather complex and continuous behavior, useful for moving about. This behavior, which requires no stimulation after its initiation due to the spontaneous activity of neurons, is called a *fixed action pattern*. It allows us to understand one simple way by which repeated, stereotyped acts can be generated by a nervous system. In all organisms, however, there is a sensory system that can modify the activity of such a motor system, which is the next topic.

RECEPTIVITY

If action is the essential characteristic of behavior, then the direction of this action is only slightly less important. Truly random, undirected behavior is rare in humans, and even the simplest one-celled organisms direct behavior toward or away from elements of their environment. In order to do this, information about the environment must be made available to the motor system. Such responsiveness used to be ascribed to the "irritability of protoplasm." Now we have examples of receptivity that occur in isolated chemical reactions involving enzyme molecules with specific receptors. This capacity of molecules to bind to some other molecules at specific sites, like keys in locks, is not confined to enzymes. The protein molecules that protrude from the outer surface of cell membranes throughout the body are specialized to do exactly this, and in this way provide a basis for all forms of communication between cells. Once specific binding has taken place, the rest of the protein molecule within the membrane is altered in some way—perhaps in shape—which then sets in motion a train of other changes in the properties of the membrane and in the function within the cell itself. Nerve cell membranes are specialized to respond to receptor binding by increased permeability to positively charged ions, such as sodium or potassium. The rapid flow of these ions into the cell is the basis for the generation of an action potential as described above and in Figure 2–1.

Thus we can begin to see how a chemical in the environment, in the form of a taste or an odor, for instance, can affect a sensory nerve cell membrane in the nose to generate a signal, which is then available to the brain. But what about other elements of the environment such as solid objects, sounds, light, and temperature? Here again, the basic receptive processes all involve the membrane of the cell, although the different forms of energy are translated into membrane permeability changes by different processes. This operation, known as *transduction*, takes place in the specialized structures so familiar to us such as the eye and the ear. The specialized receptors couple the particular form of energy to the membrane of the sensory nerve cell by chemical or mechanical means. Changes in permeability to positively charged ions may be produced by mechanical displacement of the cell membrane of one-celled organisms such as the paramecium. In the human ear, tiny hairs that can be moved by sound waves, are embedded in cell membranes and transduce the energy of sound into the electrochemical energy of the nerve impulse within the membrane. Specialized receptors are able to amplify signals enormously this way, but the basic membrane mechanisms are probably the same as those that evolved when single-celled organisms were the highest form of life (see Figure 2–3).

One result of this particular system for receptivity that has evolved in humans is that very different aspects of the environment are represented by the same signal, a nerve impulse. Since the signal responsible for activity is also a nerve impulse, the language of the nervous system is reduced to one common functional element. The design and operation of the nerve cells responsible for receptivity and for activity are also similar, giving us a common structural element as well. The

FIGURE 2-2
The oscillator network responsible for the swimming rhythm of the leech. (*a*) Coordinated contraction of segmented muscles produces wave-like swimming movements. (*b*) Excitation of cell A produces a contraction of the muscle of segment 1 and inhibition of cell B. As a result of the cessation of firing of cell B, cell C (which had previously been inhibited by cell B) now resumes discharge. This in turn inhibits cell D, which had previously been firing. Cell D controls the muscle of segment 2 so that, when cell D is inhibited, the muscle of segment 1 relaxes, and the cessation of firing also allows cell E to begin to discharge. The firing of cell E finally inhibits cell A, and the cycle has come full circle and will continue endlessly. This recurrent cyclic inhibition arranges the contraction of segment 1 of the leech to occur in a fixed time sequence with the contraction of segment 2 and generates the repetitive, wave-like swimming movements. A network of four cells will generate only a static pattern of alternate excitatory and inhibitory states in its neurons, with no cycling. It should be noted that this timing of contraction in segment 2 in relation to segment 1 is controlled by the recovery time taken by each interneuron and by the nerve impulse travel time.

advantage of this homogeneous design is that we can understand a great deal of how the nervous system works by understanding a prototypical model neuron. The puzzle is to try to understand how so many different kinds of behaviors can be produced by a system composed of similarly designed units giving nearly identical signals. The answer lies in the organization of the cellular elements, the individual characteristics of these neurons, and how they interact.

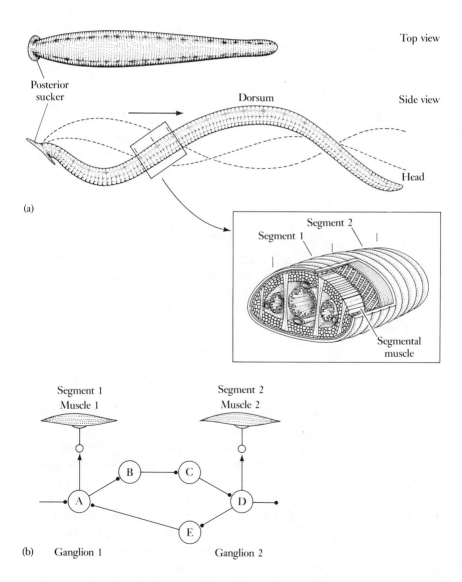

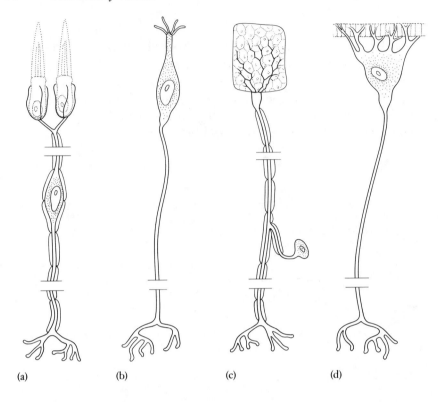

(a)   (b)   (c)   (d)

FIGURE 2-3
Some receptor neurons. *(a)* Auditory (human). *(b)* Olfactory (human).
(c) Tactile (human). *(d)* Stretch (crayfish). (After D. Bodian, "Neurons,
Circuits and Neuroglia." In G. C. Quarton, T. Melnechuk, and
F. O. Schmitt, Eds., *The Neurosciences: A Study Program.* New York: Rocke-
feller University Press, 1967).

INTEGRATION

How are activity and receptivity correlated to suit the action to the
environment? Or, going back a step, why should such integration have
evolved? The ability of an organism to move toward elements in its
environment that are necessary or useful to it and to move away from
those that are harmful is of obvious adaptive value. Even plant roots
and branches have evolved mechanisms for slowly making these adjustments to their niche. Most behaviors seem to have derived from
this simple "biphasic" response system, but in order to cope with a
rapidly changing environment, many more complex integrative capacities have evolved, conveying the ability to anticipate, remember, learn,

and communicate. Finally, humans have evolved the capacity to perform series of operations in the abstract, without overt behavior, and have thus become conscious, thoughtful, and creative. Our integrative capacities have given us the selective advantage we now have over our fellow animals.

We have already encountered examples of certain forms of integration at the level of chemical reactions (in the feedback inhibition of end products on enzymes, p. 29) and at the level of neurons (in the coordination of motor activity, p. 30). But one of the most elegant simple models of adaptive behavior in nature is the induction of an enzyme by contact with its specific substrate. For example, when increased quantities of lactose become available in the medium, certain molecules of DNA respond by transcribing increased amounts of specific messenger RNA, which in turn cause the increased production of enzymes needed for the breakdown and utilization of the lactose. It is thought that the lactose is sensed by a specific receptor site on the DNA molecule that acts to change the shape and thus the properties of an adjacent segment on the DNA molecule. In this system, the production of specific enzymes is correlated with the presence of the specific nutrient in the environment. We could say that the chemical system within the cell responds to a change in its environment with an activity suited to that change. That is, it has made a *purposeful* response to a stimulus.

The apparently purposeful character of integrated function has posed problems for theories in biology because of our tendency to conceive of purpose as having an existence outside the system, as we experience it in our minds. But apparently purposeful action is inevitable in any integrated system that is selected for its adaptive characteristics by evolutionary forces.

The function of one nerve cell is correlated with that of another by chemical processes similar to those described above. The vast majority of connections between nerve cells are not simple contact points that allow the electrical signal to pass into the next cell. Instead, a narrow gap or cleft is maintained, the *synapse*. When the wave of changed membrane potential, which is the *nerve impulse*, reaches the end of the nerve, the *presynaptic terminal*, it alters the membrane properties in this specialized region so that stored molecules are released through the membrane into the synaptic cleft (see Figure 2–4). These neurotransmitter molecules then become bound by receptors on the postsynaptic membrane of the next cell, opening *ion channels* in that membrane that cause it either to *depolarize* and thus set up an action potential in the next nerve or to *hyperpolarize* and thus inhibit ongoing activity.

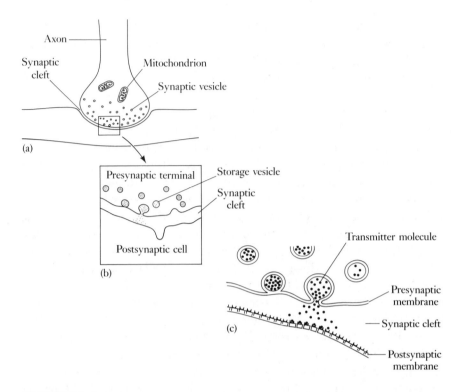

FIGURE 2-4
The synapse, showing the events following the arrival of a nerve impulse at the presynaptic terminal, at three different magnifications. Part (*b*) is drawn from an electron photomicrograph at 115,000 times actual size. Storage vesicles actually fuse with the presynaptic membrane in the process of discharging neurotransmitter molecules into the synaptic cleft. Vesicles must be reformed and refilled with neurotransmitter before they can discharge again. (After C. F. Stevens, "The Neuron," *Scientific American*, 241:55–65, 1979. Copyright © 1979 by Scientific American, Inc. All rights reserved.)

Regardless of whether the cells are motor, sensory, or connecting cells, the communication between two nerve cells is organized in the same way. The first cell acts on the second cell in the way motor cells act on muscles and glands: by secretion of a neurotransmitter onto a sensitive portion of the membrane of the adjacent cell. The second cell acts like a sensory cell by responding to the specific molecules of the neurotransmitter with a change in membrane properties. Because of the nature of these processes, communication across synapses is always one-way. Also, the processes involved in the synapse are sufficiently complex so that a number of modifying and feedback systems can act to modulate the transmission of impulses or the degree of inhibition, thus allowing for short- and long-term modification of synaptic transmission. These changes are thought to form the basis for learning and memory.

How can a given sensory neuron signal a motor neuron to produce a muscle contraction suited to the stimulus? This is determined by the way the cells are interconnected and by the unique properties of individual neurons. Thus, the organized nature of behavior is largely a result of the wiring diagram of the nervous system. The many ways these cells become connected during very early development is the subject of Chapter 8. Of course, all synapses are not equally functional at a given time, and this is the third determinant of whether or not a given stimulus will be followed by a particular action. The processes involved in modifying the function of synapses will be discussed in the next chapter.

Different categories of behavior such as sleep, feeding, and reproduction seem to be mediated by neurons with different and unique properties, as well as by neurons with characteristics common to all systems. Neurons are of two main functional categories, *excitatory* and *inhibitory*. But they can be highly individualistic in terms of their size, position, shape, pattern of connections, neurotransmitter type, and in the degree to which they are active or silent under any given set of conditions. These special characteristics of certain nerve-cell networks underlie the special functional requirements of different behaviors.

A second major form of integration between sensation and action is carried out by the circulatory system, employing chemical messengers called hormones. I have already described several different examples of chemical messengers in simple chemical processes. Synaptic transmission between nerve cells involves one form of messenger, or neurotransmitter, which is secreted by one cell and travels to the next where it acts. But the distance is very small and does not involve the circulatory system. When chemical messengers are secreted into the blood stream and thereby carried to act on distant cells, we call them hormones. Like neurotransmitters, hormones pass through membrane channels during their release and also must be bound to specific receptors at their target cells in order for them to exert their action. Literally every hormone-secreting gland is in some way connected to the sensory nervous system and is thus potentially responsive to the environment. Certain glands, such as the adrenal medulla, are directly activated by secretory motor nerves from the brain. Many others, such as the ovary and thyroid, are controlled by a series of releasing or regulating hormones linking the hypothalamus of the brain to the distant endocrine glands. Only a few cells in the body have receptors for a particular hormone and thus, although the hormone circulates everywhere, it is extremely selective in its action. This specificity is analogous to the specificity of nerve connections. An important feature of hormone action is that the brain itself is a target organ and certain cells mediating particular behaviors can be selectively affected.

Once circulating in the blood, hormones can affect behavior in two major ways. First, they play a role during early development in the organization of neural and muscular structure. Here they appear to act through selective growth-promoting properties on certain cells that have receptors for them, thus laying the groundwork for the availability of certain patterns of behavior. The early development of the neural substrates for male and female sexual behavior is an example of this kind of action, as described in Chapters 9, 10, and 15. Secondly, hormones have activating effects on certain behavior patterns by their action near the time of the behavior. Two subcategories of this kind of effect have been proposed by Leshner: (1) the priming effects of the hormonal condition before the behavior is elicited, and (2) the feedback effects of the hormonal response upon elicitation of the behavior. The increased sexual receptivity induced in female rats by ovarian hormones during the estrous cycle is an example of the first subcategory, and the reduction of aggression induced in male mice as a result of the hormonal changes following defeat in a fight is an example of the feedback type of effect. This second kind of hormonal action on behavior is the least well known but in some ways the most important for the integration of behavior. For it allows the neuroendocrine system to act like the sensorimotor nervous system in being capable of influencing future behavior on the basis of the results of past behavior.

These several properties of the neuroendocrine apparatus allow for selective and adaptive behavioral responses that suit behavior to the environment. Evolutionary selection pressures have thus tended to produce systems in which hormones, events, and actions are arranged in order to produce behavior that is adaptive within the environment in which evolution took place.

SUMMARY

The properties of some chemical reactions not only contain principles that are applicable to behavior, but also provide the mechanisms for the activities of nerve cells and thus account for the behavior of the organism. Large protein molecules selectively bind smaller molecules to specific sites on their complex structure and as a result change their shape and orientation to each other. When numbers of these molecules are organized into cell membranes, these chemical processes form the basis for the selective control of the passage through the membrane of positive and negative ions and molecules such as the neurotransmitters. The electrical charge across the membrane, the generation of the nerve impulse, and synaptic transmission of the signal to other nerves are the direct result of the behavior of these large protein molecules that make up the cell membrane. The behavior of the organism is the direct result of these special properties of motor and sensory cells and their capacity to interact with each other. The three basic features of human behavior—activity, receptivity, and integration—are thus understandable in terms of their continuity with chemical processes.

Activity, the tendency for organisms to behave, can ultimately be traced back to the forces accounting for spontaneous chemical reactions but is more immediately produced by spontaneous electrical activity of nerve cells. The rhythmicity of activity of single cells can be understood in terms of chemical processes such as feedback inhibition of enzymes and the coordination of activity by the interconnection of cells into a system in which feedback takes place at the level of the motor cells themselves. *Receptivity* is necessary for activity to have direction, and is based on the tendency for molecules to bind some other molecules at specific sites on their structure. The molecules of cell membranes transduce the impact of molecules and other sources of energy, such as touch, light, and sound, into electrical changes that can act as signals for other cells.

The *integration* between receptor and action functions is made possible by communication between neurons in two ways: at synaptic junctions between cells and by chemical messengers transported in the bloodstream. Specialized areas of cell membranes on one neuron release stored neurotransmitter molecules in response to the electrical changes of the arriving nerve impulse. The second neuron responds through the mechanisms of receptivity by binding the neurotransmitter molecules, altering its membrane potential, and initiating or inhibiting nerve impulses. Hormones are both released by certain nerve cells and selectively bound by other nerve cells, thus creating an integration with several steps involving glands distant from the brain that are nevertheless regulated by the nervous system. The crucial aspect of integration is that the specific connections made by cells and hormones come to be arranged to promote behavior that is adaptive to the environment in which evolutionary selection pressures acted. This gives behavior its purposeful character.

FURTHER READING

Bullock, T. H. *Introduction to Nervous Systems.* San Francisco:
W. H. Freeman and Company, 1977.
Kuffler, S. W., and Nicholls, J. G. *From Neuron to Brain.* Sunderland,
Mass.: Sinauer Associates, 1976.
Leshner, A. I. *An Introduction to Behavioral Endocrinology.* New York:
Oxford University Press, 1978.
Stent, G. S.; Kristan, W. B., Jr.; Friesen, W. D.; Ort, C. A.; Peon, M.;
and Calabrese, R. L. Neuronal generation of the leech swimming
movement. *Science*, 200:1348–1357, 1978.
Stevens, C. The neuron. *Scientific American*, 241:54–65, 1979.

3

The Organization
of Behavior

What do we mean by the *organization* of behavior? We are familiar with the organization of people, for example, into a political group or party. The organized units are clear in this instance, whereas the units composing the flow of behavior seem obscure. This obscurity has been a serious barrier to the study of behavior, and a later section of this chapter describes the reflex act and the fixed-action pattern, which appear to be the units that make up more complex behaviors. Each of these units has distinctive characteristics of both form and timing. Thus, the organization of behavior refers to the systematic arrangement of its constituent units so as to determine its distinctive character. But organization implies something more: it is a means of action by which some purpose is carried out or some function is performed. The word embodies the biological term *organ*, which refers to a part of an animal adapted for a particular vital function. Thus, we can be guided in our search for the principles underlying the organization of behavior by the adaptive requirements of the organism's life history.

The theme or logical thread that helps us comprehend order in behavior is that behavior is organized to serve certain purposes. The purposes in turn derive from the principles of evolution, namely, maximizing the likelihood of the individual's genes surviving into the next generation. It is dangerous to approach behavior from the point of view of its purpose because we must infer the purpose of a given behavior by logical deductions, and we can be wrong. Only evolutionary experiments can give us a clear answer, and they take too long. Nevertheless, to disregard the *purpose* of behavior (in the evolutionary sense of the word) would be to miss its most basic characteristic and could lead us far astray in our attempt to deal with its organization.

The organization of behavior can be understood in behavioral terms. But in order to determine its basic units and to analyze their interrelationships, it is useful and perhaps necessary to look also at the biological structures and processes that generate the behavior. The previous chapter described how the three basic properties of behavior—activity, receptivity, and integration—are carried out by neurons whose function has been built up out of simpler chemical processes.

This chapter outlines how complex behaviors are built up out of basic units of behavior that we can understand in terms of their neuronal and chemical functions.

THE BEHAVIOR OF A SINGLE-CELLED ORGANISM

The first stage of our life is lived out as a single-celled organism—two of them, in fact: the spermatozoon and the egg. An interest in single-celled organisms is thus neither simply theoretical nor just an exercise in obtaining perspective on our own behavior. The behavior of bacteria, for example, could be a fairly complete model for understanding the behavior of the human at the spermatozoon stage of development. As a model for human adult behavior, it obviously has limitations. Yet even here it may be useful, if one can understand the chemical processes by which a bacterium is able to discriminate, learn, and remember. For the processes by which individual cells of the adult human brain carry out these functions may involve some of the mechanisms found in bacteria, used as building blocks for the much more complex and flexible learning and memorial processes that we regard as uniquely human.

Koshland has analyzed the behavior of the typhoid bacillus to give us a model for simple forms of discrimination, choice, judgment, learning, and memory, as well as for fixed, as contrasted to adaptive, behavior. And he has been able to deduce the molecular biology of the regulation of these behaviors, within the confines of the single cell. Examples will help convey what he means by "simple forms" of these psychological processes.

A typhoid bacillus responds to very tiny amounts of nutrient in its liquid environment by moving along a concentration gradient to the source of this useful and life-sustaining substance. It is so sensitive that it can detect concentrations as low as 1 part in 100,000, and is so adaptive that it moves steadily toward the point closest to the source where the concentration is the richest, and stops there to take advantage of the situation by refueling its metabolic machinery through chemical conversion of the nutrient. In a more advanced animal such goal-directed, adaptive behavior might be characterized as intelligence. With no brain, no nervous system, and only one cell, how is it done?

Small concentrations of nutrient molecules are "sensed" by being specifically bound to protein receptors on the outside surface of the cell membrane. (At least 20 different receptors have been established in this species.) The bacterium moves by the action of its hairlike flagella, as does the human spermatozoon. In the case of the typhoid bacillus, the flagella have two modes of operation, regular wavelike motion and discoordinate movement. The first mode results in straight movement through the environment, the second in "tumbling," a series of rapid rotations and changes in direction that result in little or no movement in any particular direction. The binding of the nutrient molecule to the specific receptor sets in motion a series of conformational changes in the shape of receptor complexes and enzymes within the cell that affect the relative frequency of tumbling. The molecules of nutrient thus result in decreased tumbling, and the bacterium swims more nearly in some straight direction. But this could be the "wrong" direction. If the movement happened to result in less molecules of nutrient being available for receptor binding, tumbling would increase, and movement in that direction would slow or stop. If, on the other hand, more nutrient was available as a result of a movement (which would happen if the direction was toward the source), tumbling would be further decreased, and the bacterium would continue to move up the gradient. Finally, at or near the source, movement would cease to result in increased concentration of nutrient. In fact, continued movement through the zone of highest concentration and out the other side should result in *decreased* receptor binding, increased tumbling, and return toward the center again. This system by itself would result in bacteria moving endlessly back and forth at high speeds across the central zone of high concentration, which is not what happens. Instead, they gradually quiet down with time, and remain relatively stationary in a state of nearly constant tumbling. This kind of system explains how most of the bacteria in a culture disk are able to congregate rapidly into a tiny capillary tube filled with concentrated nutrient.

The basis for the operation of the system for this goal-directed behavior appears to lie in the nature of time-dependent chemical processes. The bacterium seems to remember what the concentration of the nutrient was in order to make a comparison with a change in this level, and it must be able to change its behavior over time (adapt, or learn not to respond) when the concentration of nutrient remains constant (see Figure 3–1). A simple chemical mechanism for this remarkable behavior has been proposed by Koshland.

The time span of this simple memory system is appropriate for the task, being the length of time it takes for a bacterium to move 20–100 body lengths. At the average speed of the typhoid bacillus, this amounts to a memory span in the range of 1/2 second, which by our standards is no cognitive feat. But the chemical processes suggested by Koshland's studies on this simple organism may form one of the

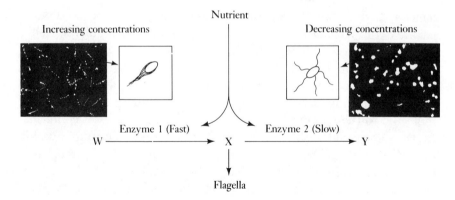

FIGURE 3-1

The patterns of locomotion of a typhoid bacterium are disclosed by dark-field multiple-exposure technique and reveal, on the left, the straight swimming tracts of bacteria in a medium to which a high concentration of nutrient has been rapidly introduced and uniformly mixed. The five flagella are streamlined and coordinated. On the right, the medium has just been rapidly diluted, and the bacteria tumble over and over in nearly the same position. The five flagella are separate and discoordinated.

Koshland's hypothetical mechanism to account for the ability of such bacteria to swim up a concentration gradient and congregate in an optimal zone is as follows: The receptor binding of nutrient molecules is thought to induce activity in two enzymes within the cell concurrently but at different rates since enzyme 1 is induced rapidly and enzyme 2 slowly. Each of these enzymes facilitates chemical reactions: enzyme 1, the synthesis of compound X; and enzyme 2, its degradation. Compound X in turn must exceed some critical level in order for the flagella to generate the smooth waves that produce straight swimming. In a declining concentration gradient, the activity of enzyme 2, and thus the degradation of compound X to compound Y, will be increasing while synthesis of compound X will be declining. Flagellar discoordination and tumbling result. In an increasing nutrient gradient, as the bacterium swims toward the nutrient source, enzyme 1, synthesis of compound X from compound W, and pool size of X will increase, producing straight swimming. Finally, when the level of nutrient stabilizes, as the bacterium reaches the zone of the nutrient source, the induction of enzyme 2 has time to catch up with the induction of enzyme 1, the rate of degradation of compound X catches up with its rate of formation, the pool size of X is reduced, and the bacterium tumbles in place.

bases for memory processes in the cells of higher organisms including people. The human spermatozoon has the uncanny ability to swim up a slow current in the fluids surrounding it (see Chapter 4) and swims more vigorously in a dense medium than in a more fluid one. Processes such as those described for the typhoid bacillus may underlie these capacities of our earliest stage of life. Other bacteria are able to swim rapidly and decisively away from certain repellant substances in the water, an avoidance response. The repellant molecules are bound to receptors and presumably set in motion chemical reactions that have opposite effects on the pool level of X shown in Figure 3–1. In addition, a simple form of learning is achieved by the induction of receptors for some compounds (ribose and nitrates) that are only rarely encountered, thus allowing the bacteria to acquire the ability to follow gradients of this substance as a result of experience with it. Other receptors form the basis of innate or constitutional responses and are present to the same degree regardless of experience.

With this welter of receptors and in the average environment filled with attractant and repellant molecules, how does the bacterium decide what to do? Many chemicals are not bound at all. Some compounds are tightly bound and therefore are detected at weak concentrations and can displace more weakly bound compounds. The number of receptors for some substances is greater than for others, and the affinity of some receptors for the intracellular components of the system can differ. Because of these and other variations, the bacterium is biased to discriminate and respond preferentially to certain elements of its environment. A hierarchy of response tendencies is thus generated, which interacts with the salience (concentrations) of the various stimuli in its present and recent environment to determine its speed of movement. Whether this constitutes a very simple form of choice and judgment is left to the judgment of the reader.

How can we use this analysis of behavior in a very simple organism? Certainly not by concluding that human psychological processes are to be understood according to the schematic diagram presented in Figure 3–1. We do *not* understand the biological basis for simple learning in human brains and are even worse off when it comes to judgment and choice. Therefore, it is helpful to begin at a level that is comprehensible, in order to give us some ways of thinking that may help us eventually understand the processes at work in more complicated systems. I will be referring back to some of the processes described for the bacterium in later sections of this chapter. Finally, it is useful to realize that very simple systems are capable of organizing and carrying out quite complex behaviors that we can describe as intelligent. This realization should help us look for the simplest possible explanations for human behavior, rather than embracing without question the most complex psychological theories as the only ones capable of explaining what we do.

THE UNITS OF BEHAVIOR

Behavior can be described in terms of its form and timing or according to its consequences. Both these qualities are represented in the term "organization," and both are needed to make much sense out of behavior. It is certainly possible to describe behavior along either of these dimensions without worrying about the question of basic units. But if we want to understand behavior in terms of its underlying biological processes, a determination of its basic units is essential.

Reflex Acts and Fixed-Action Patterns

Ethologists working at the level of naturalistic observations and neurophysiologists working at the level of cells have come to similar conclusions: that two useful basic categories of behavior can be distinguished—the *reflex act* and the *fixed-action pattern*. These units are the simplest forms of integrated activity and receptivity to occur in all multicelled organisms from snails to humans. They thus qualify as basic building blocks for organized behavior.

The reflex act requires only one sensory nerve, a synapse, and a motor nerve innervating a muscle, although almost all reflexes actually involve many sensory and motor cells connected together. The action is a graded function of the sensory input and depends entirely on sensation for its action. The fixed-action pattern usually involves an assemblage of motor neurons and is not necessarily dependent on sensory input, since time-dependent processes within its cells can determine rhythmic periods of function and quiescence (e.g., breathing). In this case it is known as an *oscillator*. In most cases fixed-action cell assemblages are connected to several sensory neurons, but are triggered in an all-or-none fashion by sensory input with none of the graded relationships found for reflexes. The motor pattern is thus stereotyped and may involve several sequential components that run out independent of any further sensory stimulation. Both reflex and fixed acts can involve a few or many sensory and motor units and can be joined together to form sequential and repeated movements. Thus, both kinds of units exist in elementary forms called *acts*, and more complex forms called *patterns*.

The different characteristics of the nerve circuits involved in reflex acts and fixed acts has been worked out by Kandel in the sea snail *Aplysia*, whose nervous system is simple and accessible enough to make such studies possible. Although the same effector organs can be involved in both types of acts, the nerve circuits mediating them are different, and some of the cells involved have special characteristics that allow us to understand the basis for the two different kinds of behavioral units (see Table 3–1).

Unfortunately, these basic units are hard to find within the stream of behavior built out of them in adulthood. However, the knee jerk and the response of the eye's pupil to light are reflex acts observable in all adults, while vomiting, sneezing, swallowing, and orgasm are familiar fixed-action patterns. In the fetus and newborn, a number of reflex acts are present as well as fixed-action patterns (see Chapter 6) but with maturation, the two types of units become combined together into sequences of behavior that coordinate reflex and fixed-action components into the trains of different behaviors we use to adapt to our surroundings and the requirements of living.

Sequences of Behavior

A larger unit made up of combinations of reflex and fixed-action patterns is the *behavioral sequence*. This results from the fact that under natural conditions, the two basic units of behavior tend to be combined in sequences and patterns that have some consistency. For example, eating usually consists of searching, consummatory, and resting phases. The form and timing of the behaviors involved is somewhat variable, and instances occur when one or another phase is shortened, changed in form, or even dropped entirely.

These sequences of behavior are sometimes called *programs*, in order to convey the fact that they seem to be arranged according to a consistent plan. The nature of these plans usually involves the purpose, goal, or result of the behavioral sequence. Thus, this unit of behavior can be expanded to include one's life's work or shortened to brushing one's teeth.

Shorter sequences can be combined into longer ones, but the criterion should remain the operational one: whether or not the sequence in question accurately describes a combination of elements that strongly tend to cluster together during the period of observation. It is a unit for which we have little or no substantiating evidence at the level of the function of the individual cells within the circuit. It is far more variable in form than the basic units and, in addition, has a complicated and variable relationship to sensory input. For it may be set in motion

TABLE 3–1   A summary of the differences in the properties of the two basic units of behavior proposed by Kandel on the basis of their cellular characteristics and connections.

	Reflex Act	*Fixed-Action Pattern*
Activity (Motor cells)	Low threshold of excitation	High threshold
	Fire in synchrony (the result of convergence of connections)	Fire in sequence (the result of initial inhibition of some cells, followed by rebound excitation)
	Firing frequency related directly to input frequency, permitting graded responses	Fire in accelerating train of spikes with after-discharges and long refractory periods, creating all-or-none responses
Receptivity (Sensory cells)	Some spontaneously active	Electrically silent
	Low threshold	High threshold
Integration (Neuronal circuits)	Different paths of connection between sensory and motor nerves, different receptive fields, and different conduction velocities allow summation of input in space	Identical synaptic input to all motor cells from connecting cells results in encapsulation of input; absence of summating connections
	Each spike from sensory cell makes connection to motor cell and these summate in time	
	Form and duration of response related to amplitude and pattern present in sensory input	Form and duration of response related to program of motor cell function rather than to pattern present in sensory input

either by sensory stimuli or by time-dependent changes in internal state; it usually has a graded relationship to the intensity of stimulation, and it often requires continued and changing sensory stimulation to sustain it. In this sense, behavior sequences are sensory-guided.

Behavior sequences may be classified according to (1) the kinds of stimuli that elicit them, (2) their adaptive consequences, or (3) their mode of development in the life of the organism or of the species.

ELEMENTARY FORMS OF LEARNING

In addition to the many developmental processes that shape behavior, there are the highly specific and reversible changes generally grouped under the term *learning*. The organization of behavior is based on the capacity to learn, which is present to some degree even in the most primitive organisms. Intimately connected with the capacity to learn is the ability to remember; that is, the capacity to retain and use information about past events.

For example, in one of the simplest forms of learning, *habituation*, an animal or person learns *not* to respond any more to a novel stimulus that is repeated several times. This change in behavior is specific to the particular stimulus, for responses to other stimuli are unchanged. The animal must be able to remember which stimulus has been repeated recently and which has not. The adaptive value of this ability is that the animal can conserve energy by not responding to events that have no meaningful consequences. This process plays an important role in early development as the infant learns which elements in its environment it can afford to ignore and which it cannot.

A second, slightly more complex form of learning involves the ability to increase the likelihood or intensity of a reflex behavior as a result of having received strong or noxious stimulation. Called *sensitization* or *facilitation*, this form of behavior change is useful in arousing certain behavioral systems so that the organism is better equipped to exploit a particular situation. Here again, sensitization can be quite specific: only certain kinds of stimuli delivered to certain sensory receptors gradually come to increase responses in another distant reflex pathway. Sensitizing stimuli act to enhance reflex responses to other stimuli and will restore a habituated response.

Both these forms of learning have been analyzed by Kandel in a simple reflex system of the sea snail *Aplysia*, involving only 35–40 cells. The analysis has enabled us to understand for the first time where and how learning takes place within a cell network. The sea snail retracts its gill and feeding siphon if touched lightly on its gill cover or "mantle," a protective reflex act. Repeated touching results in disappearance of this reflex (habituation). If this experience is repeated daily for four days in the same way, the animal will not respond at all to that particular stimulus for days afterwards, and the response will be 50 percent diminished even 3 weeks later (long-term habituation). On the other hand, if another animal is given repeated strong stimulation to the region of its head for a 4-day period, the gill-protective reflex to touch, when tested a week later, can be elicited by lighter touch and is much more prolonged than before the sensitizing stimulation. Thus, the sea snail has learned to respond *more* vigorously to the same stimulus as the result of one experience and to respond *less* vigorously or not at all as a result of the other experience (see Figure 3–2).

FIGURE 3-2
The sea snail *Aplysia* and the structures primarily responsible for the learning involved in the habituation and sensitization of the gill mantle withdrawal response as described by Kandel and co-workers. Weak stimulation of the siphon or mantle shelf (e.g., by a water current [a]) results in retraction of the siphon and gills underneath the cover of the mantle *(b)*. Repeated weak stimulation leads to habituation of this response. Strong stimulation of the head (e.g., by electric shock) leads to sensitization of the mantle shelf reflex. The terminal of the mantle shelf sensory neuron on the gill motor neuron cell body (stippled) is thought to be the common locus for the synaptic changes responsible for these effects. In the case of habituation, repeated stimuli cause a progressive and sustained reduction in the amount of neurotransmitter released per nerve impulse at this type of terminal and at no others. Long-term habituation is the result of many of these terminals being virtually inactivated by this process of *synaptic depression*. In the case of sensitization, the pathway involves several interneurons found to synapse on the presynaptic terminals of the sensory neurons. Although strong, repeated stimulation of the head of the animal or experimental stimulation of this interneuron produces little or no synaptic activity in motor or sensory cells, it greatly increases the quantity of neurotransmitter released from the presynaptic terminal of the sensory neuron by each sensory nerve impulse from the mantle shelf sensory neuron. This interaction of a modulatory synapse on a mediating synapse appears to be the process responsible for sensitization in this system. The membrane mechanisms by which neurotransmitter release is regulated by the presynaptic terminal are not well understood, but appear to involve changes in membrane conductance to the calcium ions that participate in the discharge of neurotransmitter into the synaptic cleft.

By a series of analytic experiments it was possible to isolate the processes underlying both sensitization and habituation to the synapse between sensory and motor cells, and to the presynaptic terminal of the sensory neuron in particular (stippled, in diagram Figure 3–2). It is worth noting that both short- and long-term memory in habituation have been traced down to the same site, the presynaptic terminal of the sensory cell. Since sensitization exerts its action on the same area of cell membrane by producing opposite effects, the understanding of memory storage in this animal hangs upon greater understanding of this interesting structure.

Although there might appear to be an unbridgeable evolutionary gap between the sea snail and the human, Thompson and his associates, working with a cat's spinal cord system, had previously found evidence for two separate systems of interneurons that mediate habituation and sensitization. The similarities between the snail and the cat are striking, both in the characteristics of the behaviors and in the neural mechanisms underlying them. Special technical advantages of

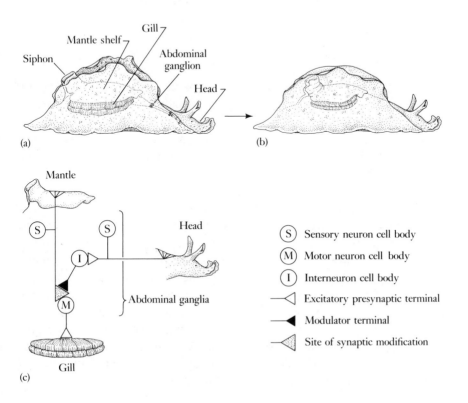

(a)

(b)

Mantle shelf

Gill

Siphon

Abdominal ganglion

Head

Mantle

Head

S Sensory neuron cell body

M Motor neuron cell body

I Interneuron cell body

Excitatory presynaptic terminal

Modulator terminal

Site of synaptic modification

Abdominal ganglia

Gill

(c)

the invertebrate snail neurons allowed further analysis leading to identification of the cellular site at which the plastic changes take place in
this species. Judging from the fact that human neurons employ the
same neurotransmitters and have similar structural features of synapse, axon, and cell body, it seems likely that our brain cells use some
of the same processes in order not to respond to irrelevant events or
to become sensitized as a result of traumatic experiences. Other mechanisms are no doubt involved in more complex forms of such simple
behaviors, but these discoveries give us a way to conceptualize what
may be going on in the brain during learning.

HIERARCHY IN BRAIN AND BEHAVIOR

The idea that some elements in an organized system control others
and that some goals take precedence over others at a given time is a
familiar one. In the structures of the units of behavior described above,
sensory cells control the function of motor cells, although the mode
of control is very different for reflex and fixed acts. In the behavior of
the bacterium, choice is made possible by a hierarchy of values established by the characteristics of innate and acquired membrane receptors and the relative concentration of various substances in the fluid
medium surrounding the organism.

Simple reflex acts and fixed-action patterns are much more evident
in human embryos and newborns than in adults. This is not due to
the disappearance or replacement of the neuronal circuits; infantile
reflexes such as rooting, sucking, and grasping reappear unchanged in
adults when injury occurs to the frontal areas of the brain. These, and
a number of more complex fixed-action patterns such as neonatal walking and reaching, normally disappear during the first few months of
life (see Chapter 6) as a result of the gradual maturation of brain circuits
that take over control from the simple sensory circuits that elicit the
behavior in the infant. The reflex and fixed acts become incorporated
into more complex patterns of behavior. Particularly dramatic examples of the development of this kind of hierarchy can be found in the
phases of development of very simple behavior by fetuses (see Chapter
5). The earliest behaviors involve only a few sensory and motor units,
consist of very simple isolated muscle twitches, and are mediated by
very simple circuits in the spinal cord. As higher brain stem circuits
mature, these very simple movements are first inhibited entirely so
that the fetus becomes unresponsive for a few days. Then responses

resume but are different in form: they involve more sensory and motor units in more complex and coordinated sequences of movements. This process of repeated subordination of simpler types of behavioral organization by more complex and far reaching patterns of control continues throughout development to adulthood. This hierarchical pattern is established slowly as a result of maturation of the nervous system and its many developmental interactions. These progressive steps in the integration of simpler units organize the behavior of the human at each stage of life. The wisdom of old age is probably the high point of these processes, although organizations typical of other stages in life are also admirable for other reasons.

Early in development, as the brain becomes organized so that the fetus is able to do several different things, the element of a functional hierarchy is introduced. That is, certain behaviors begin to have higher priorities than others in certain situations. Like the bacteria, humans have to decide what to do before developing any concept of choice or purpose. Our solution to this problem is not so very different from the bacterium. As fetuses and newborns, we have sensory receptors that are tuned to certain forms of stimulation and do not respond to others, and we have time-related processes taking place within the cells of our brains and bodies that cause them to be predisposed to certain motor acts at some times and not at others. These early states have rhythms of transition that relate priorities for action to time. These processes account for a baby sucking more readily and vigorously 4 hours after a meal than one or two hours earlier. Certain behavioral responses, such as struggling in response to strong stimulation, take precedence over all other behaviors in the hierarchy of organization because such circuits have widespread inhibitory connections upon circuits for other behaviors.

The fetus by the sixth month of life is seething with incessant activity, while the infant six months after birth spends most of its time quiet. What seems to characterize the establishment of hierarchical organization is the widespread inhibition of behavioral activity. Neuronal circuitry for a variety of behavioral acts apparently is then held in a potential form, but is inhibited from expressing itself until activated as a part of a larger behavioral sequence. The organization for such complex sequences is such that they are not elicited except in response to certain specific combinations of internal and external inputs. In this way the inhibitory action of nerve cells upon each other is the basis for the hierarchy that occurs during development and for the hierarchy of priorities of different behaviors at any given time.

STATES OF AROUSAL, MOTIVATION, AND EMOTION

One of the most fascinating and frustrating aspects of the study of behavior is that an animal or person may respond entirely differently at different times to the same stimulus or event. Internal changes alter the tendency of an organism to behave, predisposing it to some kinds of behavior and causing others to be difficult or impossible to elicit. These time-related changes in the internal condition of the animal are generally called *states* if they persist for any appreciable length of time.

The fetus, having first behaved as a collection of simple reflexes and fixed acts, coordinates these along the principles of a simple hierarchy. The next step in the organization of its behavior is the differentiation of states. Spontaneous behavior begins to occur during certain time periods and not during others. Responses can be elicited during active periods and not so easily when the fetus is quiet. This new departure takes place between 24 and 27 weeks of the 40 week gestation period, and marks the earliest precursor of what we will later refer to as "drive," "motivation," and "emotional" states. What do we really mean by state? *Any* stimulus alters the probability that responses will occur—at least for fractions of a second. Also, neurons fire spontaneously due to changes in time-dependent chemical processes within the cell that amount to *very* short changes in intracellular states. But states as we ordinarily consider them, last for minutes, hours, and even days and have been shown in cellular studies on simple organisms to depend on long lasting forms of the same membrane changes that underlie the much shorter events of reflex and spontaneous neural activity. States can be produced by internal or external stimuli (as in hunger or fear) and can turn themselves on and off in a rhythmic cycling pattern (as in the states of sleep and wakefulness). They are terminated by altered conditions in the internal or external environment.

Most important, states are conditions of the nervous system that predispose to certain characteristics of behavior. They can control the level and intensity of a number of behaviors or their specific units and sequences. It is because of this capacity that states are called "motivational," "arousal," or "emotional," and are referred to as *the drives*. But we must be careful how we use the concept of a motivation or drive for any given behavior. For a long time, behaviors were attributed to instincts, and debates raged over how many different instincts really existed and what they were. But instincts (and drives) as explanations do not carry us very far and lead into circular paths of thinking. It is too easy to deduce that a person must be angry because he or she hit a friend and then explain this action as the result of being angry. States (drives) cannot *cause* behavior; they are steps on the way from a set of internal and external factors to the behavioral act. We must look to these factors for an understanding of how a given behavior is caused.

States are inferred at the behavioral level by observation of a pattern of posture, facial expression, ongoing motor activity, and other signals such as spoken language and even body odor. They can also be inferred by reference to some preceding event or stimulus that has a predictable long-term relationship to future behavior (for example, raising the temperature of the environment). Our inferences are confirmed by the behavior that ensues. We can also attempt to specify the physiological changes that characterize the various states and attempt to find those variables responsible for the behavioral predisposition.

I will discuss the general characteristics of three main categories of states: the nonspecific arousal states (e.g., sleep), the specific motivational states related to regulation of the internal environment (e.g., hunger), and those related to the external and social environment (e.g., sex, aggression, and fear).

Nonspecific Arousal

The two main stages of sleep and the degrees of waking alertness are relatively nonspecific states in the sense that they predispose to a broad spectrum of behaviors, specifying the level of responsiveness and the intensity of behavior more than the specific units or sequences of behavior. This is not only true for the awake state as compared to being asleep, but also for the differences between the two sleep stages. "Rapid-eye-movement" (REM) sleep contains the most motor activity in some systems, particularly of eye and middle ear muscles. Physiological activity in a variety of systems shows many rapid fluctuations, and the electrical activity of the cerebral cortex shows a highly activated pattern. Our most clear and vivid dreams occur in this state. Yet the threshold for being awakened is high and the general level of muscle tone is diminished even below that found in slow wave sleep. We do not know how these periods of intense internal arousal combined with inhibition of motor outflow may be useful to us, but they stand in strong contrast to the low and steady levels of internal and motor activity in slow wave sleep.

These arousal states, like activity itself, occur with a definite periodicity or rhythm, are relatively independent of environmental stimulation, and are best understood in terms of the time-dependent chemical processes taking place within cells of the brain described in the previous chapter. The onset of these cyclic processes is set or entrained by the occurrence of stimuli and interactions with the environment. Meals, light, physical exertion, social interactions, and centrally active drugs are some of the events capable of setting, resetting, and thus entraining these rhythms to coincide with the patterns of our life. But these arousal states also show cyclic fluctuations in a constant environment. In this situation, they may lose the lawful and regular relationship they once had with the environment (e.g., sunrise) and with each other. They are then called *free running rhythms*. The cycle length of each rhythm under free running conditions tends to be reasonably close to the period observed under natural conditions, suggesting that we fit the rhythms of our lives to the rhythm of internal biological clocks.

Regulation of the Internal Environment

Changes taking place in the organ systems of the body produce chemical, hormonal, and neural signals that act on the brain, altering its functional state so as to predispose to certain sequences of behavior. The behaviors are relatively specific and ordered to restore the internal systems to their previous levels of function. The purposeful nature of these sequences and their evolutionary origins have been discussed above. Their relationship to specific states is referred to as the drive or motivation for the behavioral sequence, and we say "the behavior satisfies the need." Breathing, thermoregulatory behaviors, or the searching out and consuming of food and water are examples of internally motivated systems of behavior, as is the artificial craving found in drug addiction.

Much current research is aimed at trying to understand what the internal signals are and where the receptors may be. We are also trying to understand how the set level is determined and how optimal and present levels are compared to determine when the behavior is released. The problems are very much like those previously encountered in trying to understand how a bacterium swims up a nutrient concentration gradient.

Regulation of the External and Social Environments

Changes taking place outside the organism also alter neural and hormonal signals that act on the brain producing relatively long lasting changes in the predisposition to certain behaviors. Again, the specific behaviors are ordered to achieve certain goals for the organism within its environment. A need or motivation to behave in certain ways is thus set up by specific features of the environment. Sexual, aggressive, and flight behaviors are examples of these kinds of motivated behavior systems. The states associated with these behaviors are usually referred to as *emotional states*, such as lust, anger, and fear, identified according to our inner experience of these states. Other changes in the environment, such as painful stimulation, loss of companions, unchanging monotonous stimulation, and novelty all may be considered as inducing relatively well-defined states, such as grief or boredom, and associated behaviors. But the problem here is that categories begin to overlap, associated behaviors are often not highly specific or reliably predictable, and the states themselves cannot always be accurately specified in terms of posture, facial expression, or other behavioral signals. Even spoken language is unable to do justice to the complex interweaving of many emotional states.

These states are generally easier to identify by the signals or events inducing them than by their behavioral or physiological characteristics. But external factors are not enough, for several states in this category show some evidence of endogenous rhythms. In the case of sexual behavior this can be related, for example, to the monthly cycles of female hormones. But in the case of aggressive and fearful behavior, the effects of internal factors and cycles are not so well established for humans as for animals.

Like the motivational states associated with regulation of the internal environment, emotional states appear to be organized around equilibrium points or levels. Specific behaviors are utilized to avoid certain emotional states and to achieve and maintain others. The pursuit of sex and the avoidance of pain are obvious examples. The way in which such pleasurable and unpleasurable emotions are organized with their appropriate behaviors is to maximize adaptive fitness within the individual's physical and social environment. The bottom line determining what is adaptive is, of course, that the individual's genes are perpetuated. This has been the force molding the organization of these behavioral states during evolution and is the ultimate cause of their particular nature.

The Physiological Basis of States

At the behavioral level, states are inferred rather than observed and are useful for prediction but not amenable to measurement, as is overt behavior. However, if the physiology of nerve cells, muscles, and hormones is studied during these inferred behavioral states, distinctive patterns can be found peculiar to some of these states. That is, a set of measurements can be made at the physiological level that characterize certain states. But only some of these physiological measures are in fact causally related to the behavioral predispositions of the state; for example, levels of testosterone predispose to sexual behavior but levels of heart rate do not. Many measures are simply *correlated* because they reflect function in a shared underlying system. One of the tasks in trying to understand the biology of states is to find the physiological measures that actually account for the behavioral predisposition.

In simple systems such as those of the sea snail *Aplysia* (see above), where all the nerve cells involved in a behavior are known and can be studied, it is possible to measure these networks in terms of the levels of electrical potential across cell membranes, for example. Since membrane potentials indicate how close that membrane is to threshold level for firing, this measure can tell us how predisposed a given cell may be to initiate a nerve impulse at any given time. Such a measure gets us a great deal closer to the specification of state in measurable terms that can be causally related to behavior. But the prospect of defining states this way when tens of millions of cells are involved does not encourage optimism for this approach. Nevertheless, it allows us to conceive of what the cellular basis for states may be and can orient our thinking toward better means of defining and measuring them in more complex organisms.

Factors Terminating States: Consummation

The endogenous arousal states cycle in rhythms that have considerable regularity. Thus, they are organized to terminate themselves by switching to another state. In fact, as the person spends longer in a given state, the predisposition to change to another becomes more and more powerful until it assumes control over all other behavioral systems, at which time the previous state is terminated and the new state is consummated. For example, after an all-night vigil we may fall asleep instead of eating breakfast. With arousal states, and some motivational states, the stimuli that induce one state are those that terminate the previous one. This arrangement allows lengthy sequences and cycles to be organized. The behaviors characteristic of the arousal states tend to lead to termination of the state mainly by creating a set of conditions that elicit another state in the cycle. For example, after a long hard day we look around for a quiet place to sleep.

Motivational states are usually terminated by the action of specific stimuli that are experienced as a result of the behaviors characteristic of the state. For example, the sensations involved in swallowing food terminate the searching and eating, or the physical contact of the young child with the mother terminates its restlessness and crying. The last act prior to termination is often called a *consummatory act* and the signals involve *consummatory stimuli*. But there are two other ways by which motivational states can also be terminated. First, the factors responsible for the state may change: for example, the weather may turn warm again after a cold spell and heat-conserving behavior will be terminated as a result. Second, the organism may adapt through internal processes so that the predisposition to behave in certain ways wanes and disappears. For example, a person will cease to search for food after a prolonged period of fruitless activity due to fatigue and habituation, or a person will adapt physiologically to cold and no longer search out warm places throughout the day.

Emotional states are thought to be terminated by the same three kinds of events as motivational states, but there is evidence for considerable overlap in the consummatory acts of different emotional states. A sexual state may be terminated by an aggressive act, for example. It is not yet clear what the basis is for this fluidity in the organization of these behavioral systems, but it is of considerable importance clinically (see Chapter 15).

The behaviors associated with emotional states can be inhibited, and the emotional feelings can be prevented from reaching consciousness in people. This form of termination is ascribed to psychological *defenses* in clinical work with patients. The lives of animals as well as people can be lived without sexual, aggressive, or parental behavior, and without love, anger, or pleasure. It is not clear how we should consider the states to have become modified under these conditions, and this is the topic of considerable psychological theory.

Vicissitudes of Motivation and Emotion

It should be clear to the reader by now that nature's plan for the motivational states does not work as well as I have suggested it should. People overeat, seek out danger, batter their children, give away all their money, require pain with sex, and commit suicide in a variety of ways, both slow and fast. Why is this?

Attempts to find an answer have led to religion and philosophy as well as science. For the biologist, the ultimate question is how evolutionary forces have allowed or fostered such apparently maladaptive behavior. For the person entering the healing professions, the question is a more immediate, developmental one. What happened in the person's life that would lead to this behavior? An understanding of the many complex processes of development should provide a basis for trying to answer this question.

ADAPTIVE BEHAVIOR

So far, the organization of behavior I have described is primarily suited to a regular or predictable environment. This will obviously not do for living in most areas of the world and certainly not within a social system. However, for one stage in our life—the intrauterine period—it is probably sufficient. So long as we can move about to avoid uncomfortable positions and regulate our internal environment within the relatively fixed conditions of the womb, we will do quite well. But after birth it is another story. Almost nothing stays the same and almost nothing is under our control: we must adapt or perish.

A Simple Model System

The first of these postnatal adaptations is in breathing. I will describe this system in some detail as a prototype of adaptive behavior organization. The fetus "breathes" amniotic fluid rhythmically in and out of its upper airway, particularly during REM sleep, but the amplitude of these breaths is not very deep (see Chapter 5). At the time of birth, the placenta ceases to function as a lung for the infant, and the infant's nervous system must take over regulation of the two main gases carried by the blood, oxygen, and carbon dioxide. This behavioral system is organized so that it senses the low oxygen levels and high carbon dioxide levels that have resulted from ongoing metabolic processes in the body. It must be able to compare these levels to some standard or set point range and activate an appropriate behavior—deep rhythmic breathing. It must be able to sense when these levels have been returned to the set point range and modify breathing behavior thereafter

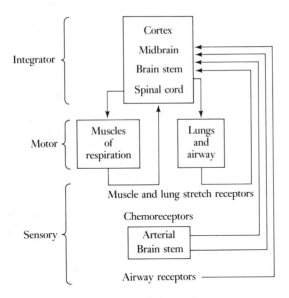

FIGURE 3-3
Plan for the respiratory control system, showing the subunits subserving the three basic properties of behavior in this system. (After A. J. Berger, R. A. Mitchell, and J. W. Severinghaus, "Regulation of Respiration," *New England Journal of Medicine*, 297:92–97, 1977.)

by controlling its frequency and amplitude so as to compensate for changes in blood gas levels above or below the optimal set point range. But this is not all: the organization for breathing also has sensors in the nose and mouth that respond to certain noxious molecules in the air by setting off reflexes that temporarily inhibit respiration (see Figure 3–3).

This capacity, useful as it is, can generate a conflict between two opposing response tendencies, producing an alternation between abbreviated responses of the two sorts, gasping and breathholding. Such a situation can only be resolved by bringing in a higher system in the form of voluntary control of breathing, a system that has access to information that goes way beyond those signals from blood and nose that are in conflict, and has access to other behavioral response systems as well. The solution for the infant may be to scream, which will bring the parent to help, or for the older child to hold its breath and run before trying another breath.

The basic elements in the organization of the control of breathing behavior are present in all complex goal-oriented and motivated behaviors, so they can serve as a model for the principles at work in: thermoregulatory behavior, eating, drinking, and even in social attachment, sex, aggression, and parenting. I have chosen breathing because we know more about the specific internal and external factors that cause it and how they are translated into action.

What are the basic elements of this model behavioral system? Illustrated in Figure 3–3 is a schematic plan of the various basic elements involved. First of all, there must be a motor system, the source for the basic function of activity. In the case of respiration, this is located in the brain stem. The origin of rhythmic respiratory movement has been traced to a small group of cells in the nucleus tractus solitarius that are organized to produce cycles of excitation and inhibition. The motor outflow of these cells passes to another brain stem cell group and through the spinal cord to the muscles of the chest and diaphragm, alternately inflating and deflating the lungs. A second motor pathway along the vagus nerve controls the accessory muscles of the upper airway. There are two levels of control over these medullary centers, originating higher in the brain stem. One exerts mainly inhibitory effects while the other is excitatory. These and even higher systems in the midbrain and cortex integrate a large variety of feedback signals that play roles in the respiratory adjustments during exercise, fever, and disturbances of acid–base balance. The result of this arrangement is that the same behavior—breathing—can be controlled through different neural systems under different conditions.

The receptors also are multiple and allow several overlapping sources of feedback control. The best known are the tiny groups of chemoreceptor cells in the carotid and aortic arteries. These cells are sensitive to small changes in oxygen, carbon dioxide, and acidity of the blood, and respond to changes in these levels by changes in the frequency of nerve impulses passing back to the several levels of brain stem motor control systems. But if these systems are cut, the animal continues to regulate its breathing in response to changes in carbon dioxide in the blood. The receptors for this back-up system have been traced to the surface of the brain stem where cell groups have been found that respond sensitively to changes in spinal fluid bicarbonate and blood acidity. A third set of receptors for the control of breathing respond to airborne irritants from the environment and are distributed widely in mucous membranes of the nose, pharynx, larynx, and lung. Stimulation of these, for example, with ammonia or smoke, produces widespread visceral and somatic responses including cessation of breathing, coughing, sneezing, sharp inspiration, contraction of the bronchioles, and increased blood pressure (which is probably the key to the helpful effects of "smelling salts" in fainting attacks, during which blood pressure has fallen too low to maintain consciousness). Finally, there are stretch receptors in the lungs and in the chest muscles of respiration that relay signals about the degree of expansion of the chest wall and lungs themselves.

The integration of these receptor and motor systems takes place at the level of the spinal cord and at the several levels of motor control in the brain stem and above. This is the part of the system that we can localize and understand least well. It is indicated by the term "integrator" in Figure 3–3. The areas responsible for simple reflex integration are at or near the small groups of motor neurons in the brain stem. But the function of integration takes place at several different levels of the nervous system, and higher integration areas in midbrain and cortex are not well localized. There are also local spinal reflexes from chest muscle stretch receptors that affect spinal motor neurons and projections from lung stretch receptors that project up to the brain stem motor cells. These are in addition to the better known arterial and central chemoreceptors projecting to all three brain stem motor systems.

We do not know exactly how set point ranges are maintained by integrator units for chemical levels in the blood or for degrees of inflation of the lungs or for amount of irritants in the air. From knowledge of simpler systems we can suppose that these are represented in the cells of the integrator areas as membrane thresholds for excitation and inhibition of nerve impulse generation. But how are systems of cells arranged to keep track of all the incoming information from the various receptors, to synthesize this information, and to program an adaptive respiratory behavior suited to each of a wide variety of environmental situations? How are the priorities maintained, and how are choices made when conflicting signals are received? We are not yet ready with answers to these questions, but we are beginning to be able to ask them in experiments on simpler systems.

We do understand enough about this model system to see the way in which it is organized out of the component parts described in previous sections. The basic units of behavior—reflexes and fixed-action patterns—are arranged in a hierarchical system. The action of specifiable stimuli in the internal and external environment acts on known receptors to elicit states that predispose to certain kinds of behavior.

In this system, the states are clearly steps toward the behavior. But a person in the state induced by low oxygen and high carbon dioxide in the blood (for example, asthma from smoke inhalation) is clearly in a describable state. Both the behavior and the inner experience, which a person can tell us about, are specifically descriptive of the state. The person is highly motivated to perform a number of behaviors that are likely to return the internal signals to their set point range. That is, the person may go to an open window or ask someone else to fetch a doctor; or the posture and respiratory behavior can be changed. Different acts are all organized around a central specifiable goal or purpose.

One of the striking characteristics of this relatively simple behavioral system is the variety of levels on which it operates. At the spinal and brain stem levels, the basic rhythm is generated by a small assemblage of cells, while sensory feedback projects directly to groups of motor cells, much the way it has been found to do in the neural systems of the invertebrate sea snail. But superimposed on this organization of reflex and fixed acts are a series of higher integrating systems, culminating in the so-called "voluntary" level, mediated by the vast integrator assemblages of the cerebral cortex. These systems, although interconnected, remain distinct: localized injuries to the spinal cord result in people with normal respiration except that they lose voluntary control over breathing or who do not breathe adequately *except* by maintaining conscious control (or employing an artificial respirator). The different levels are characterized in terms of the receptor systems from which they receive signals and the motor systems they command. For example, the brain stem does not control language and locomotion, whereas the cortex receives more extensive and direct feedback from nose and throat receptors than from the arterial blood gas receptors that project exclusively to the brain stem.

The other notable characteristic of this system is the extent of the feedback provided to the higher integrative areas from motor as well as sensory systems. All skeletal muscles, like those of the chest wall, have sensory organs called *spindles* within them that convey information on the extent of muscle stretch currently being experienced. These spindle organs can be tuned by their own motor (efferent) nerves to be more or less sensitive, and this is how muscle tone is maintained and adjusted to allow postures to be maintained in their characteristic form. Likewise, most ordinary sensory receptors, including the eye and the ear, can be tuned by their own efferent nerves to filter out or

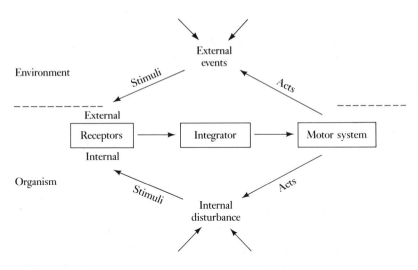

FIGURE 3-4
A simple general plan for the organization of adaptive behavior. (Modified from W. T. Powers, *Behavior: The Control of Perception*. Chicago: Aldine Publishing, 1973.)

selectively respond to certain stimuli. Thus, both motor and sensory systems are first modified at their most peripheral outposts, the muscles and sense organs, as the result of the feedback provided to the integrative systems. This peripheral level of regulation is only the first of a series of feedback control loops that serve to stimulate, guide, and modulate behavior. Each level plays a special role in the complete sequence of behavioral adaptation, some essential and others merely contributory. The analysis of the interplay of sensory control systems in the generation of complex behavior is an area of current intensive study.

A General Plan

The details of the control system for respiratory behavior obviously do not generalize precisely to other systems, but its general principles can be useful in trying to understand other behavioral systems. A simple schematic diagram (Figure 3–4) illustrates the conceptual relationships involved. Keep in mind that many of the processes are inferred rather than demonstrable, so the diagram should serve only as a conceptual model. I will apply it to eating behavior to show how it works. As with respiration, there are different sources and types of stimuli, both external and internal; for example, the level of blood sugar, the amount of fat in cells, ambient temperature, and the smell, sight, and oral sensation of food. There are different motor pathways, some of which control meal size, some the speed of eating, and others the intervals between meals. Motor output is not confined to eating, for the general level of muscular activity and the level of internal metabolism also contribute to the regulation of body weight. The control of eating activity, like respiration, is integrated at midbrain (hypothalamic) as well as at cortical levels. The rhythm or cycle for breathing is of course much shorter than for eating, a time frame of seconds instead of hours. Internal and/or external stimuli impinge on their receptors, which create neural input to the integrator system. These sensory signals are compared by the integrator to a reference function, set point level, or sensory "schema." If these do not match or balance, the motor system is activated according to a sequence of behaviors that we might call a strategy, since they are organized around the purpose of finding and swallowing food. These actions by the motor system change both external and internal events, leading to changed feedback from the receptors, alteration of the input signal to the integrator, and ultimately to a match or balance within the integrator. At this point, equilibrium is restored, and the motor strategies for the behavior are no longer activated by the integrator. In this system, the motivational state of hunger is generated by the condition of mismatch or disparity between sensory stimuli and the reference function. Note that the specific motor activity is generated by the same condition of mismatch, hence the relationship discussed in the previous section between motivational state and its specific behaviors. This generalized plan for the organization of adaptive behavior can also be applied to other early behaviors such as infant attachment to parental figures. In these cases, however, we know even less about the possible internal and external signals or stimuli, their receptors, or the various motor pathways. However, this conceptual scheme can be a useful way to order the information we do have and to indicate new directions. Similar models and their implications for theories of motivation and learning have been developed by Powers and Bindra.

This model shows us where our greatest ignorance lies: the integrator. As indicated for the regulation of breathing, we do not have a biological process to explain the matching that seems to go on between receptor signals and some kind of internal standard. We can understand how a household thermostat matches room temperature with the point set by the householder, but this is only an analogy. The twin enzyme systems in Koshland's typhoid bacterium and the nerve cell membrane threshold for action potential previously described suggest mechanisms that we can imagine as working to provide an internal standard for comparison to a blood level of a chemical substance or a level of neural input from a particular environmental stimulation. But how are we to conceive of the matching that goes on in the specific attachment of a child to its own mother or the regulation of aggressive encounters? In these cases, the match is between highly specific patterns of stimulation and some kind of acquired internal representation of that pattern. We can call these *schemas* and, although we admit we do not understand their neural basis, they are useful for conceptualizing such behaviors in the same frame of reference that we use for understanding simpler systems such as the control of respiration.

The systems for behavioral adaptation are generally not fixed in their mode of operation. Both the motor strategies and the sensory reference functions or schemas can change as a result of experience. When this form of plasticity is specific and reversible we call it *learning;* when it is less specific and involves long-term changes, particularly in early life, we call it *the developmental effects of experience;* and when it occurs as a result of damage to the nervous system we call it *neural regeneration.* The actual cellular mechanisms in these three kinds of effects may share some basic features, but our knowledge on this score is still too scanty to allow us to unify them under a single heading. The developmental effects of experience are dealt with at length in later chapters. Simpler forms of learning have been discussed above. More complex forms of learning by association of stimuli and by consequence of actions (classical and instrumental learning) enable the organism to change or reorganize its adaptational system as circumstances demand. Both forms of learning involve properties of memory that go well beyond the simple processes outlined above. The biological processes for these functions are essentially unknown, although interesting clues and theories abound and are being actively pursued in current research. (The origins of these learning and memory processes in early infancy are discussed in Chapters 9 and 12.)

CONSCIOUSNESS

So long as we deal with the organization of behavior, it is possible to build a coherent conceptual framework that can deal with infants as well as adults and with animals as well as humans. But as soon as we enter the realm of our inner experience, we get into severe difficulties. Numerous questions arise. Is there inner experience before language, and what is it like? Does the fetus experience its extraordinary world? What kinds of inner experiences do animals have, if any at all, and what difference does that make in comparing their behavior to humans'? What features of brain function are responsible for our inner experience?

The Oxford English dictionary defines consciousness as "a concomitant of thought, feeling and volition, knowledge as to which one has the testimony within oneself." If we accept this definition, we have stepped into a realm outside the empirical, observable world that we have been dealing with in this book. It is not surprising, then, that we have no idea of how biological events in the brain may be translated into such experiences. Furthermore, our own inner world is in many of its aspects very difficult to convey fully and accurately to others, even with words. For those without words, like infants and animals, the difficulty of assessing the nature of their consciousness appears almost insuperable.

It is sobering to realize how much of behavior regulation can take place without consciousness, and in fact does so in our daily lives. Perceiving and reacting do not have to be conscious to be effective, nor does learning or the formation of concepts. Even the mental processes for simple judgment—for example, which of two objects held in our two hands is heavier—are not conscious; the answer just pops into consciousness. Thus, consciousness is not very extensive and is certainly no mere copy of experience. It is rather perceived as an imaginary space in which we behave mentally in ways analogous to our behavior in the real world. We can use this space as a test arena for trying out possible alternative courses before acting in the real world. This ability may have been the crucial property of consciousness that gave it the survival value necessary to have evolved. But the rules governing events in our inner world are not those of the outer world. We can escape into an inner domain of our own construction where anything can happen. Visual, tactile, and even olfactory images are present in consciousness, in addition to numbers and words. Many of these inner representations are attached to very specific feelings, and indeed the whole of consciousness is pervaded by more long-lasting feeling tones that we call moods.

The relationship of this inner world to our behavior is a complex and controversial one, and it is difficult to relate it to the world of biology and early development. Yet the recent discovery of sign language acquisition by chimpanzees has again raised the question of consciousness in other animals and has reminded biologists of the importance of this phenomenon.

Studies on surgically damaged patients have opened up a new approach to the biology of consciousness in humans and have shed new light on the relationship of consciousness to the organization of complex behavioral organization. Sperry and Gazzaniga studied patients after their two hemispheres were surgically disconnected to prevent the repeated spread of epileptic seizures. Due to the anatomy involved, this resulted in two semi-independent behavioral systems within one human being. The left hemisphere alone is known to control the right arm and to perceive the right half of the visual field of each eye. Thus, through special contact lenses, visual communication could be set up with either of the two hemispheres separately, and its unique function assessed by observation of the behavior of the appropriate arm. Communication with the left hemisphere in most of these patients was much easier because language functions were localized there. However, the right hemisphere could be confronted with manual tasks involving identification or assembly of objects presented visually to that hemisphere and with simple arithmetical or verbal puzzles. The right hemisphere was found to be superior to the left on problems involving spatial relationships and recognition of patterns, but could only add to ten and was severely limited in its use and comprehension of word combinations to about the level of a 2-year-old. For example, nouns could be used and understood far better than verbs. The left hemisphere could speak, write, and calculate; furthermore, it excelled in problems requiring logic and an analytic conceptual approach. The right hemisphere, in contrast, utilized a more global or "gestalt" approach to problem solving, reacting immediately to whole constellations.

These classical studies are exemplified by a certain patient who was studied while his hands were screened from his view. His left arm rapidly solved a block assembly task according to a diagram presented visually to the right hemisphere. The same task was then presented to the right arm and its left hemisphere. There were several false starts and hesitations. During one of these difficult periods, the left arm darted over, felt the half-assembled design briefly, and rapidly corrected a crucial misaligned block. Although prevented, in this particular test situation, from observing the actions of his hands, either hemisphere could learn rapidly by watching the other hemisphere perform a task it had learned independently.

However, both hemispheres in these patients seem to be united at the level of emotional experience. A celebrated example is that when a sexually suggestive picture was unexpectedly presented by a tachistoscopic viewing machine only to the right hemisphere, the patient giggled and blushed but stated that she had only seen a flash of light. When asked why she was giggling and blushing, the patient exclaimed, "Oh, Dr. Sperry, you have some machine!" When the left hemisphere was shown the picture, the patient was also embarrassed, but had no difficulty in describing what she had seen. Another patient declined responsibility for the actions of his left arm, which occasionally made advances toward the nurses, and his left hemisphere stated: "Now, I know it wasn't me that did that."

The sense conveyed by these experiments is of one person with two minds, the left hemisphere mind being the one which we hear the most about because of its capacity for language. In a recently studied patient whose language function was present to a greater degree in the right hemisphere (due to injury to his left hemisphere at an early age, see Chapter 13), more could be asked of the normally mute half of the brain. Moods and simple feelings could be described in single words. When this patient's right hemisphere was asked to complete the sentence, "I want to become a . . . ," that hemisphere spelled out "auto racer" from Scrabble letters with the left hand. When the same question was put to his left hemisphere, the answer was "a draftsman."

What can we make of all this? Certainly it does not tell us how the normal human brain produces consciousness. Communication between the two sides of the brain had been cut in these patients, whereas in normal people information and strategies of processing are rapidly shared between the two hemispheres. However, it serves to focus our thinking about our own consciousness when we ask ourselves whether the disconnected right hemisphere of such a patient is conscious. This unit can learn, remember, judge, conceptualize, abstract, and reason. It can also feel at least those emotions that it can put into words. However, it clearly is capable of less than the whole brain, in both performance and inner experience. How different is this situation from what we confront when we ask whether an infant or a chimpanzee or a rat is truly conscious? To what extent does it fulfill the dictionary definition?

The implication of the split brain work, I think, is that we should view consciousness in relative terms and be quite specific about which of its attributes we are considering when we ask questions about it. Different people tend to be more or less aware of their inner feeling states, their sexual urges, or their angry or parental feelings, and have different kinds of fantasy lives and tend to approach problem-solving differently. They possibly use different brain functions to varying degrees. Infants—or fetuses, for that matter—organize their behavior differently from adults and thus give us clues that their consciousness is likely to be quite different. The individual will grow, through life experience and predispositions, into a complex balance or organization of the interdependent systems within the brain that will give a unique stamp to the mind and personality. A person's conscious inner experiences are a part of the system for behavior organization, and we can get important clues as to the organization of behavior through conversation. But "actions speak louder than words," and in order to understand an adult as well as an infant, we must take account of what is perceived and what is done with that perception.

Clearly, much of what the brain does is beyond our inner experience; that is, is unconscious. Apparently we learn to become aware of feelings and motivational states, much the same way we learn to become aware of fine perceptual discriminations or cognitive strategies. Through different life experiences and different predispositions, some people become aware of more or different aspects of their mental functioning than others. Even as adults, we can learn to become aware of certain aspects of our inner experience that had been previously neglected or avoided.

The functioning of the disconnected human right hemisphere can be viewed as a model for conceptualizing a dynamic unconscious in normal human functioning. The Sperry studies demonstrate that the sense of self, the "we" in the previous sentences, can carry on without any awareness of the complex mental functioning going on in other parts of the brain. The unified sense of person expressed by these patients' left hemispheres does not seem to be nullified by the existence of the other mind under the same roof. The extent to which this divided consciousness occurs in the lives of normal people has been studied by many different approaches. A number of principles have been worked out by which thoughts, feelings, and motives appear and disappear from our conscious awareness. These principles form the basis for clinical approaches to an understanding of the psychological problems presented by patients.

The story of early development in this book describes the processes that gradually forge the machinery for inner experience or consciousness. Without percepts, actions, states, and their integrative organization in relation to the outside world, there would be nothing to be conscious of. Whether all this behavior organization can exist without consciousness is a question we cannot yet answer. Certainly there has never been a case of a person developing complex spoken language without consciousness.

The best bet we can make at present is that consciousness, or inner awareness, is built up by degrees during early development along with the capacities for complex behavior organization described in other chapters of this book. Infants and children are likely to have degrees and qualities of consciousness commensurate with the extent of their higher cognitive and emotional capacities. The goals and dreams of our inner world usually involve the further extension of the domain of consciousness and embody some perception of its full potential that remains as yet unrealized.

SUMMARY

The organization of behavior is illuminated by the idea that all of our actions carry out some purpose in an evolutionary sense. The three basic properties of behavior—activity, receptivity, and integration— are found in the behavior of a single-celled organism, the typhoid bacillus, and of an invertebrate, the sea snail, as well as in the first new adaptive behavior of the human infant after birth: breathing. The basic units of behavior are thought to be the reflex and the fixed-action pattern. These are put together into behavioral sequences, longer units of more complexity.

The capacity to change behavior on the basis of past experience is a vital aspect of the organization of behavior and can take place at the level of the simplest behavior, the reflex act. Two elementary forms of learning, habituation and sensitization, have been traced to alterations in specific cells in the central nervous system of higher mammals as well as in the invertebrate sea snail. In the latter, the actual site of plasticity can be sought after and appears to be localized at a particular type of synapse that undergoes two different forms of modulation, synaptic depression and presynaptic facilitation, which account for the two forms of learning. In building more complex sequences out of the basic units of behavior, the concept of hierarchical levels of control is important. The principle has implications for understanding development as well as adaptive behavior.

The dynamic relationship between activity, receptivity, and integration determines the state of the organism. States can be roughly divided into three categories—arousal, motivation, and emotion—although there is some overlap between them. It is through an understanding of states that we can account for the variability of behavior, for these time-related changes in the internal condition of the organism determine not only the level and intensity of behavioral acts but also predispose toward specific units and sequences and against others, thus regulating the type of behavior likely to occur.

How these different aspects of the organization of behavior are brought together in order to cope with a rapidly changing environment is illustrated by an analysis of one of our first adaptive behaviors— breathing. This model contains most of the elements of the more complex adaptive behaviors of an appetitive, sexual, or aggressive sort. The units of behavior are organized in a hierarchical system, the stimuli from internal and external sources are sensed at several levels in the central nervous system, and compared with set points by the integrator systems. Motor acts are selected by the integrator system on the basis of this comparison; these motor acts affect both external and internal environments, bringing the chain of events full cycle. The existence of several different sets of these elements at different levels of the nervous system creates a redundancy that allows the same behavior to be carried out with varying levels of access to complex functions such as stored memories and integration with other events in the organism's environment.

At the highest levels of integration, the phenomenon of consciousness allows the widest possible range of information to be brought to bear in analyzing sensory input and selecting appropriate behavior. At this level, states, percepts, memories, and action strategies can somehow be experienced by an inner awareness that totally eludes biological description. The evolutionary purpose of this aspect of the organization of our behavior may lie in the competitive edge provided by the ability to try out behaviors on models of the world in our minds before we use them on the real world outside. The more sophisticated behaviors made possible by the capacity for this mental activity, such as verbal language and scientific experiment, have carried us to the point where we can attempt to understand ourselves.

FURTHER READING

Berger, A. J., Mitchell, R. A., and Severinghaus, J. W. Regulation of respiration. *New England Journal of Medicine*, 297:92–97, 138–143, 1977.

Bindra, D. How adaptive behavior is produced: a perceptual-motivational alternative to response-reinforcement. *Behavioral and Brain Sciences*, 1:41–52, 1978.

Galin, D. Implications for psychiatry of left and right cerebral specialization. *Archives of General Psychiatry*, 31:572–583, 1974.

Gazzaniga, M. S., and LeDoux, J. E. *The Integrated Mind.* New York: Plenum Press, 1978.

Granit, R. *The Purposive Brain.* Cambridge, Mass.: MIT Press, 1977.

Groves, P. M., and Thompson, R. F. Habituation: a dual-process theory. *Psychological Review*, 77:419–450, 1970.

Hilgard, E. R. *Divided Consciousness: Multiple Controls in Human Thought and Action.* New York: Wiley, 1977.

Hinde, R. A. *Biological Bases of Human Social Behavior.* New York: McGraw-Hill, 1974.

Kandel, E. R. *Cellular Basis of Behavior.* San Francisco: W. H. Freeman and Company, 1976.

Koshland, D. E. Bacterial chemotaxis in relation to neurobiology. *Annual Review of Neuroscience*, 3:43–75, 1980.

Marler, P. R., and Hamilton, W. J. *Mechanisms of Animal Behavior.* New York: Wiley, 1966.

Powers, W. T. *Behavior: The Control of Perception.* Chicago: Aldine Publishing, 1973.

Shepherd, G. M. *The Synaptic Organization of the Brain.* New York: Oxford University Press, 1974.

Sperry, R. W. Lateral specialization in the surgically separated hemispheres. In F. O. Schmitt and F. G. Worden (Eds.), *The Neurosciences: Third Study Program.* Cambridge, Mass.: MIT Press, 1974. Pp. 5–19.

Thompson, R. F., and Spencer, W. A. Habituation, a model phenomenon for the study of neuronal substrates of behavior. *Psychological Review*, 73:16–43, 1966.

Young, J. Z. *Programs of the Brain.* Oxford: Oxford University Press, 1978.

Part II
FROM CELL
TO PSYCHE

This section tells the story of our development from a pair of cells into an infant that begins to have a mind of its own. It is hard to imagine a more remarkable transformation. No wonder our comprehension of its basic processes is so incomplete.

The cellular and organ structure aspects of embryology have been studied extensively for many years, but the behavior of the embryo has been neglected by all but a handful of laboratories. The individuality of spermatozoan behavior and the consequences of individual sperm behavior for the selection of our particular genetic constitution have escaped attention until very recently. Few of us pause to consider that the earliest stage in our life cycle involves a single-celled creature, swimming with the aid of a whiplike tail. A few realize that our first behavioral responses occur in the earliest part of fetal life at 7–8 weeks gestation, when our mothers have just become sure they are pregnant. Possibly, we do not like to become aware of our direct continuity with such primitive forms of life any more than we readily accept the evolutionary continuity between our own behavior and that of other animals.

In contrast to our neglect of our earliest developmental origins, newborn babies have been the object of a truly prodigious amount of research and even greater quantities of speculation and fantasy. Adults in all human cultures are drawn to newborns as if by magnetism, and the same phenomenon is seen among nonhuman primates. To add to this attraction, most women in the United States have their babies in hospitals where they remain for several days with little else to do than participate in research studies. Home deliveries in other cultures make neonatal research more difficult.

I have tried to redress this balance in the following chapters by including as much information as I could find about behavior prior to fertilization and during fetal life while summarizing and selecting from the vast literature on the newborn. Even so, I have devoted a comparable number of pages to the newborn as to the entire 10 months prior to birth. I would like to achieve the perspective of the newborn's behavior as a natural outgrowth of the trajectory of fetal behavior development and not as an unprecedented new phenomenon. I have not interrupted the continuity of the story by including a discussion of the interacting events that shape and determine the course of behavior development. However, behavior plays a role in the process of its own development, and this interesting form of auto-regulation will be discussed at intervals throughout the ensuing chapters. The interplay between the environment and the developing organism will be the subject matter of Part III.

The predispositions of the newborn are an outgrowth of prenatal life, while the plasticity of the newborn's behavior provides the basis for mental representations. By describing the organization of the newborn's behavior, the transition is almost imperceptibly made from the world of biology to the world of psychology. I will follow in some detail the way in which this transition is accomplished as we try to describe and understand, through known biological processes, some of the infant's more complex behaviors. The distinction, then, between biology and psychology is not to be found in the infant's behavior or simply as the result of the transition from one stage of development to another, but in the kinds of processes we infer as organizing the behavior we observe.

4

The Sperm
and the Egg

Most of us would begin our life history at the moment of our birth, without giving it another thought. If we paused to think about our biological beginnings, we would probably begin with conception. But if we are interested in our first behaviors and in precisely how the environment and our genes interact to determine who we become, we must go back to the period that concerns our germ cells and their separate origins within each of our parents. The story is so far beyond our ordinary experience that we tend to regard it as unrelated to our nature and perhaps even prefer not to think about it. But, in reality, it makes a dramatic tale, one which is essential to a full understanding of our developmental origins.

ORIGINS AND LIFE HISTORY

How early were the genes formed that contained the blueprint for our development? If we look on the maternal side, the answer is that in this sense we are almost as old as our mothers! The fact is that the ovarian structures that contain the genetic materials for the eggs were formed during the fetal life of our mothers, and this process ceases before birth. Primordial *follicles* are present in babies at birth but remain dormant for years, further changes being normally postponed until puberty or after. These germ cells are ready to become mature, for it has been documented that the ovary responds appropriately to pituitary hormones at 9 months of age and 5-year-olds have given birth to normal children.

While these follicles wait for puberty to rouse them into action, more than 80 percent are lost by attrition, but about 5 million are left when pituitary hormones first begin their cycles of stimulation. Throughout this period, the eggs have the full chromosome complement of 46 *(diploid)*. It is not until the midmenstrual cycle surge of pituitary luteinizing hormone that reduction division takes place and the germ cells of the egg become *haploid* (23 chromosomes). A few hours later the egg is popped out of the wall of the ovary into the

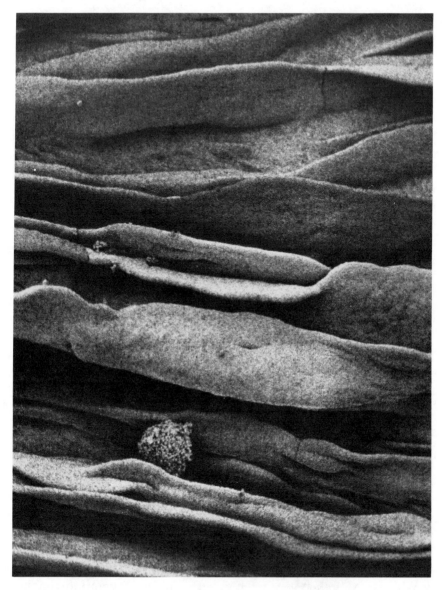

FIGURE 4-1
Unfertilized ovum in the folds of the fallopian tube. Those follicle cells surrounding the ovum at the time of ovulation still remain as an outer envelope. The folded mucous membrane secretes enzymes that gradually cause this cellular envelope to loosen. (Photograph 100X by Lennart Nilsson.)

protective embrace of the fallopian tube. It is still a mystery how just one or two eggs are "chosen" for ovulation each cycle from so many.

So at midpoint of our mother's menstrual cycle, her contribution to our biological inheritance was launched. Recent successful test-tube babies are proof of how independent the egg is after ovulation. Unlike the spermatozoa, the egg has no means of moving and is carried along by poorly understood local fluid currents within the ciliated lining of the fallopian tube. The egg is changed by the fluid in the tube so that it is ready for fertilization within 2 hours of ovulation; it remains in the tube, ready for fertilization, for 1–2 days. If not fertilized by sperm, it disintegrates and is reabsorbed from the female genital tract.

Conception is certainly a special event; in fact, it is comprised of a series of events or processes beginning with the arrival of the sperm in the vicinity of the egg and culminating in implantation of the fertilized egg in the wall of the uterus. But how do the sperm get there and what are their beginnings?

Sperm lack the long history of the egg but present the special feature of motility. That sperm move makes them of considerable interest to people concerned with behavior, and the long and perilous journey of this particular phase of our life arouses our curiosity. Cells that line specific passages within the testis produce hundreds of millions of sperm every day. On our father's side, the cell carrying the other half of our genetic heritage was laid down about 60–90 days before our mother's egg popped into its independent existence. For sperm, the reduction division occurs at the point when four immature sperm are formed from a precursor cell in the testis. They are not functional yet and undergo further maturational changes that involve alterations in the shape of the nucleus and of the sperm head. Finally, functional maturation of the nucleus takes place under the influence of fluid in ducts lying next to the testis.

THE GREAT SPERM LOTTERY

The nature of sperm formation is interesting because it determines what kinds of processes we can expect will play a role in the crucial outcome question: which sperm fertilizes the egg? For we know that there is great diversity among the 350 million sperm released during a single ejaculation, and many aspects of our nature will be strongly influenced by which one actually joins its 23 chromosomes with the

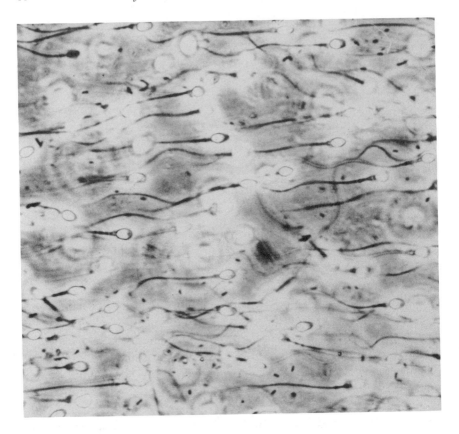

FIGURE 4-2

The long journey. Sperm swim together almost in formation. All tails point in the same direction and all heads are turned forward. These sperm are on their way into the uterus through the protective mucous plug in the cervix, the neck of the uterus. This mucus varies in consistency during different parts of the menstrual cycle. Most of the time it is thick and viscous. Around the fourteenth day of the menstrual cycle, when the ovum is to enter the fallopian tube, the mucus is as clear as glass and half liquid. Its molecules then stretch out in a pattern that allows the sperm to pass between them, farther on into the uterus. Sperm that do not arrive at this time are less fortunate. It is difficult for them to penetrate the viscous mass of entangled mucous molecules that present an effective barrier during most of the menstrual cycle. (Photograph 500X by Lennart Nilsson.)

23 chromosomes of the egg. It is estimated that 70–80 percent of the variability found in size and shape among sperm of the human species is accounted for by variation within the range of types from any single

male. Thus, there are marked differences in shape, motility, and capacity to fertilize eggs within the population of sperm in a single human ejaculate.

Until very recently, sperm were regarded as detached portions of the male body, and characteristics of their shape and activity were thought to be determined solely by the genes of that body. It was thought that the genetic material in the nucleus was simply being delivered to the egg by the motile body, much as a rocket delivers its warhead. This view is now being challenged by a number of experimental findings that suggest that the characteristics of sperm are initially determined by the special genetic properties of local patches of tissue (clones) in the testis and that the particular genetic content of each sperm may affect the character of the sperm themselves. For example, it has been found that sperm carrying a gene for very short tails in mice, when competing with sperm carrying genes for normal tails, will have a much greater success in fertilizing eggs if inseminated a number of hours after ovulation than when inseminated at the time of ovulation (1). The competitive balance between diverse sperm, therefore, can be shifted by an interaction between individual genetic characteristics of the sperm and time-related variations in characteristics of the female genital tract and egg.

We do not know how the tail allele in these experiments alters its competitive ability. However, it has recently been discovered that human Y- and X-carrying sperm can be distinguished on the basis of a surface characteristic revealed by the biochemical technique of immunofluorescence. Possibly surface tags or indicators exist on the surface of different sperm—clues to the specific genetic make-up of the individual sperm—and handles by which they can be differentially affected by their environment.

If the characteristics of individual sperm are the expression of differences not only in their cell line of origin but also in their own genes, this would have far-reaching implications. The many possible interactions between the physical and behavioral characteristics of the individual sperm and the environment provided by the female genital tract constitute a complex and powerful mechanism for genetic selection. The "many are called but few are chosen" nature of this phase of our life history suggests several ways by which the environment can influence the genetic makeup of children. For example, the hormonal state of the female affects characteristics of mucous flow in her uterus and cervix, and neural influences affect uterine contractions, both of which are important for sperm transport. Sperm of different genetic constitution will be differently affected by alterations of these characteristics of the female genital tract in their competition to fertilize. The woman's central nervous system, in turn, acts to alter those neural and hormonal messages that so affect the nature of the challenges to be encountered by the sperm in their journey toward the egg.

Thus, characteristics of an individual female's genital tract can exert a preferential action on sperm of a given genetic makeup, and different females may differ in such preferences. For example, it has recently been reported (2) that 65 percent more boy babies are born to women who have intercourse two days after ovulation than in those whose timing is closer to ovulation. Y sperm, then, would appear to be favored by the characteristics of the female genital tract and/or egg at certain points in the menstrual cycle.

THE BEHAVIOR OF SPERM

In addition to this population selection process, the realization that sperm are in fact individual, haploid, *human* organisms—each with its own structural, chemical, and behavioral characteristics—jars the mind. But should we use the word "human" here? If not, how are we to indicate that we are not referring to bull or mouse sperm? What ethical problems are raised by this view of the nature of sperm? Beyond these unanswerable questions lies a fertile area for exploration of the genetics of behavior. For we have recently learned that sperm, if quiescent, respond to stimulation by becoming motile. If challenged by increased viscosity in their surrounding fluid, they increase the amplitude of their tail motion. And when finally approaching the egg, sperm have been observed to increase the speed of their tail movements. Bull sperm have as high a concentration of the neurotransmitter enzyme *acetylcholinesterase* as does bull brain, and motility of sperm is markedly affected by low concentrations of drugs that are active in cholinergic systems. The mechanism of flagellar (tail) motion has recently been shown to involve a doublet protein, forming a complex that changes shape in the presence of sources of chemical energy (ATP), much the way the protein complex of actin and myosin in human muscle causes muscular contractions. Thus, we have a very small, single-celled organism, capable of locomotion and reactive to its environment. Almost everything about the determinants of its behavior remains to be discovered.

But we do know what the sperm has to do. Sperm swim at 5 mm/ minute, a speed which, if adjusted for relative body size, would be approximately the speed of a jogger, a 10-minute mile. This motility is induced in the nonmotile testicular sperm by the addition of prostatic and seminal fluid at the time of ejaculation and by the action of cervical and uterine fluids. Nevertheless, this speed cannot account for the transit time achieved by the first few sperm that pass the entire length of cervix and uterus in a few minutes to enter the fallopian tube. Since the flow of uterine mucous is against them, uterine contractions may be the answer, but the sperm would have to swim across the current to the mucosal wall in order to get a ride up. Actually, sperm tend to swim upstream, even in a constant current (3), a feat that requires relatively sophisticated navigational equipment, well beyond what sperm are supposed to possess. Two sperm sticking close together swim faster than one, and physical hydraulic considerations predict that this saves energy. Thus, factors such as those promoting schooling of fish may also govern the behavior of sperm. In any case, after vaginal insemination, equilibrium in distribution of sperm throughout the female genital tract is reached in about six hours, with the vast majority of sperm remaining in the cervical mucous where they can survive for 5–7 days.

FEMALE SELECTION MECHANISMS

Only about 1/10 of 1 percent of the 350 million sperm actually get as far as the fallopian tube where the egg is. This is the first stage of a powerful selection process whose precise workings are only dimly understood. Recent evidence from Cohen and others suggests that the female immune system coats nearly all the sperm in the uterus with antibody, thus incapacitating most for fertilization by stabilizing their head membranes. Thus, the female may selectively "choose" a small uncoated population of sperm with which her egg will be allowed to combine. The functional significance of this newly discovered mechanism is as yet unproven, but highly specific material selective processes such as this must exist to account for the kind of effects described for the tail allele for mice. In addition to such "allergic" responses, the hormones of the ovary have regulatory action on sperm movement. Removal of ovaries in female animals completely halts sperm transport. Very small doses of estrogen enhance sperm transport in such animals. The pituitary hormone oxytocin, sympathetic and parasympathetic neurotransmitters, histamine, progesterone and prostaglandins have also been implicated in sperm transport. These substances are all under the control of the female's nervous system and are thus liable to be altered during emotional states and in response to changes in her environment or in her behavior. It is by such a chain of events that a particular female might exert a particular preference for sperm of a particular genetic makeup.

The final phase of our sperm's journey involves another selection process in which only one sperm fertilizes an egg, although many potentially fertile sperm may be in contact with it. The local mechanisms for membrane fusion and penetration of the head of the sperm into the egg have been greatly illuminated by recent electron microscopic studies, but the processes by which the single sperm is selected remain a complete mystery. The exquisite coordination of three processes—maturation of the fertilized egg, modification of the uterine wall to receive the egg, and fallopian tube transport—results in successful implantation of 70–75 percent of fertilized eggs, and the next stage of development begins: the prenatal period.

SUMMARY

In looking back at this earliest stage of our biological development, it is clear that many environmental interactions help determine the genetic makeup of the embryo. The mother's behavior and emotional state may affect this interaction by altering the environment through which the sperm must move and thereby act to select which sperm have the greatest chance of fertilizing the egg. The genetic content of the sperm itself may influence this selection process, either by gross structural, ultrastructural (antigenic), or even behavioral means, through modifications of motility. Even after the selective processes of mating, both the behavior of the mother and the behavior of the sperm are factors in the critical selection process by which our genetic endowment is determined. Of course, chance plays an enormously important role, and the precise workings of environmental influences on these processes remain to be elucidated.

The biological processes described in this chapter suggest possible ways by which we may be able to understand some puzzling phenomena: shifts in the sex ratio of births during wars or other social upheavals (4) and animal experiments demonstrating transmission to offspring of alterations induced in their parents prior to mating (5). Biochemical changes in the mucus of the female genital tract that favor X-bearing spermatozoa could be produced, for instance, by altered hormonal balance as part of the female's nutritional state and emotional response to environmental devastations. The transgenerational effects in animals can be illustrated by the following example. Female *or* male rats made diabetic by a toxic chemical (alloxan) produce offspring with higher than normal incidence of diabetes in subseqent generations (5). Such examples of the inheritance of acquired characteristics need not imply alteration of genetic material. When transmission is through females, such effects may be produced by persisting changes in the uterine environment. Equally plausible is the possibility that persisting changes in the female genital tract could bias the selection of sperm. What about the male rats made diabetic? Could the alloxan or the ensuing metabolic derangements of the diabetes have affected the behavioral characteristics of some of the sperm and shifted the likelihood of fertilization by sperm carrying genes for diabetes?

A greater awareness of the interesting unsolved problems in the behavioral biology of this, the earliest phase of our development, may lead to new ideas on how individuals are formed.

FURTHER READING

Beatty, R. A. Sperm diversity within the species. In B. A. Afzelius (Ed.), *The Functional Anatomy of the Spermatozoon*. Proceedings of the Second International Symposium. Oxford: Pergamon Press, 1975. Pp. 319–327.

Bishop, D. W. (Ed.) *Spermatozoon Motility* Am. Assoc. for Adv. of Sci. Publ. No. 72. Washington, D.C. 1962.

Cohen, J. Gametic diversity within an ejaculate. In Afzelius, op. cit., pp. 329–340.

Nelson, L. Chemistry and neurochemistry of sperm motility control. *Federation of American Societies of Experimental Biology*, 37:2543–2547, 1978.

Noyes, R. W. Disorders of genetic transportation and implantation. In N. S. Assali (Ed.), *Pathophysiology of Gestation*. Vol. I: *Maternal Disorders*. New York: Academic Press, 1972. Pp. 63–143.

Phillips, D. M., and Olson, G. Mammalian sperm motility: structure in relation to function. In Afzelius, op. cit., pp. 117–126.

REFERENCES CITED

1. Braden, A. W. H. T-locus in mice: Segregation distortion and sterility in male. In R. A. Beatty and S. Gluecksohn-Waelsch (Eds. and Organizers), *The Genetics of the Spermatozoon: Proceedings of the Second International Symposium held at the University of Edinburgh, Scotland on August 16–20, 1971*. Edinburgh: First published 1972 by the Organizers. Pp. 289–305.

2. Harlap, S. Gender of infants conceived on different days of the menstrual cycle. *New England Journal of Medicine*, 300:1445–1448, 1979.
3. Rothschild, L. Sperm movement—problems and observations. In Bishop, op. cit., pp. 13–29.
4. Trivers, R. L., and Willard, D. E. Natural selection of parental ability to vary the sex ratio of their offspring. *Science*, 179:90–92, 1973.
5. Spergel, G., Khan, F., and Goldner, M. G. Emergence of overt diabetes in offspring of rats with induced latent diabetes. *Metabolism*, 24:1311–1319, 1975.

5

Prenatal Behavior

If biology were different and humans ordinarily observed the development of their young from implantation of the fertilized egg to the time of birth nine months later, we would probably have very different conceptions of our nature and of the processes by which we come into being. As it is now, birth is regarded as the event that begins our recorded life. Newborn babies are essentially human and by their appearance do not suggest the idea that our origins might have any features in common with other species.

In the late nineteenth century, however, when early embryologists began to observe prenatal stages of mammals including humans, as well as early developmental stages of birds, reptiles, and invertebrates, they were forcibly struck by the similarity in appearance of embryonic forms of such widely divergent classes as fish, chicks, pigs, and humans. With the excitement of Darwin's new evolutionary theory, it was not long before the idea emerged that in human embryologic development, all the stages of evolution were rapidly passed through. The idea that ontogeny recapitulates phylogeny is so appealing that it was still being taught in high school biology courses a decade ago, despite the fact that knowledgeable embryologists had long abandoned it. As Gould points out, it was only the discovery of the genetic basis of heredity that short-circuited this popular analogy by illuminating the real source of control for the structure of organs. By discovering that the rates of development of structures were determined by enzymes dictated by genes, it was learned how the *appearance* of recapitulation was produced as well as the many exceptions to this generalization. What was left, then, was the observation that vertebrates share a common embryonic stage with each other and with some invertebrates. This is currently taken to indicate descent from a common ancestor and to demonstrate the conservative nature of evolution.

Partly because all the early stages of human development have been hidden from view, we are far behind in our understanding of the processes and principles governing this period of life. Even in other mammals, techniques are still inadequate to the task of exposing the fetus to the experimenter for days on end while maintaining its delicate maternal support system. As a result, the fetal bird, developing outside the mother in its thin-shelled egg, has become a favorite model for asking basic questions about early vertebrate development.

THE EMBRYONIC PERIOD: BEFORE 7 WEEKS

What is our first behavior? Do we move before we are stimulated or are we primarily responsive creatures? When we do make our first response, is it toward the stimulus or away from it? Which skin areas become sensitive first? Which internal functions start earliest? These questions are sometimes asked in the hope that the answers may tell us something about the basic nature of humans, since what develops first must be fundamental to all subsequent characteristics. There are answers to the specific questions, if not to the one about our basic nature. Yet there remains a major mystery in prenatal life—the question of why sensory and motor functions develop and exhibit activity, weeks and even months before they have any clear usefulness to the baby. We find it hard to accept that there is all this function without some purpose. But let us see what our life is like before we ask why it might be this way.

The very first movement that an observer would be able to detect is the beating of the heart, but a magnifying glass would be needed because the embryo is about 1/4-inch long at this point. Our observer would also have to start looking very early—even before the mother knew she was pregnant—because the heart begins beating a week after the first menstrual period is missed, when the embryo is only 3 weeks old. Already, the two-layered embryonic disc has become transformed into a recognizable body resembling a worm, a fluid-filled amniotic sac, and a stalk connecting the embryo to the wall of the mother's womb. The first primitive movements are spontaneous and originate within the muscle cells of the heart, since the nervous system has not yet begun to form. A few red blood cells can be seen, shuttling ineffectively back and forth with each irregular contraction of the single-chambered, tubelike heart. Gradually the movements become more regular, a rhythm is established, and there is a jerky progression of corpuscles to and from the three arcs of the early circulatory system: the yolk sac where corpuscles are formed, the chorion where they pass close by the mother's blood vessels, and within the embryo itself. This

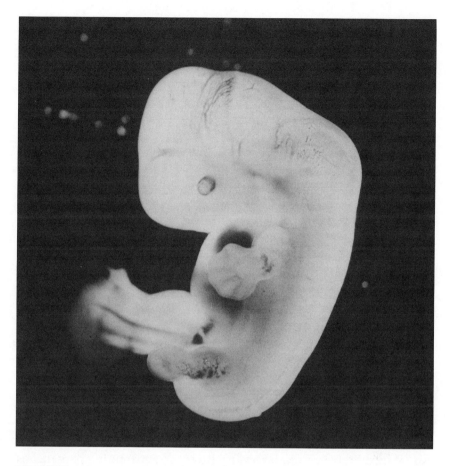

FIGURE 5-1
The embryo at 5–6 weeks, about ⅜ inch from crown to rump. (Photograph by Lennart Nilsson.)

early start gives the developing heart a predominant position in the ensuing days, so that by 5 weeks of age it is almost as big as the head, bright red, and its powerful regular movements shake the entire embryo at each contraction (see Figure 5–1). Those who have seen early vertebrate embryos cannot help being struck by the power of this early source of rhythmic stimulation, arising within the developing organism itself. The role of this very early spontaneous rhythmic behavior and the effects of the stimulation it provides may go well beyond its obvious function as a pump, but are at present wholly unknown.

THE EARLY FETAL PERIOD: 6–16 WEEKS

Only after the heart begins to function does the nervous system start to develop. Then limbs begin to form, and muscles within them differentiate. By six weeks, the embryo is clearly not going to be a fish, although it appears as likely to become a frog or a rat as a human being, its tail having not yet regressed. This age is considered to be the end of the embryonic and the beginning of the fetal period. It is the age at which the organism first responds to stimulation. But the response is given only to strong direct stimulation of muscles and consists only of a local contraction, the *myogenic response*. Since this behavior is not spontaneous, does not involve the nervous system, and is hard to see, we are inclined to be less interested in it; however, the role of muscular contraction prior to innervation remains to be explored.

Finally, we come to a question that still captures the attention of behavioral embryologists. Is the earliest behavior spontaneous, or is it responsive? Are sensory pathways necessary for motor systems to initiate function? It has become clear that it is enormously difficult to prove that any motor act is truly spontaneous, for one cannot easily rule out the possiblity that some unappreciated stimulus, either neural or hormonal, preceded and elicited the motor burst. However, the task is made easier for us in the human, since apparently spontaneous movements have never been observed earlier than the age at which responses can be elicited by stimulation. This is not the situation in fish or bird embryos that show a pattern of apparently spontaneous movements for several days before responses can be elicited by stimulation, a pattern that develops unchanged even when the sensory system is surgically disconnected from the motor system. Mammals show reflex responsiveness at or before the time of "spontaneous" movements. Obviously one would have to watch carefully and continuously in early fetal life to be sure that earlier spontaneous movements were not being missed. This has not been done systematically in the human, but in the guinea pig the first spontaneous movements occur 10–14 hours *after* reflex responsiveness first occurs, a time period equivalent to about a week in the human gestation period.

The first neuromuscular behavior of the human fetus has been recorded at 7½ weeks gestation by Hooker in his classic studies during the late 1930s, which, together with the later studies of Humphrey, remain the best behavioral observations on early human fetuses. He studied fetuses as they were being removed for therapeutic abortion

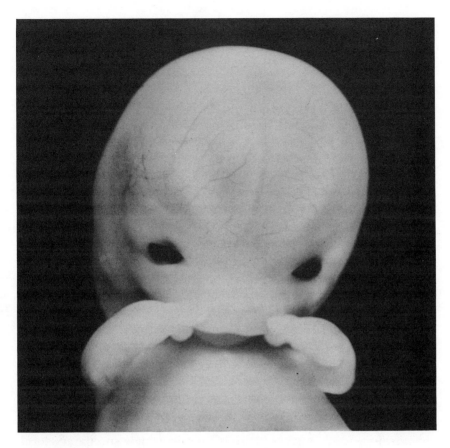

FIGURE 5-2
The fetus at 8–9 weeks, about 1 inch from crown to rump. (Photograph by Lennart Nilsson.)

while their mothers were under spinal anesthesia. The first movements were in response to light stimulation around the mouth and involve the head and neck, which flex *away* from the site of stimulation. By 8–8½ weeks some quivering of the arms and flexion of the upper trunk were noted. Mouth opening accompanies these early responses in many cases. At this point, the fetus is only an inch long, but stubby fingers have formed and joints have appeared along the limbs (see Figure 5–2). Hooker also observed slight spontaneous movements of the upper trunk, but if these movements occur in the womb, they are not felt by most mothers until 16–17 weeks.

On the sensory side, at 8–9 weeks the fetus responds behaviorally to a fine hair being drawn across its lips. This is even before the growing sensory nerves have reached the basement membrane of the skin and well before the development of the specialized touch receptors of the skin (12 weeks). But this is true only around the mouth and nose; other areas of skin do not become responsive until about 3 weeks later.

Over the next 2 weeks (9–11), an expanding pattern of reflex behavior can be elicited by oral stimulation. Extension of the arms at the shoulders and rotation of the pelvis to the opposite side come to accompany the head and neck movements. This triple response is stereotyped and can only be elicited from the one skin area. At 10½ weeks, stimulation of the palms of the hands elicits transient finger closing, the earliest beginning of the grasp reflex. By 11 weeks, stimulation of the sole of the foot elicits downward curling of all the toes, and stimulation of the eyelids causes forcible closing of the muscles around the eye. Still, only the oral region can elicit the generalized pattern, other sites giving the local responses described.

Between 11 and 17 weeks, there develops an increasing variability of the limb and trunk responses elicited by oral stimulation and the first appearance of local responses of facial muscles to the stimulus. In addition, body movements are flowing and graceful instead of mechanical; flexion toward a gentle stimulus occurs more frequently. Responses can be elicited from any part of the body, except the back and the top of the head. These responses are increasingly specific and local, such as the appearance of fanning of the toes and upward flexion of the great toe (the Babinski sign) in response to stimulation of the sole of the foot. By the sixteenth week, a sustained grasp reflex is present to palm stimulation. Spontaneous movements are frequent, vigorous, and varied with slower squirming ("athetoid") movements as well as jerks and thrusts. These movements are often felt by the mother, the fetus being about 7 in. long at 17 weeks. A fetus this age may suck its thumb if it comes in contact with its mouth; other patterned movements are reminiscent of later behaviors such as wriggling, reaching, and kicking. Facial grimacing and pouting occur, and the first recorded swallowing of amniotic fluid is at the thirteenth week.

We have seen that heartbeat begins very early and is essential for transport of nutrients and removal of cellular waste products. What about respiration? Oxygen and carbon dioxide are carried out in the placenta so that respiration is not essential and yet shallow, periodic inspiratory and expiratory movements of chest and abdomen have been detected by ultrasonic techniques during the second trimester, about the time we have just been describing. Analysis of similar respiratory movements at the same stage in the fetal lamb have shown that there is no net movement of amniotic fluid in the trachea and lungs, the chest moving (passively) in as the diaphragm moves down with no change in intrathoracic pressure resulting. These movements at first occur only during or after periods of generalized activity, like an animal out of breath, and are not regulated by changing fetal blood gas levels as they are in the newborn. In fact, lowering fetal oxygen supply reduces and finally stops them long before other movements cease. As for other internal movements, those involving smooth muscles such as stomach contractions and peristaltic bowel movements have been observed in the youngest fetuses showing neuromuscular behavior, as early as the seventh week.

A FUNCTIONAL ROLE
FOR EARLY FETAL BEHAVIOR?

The midpoint of pregnancy has not yet been reached, and yet the fetus has been active for more than half of this time and has become extremely active in systems that it will not need for another five months. This has been noted by behavioral and physiological embryologists for many years but remains a mystery to which has been given the name *anticipation.* Nature has few examples of activity without adaptive purpose and it seems likely that these early behaviors are somehow essential for proper maturation of behavioral mechanisms. The first tests of this idea were done on simpler vertebrates such as the amphibian *Amblystoma* by Carmichael in the 1920s (see Gottlieb).

Prevention of their early embryonic movements by prolonged anesthesia with chloretone placed in the embryo's water bath revealed that embryos thus deprived prior to the free swimming stage of development nevertheless were able to swim. Recent tissue culture techniques developed by Crain have enabled a limited test in a mammalian system. Fetal rodent spinal cord and midbrain explants form complex synaptic networks in a culture medium and develop equally complex bioelectric discharge patterns that can be stimulated and recorded electronically. Prevention of all electric activity for several weeks by the presence of a local anesthetic, xylocaine, in the culture medium did not prevent the formation of normal synapses or the production of complex neuronal firing patterns in response to the *first* electric stimulus applied after withdrawal of the anesthetic. The neural structure of these tissues was similar to normally developed explant systems even when viewed under the electron microscope, and the evoked electric potentials from cerebral tissue were similar to those seen in normally developed explants. Thus, whereas patterned and repetitive neural discharge patterns seem to be a consistent feature of developing nervous systems from amphibians to humans and even occur in artificial test-tube systems, this function does not appear to play an absolutely essential role in the maturation toward more complex neural function.

This capacity of neural tissue to organize itself during maturation in anticipation of the need for more complex functioning is an important biological tendency that underlies much of development. How independent this organizational process may be from the consequences of its own functioning is an unsettled question, despite the experiments just cited. First, although gross behavior patterns may not be dependent on previous function, modulation, threshold levels, and more complex properties of advanced behavior may be more dependent on the effects of practice. For example, the amphibian embryo studies have been repeated and have shown that the previously paralyzed embryos give shorter swimming responses to stimulation and the forward movement achieved by their efforts was reduced in comparison to controls that had exhibited early spontaneous movements for several days prior to testing. Secondly, the natural course of structural development in the nervous system appears to be modified by muscle function during the embryonic period. Spinal cord motor neuron number normally declines by about 25 percent in chick embryos (and mammals) during the first half of the prehatching period. Immobilization of the embryo with curare-like drugs during this period prevents the phase of natural cell death and results in muscles with increased numbers of motor endplates and in spinal cords with increased numbers of motor neurons (1). So far, it has been impossible to keep such creatures alive long enough to see how their behavior is affected by such abnormalities of structure, but it is a vivid example of the role of the behavior of the embryo in the formation of its own nervous system.

Convincing evidence for a vital role of prenatal activity in behavior development comes from two other lines of experiments on muscle function. The first attempt in higher vertebrates to prevent prenatal activity (2) produced a startling and inconvenient finding. Chick embryos prevented from early behavioral activity by intravenous infusion of curare or succinyl choline were unable to move later in development, not because the nerves or muscles failed to develop normally but because their joints had become fixed into rigid structures. As little as one to two days of paralysis led to severe contractures of the soft tissues in and around the joints of the neck as well as of legs and toes. Apparently, fetal movements are necessary to the development of flexible articulations between the bones. In some cases, fibrous adhesions had developed between the surfaces of the joints.

This unplanned venture into experimental orthopedics made it clear that deprivation by paralysis was not the best way to find out more about the developmental function of anticipatory prenatal activity in vertebrates. The experiment did establish one important function for all this prenatal movement: to keep the fetus from ossifying in the fetal position. The limited range of limb movements found in human newborns that have been anesthetized prenatally due to high maternal alcohol intake suggests that we are as vulnerable as chicks in this regard. Another site where fetal movement may be important for structural development is in the mouth. It is during the early period of spontaneous mouth opening between 8½ and 11 weeks of age that the bones of the hard palate change from a vertical to a horizontal position over the tongue and come in contact with each other and with the nasal septum for fusion. Movement of the mandible forces the tongue against these bony ridges, creates suction above the tongue, and produces movement of amniotic fluid in and out of the mouth. These forces exerted upon the elements of the palate during the critical period before bony fusion have been thought to be important in normal tissue union and in the abnormality of cleft palate deformity. Recent experiments with mice have shown that tongue removal during this period in their prenatal life in fact led to an increased incidence of palatal abnormalities (3).

Another set of experiments (4) investigated the effects of patterns of nerve impulses on the behavior and biochemical makeup of muscles. In mammals, muscles of different types give either fast or slow twitches to a standard nerve stimulation. The slow twitch muscles are innervated by tonic neurons discharging at a slow rate, the fast muscles by phasic neurons firing at a faster rate. If a nerve normally innervating a fast muscle is transplanted so that it now innervates a slow muscle, that muscle will change both its twitch characteristics and its protein makeup. The reverse is also true. This was thought to be due to specific *trophic factors* characteristic of the nerves until a normally innervated fast muscle was stimulated for three weeks at a slow rate pattern. It became transformed into a muscle that gave slow twitches and was induced to synthesize protein components normally found only in the slow muscle. These experiments were done on mature rabbits; muscles are likely to be even more sensitive to neural firing patterns earlier in development. The implication is that functional activity of the nervous system during early fetal life may have a determining effect on biochemical and physical characteristics of the muscles innervated, leading to the functional specialization necessary for complex motor acts later in life.

Another more speculative function of these high levels of prenatal activity is the stimulation they provide to the developing fetal sensory receptors. In the human, specialized nerve endings in the skin (Pacinian corpuscles) reach structural adequacy, as judged under the microscope, by 12 weeks in the area of the lips and 16 weeks in the fingers. The simple nerve endings are already responsive at 7–8 weeks; the vestibular apparatus (responsive to alterations of position in space) by 14 weeks; all parts of the auditory apparatus are present and morphologically mature at 6 months, while photoreceptor development in the retina is not complete until birth. The first evidence of auditory function has been obtained by evoked electrical response at 21 weeks and in the visual system at 26 weeks.

This order in development of the sensory systems is present in most mammals: cutaneous, taste and olfactory, vestibular, auditory, and visual. We do not know much about the extent to which normal development of structure and function in these specialized sense organs is dependent on the stimulation provided by fetal movements and other stimulation present in the uterine environment. In Chapter 10 I will deal with some of the evidence we have on this subject.

In summary then, fetal body movements begin before the second missed menstrual period and can be elicited by sensory stimulation in the mouth area at about the same time that they first appear spontaneously. Early movements are limited, weak, jerky, uncoordinated, and stereotyped. Beginning in the region of the head and moving down the body, movements gradually become stronger, smoother, more integrated, and individualized over the next two months. Some elicited movements are generalized and involve most of the body parts early, becoming more discrete and localized later. Stimuli to other skin areas elicit only localized movements first, which become parts of more generalized, coordinated patterns later on. Earlier theoretical formulations attempted to assert one or the other of these patterns exclusively, but the evidence in a variety of species demonstrates that both local and generalized patterns of movement coexist during development. The basis for any particular sequence must be traced to the underlying schedule of neural development, as these change over time. An example of this will be given in the next section.

The main concept that has been generated by these observations on the very earliest beginnings of our behavior development is that it is *epigenetic;* that is, motor and sensory capabilities do not arise at once. Development is characterized by transformations in which certain functional patterns come into being that are not found in previous or even in subsequent stages. Functionally as well as structurally, it is not the same creature at two different stages of its own development. The differences between stages of development in a single animal are almost as profound as those between species of vertebrates. The implications of this fact are difficult for adults to fully grasp, accustomed as we are to relative stability in our remembered past experience. It means that we cannot generalize about the mechanism of an action, the effect of a stimulus, or the long-term impact of an experience from one stage of development to another. We have to understand exactly how the developing infant interacts with its environment separately at each age. The demarcation into the major stages for a given behavioral system and the determination of the nodal points of transition are tasks that currently occupy much of the attention of developmental researchers. Both maturation of brain mechanisms underlying behavior and crucial interactions with its environment cause progression to a subsequent stage and are the dynamic forces that drive development forward. I will continue to give the available evidence on how these forces work as we move on through the major stages of development.

THE FIRST DISCONTINUITY: 17–22 WEEKS

An extraordinary change takes place in the pattern of behavior development at 17 or 18 weeks of gestation. The level of activity that had progressively risen over the past two months becomes stilled. Elicited movements are sluggish, and spontaneous activity is limited to levels previously reached a month earlier. This period of inhibition lasts until about the twenty-fourth week of gestation, when the trend toward increasingly complex activity is resumed. This is the first instance of what have been termed *discontinuities* in behavioral development. A close look at exactly what happens reveals that the elements of a complex elicited response do not disappear all at once, but rather one by one. For example, the earliest response to develop—the flexion re-

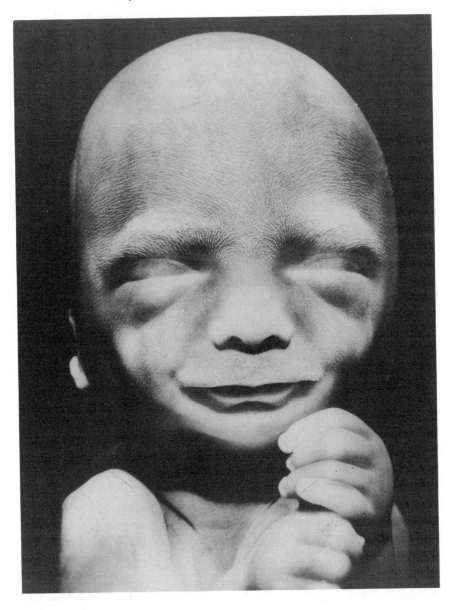

FIGURE 5-3
The fetus at 18 weeks, about 7 inches from crown to rump. (Photograph by Lennart Nilsson.)

sponse away from stimulation—is the first to be affected: it reaches its height at 11 weeks and then parts of the action disappear in a specific order, starting with the lower trunk and progressing toward the neck until the entire reflex is elicited only with difficulty. The fetus, in this respect, appears to have regressed functionally to a much earlier level. But this appearance is in some ways misleading, for if the fetus at this age of quiescence is subjected to partial anoxia, the response will be facilitated instead of suppressed entirely as in earlier days. But the response, once facilitated, can be seen to be qualitatively different from a response of the same intensity at an earlier age. The movements are more limited, coordinated, and stimulus-related, more nearly purposeful in the eyes of the observer. At the end of the quiescent period, responsiveness reappears in the order in which it first appeared, starting with the head and neck, progressing to arms, and finally involving the lower trunk. Expressive facial movements have been added to these rather diffuse trunk and limb movements, with a scowl, tightening of muscles around eyes, and wide mouth opening.

How can this unusual era in our development be accounted for, and what does it tell us about subsequent stages in our development? Here again, we must rely on animal experiments to shed light on puzzling and important questions about our early life. For a time this quiescent period was ascribed to the low levels of oxygenation typical of fetuses at this stage. The fact that worsening the anoxia reestablished activity was of course disturbing to that explanation. Through neuroanatomical studies in animals and physiological work on sheep, it has become clear that the quiescence reflects the maturation of descending regulatory fibers originating in the dorsal thalamus and striatum. As these higher regions become dominant, the midbrain systems previously regulating movement are first brought under control by inhibition, creating the quiescent period, and then activated, bringing the pause to an end. Barcroft was able to test this theory by making cuts just below the midbrain of sheep fetuses that had entered their quiet period, and returning them to their mothers' wombs so that they developed normally for the next ten days. At the end of this period, he found that their mental age had been reduced 30 percent: their spontaneous and elicited behavior was that of a fetus prior to entry into quiescence. Cut off from the influence of developing midbrain centers, behavior persisted at its earlier level of organization, determined by spinal and bulbar regions.

The puzzling effects of anoxia were explained by the finding that the most recently developed systems are the most suppressed by anoxia, the apparent facilitation of behavior being the result of partial release of the relatively anoxia-resistant, long-established spinal system from the inhibitory influence of the newly-formed, anoxia-susceptible descending midbrain system.

The extent and importance of inhibitory neural systems in fetal development has not generally been appreciated. Electrophysiologic evidence of inhibitory activity appears in the cortex of fetal cats and dogs a few days *before* evidence of excitatory activity. Fish and amphibian larvae show enhanced swimming activity when agents such as strychnine are introduced into their water—agents that selectively block inhibitory neural cellular mechanisms. Strychnine releases the potential for stimulation to produce the typical, elaborate, synaptically-mediated discharge patterns seen earlier in development of the tissue explant.

It is clear how useful such behavioral inhibition must be at a stage in life when we must remain in as restricted a space as the womb. The fetus is growing rapidly in relation to its living space, so that it is becoming progressively more cramped. The appearance of inhibition of total activity by higher centers is well-timed from this point of view, and when fetal activity begins to increase again it no longer involves most of the parts of the body simultaneously. Generalized or total pattern activity has been replaced by individual limb or trunk movements, sometimes in sequences but not expressed simultaneously in mass action patterns as before. This is an expression of the regulatory action of descending pathways now functioning. These movements are more suited to the close quarters the fetus will remain in for the next four months, although the fetus's kicks may become powerful enough to occasionally wake the mother from her sleep.

Fetal movements in response to stimulation gradually begin to resume their vigor and extent starting at 22–24 weeks. More fluid and coordinated, activity at this stage is not grossly different from newborns' and, indeed, the fetus is approaching the age at which it can first live outside the womb. The general sequence in which elicited movements reappear after the period of inhibition is the same as the one by which they originated weeks earlier. This is likely to be due to the fact that motor neuron systems that have been active for a longer period of development are more easily fired and become activated earlier by descending systems than those that matured more recently.

THE ORIGINS OF STATE ORGANIZATION
AND RHYTHMS IN BEHAVIOR: 24–32 WEEKS

Thus far we have described the behavior of the fetus in a qualitative way and by crude efforts at quantitation that partially reflect the very great practical difficulties of observation and the limited data available.

We might well ask whether the fetus is equally active all the time or whether there are periods of rest and activity. The rhythmic quality of our behavior is so familiar to us that we tend to take it for granted, and the organization of behavior into periods during the day is a fundamental characteristic of functioning in mature biological systems down to the single-cell. Once recurring periods of increased or decreased levels of behavior become established in early development, we begin to use the concept of *state* to refer to these periods of differential activity. It could be argued that the world inside the womb is so protected and its conditions so constant that there is no need for changes in state by the fetus. Yet here again we have an example of anticipation.

The earliest observed rhythms in human fetal behavior have been found in the fifth month by continuous recording from sensors placed on the mother's abdomen during her sleep (5). Fetal movements were not evenly distributed throughout the night but showed an irregular alternation of peaks and troughs. No systematic trends in the level of this activity or its periodicity were observed over the 4-month period to term, although the quality of the movements altered slowly from sudden jerks to more sustained activity. By sensitive computer techniques, two basic cycles were extracted that seemed to underlie these apparently irregular fluctuations: one recurring at about 40 minutes and another, weaker one at 96 minutes. Interestingly, the 96-minute cycle drops out immediately after birth, so that it is likely to be caused by a maternal cycle, possibly the REM sleep cycle, known to be almost exactly this duration in adults. Clearly, the infant is more predisposed to be active at some times than others and this state recurs in cycles, the most clear-cut one being about 40 minutes between peaks of activity. It appears that this cycle remains at this length until about 2 years of postnatal age and then gradually increases until it reaches adult length of 90 minutes by about age 10.

This, then, is the first evidence of temporal organization imposed on fetal behavior. Thus begins a form of organization of behavior that will underlie and influence all behavior in the months and years to come. But it is barely discernible at 24 weeks of age when the first detailed long-term observations of behavior and electrophysiology of premature infants have been made (6). Before 27 weeks, no infants have survived longer than a few days. The observations were made on infants over the first day and a half of life while they were still in relatively good condition, in incubators made to reproduce conditions in the womb as closely as possible. These 1½–lb infants were continuously active, with only the barest suggestion of phasic fluctuations. Sudden jerks alternated with slow local movements (e.g., mouthing, hand clenching) as well as very slow (5–10 seconds) limb movements (elevation and slow lowering) and diffuse movements. Repetitive facial movements were noted in bursts of about ten second durations. Muscle tone between movements was very low. Brain waves were recorded and showed only occasional short bursts of irregular and nondistinctive fluctuations between longer periods of silence. Breathing was very irregular most of the time, but showed few pauses longer than 10 seconds. Heart rate was fixed at rates around 100 beats/ minute. Crying was observed in three of the five infants but only lasted 20 seconds. Occasional grunts, sighs, and yawns were heard. Eye movements were very rare and the electromyogram was flat between episodes of movement. Without elaborate averaging techniques, no alterations of state were evident. These premature infants were mostly in one state the whole time. And what is this first state like? It does not fit the description of any of the three major states found in full-term infants and adults—wakefulness, REM sleep, or slow-wave sleep—and probably should be considered a common precursor from which the three major states gradually differentiate themselves.

Two major trends characterize the development of state organization in the weeks from 24 to full term at 40 weeks: (1) the appearance and increased duration of quiescent periods and (2) the increasingly close association of specific patterns of body movements with specific patterns of function in other systems as indicated by respiration, EEG, heart rate, and electromyogram. The first of these trends to become evident is the development of periods of clear-cut motor inactivity at 28–30 weeks. Prior to this, all that was evident was the waxing and waning of a continuous level of movement. Now the infant is actually motionless for longer than a few seconds at a stretch. By 32 weeks, body movements are absent in 53 percent of 20-second epochs of continuous recording in premature infants, 60 percent at full term, and 81 percent at eight months after birth.

In terms of patterning, by 28–30 weeks repetitive bursts of eye movements appear for the first time. These occur in association with the body movements, irregular respiration, and flat electromyogram that have been characteristic of the fetus for several weeks. Although the EEG is still primitive, most of the criteria for rapid eye movement or REM sleep are now present.

The periods of motor quiescence are still not at all typical of later quiet or slow-wave sleep because respiration remains irregular, EMG is flat, and slow waves are not seen on the EEG. The association of patterned functioning that will become quiet sleep develops out of the periods during which there are no eye movements and no body movements. From about 30 percent of the time at 32 weeks, this pattern increases until it is seen 45 percent of the time by full term and 76 percent of the time by 8 months postnatal. Respiration does not become regular during these periods until full term, and slow waves do not appear on EEG until 3 months postnatal.

The awake state becomes differentiated out of the precursor state with the opening of the eyes at about 30 weeks and the advent of sustained muscle tone at about 36 weeks. For the first time body movements occur during periods that do not contain the bursts of short, darting, vertical eye movements characteristic of REM sleep. The EEG of REM sleep is virtually indistinguishable from that during wakefulness in young infants, so that the profound loss of tonic muscle tone and the high threshold to stimulation during REM sleep become the major criteria for distinguishing these two very different states. The fetus spends 70–80 percent of its time in REM sleep at 32 weeks of gestation, falling to 50 percent at full term, with non-REM sleep and wakefulness sharing the remainder of the time about equally. By 6 months postnatal age, REM percent has decreased to 30 percent.

Why does the fetus spend so much of its time in REM sleep? Can the rapid decline in proportion of REM sleep to wakefulness throughout the late fetal period be a hint that the infant needs this state particularly at this time? Howard Roffwarg suggested that during this period of minimal outside stimulation, the developing nervous system required the internal stimulation produced during the state. For the REM state is characterized by diffuse activating volleys from the brain stem to higher centers and localized bursts of activation of eye muscles, ear muscles, heart rate, blood pressure, and other vital systems. Neither quiet sleep nor waking provides anything like this extensive, spontaneous, internal activation. Since no means of selective deprivation of REM state has been discovered, this attractive idea remains a plausible hypothesis. It provides another possible role of very early brain function in contributing to and regulating its own development. Presumably, as the infant grows older, its interactions with the environment increasingly take the place of this internal stimulation. And, in fact, REM sleep proportion declines rapidly during the first postnatal year.

A specific example of stimulation of vital pathways by the REM sleep generator in the fetus is the finding in sheep that fetal respiration during the last trimester of pregnancy occurs in bursts, confined to periods of REM sleep (7). These periods of rapid irregular breathing, as in humans, do not move the amniotic fluid in and out of the lungs, but they do generate large changes in intratracheal pressure and to-and-fro flow within the bronchial tree. The apparatus is thus prepared and exercised before it is needed by the phasic event generators that are uniquely active during REM sleep.

The three major states have fundamental importance in the early development of behavior regulation. Major vital functions such as respiration, body movement, heart rate, and muscle tone gradually tend to cluster together into specific patterns of function in association with specific patterns of central neural function detected by surface EEG and depth electrodes. This basic form of biological organization, developed in the womb, will continue to regulate our behavior throughout life. The development of these states are functional evidence of maturation of brain inhibitory and feedback controlling mechanisms made possible by the increasing complexity of neural structure at all levels of the central nervous system.

Although the differentiation of states is the most obvious new development of the last trimester of pregnancy, the infant's posture, spontaneous behaviors, and responses are changing also. We left the fetus at 24 weeks, when spontaneous behavior appeared to be due to the continuous play of randomly activated local muscle groups. There were two types of movements, fast and slow. The fast movements were sometimes loosely coordinated and resulted in changes of posture. Because of the unpredictable, intermittent, continuing nature of spontaneous behavior, it was virtually impossible to tell whether the infant responded to a given stimulus or not. This is not a very satisfactory sort of behavioral organization, even for interacting with a nurturing parent and, in fact, parents have an extremely difficult time dealing with prematurely born infants or establishing relationships with them.

By 28–32 weeks, fetuses are viable, although they weigh only 2 lb and must be protected in a womblike incubator. Their skin has outgrown their fat and they have a thin, wizened appearance with wrinkled faces giving a false sense of great age. Individual movements are still fleeting and weak but occur nearly continuously with periods of waxing and waning of intensity. Transitions from activity are gradual and poorly defined. A postural reflex is now clearly present for the first time, providing a recognizable pattern of limb and head positions that recurs periodically. Called the tonic neck reflex, this is a pattern of coordinated muscular innervation that extends the arm and leg on the side to which the head is turned while flexing the opposite arm and leg. This is a fundamental pattern that will recur every time the head is turned rapidly to one side, from this period until 6–8 months postnatal age. The grasp reflex is so strong at this age that the fetus can hang from a bar like a gymnast. Light, sound, and sudden jolts produce a slight flinch followed by a predictable intensification of random and diffuse activity. The facial muscles at this age, in Arnold Gesell's words, are "as busy as so many separate workshops." Eyes, forehead, and mouth muscles flash fragments of smiles, grimaces, and frowns, and these bouts of facial activity tend to occur when the infant's head turns.

THE ORIGINS OF POSTURE, INTEGRATED BEHAVIOR, AND FACIAL EXPRESSION: 32–36 WEEKS

By 32–36 weeks, fat has filled out the infant's skin and it starts to look like a baby. Thick pads have developed in the cheeks that 8 weeks later will prevent their bending in with the negative pressure generated by nursing. Periods of real quiet at last can be observed and transitions are clearly defined. Movements are more vigorous and sustained without the "fading out" character of a month earlier. The infant cries lustily, sucks its thumb, yawns, and grunts. A new development is the state of quiet alertness in which eyes are open and will flicker at a moving object, although head turning and following will not yet occur. Prior to this, the infant had its eyes open and appeared attentive only when active, while all quiet periods brought closed eyes and visual inattention.

The infant is now only a few weeks from the normal time of birth and seems little different from full term. The changes that occur in the next month involve smoother transitions, greater coordination, and sharper differentiation of postures, states, and movements. If we look back over the course of the development of behavior outlined in this section, the first thing that strikes us is the amount of behavior that has gone on before birth. For 7 months, the infant has been moving about, exercising the more than 400 muscles in its body, the countless junctions of nerve and muscles, and the unimaginable numbers of connections between its nerve cells. This exercise provides many of the shaping influences on the development of the neuron, as described in Chapters 8 and 9. The growth of bones and tendons is greatly dependent on the physical tensions generated by the contracting muscles. Bones are shaped in part by the uses to which they are put, and a bone disconnected from muscles, even in postnatal life, grows only to half its usual thickness and contains few of the inner architectural features that ordinarily give it strength. It remains a thin tube closed at both ends. Tendon fibers are few, thin, and fail to grow parallel without the organizing force of muscle tension exerted on them. The mouth opening at 8½ weeks appears to play a role in closure of the palate at that time; swallowing amniotic fluid from 13 weeks on facilitates development of the intestinal tract and later is an important regulator of the amount of amniotic fluid. All this prenatal behavior is utilized for the shaping, moulding, strengthening, and organizing of growth in neurons, muscles, and bones—the machinery of behavior.

But the diffuse and intermittent activity of the 3-month-old fetus would be enough to accomplish these effects. Another developmental process is going on that is still very poorly understood. That is the progressive takeover of control of behavior by centers above the spinal cord. Spontaneous behavior and elicited responses develop with certain characteristics, and then these characteristics are lost and are replaced by behavior with new characteristics. Some behaviors merge imperceptibly into new forms while others disappear entirely and even abruptly, never to be seen again in recognizable form. In fact, very few behaviors, once developed, maintain a fully stable form (for example, the eyeblink to a close, rapidly approaching object). These repeated phases of inhibition accompanied by reorganization are clearly evident in the prenatal period and continue well into childhood. They coincide with the development of complex structures in the cell bodies of neurons, the completion of the outgrowth of axons and dendrites, and the formation of cell connections taking place in progressively higher regions of the brain. The neural tube closes first in the neck and maturation proceeds rapidly down the cord but only slowly upward through the hindbrain, the midbrain, and finally the forebrain. The transition from total to local reflexes at 9–10 weeks of gestation coincides with differentiation of bulbar and midbrain regions and establishment of long descending pathways connecting these cell assemblies with the sensory and motor cell systems of the spinal cord. The height of midbrain regulation at 14–15 weeks is followed by a clear-cut period of wholesale inhibition coinciding with maturation of dorsal thalamic and striatal systems and their connections with midbrain and spinal systems. Once fully established, behavioral responsiveness returns and gradually becomes reorganized again with the clustering of activity and inactivity and their temporal patterning as states. However, since the period of maturation of cortical systems has not fully occurred prior to birth, this takeover is yet to come.

Since cutting the connection of these higher centers, even in the adult, results in a return to certain reflexes and behaviors characteristic of much earlier periods of development, it is difficult to escape the conclusion that the stepwise progression of development is due to the stepwise maturation of structure and function in progressively higher systems of the brain; and that when these take over, they use and add to (without destroying) the simpler organization at the lower level.

The implication is that the brain is organized for behavior at several different levels—that a hierarchy is built up during development and substantially different organizations are built into each level. The characteristics of organization at each level can be determined by careful study of the behavioral repertoire of the fetus or infant at a given age. By maturation of progressively higher centers, new capacities and new forms of organization are brought to bear upon behavior: new motor patterns, new sensory capacities, and above all, new forms of coordination between the two. Because of the relative constancy of the intrauterine environment and the extremely meager opportunities for anything the fetus feels or does to be related to any events in the environment, there is little chance for us to assess how adaptive fetal behavior may be. All the evidence we have on behavior organized at bulbar and midbrain levels in fetal development in experimental animals points to the conclusion that it is rigidly fixed and not influenced by experience except for some waning of responses with repetition (habituation) and recovery with additional kinds of stimulation (sensitization). However, we really do not know enough about the kinds of environmental events that are capable of influencing behavioral organization in the prenatal period. As we shall see in the life history of neurons, the cellular environment is a very potent shaping force at the earliest stages of development; there are several known ways by which the environment outside the fetus can affect its cellular environment and, thus, influence developing neural organization (e.g., effects of prenatal hormones on behavior).

The behavioral characteristics that form during the last phase of fetal life are not so rigidly prescribed, as we shall see in the next section; yet the infant brings to the world at birth a system that is already organized to behave in certain specified ways and to respond according to a certain specified set of rules. The potential for plasticity is very much there but cannot be seen unless we look carefully for it.

SUMMARY

We have now followed the development of the fetus to the point when it is ready to be born and to survive. The dominant feature of the first phase was the advent and spread of spontaneous and elicited movements from 7 to 17 weeks gestational age. The second phase (17–22 weeks) was marked by the appearance of widespread inhibition resulting from regulation of behavior by descending pathways above the spinal cord. The third phase (beginning at 24–27 weeks) was marked by the first evidences of state organization and the periodic rhythmic alternation of states. The fourth phase (32–36 weeks) was indicated by the development of muscular tone, the coordination of limb movements into postures, and the advent of effective limb movements and recognizable facial expressions. Some sensory capabilities arise as early as spontaneous motor movements, beginning with cutaneous sensitivity in the region of the mouth and nose. Taste and olfaction are next, followed by vestibular and then auditory function by midterm. Some visual functions soon follow, but are the last to mature. The story is one of progressive imposition of structure on the flow of behavior by the maturation of regulatory systems within the central nervous system of the fetus. The occurrence of behavior so long before birth appears to be necessary for the development of joint and bone structure and muscle function and for life within the confines of the womb.

FURTHER READING

Barcroft, J. *The Brain and Its Environment*. New Haven, Conn.: Yale University Press, 1938.
Bradley, R. M., and Mistretta, C. M. Fetal sensory receptors. *Physiological Reviews*, 55:352–382, 1975.
Crain, S. M. Tissue culture models of developing brain functions.
   In G. Gottlieb (Ed.), *Studies on the Development of Behavior and the Nervous System*. Vol. 2: *Aspects of Neurogenesis*. New York: Academic Press, 1974.
Gesell, A., and Amatruda, C. S. *The Embryology of Behavior*. New York: Harper, 1945.
Gottlieb, G. (Ed.) *Studies on the Development of Behavior and the Nervous System*. Vol. 1: *Behavioral Embryology*. New York: Academic Press, 1973.
Gould, S. J. *Ontogeny and Phylogeny*. Cambridge, Mass.: Harvard University Press, 1977.
Hooker, D. *The Prenatal Origin of Behavior*. Lawrence: University of Kansas Press, 1952.

Humphrey, T. Postnatal repetition of human prenatal activity sequences with some suggestions of their neuroanatomical basis. In R. J. Robinson (Ed.), *Brain and Early Behaviour: Development in the Fetus and Infant.* London: Academic Press, 1969. Pp. 43–84.

Humphrey, T. The prenatal development of mouth opening and mouth closing reflexes. *Pediatric Digest,* 2:28–40, 1969.

Nilsson, L., Furuhjelm, M., Ingleman-Sundberg, A., and Wirsén, C. *A Child Is Born.* Revised ed. New York: Delacorte Press, 1977.

Parmalee, A. H., and Stern, E. Development of states in infants. In C. D. Clemente, D. P. Purpura, and F. E. Mayer (Eds.), *Sleep and the Maturing Nervous System.* New York: Academic Press, 1972. Pp. 199–228.

Roffwarg, H. P., Muzio, J. N., and Dement, W. C. Ontogenetic development of the human sleep–dream cycle. *Science,* 152:604–619, 1966.

REFERENCES CITED

1. Pittman, R., and Oppenheim, R. W. Cell death of motoneurons in the chick embryo spinal cord. *Journal of Comparative Neurology,* 187:425–446, 1979.
2. Drachman, D. B., and Coulombre, A. J. Experimental clubfoot and arthrogryposis multiplex congenita. *Lancet,* 2:523–526, 1962.
3. Walker, B. E., and Quarles, J. Palate development in mouse foetuses after tongue removal. *Archives of Oral Biology,* 21:405–412, 1976.
4. Streter, F. A., Gergely, J., Salmons, S., and Romanul, F. Synthesis by fast muscle of myosin light chains characteristic of slow muscle in response to long-term stimulation. *Nature New Biology,* 241:17–19, 1973.
   Streter, F. A., Luff, A. R., and Gergely, J. Effect of cross-reinnervation on physiological parameters and on properties of myosin and sacroplasmic reticulum of fast and slow muscles of the rabbit. *Journal of General Physiology,* 66:811–821, 1975.
5. Sterman, M. B., and Hoppenbrouwers, T. The development of sleep–waking and rest–activity patterns from fetus to adult in man. In M. B. Sterman, D. J. McGinty, and A. M. Adinolfi (Eds.), *Brain Development and Behavior.* New York: Academic Press, 1971. Pp. 203–228.
6. Dreyfus-Brisac, C. Sleep ontogenesis in early human prematurity from 24 to 27 weeks of conceptional age. *Developmental Psychobiology,* 1:162–169, 1968.
7. Dawes, G. S. Breathing and rapid-eye-movement sleep before birth. In *Foetal and Neonatal Physiology.* Proceedings of the Sir Joseph Barcroft Centenary Symposium, Cambridge, England, 1972. Cambridge: Cambridge University Press, 1973. Pp. 49–62.

6

The Newborn

Through the ages, humans have stood in awe of birth and regarded the newborn at first with hesitation and puzzlement. The event of birth has become the occasion for celebration, and it can be a relief to rejoice in the new arrival rather than attempt to comprehend it. Full of contradictions, the newborn is at once fully human and not at all like us. It elicits powerful emotional responses without giving any obvious signals and appears absolutely helpless but is extraordinarily good at a number of things. The newborn is a specialist, but more open to change than ever again. We continue to be bothered by questions such as whether a newborn can think or feel and whether under any circumstances we could remember what it was like to be that age. In our uncertainty, the newborn has tended to become an object onto which adult humans have projected all their fears and all their hopes about themselves. Looking back over the enormous literature on infancy that has evolved in the past century, the kinds of observations made as well as the conclusions drawn reflect the varying beliefs of the authors on human nature. The contradictions and confusions on the part of scientists are fortunately shared to a lesser degree by parents. We can become a part of a natural system without understanding it.

In this chapter, I will first describe the newborn as the natural outcome of the prenatal developmental processes outlined in the previous chapters. Second, since birth precipitates the newborn into a very different world, I will show how it is equipped to deal with that world. Third, I will explain what capacities enable the infant to acquire new and progressively more adaptive ways of dealing with its environment.

BIRTH

Much has been made of the traumatic character of birth, and certainly we would do everything possible to prevent an infant from having to go through such an experience a second time. Brain hemorrhage and periods of reduced oxygen supply caused by difficult delivery have been related to a wide variety of abnormal patterns of brain and behavior development. Nevertheless, the fact remains that the actual experience of full-term pelvic delivery does not have any discernible effects on development beyond the first few days post partum. Comparing full-term infants with others born by Caesarean section or delivered a month premature (when pelvic delivery is so much easier) has not revealed any differences in any measures of performance after the first month or two.

The major impact of birth appears to be the sudden change in environment, which of course is shared by all methods of delivery. This environmental disruption sets in motion a wide variety of changes within the infant. The circulation of blood undergoes the most dramatic shift with the closing of the hole between the auricles (the foramen ovale) and the redistribution of blood flow from the placental bed to the pulmonary system. The lungs fill with air, instead of amniotic fluid, the skin loses its fluid covering, and the limbs are free to move. The background sound level is much reduced while the light level is increased and ambient temperature falls. The effect of all these changes on the infant's behavior is not well understood. The infant loses 6–9 percent in body weight during the first 4 days, not regaining birth weight for a week to 10 days. The moulding effects of the uterus and birth canal are evident in the shape of the head, the rounded back, and the limbs, which are kept in the flexed position for several days. The state of the newborn is highly variable the first day or two, fluctuating between irritability and somnolence with an unusual amount of hiccups, tremors, discoordinated eye movements, gagging, and crying. Irregular breathing, regurgitation, and apparently random oscillations of body temperature and skin color suggest a lack of stability of internal physiological regulation. These irregularities disappear in a day or two and are not simply evidences of immaturity, since they are not seen in like-aged infants who were delivered prematurely several weeks earlier. The questions that need to be considered include how much of the observed behavior of the newborn could be observed 3 days earlier in the womb? Conversely, are there behaviors and sensory capacities that were present in utero but were lost temporarily or permanently due to the effects of the environmental change at birth? Answers to these questions would require ingenious new methods of behavior testing, which could be done in animals. The point I would like to emphasize is that we must not lose sight of the continuity of development from prenatal to neonatal periods or of the relatively unknown effects of the extraordinary environmental changes imposed by birth.

THE ORGANIZATION OF SLEEP–WAKE STATES
AND BEHAVIOR

After the newborn has had a day or two to settle down following birth, we can observe the regularities and patterning of its behavior while it lies unattended between feedings. The organization has not changed dramatically since we last described it in late fetal life, but there are some interesting features that we did not see in the fetus.

First, the newborn's pattern of state transitions is of necessity interrupted by periodic feedings. The fetus did not have this periodic event to interact with, and the timing of the newborn's awakenings and its readiness to be fed are at first extremely irregular. The event of feeding is one of the most salient post-natal environmental rhythm-givers, and the cycle of many behavioral and physiological events of the newborn is not organized around the day but around the inter-feeding interval. In some cultures, this is as frequent as every hour but in our culture usually ends up being every 4 hours. The infant seems to be able to adjust its own rhythms to cycles of a range of lengths within limits of about 1–6 hours. This organization of a basic rhythm of behavior by interaction with its environment is one of the first of a vast number of such shaping experiences.

Beginning as a 40-minute period of waxing and waning activity in the prenatal period, active sleep, quiet sleep, and wakefulness become differentiated. By the newborn period, wakefulness can be subdivided into quiet inactivity, waking activity, and crying. The infant spends about one-third of its time in each of the three states—REM (or active) sleep, quiet (or slow-wave) sleep, and awake. Alternating between active and quiet sleep on a 15-minute cycle, the baby awakens every 1–6 hours and will then become diffusely active and finally cry unless fed.

Second, incessant activity was the hallmark of prenatal life, and the newborn continues to show a variety of spontaneous behaviors even while the eyes are closed and the infant is in one or another of the stages of sleep. Diffuse motility, smiles, and penile erections occur much more in active sleep than in either quiet sleep or wakefulness, while spontaneous "startles" occur predominantly during quiet sleep. Mouthing movements occur most often when the infant is awake but drowsy. These spontaneous behaviors are not just occasional, fleeting, or random events. They tend to occur rhythmically, with a characteristic interval, as if generated on a cycle. Sometimes they come very frequently, as often as every 15 seconds for penile erections and every 45 seconds for startles. These repetitive behaviors tend to occur at the time that the infant closes its eyes in transition from wakefulness to sleep but not when slowly awakening, suggesting that the sensory input of wakefulness, particularly vision, normally inhibits spontaneous discharge processes.

Wolff has shown that these behaviors have at least three interesting properties. First, they can substitute for each other: when penile erections occur frequently, startles are very rare, and vice versa; sucking on a pacifier in sleep totally inhibits startles and erections. Second, if a behavior is elicited by outside stimulation at a frequency slightly higher than the spontaneous rate, the behavior ceases to occur spontaneously. This equivalence between spontaneous and elicited behaviors can be clearly shown with startles. By a slight, sudden jarring of the crib, the infant's vestibular motion receptors are stimulated and a startle occurs (with sudden forward reaching of arms and arching of the back, the Moro reflex). When this is repeated every 2 minutes, the number of spontaneous startles is dramatically reduced while the occurrence of mouthing, diffuse activity, and erections is not affected. Third, in the period immediately following a spontaneous or an elicited behavior, a stimulus is temporarily ineffective, suggesting the existence of a refractory period. In the case of the jarring stimulus described above, this refractory period lasts for 2–3 minutes after elicited or spontaneous startles, thus limiting the amount of behavior that can be elicited.

Relationships like these between stimulus, response, and spontaneous activity are found in simple neural networks, suggesting that certain aspects of the newborn's behavior can be understood in terms of known properties of its underlying neural machinery. The effects of these principles of organization can be found in characteristics of much more complex behaviors later on, so that they appear to be reflections of a basic structure that the infant will take with it into the rest of life.

Another form of organization is imposed by the strong tendency of certain behaviors to occur during certain states, the states themselves being composed of patterns of brain activity, muscle tone, and internal regulation of breathing, heart rate, and so forth. This patterning of behavior becomes more and more clear-cut with maturation and experience. The newborn spends two-thirds of its time asleep or drowsy and almost all of its awake time either nursing, diffusely active, or fussy and crying. There is very little time spent in the quiet attentive state so characteristic of older children and adults. The transition from this neofetal phase to infancy involves a remarkable differentiation of the awake state into a number of substates, each of which carries with it certain behaviors likely to occur in response to the environment. Furthermore, a given behavior is likely to have certain qualities in one state that it will not have in another. Thus, the variability of behavior and even the likelihood of its occurrence are closely tied to the underlying state. For example, in the newborn, a stimulus that elicits a turning of the head in an awake infant will have no effect if it is drowsy, is likely to set off a whole body startle response if it is in slow-wave sleep, and can elicit a smile if the infant is in active sleep.

Internal and External Regulation of States

Certain environments are conducive to particular states but do not have final control. Most important, the infant clearly needs to spend a certain proportion of every 2–4 hour period in each state. If time is too prolonged in one state, another will become increasingly preemptive until it takes over, despite the environment. This is familiar to anyone who has tried to entice a newborn infant to stay awake for a late visitor or sleep through the night for its tired parents. Thus, the alternating transitions from one state to another that characterized late fetal life (and that were then wholly independent of the environment) come under partial control of the stimulus world of the neonate. The short-term distribution of time spent in one state relative to others can be altered, but the structure of the long-term pattern sets certain limits that cannot be overcome. The option and the limit are basic principles of the organization of human behavior clearly evident in neonatal state organization.

In the prenatal period, the infant changes states and thus alters its behavior systematically, even in a situation where its needs for nutrition, warmth, and waste elimination are steadily and constantly provided and when external stimulation is virtually changeless. After birth, these patterned state transitions come under the influence of changes in internal as well as external stimulation. It is very difficult to study this relationship to internal factors, however, because the stimuli are hard to measure (e.g., bladder wall tension) or complex and poorly understood (hunger). It becomes increasingly difficult, therefore, to say whether an infant is in a certain state and behaves in a certain way because it is hungry or because its arousal state has shifted, independent of hunger. Evidently the two forces are organized to be in conflict some of the time. No matter how hungry an infant, it will fall asleep if it has been awake long enough but will waken again sooner than if it were not hungry. Certain expectable relationships hold true: the passage of time since the last meal decreases the likelihood of regular sleep and increases the level of diffuse motility, and finally results in crying.

The Gradual Emergence of Wakeful Behavior

Compared to sleep, which occupies two-thirds of the newborn's day, the awake state is unstable and difficult to study because most of this time is spent in feeding. And even during nursing, the infant is asleep some of the time. Thus, the newborn infant does not stay quietly awake for more than a tiny fraction of the day. It is as if it were a brief transitional zone between sleep, the diffuse activity of fussing, and the channeled activity of feeding. Even smiling and the startle response do not initially arise out of the awake state. This is not to minimize the importance of the brief periods of quiet awake for future development; they are crucial, as we shall see shortly. Facial grimacing, mouthing, kicking, head turns, arm reaching, and eye movements occur during the awake state. All of these behaviors, as well as crying, can occur without any apparent external or internal physiological stimulation (e.g., full bladder, empty stomach). Most of them can be stimulated as well and are then usually referred to as *reflex behaviors*. The relationships between stimulus, response, and spontaneous behavior are similar to those shown for behavior during sleep. The rule continues to be that if the environment does not elicit a behavior, the infant will generate something like it on its own. As we shall see below, stimuli do not simply set off behaviors, but modulate the characteristics of the behavior so that there is never an *exact* equivalence. However, the substitution and shared refractory period described above strongly suggest a shared neural substrate underlying stimulated reflex and spontaneous behaviors at this age.

Two further general characteristics of waking behavior in the newborn are interesting. First, although generally more responsive to stimuli when awake than asleep, the newborn is practically unresponsive when crying. The only similar degree of unresponsiveness comes during quiet sleep. Thus, both quiet sleep and crying tend to buffer the infant from the environment. Only sudden vestibular (balance and motion receptors) stimulation seems to be effective in these states, producing startles in quiet sleep and calming the crying infant. The second characteristic is that repeated or constant stimulation in most modalities tends to elicit decreases in activity in wakeful infants. If the infant is already quietly awake, sleep is induced. White noise has been found to shift an infant from active to quiet sleep. Swaddling, rocking, singing, and even the baby's ear pressed to the mother's heartbeat are time-honored exploitations of this basic property of organization of the infant's behavior. I have already described how eye opening seems to suppress diffuse activity. This inhibitory effect of visual stimulation on levels of spontaneous behavior seems to be a critically important property of newborn behavior and is an essential ingredient of what we call attention.

Adaptive Characteristics

In the newborn, specific and diffuse behaviors occur spontaneously with considerable frequency. Many of these behaviors can be produced in response to stimulation and can thus substitute for their spontaneous occurrence. The likelihood of a given behavior occurring either spontaneously or in response to stimulation is determined by the state the infant is in at the time. The state in turn is the result of external environmental and internal physiological influences acting to support or oppose the rhythmic pattern of alternation of states, a pattern established during prenatal life and characterized by flexibility within certain strict limits.

What use to the infant are such characteristics of behavior organization? First, the wide variety of spontaneous behaviors guarantees that the infant will have an impact on its environment, will be likely to affect its caretaker, and change its immediate environment. Second, they mean that from the first the infant can *initiate* an interaction and not simply respond, can cause things to happen and not simply receive stimulation. This provides the crucial ingredient for the discovery of cause and effect, the basis for the development of learning and thought. Thirdly, the infant is capable of operating in different modes or states that allow it to perform certain specialized functions in a coordinated and focused manner, temporarily excluding other functions. The occurrence of certain minimal amounts of each of these states every few hours is guaranteed. In addition to promoting specialized functions, this property gives the infant a way of avoiding fragmentation of effort and overloading of sensory pathways. The possible function of the REM sleep state in providing stimulation necessary for neural maturation has been discussed above. Finally, the close correspondence between elicited and spontaneous behaviors at this age suggests a shared neural mechanism and provides an organization suitable for the shaping of behavior to the environment and for the development of purposeful behavior (see below).

SENSATION AND RESPONSE

So far, I have considered the newborn in the way I described the fetus, emphasizing the characteristics, organization, control, and usefulness of spontaneous behavior and giving less time to the nature of behavior elicited by stimulation. I described the early development of sensory structures and function and how the long history of spontaneous behavior served to stimulate receptors and sensory pathways and thus can facilitate their development. What is the result of this long preparatory period? How is the infant's sensory system organized at birth to receive stimulation, and to what degree are behavioral responses suited to the stimuli?

We know much more about the visual system than other sensory systems in the newborn, and it is certainly one of the most important in establishing a relationship with the mother. For eye-to-eye contact is the main way we judge whether there is a "person there" and whether we are important to that person.

Both color and brightness vision are functional two months before birth. The pupillary reflex, which adjusts the amount of light admitted by the eye, is slow but at least partially functional at birth. The infant turns its head to avoid strong light. The infant however cannot change the shape of its lens to focus images on its retina and only objects close to 8 inches from its eyes are sharply enough projected not to be blurry. That distance is about the distance between the baby and mother's face during nursing, a coincidence that may in fact be an important preadaptation. The infant can control the movements of its eyes, and they normally move together and converge on objects within their clear visual range. If the object moves slowly, the infant can follow or track it, although when it changes direction unpredictably, the newborn overshoots and back-tracks much more than an older infant. Best estimates are that the infant can distinguish something as small as a one-eighth inch wide stripe, and that its visual system tends to repeatedly scan sharp edges and angles rather than relatively shapeless objects.

The infant turns its head toward any novel stimulus but turns more frequently toward some objects and gazes at them in preference to others. This property has allowed us to determine the discrimination abilities and the preferences of the newborn, prior to its experience with the world of objects. Fantz and others have shown that the infant comes into this world with a tendency to look more at bull's-eyes than squares, symmetrical figures more than asymmetrical, and complex designs more than very simple ones. Reports that the newborn prefers a set of human facial features to the same features scrambled and thus has an innate "template" or "schema" for its mother's face seem now to be explained on the basis of individual design features such as symmetry. Even so, the tendency of the newborn is to look preferentially at just those features found in the human face, prior to any experience with its mother. These properties of the newborn's visual, sensory, and motor system do not have the stereotyped, rigid character we associate with reflexes like the knee jerk; they are characteristics based on probabilities. In this way they appear to be examples of biological preadaptation for the relationship with the mother. In addition to the responses mentioned, spontaneous head-turning and scanning gaze with wide open bright eyes also occurs during the quiet alert state described above, most often a few minutes after a feeding. This means that the infant will spontaneously search for things in its environment around the time of feeding when the mother is likely to be there.

Thus, the newborn's visual behavior is organized both with a definite probability that certain behaviors will occur, even in the absence of environmental cues, and with a set of probabilities of responding in certain ways to certain kinds of stimuli. The principles illustrated in the visual system apply to other sensory systems as well, although the degree to which stimuli are specified at birth may be less or more complete and the elicited patterns of behavior less or more specific. Newborn behaviors vary a great deal in the degree to which they are modifiable as the result of experience, in the degree to which they are dependent on experience for their continued existence, and in their susceptibility to modification or even disappearance. For example, the spontaneous and elicited Moro startle response vanishes by 6 months in normal infants, regardless of continuing elicitation, and the eyeblink response to a sudden approaching object continues virtually unchanged from birth to old age, despite wide variations in experience. Most behaviors lie somewhere between these extremes and contain interesting interactions between neural maturation and experience.

Although much less is known about auditory and olfactory senses in the newborn than about vision, they may turn out to be at least as interesting. It has recently been found that newborn infants have an adult's auditory threshold, can discriminate the loudness and pitch of sounds, will turn their eyes toward the direction of sound, and show more limb motor activation to the human voice than to other sounds. A recent report indicates that newborns with only 12 hours of intermittent postnatal experience of their mother's voice will respond to a recording of her voice in preference to an unfamiliar voice (1). Work by Turkewitz suggests that newborns process sounds differently depending on which ear and thus which side of the brain is used. The threshold for the eye-turning response to sound is lower in the right ear, and discrimination of fine differences in sounds is better for speech on the right but is better for nonspeech sounds, such as white noise or music, on the left. Thus, newborns show auditory as well as visual preadaptations, and begin life by processing human speech and sounds differently from other noise, with an early lateral specialization of auditory function for language.

Recent observations suggest that blind babies as young as 6 weeks of age use echoes to detect the presence of objects. In one of the first of these studies, reported by Bower, the parents had noticed that the baby could turn its head and eyes toward objects dangled silently in front of its face. The baby then was observed to be making a number of clicking noises with its tongue as it sensed the object. The echo location idea was later tested with a sophisticated sound generating device worn on the baby's head. With this aid, a 16-week-old blind baby could reach with some accuracy for objects as small as a pencil. This potential for auditory localization using differential input to the two ears may have had evolutionary survival value as a means of navigating in dense fog and darkness.

Olfaction is certainly an under-studied sense in humans of all ages. We do know, however, thanks to MacFarlane, that in the neonate it is a sense by which the infant is able to discriminate its own mother from all other persons. By 10 days of age, a newborn will turn its head preferentially toward the side of the crib on which rests a breast pad from its own mother, even if the other side of the crib has a breast pad from another lactating mother. Newborns have no preference at first, but by 4 or 5 days after birth they will turn toward a used breast pad in preference to an unused one. Thus, this appears to be an example of very early learning of a highly specific scent, obtained through the process of nursing. It does not appear to be milk on the breast pad to which the infant is responding, but rather the scent from the glands of the skin of the breast around the nipple (Montgomery's glands). By olfactory processing, the newborn appears to have quickly built up a sensory schema for its own mother that is so highly specific that it can respond to her in preference to anyone else. An interesting question would be whether other scents could be as rapidly discriminated; that is, whether or not learning is set to occur quickly with these particular stimuli.

The tactile sense of the newborn is highly developed, having been the first to emerge during prenatal life. Its participation in the infant's adaptive behavior will be covered in the next sections of this chapter, for the sense of touch is a crucial element in the control of so much that an infant does.

DISAPPEARING BEHAVIORS

One of the most puzzling aspects of behavior development in infancy is the tendency of the newborn to lose certain advanced capabilities that are present at birth. Reaching and walking are two of the most interesting early behaviors and, although both of these responses can be easily elicited in newborns, they are virtually absent in most 2-month-olds. The probable explanation for this apparent deterioration involves a process that has become familiar from what we have learned about prenatal life. Discovery of conditions under which these behaviors can be maintained reveals an important developmental process.

A newborn will reach out and grasp an object that it sees. Although it misses half the time, when successful, this appears to be a very precocious skill. The infant's hand opens the right amount according to the size of the object and starts to close just before reaching it. If fooled by a visual illusion, the neonate will fuss and cry upon closing its hand on thin air. The most extraordinary thing about this pre-adapted newborn behavior is that it disappears within 4 weeks of birth! We have to wait about 5 months before reaching is readily elicited again. Now it is almost 100 percent accurate, but there are other differences, as Bower has shown. There is *less* hand closure anticipation. The infant touches the object *before* the hand closes and does not close with full pressure immediately as it did as a neonate. When encountering a virtual object illusion, the hand does not close and the infant is not upset. Reaching is still under visual control, but grasping has come under graded tactile control, providing greater adaptability. If the lights are turned out, just as the infant starts his reach at this age, the old pattern of anticipated full force grasp reappears.

These apparently puzzling developments can be understood in the light of what repeatedly occurred during the prenatal period. Here we saw elicited behaviors cease to occur and then reappear, but with some new qualities. The old behavior, however, could still be elicited under certain conditions. This pattern was explained for the fetus by the maturation of descending pathways from higher control centers that inhibited the behavior for a period prior to taking over control with a revised pattern of organization.

The period of inhibition is relative and flexible, however, in the case of reaching. For in other cultures or by design of experiments, if infants are given sufficient daily experience in reaching for objects, no decline in reaching takes place; instead there is a gradual transition from the neonatal to the 5-month types of reaching. Between 1–5 months, infants who are given regular experience show an intermediate pattern: they will reach and touch an object without closing their hands at all. Apparently, the repeated experience somehow maintains the behavior against a tendency for it to drop out. But even if the behavior is not given sufficient use to maintain it, it will reappear. What seems to be altered during the period of inhibition is the *threshold* for eliciting the behavior. This threshold apparently can be kept low through experience, possibly by neural processes of facilitation.

A somewhat different pattern is observed for reaching toward an object that makes noise when the infant cannot see because it is dark. This behavior can only rarely be elicited in the newborn period, but rises to a peak at about 16 weeks of age and then drops off sharply to the point that it is not at all observed at 25 weeks of age. There is a slow regaining of the response over the next many months. Attempts to maintain the behavior by practice in normal infants have not been made, but the development of blind infants is of great interest on this point. Blind infants at 16–20 weeks of age will turn head and eyes, appearing to look at a sound and will successfully reach and grasp noisy objects like bells. They will also appear to follow their hands moving silently in the air in front of their faces! This behavior rapidly disappears in the next weeks, even though reaching for noisy objects is repeatedly reinforced in blind infants. One could argue that it drops out in sighted infants because it is rarely used and sighted reaching replaces it. But how to explain the lapse in blind infants? Apparently such reaching cannot reappear until other capacities have developed such as the concept of object constancy.

It is not generally known that newborns can walk if held upright. This stepping gait is rigid and automatic in appearance, not compensating for uneven terrain. But very young infants will walk across a room like soldiers while being supported lightly by a parental hand under each armpit. Explained as a "statokinetic reflex," such automatic, repetitive, gravity-resistant postural adjustments are thought to be typical of midbrain levels of neural organization. We may expect this reflex to become inhibited with maturation of higher control centers, and indeed this is the case—unless it is practiced regularly, in which case it becomes progressively easier to elicit and the number of steps possible increases from one or two to as many as 30 consecutive steps by the second month of life. Zelazo has recently shown that as little as 10 minutes of supported upright stepping practice each day will increase this behavior remarkably in the first few weeks and then maintain it for as long as practice is continued. Under normal conditions, without this special experience, and with parents who wait for the infant to walk "on its own," the infant will do so at about 12 months. Meanwhile, in the intervening period, walking is impossible to elicit.

The next question is whether practice of this sort can improve or hasten the appearance of unsupported walking. The answer to this appears to be no. Studies on identical twins given radically different amounts of practice do not support such a notion in this case. The behavior can be induced to appear at any age with repeated practice, but the advent of unsupported walking is not affected by this. Apparently the stepping behavior does not disappear but continues to exist as a *potential* behavior that can be induced by repeated practice.

How is newborn stepping (or reaching) lost before it is regained in its new form? We are just beginning to learn about the cellular events that act to maintain neural function at certain levels and to determine thresholds. Repeated use alters the readiness with which some synapses can subsequently be fired. And cellular events occur that cause synapses to become progressively less responsive, if they are not used for periods of time. Presumably, it is these kinds of events that determine the unusual course of these neonatal behaviors.

More mysterious still is the process by which walking (and reaching) reappear at about 1 year of age. This is associated with the maturation of a number of cortical and subcortical systems (including balance coordination), but involves qualitative changes in the adaptability of walking to changes in terrain, its smooth coordination with eye and head movements, and the way in which the behavior is used. Walking is no longer elicited by pressure on the soles of the feet, but is initiated in order to achieve some goal (e.g., a hug from the mother or a toy on a table across the room). Walking has become *voluntary*. Such transformations of organization of behavior will be discussed in following chapters.

AFFECTIVE BEHAVIORS AND STATES

There is a class of behaviors that are unlike the preceding because they are of no importance to the infant in dealing with its inanimate environment, but are extremely important in dealing with its human environment—the parents. They have come to be known as *affective behaviors* because they affect us, change our way of feeling and what we do. Fussiness, grimacing, and crying are prototypical behaviors of this sort. The transition from these behaviors to a state of quiet wakefulness with regular respirations and responsive eye movements appears to form the earliest beginnings of comfort and pleasure.

Facial expressions of a grimacing sort and partial versions of the crying face go along with greater restlessness and early whimpering, prior to full-blown crying. The infant has at least three kinds of cries in its first few hours that can be identified by electronic recording (sonogram) and by experienced parents: the first cry at birth, the pain cry, and the rhythmic (hunger) cry. The last of these is the basic cry that the others revert to after a short time. Facial expressions associated with quiet attention, such as wide eyes and quizzical eyebrow lifts, are clearly associated with a receptive state in which the infant will gaze at the mother's face for long periods and will follow moving objects with its eyes. The mother's actions, talking, and smiles will elicit vigorous limb movements and reaching for the mother's face or hand while the infant is in this state. Such responses are very appealing to someone who is trying to "get through" to the neonate and begins the play interaction that is such an important part of the baby's first relationship.

These affective behaviors are distinctive features of the newborn's states that I described above. The coherent, organized nature of such states allows us to use affective behaviors as cues in order to make a number of highly useful predictions about what the infant (or grown person) is likely to do and what it needs in order to maintain that state or change to another.

As I described above, these states alternate in a pattern of transitions that have a rhythm partially controlled by external and internal stimulation. The infant's own inner cycle of states probably accounts for the so-called unexplained fussing and crying that occur periodically during the first few months after birth, ranging in amount from 10 minutes to 3 hours per day for different babies.

Hunger is, of course, the best known inner event eliciting crying. Cold, exposure of the skin to air, and strong, or sudden stimulation tend to produce crying, fussiness, and turning away of head, eyes, and limbs. Mild, slow, and rhythmic stimulation leads to attentiveness, calming, and turning toward or reaching. These are the pieces of evidence we have for the beginnings of negative and positive affects as we first emerge into the world.

Comfort, that is returning the infant to the quiet awake or sleep states, can be accomplished by warmth, covering the skin with a textured cloth, by rhythmic mild stimulation in any modality, but particularly vestibular stimulation (e.g., rocking), by inducing rooting, placing, and sucking and also by swaddling, which is thought to work by reducing proprioceptive stimulation from the limbs.

These changes in state and the facial, vocal, and postural behaviors that signal them are the language of the newborn, by which it communicates its needs to its caretaker and elicits, in turn, stimulation, comfort, and feeding. These behaviors operate on the human environment more effectively than any other and become involved as a result in crucially important affective learning experiences about which I will have more to say below.

The affective expressions of positive and negative, or approach and avoidance states, are not exclusively aroused in interpersonal situations. From the very first systematic observations of learning in the newborn, attentive and quieting expressions take place while a stimulus is novel and then again when the infant shows the first signs of learning the task. Fussiness and grimacing occur when learning is long or difficult and when the rules are changed so that the old response no longer works. These affective expressions take place with no other humans in the room; the only thing the infants are responding to are the changing contingencies of the learning task. Thus, affective behaviors of pleasure and distress appear to be connected with the learning experience at birth. Some of the implications of this relationship for the development of mind will be discussed in the next chapter.

Smiles do occur in the newborn but at this age are generated spontaneously as a part of the REM state. Emde has called these *endogenous smiles*. They are not elicited clearly by any stimulation and are regarded as one manifestation of a substate that has been called *waking*

REM because the eyes are open. Fussing, crying, and other facial expressions also can occur spontaneously in this state; indeed, almost every identifiable facial expression has been observed in the infant's spontaneous productions. Smiling is five times more frequent in 30-week-old prematures than 10 weeks later at full-term. Within the month or so after birth all smiling disappears, until the next form of smiling begins to occur at 1½–2½ months. In this second phase, the smiling is elicited by any mild stimulus equally well and occurs in the awake state. Being bounced will elicit a smile as readily as the sight of the mother's face at this stage. Very soon, the infant begins to smile selectively and then exclusively to the human face, finally only to a very familiar face.

The smile begins as a spontaneous behavior organized within a state in which the infant is generally unresponsive to the environment. Like the spontaneous Moro or startle response, smiles gradually cease to occur in this way. Again like the startle response, smiles reappear, but in the awake state and in response to stimulation. Once organized within this second phase, facial expressions become dependent on their environment for differentiation and even for their continued existence, as we shall see below in the case of blind children.

In summary, two basic aspects of emotion are evident from birth, and indeed from the late fetal period, in the form of states associated with bodily movements of approach or avoidance. These states alternate on an independent cycle but are also influenced by external and internal stimulation. Facial expressions similar to adult expressions of distress and contentment are closely associated with these states from their beginnings. Another dimension, intensity, is reflected in the posture, the vigor of the bodily movements, and in the fullness of the facial expressions. Specialized facial expressions like the smile have a somewhat different history. In newborns they are produced, like fetal behavior, without relation to external or internal stimulation as part of a state that is tightly controlled by an endogenous rhythm generator. It is several months after birth before they begin to appear in the waking state and in association with specific stimuli and contexts.

NURSING

Sucking is a behavior that is normally practiced every day and, possibly as a result, does not show obvious discontinuities in development. The newborn has been making rhythmic spontaneous sucking movements and swallowing amniotic fluid for months before birth. Thumb-sucking is commonly observed in X-rays of fetuses, for the fetus will turn its head toward a stimulus on the cheek (e.g., its own hand) and will open its mouth to take in a thumb or finger as early as 25 weeks of gestational age. Thus, the newborn is experienced with all the components required for nursing. But recent evidence has shown that even the first feeding of a newborn is not simply the playing out of an automatic stereotyped reflex sequence.

There are four separate reflex actions that must be coordinated: head turning toward cheek stimulation (rooting reflex), opening and closing the mouth to grasp the nipple (placing reflex), sucking, and swallowing. Breathing must be coordinated with the swallowed milk. All these actions can be separately elicited by appropriately placed stimuli in the regular and automatic way typical of reflexes. But they are not so automatic as they seem. For example, the rooting reflex is frequently not elicitable after a feeding, when turning *away* from cheek stimulation is a more common response. In addition, rooting and placing are more vigorous and elicited with less stimulation after a long interfeeding interval if the infant is not too upset. Thus, we can say that these reflexes seem to be affected by some aspect of the infant's *state*, or more precisely *substate*, within the awake state. A second attribute of these reflexes is that they continue until some result is achieved and then stop. The infant will turn its head back and forth, opening and closing its mouth until the nipple is firmly grasped and positioned well into the mouth, at which point rooting and placing stops.

This is clearly an example of a goal-directed behavior and goes well beyond the knee jerk in complexity of organization. The advanced features are a means of repeating the movements and a set of sensory conditions (nipple in the mouth) that turn off the repetition. The set of sensory conditions resulting from the nipple in the mouth releases the sucking reflex. Milk in turn releases swallowing.

For a long time sucking and swallowing were thought to be simple reflexes over which the environment had no more than on–off control. For example, the infant sucks in a stereotyped rhythm of about two sucks per second in a pattern consisting of between 5 and 20 sucks followed by a pause of 5–15 seconds without sucks. Individual infants have their own characteristic variation within this basic rhythm, and it is the same pattern whether elicited by a pacifier while awake or if occurring spontaneously during regular sleep. If a string of sucks is begun on a pacifier it will continue through the regular number of sucks, even if the pacifier is suddenly removed. This looks like the output of a generator of machine-like fixity. However, if the flow of milk rises above a certain rate, sucks are emitted in a continuous stream, rather than the burst–pause pattern. In the first day of life, infants suck differently when they are receiving breast milk from a bottle than if it is cow's milk. If given a bottle of milk with an artificial nipple or an empty tube for short periods of time in repeated alternation, newborns will suck progressively more on the nipple and less on the tube, indicating that their sucking is selectively influenced by their prior experience.

It is in the natural situation with the mother that these features are most dramatically evident, as described by both Gunther and Lipsitt. On her first breast feeding, the mother's nipple must be inserted far enough into the infant's mouth or sucking is not elicited. The ordinary bottle nipple is "supernormal" in terms of length and contour, and this dependence of sucking on rather strict rules of stimulus configuration is another example of preadapted sensory requirements. Occasionally the baby's upper lip may become inadvertently pressed against its nose by breast tissue, sealing its nostrils. The baby cannot breathe and rapidly reacts as it does to any airway obstruction: by throwing its head backwards and repeatedly wiping or beating with its hands in front of its face. The mother may not be aware of the problem and if the same thing happens several times in a row, the infant will turn away from the breast instead of rooting and placing. If this continues to happen on subsequent attempts at feeding, the infant will begin to fuss when picked up for its feedings and resist attempts to nurse. If not aware of the trouble, it is difficult for the mother not to take this sort of thing personally and the whole relationship is off to a poor start.

From its earliest beginnings, the whole sequence of nursing is clearly open to modification as the result of experience, even though each component has some of the characteristics of automatic reflex responses. The extraordinary adaptive capacity of this system in the infant has been dramatized by Siqueland's finding (see Stone) that infants as young as 3 weeks after birth will suck harder and faster on an artificial nipple in order to increase the illumination of a 35 mm slide projector so that they can see the picture better.

INDIVIDUALITY

It should not be surprising that newborns are very different from each other, considering the enormous range of genetic possibilities prior to fertilization and the long and eventful history that precedes their birth.

Indeed, in all the aspects of behavior described in this chapter, a range of individual differences can be found. Combining these into patterns as a basis for classification into types or temperaments has been a fascinating but frustrating occupation for researchers and parents alike. The greatest difficulty is in defining patterns that have stability over time, and thus become convincing as aspects of the enduring personality. Perhaps the greatest problem is in deciding which aspects of behavior at a later age are direct outgrowths of a particular behavioral characteristic of the newborn. For example, Bell studied the responses of newborns to the sudden unexpected removal of a pacifier nipple and later in the preschool period observed their behavior in a social situation. What he found was a developmental inversion: infants who showed rapid, intense responses to removal of the nipple later showed slow and reduced responsiveness in the research nursery school (low interest, participation, assertiveness, gregariousness, and communicativeness). It is difficult to know surely what such findings mean. Such inversions may be explained by some of the developmental processes to be described in the next section on interactions and in Chapter 12. On the other hand, the measures used in the preschool period may not have tapped the same aspect of the individual as the response to removal of the nipple during the newborn period.

Thus, consistent individual differences are easiest to demonstrate and understand over short periods of several weeks during the first postnatal year. They are obviously of enormous importance, since they will affect so many encounters of the infant with his or her environment and will thus exert an important effect on future development through changing social relationships and altered perceptual experience.

SUMMARY

Birth marks our first major environmental shift. The organization of behavior and the maturation of sensory functions that took place during the prenatal period provide the newborn with a number of capabilities that are suited to life outside the womb. The establishment of spontaneous behaviors as a part of the organization of sleep–wake states guarantees that the infant will act upon his or her environment as well as simply being able to respond to it. The embedding of different behavioral characteristics in different states and the rhythmic ordering of state transitions provide the basis for the specialization of behavior according to different environmental demands and for the achievement of a cycle during which behavior characteristics differ markedly at different times of day.

The infant's visual and auditory systems have certain characteristics that predispose them to perform particularly well with the human face and human voice. The extraordinary sensitivity of the olfactory system provides the first way in which the newborn can recognize important other indiviudals.

Motorically, the newborn is equipped with at least two behavioral capabilities, reaching and walking, which it loses if not required by its particular environment. These are particularly good examples of the precocious endowment of newborns and their dependence on practice indicates their adaptive nature.

No other behaviors are more important to the survival of the infant than affective communication and nursing. The occurrence of these behaviors in the newborn is guaranteed both by their organization as a part of sleep–wake states and as reflex responses to sensory stimulation by the mothers. However, they both have considerable potential for change, according to the infant's particular experience. It is this plasticity that forms the basis for learning and finally for knowing, as will be described in the next chapter and in Chapter 12. Finally, we are individuals from the beginning and behave differently from other newborns in all these different areas. This allows us to begin to determine our own futures, at least within the limitations of the newborn's world.

FURTHER READING

Bell, R. Q., Weller, G. M., and Waldrop, M. F. Newborn and preschoolers: organization of behavior and relations between periods. *Monographs of the Society for Research and Child Development*, Vol. 36, Nos. 1–2, Serial No. 142, 1971.

Bower, T. G. R. *Human Development*. San Francisco: W. H. Freeman and Company, 1979.

Dunn, J. *Distress and Comfort*. Cambridge, Mass.: Harvard University Press, 1977.

Emde, R. N., Gaensbauer, T. J., and Harmon, R. J. *Emotional expression in infancy: a biobehavioral study. Psychological issues*, Vol. 10, Monograph 37. New York: International Universities Press, 1976.

Fantz, R. L. Visual perception from birth as shown by pattern selectivity. *Annals of the New York Academy of Sciences*, 118:793–814, 1965.

Gunther, M. Infant behaviour at the breast. In B. Foss (Ed.), *Determinants of Infant Behaviour*. Vol. 1. London: Methuen, 1961. Pp. 37–44.

Humphrey, T. The development of human fetal activity and its relation to postnatal behavior. *Advances in Child Development and Behavior*, 5:1–57, 1970.

Korner, A. F. Individual differences at birth: implications for early experience and later development. *American Journal of Orthopsychiatry*, 41:608–619, 1971.

Lipsitt, L. P. (Ed.) *Developmental Psychobiology: The Significance of Infancy*. Hillsdale, N.J.: Erlbaum Associates, 1976.

MacFarlane, A. *The Psychology of Childbirth*. Cambridge, Mass.: Harvard University Press, 1977.

Mussen, P. H. (Ed.) *Carmichael's Manual of Child Psychology*. Vol. 1, 3rd ed. New York: Wiley, 1970.

Peiper, A. *Cerebral Function in Infancy and Childhood*. New York: Consultants Bureau Enterprises, 1963.

Rexford, E. N., Sander, L. W., and Shapiro, T. (Eds.) *Infant Psychiatry: A New Synthesis*. New Haven, Conn.: Yale University Press, 1976.

Stone, L. J., Smith, H. T., and Murphy, L. B. (Eds.) *The Competent Infant: Research and Commentary*. New York: Basic Books, 1973.

Turkewitz, G. The development of lateral differentiation in the human infant. *Annals of the New York Academy of Sciences*, 299:309–317, 1977.

Willemsen, E. W. *Understanding Infancy*. San Francisco: W. H. Freeman and Company, 1979.

Wolff, P. H. *The Causes, Controls, and Organization of Behavior in the Neonate*. *Psychological Issues*, Vol. 5, No. 1, Monograph 17. New York: International Universities Press, 1966.

Zelazo, P. R. From reflexive to instrumental behavior. In L. P. Lipsitt (Ed.), *Developmental Psychobiology*. Hillsdale, N.J.: Laurence Erlbaum Associates, 1976. Pp. 87–104.

REFERENCE CITED

1. DeCasper, A. J., and Fifer, W. P. Of human bonding: newborns prefer their mothers' voices. *Science*, 208:1174–1176, 1980.

7

From Biology
to Psychology

At this point in our story of human development, we are at a threshold of transition from behavior that can be understood in terms of our knowledge of biological processes to behavior that cannot be described in purely biological terms. In an attempt to deal with complex behavior, concepts have been developed that use different language and different properties than any known biological events. These concepts help to order the observations in our minds, supply an intellectual system that gives a sense of understanding in terms of principles of action, and above all, allow prediction of how the infant will behave in the future in similar and even in new situations. The problem with many of these concepts, for the biologist, is that they use language that is either unfamiliar (for example, "reinforcement") or although familiar (e.g., "inhibition") are applied to behavior without any evidence that the biological process suggested is actually at work in the nervous system at the time. Such concepts can sometimes be rigorously and even operationally defined in terms of biologically relevant variables (e.g., rate, time since last meal). But the steps are missing between the biological and the psychological levels to a degree that is not present between cell, organ, and physiological regulatory levels. In this way, a gap has grown up between biology and psychology, an apparent but unreal discontinuity, the roots of which are deeply engrained in our language, our culture, and our necessary lack of perspective on our mental functioning.

In the previous section on sensory and motor capabilities of the newborn, I described some of the changes that ensue in the functioning of these systems during the newborn period and, in one case, up to a year after birth. Two main processes that had been observed prenatally were discussed: the repeated waves of maturation of progressively higher neural systems and the stabilization or moulding of function with continued use.

Newborn behavior is organized so that certain behaviors are highly likely to take place and certain responses are guaranteed. Specific stimuli and patterns of stimuli are preselected so that certain responses are preferentially linked to those stimuli at the first encounter between the infant and its environment. But these preadaptations are the exception rather than the rule and most behavior must be acquired by experience. In fact, some preadapted behaviors, like reaching, actually disappear if they are not used, so that even they are not rigid, inevitable, and automatic. Two processes of change take advantage of the intrinsic organization of the newborn, working with and upon the spontaneous and elicited behavior repertoire: learning and imitation. Other processes of change, resulting from interaction with the environment, will be discussed in Part III.

PROBLEM SOLVING

The oral region of the body and the motor systems of the head and neck were the first to show any behavior, way back at the eighth week of gestation, and it may be no coincidence that the first clear-cut demonstration of learning in the newborn 32 weeks later involves this system. We do not know why such a long period is necessary before learning becomes possible. Indeed, recent animal studies suggest that learning may be possible during the latter half of fetal life: for newborn rats, 1 day old, can be shown to perform a discriminative learning task (1) on the first day after birth, when they are at a stage in neural maturation roughly equivalent to a human fetus of 6 months gestational age.

I will describe the changes in behavior that we call learning in some detail as they occur for the first time in the newborn, for this adaptive capacity is fundamental to so much developmental change that follows. In the experimental situation used by Papousek, newborns are placed on their backs in a bassinet equipped with milk bottles and rubber nipples that can be made to move forward and stimulate the infant on the cheek from either side. An auditory signal is used to tell the infant when the milk is about to become available for a short period of time. If the infant turns its head to the signal, there will be enough time to suck from the nipple before it is retracted between trials.

The first form of learning, *habituation*, develops rapidly to the auditory signal given alone: the newborn gradually ceases to turn its eyes or breathe irregularly in response to the repeated signal. When the nipple is first made to touch the cheek a few moments after the sound signal, only a few newborns turn to the touch of the nipple. After a few pairings of sound and touch, the infant responds to the sound with increased activity and a growing number of partial responses; for example, turning the eyes to the side of the signal or contraction of one side of the mouth. Responding to the touch of the nipple becomes more consistent. Eventually these fragments become part of a head turn to one side in response to the sound, allowing the infant to suck as soon as the bottle is presented. Until this is achieved, the infant shows much fussing and grimacing in response to the auditory signal.

The learned behavior is at first very erratic in newborns; they cannot produce more than one or two consecutive responses. Head movements occur between trials and the whole body is used in the response. But as soon as a few consecutive responses have been produced, the infant is no longer fussy when the sound signal goes on and between trials shows regular breathing, an attentive expression, a quieting of general movements, and regular respiration. The response becomes more rapid, forceful and more discrete, involving only head and neck, with the rest of the body relatively quiet.

When the bottle is no longer provided following the tone, there is an increase in general activity, with fussing, crying, and the appearance of vigorous head turns during the time between sound signals. Responses to the sound signal become fragmented again, as in the early acquisition phase, with eye turns and mouth contractions that may remain for a number of trials. The infant does not stop turning its head all at once, but begins by ceasing to respond sporadically, then once or twice consecutively, but with reappearance of the response at intervals. At this stage, responses to the opposite side may occur for the first time. A sudden noise, such as slamming the door, will cause the response to return regularly for a few trials. Finally, when the response is regularly absent, the infant's whole body can be noted to be very quiet, and the infant lies with motionless open eyes and slow, rhythmic breathing.

Infants only 1 day after birth can learn in such a situation to turn their heads to a bell and not to a buzzer. Less controlled observations suggest that learning is rapid during the first few nursing bouts within hours of birth, but the phases in the process cannot be distinguished nearly as well. Likewise in 3-month-old infants, learning this head-turning response is so rapid that it is hard to see how it takes place.

Two other characteristics of learning in 2–3-month-infants are worth mentioning here. First, once the task is learned, the infant may continue to respond by head movements, even though it is too full to take any more milk and indeed does not suck on the rubber nipple. Smiling, cooing, and bubbling accompany repetitive performance of the head turn response to the sound, reinforced only by the appearance of the bottle brought about by this behavior. Second, although signs of distress are nearly absent during acquisition in older infants, pouting, grimacing, and whimpering appear when the infant is suddenly required to make a discrimination between two different auditory signals, each denoting head turns to opposite sides. Intensification of diffuse motor activity, orienting behavior, and the production of novel responses or sequences accompany these affective expressions, until the new requirements are met, again bringing affective expressions of pleasure.

These relatively simple observations of newborn behavior are extraordinarily difficult to explain according to biological processes known to operate in cell, organ, and even in organismic regulatory systems. The promise of neurobiology is the discovery of neural processes that can explain such a series of behavioral changes. Meanwhile they can be viewed in terms of broader biological concepts derived from studies of ecological adaptation and the regulation of physiological systems.

Lacking a preadapted reflex solution to the task posed by the experimenter in the example above, infants' adaptive capacities must be fourfold. They must have some mechanism that will allow them to select the relevant stimuli from among all the sensory information coming into the brain—a sensory processing plan. They also must have a set of actions that are appropriate to this stimulus—a strategy. Both sensory and action plans must be stored and available for future use. They must have a mechanism for comparing the outcome of their efforts with some optimum state, and for revising the selection of sensory and/or action strategies if that comparison detects a discrepancy.

This is a formidable number of capabilities for which we have no comprehensive physical model. Yet certain aspects of such an organization can be found in simple systems like the familiar household thermostat. Selection of the relevant stimulus is no problem; it is prewired to be room temperature, sensed by a thermometer. The action strategy is also simple, closing the switch on the furnace. Both plans are permanently stored in the system. The optimum state or goal of this system is variable and set by the person living in the house. If room temperature has fallen below the setting (roughly analogous to an infant not having been fed for several hours) the discrepancy between optimum state and current outcome is sensed, and the action strategy is activated. The heat continues to be produced until the discrepancy is no longer present, at which time the action is terminated and the furnace shuts off. This kind of model is useful in thinking about simple purposeful behaviors such as rooting and nipple attachment, and applies equally well to the regulation of pituitary hormones or body temperature in the infant. It is not too hard to translate into what we know of how neural networks are organized to interact.

Two important features are missing in this household thermostat model—plasticity and storage (memory). Somehow an adaptive system must be able to select one or another sensory pattern and one or another plan of action from all those available (in storage) on the grounds of the degree to which it is likely to maximize an optimal state. Some sort of feedback must facilitate transmission along the sensory and motor pathways that are successful in reducing the discrepancy between present and optimal states, while inhibiting other sensory and response systems. Studies on synaptic mechanisms are attempting to establish what this feedback and these facilitating and inhibitory mechanisms may be at the cellular level. Likewise, we are beginning to understand the basis of memory in cellular and neural network function.

Research with kittens (2) is gradually increasing our understanding of how experience produces the sensory plan or neural representation of visual space. It was first observed that when kittens that had been raised in the dark for the first 7 weeks after birth were brought out into the light, they collided with objects, walked off edges, and were unable to reach out accurately to touch objects with their forepaws. This discovery demonstrated that there is more to using one's eyes than simply looking and inspired a great deal of interesting work on the neural basis for early visual perception. But Hein has recently added a new dimension by finding that *normally* reared kittens had the same difficulties if their eye movements were prevented by nerve section at birth. Marked difficulties in visually guided behavior persisted for many months in these animals, while other kittens whose eye muscle nerves were cut at 7 weeks showed little or no impairment. Apparently by 7 weeks of age an immobilized eye is capable of mediating visually guided behaviors, but Hein's cats were missing something else. They seemed not to have developed the plan or *schema* for visually guided behavior, as a result of not having been able to move their eyes during the developmental period before 7 weeks. The persistent difficulties of the early lesioned animals indicate how difficult it may be to acquire certain behaviors if the early representation is not properly laid down. The missing ingredient here appears to have been the feedback from eye muscle movement during the early experience with visually guided behavior.

We can thus begin to account for some aspects of complex behavior on the basis of properties that are known to exist in biological systems. There are many gaps and uncertainties, but one has a sense of what needs to be done in order to find out whether this approach will give a satisfying degree of understanding of this adaptive behavior in terms of biological processes.

But there are other aspects of the infant's behavior, given in the first example above, that go even further beyond current biological principles. For example, what do the affective expressions mean in this problem-solving context? Why does the infant continue to respond when it no longer takes milk from the bottle? Attempts to answer these questions take us squarely into the realm of psychology, into theories of cognitive and emotional development, into the world of the mind.

IMITATION

Behavior that seems to be imitative has recently been discovered to occur in infants only a few days old, but how the infants do it is an unresolved question. The actions reported to be imitated so early involve only the facial musculature. For example, a mother protrudes her tongue and opens her mouth; within a few moments the infant will do likewise. A more rigorous and demanding test (3) exposes the infant to a stranger who makes a predetermined standard facial gesture (e.g., opening the mouth or raising the eyebrows and lids) while the infant is sucking on a pacifier. Sucking prevents immediate response until the pacifier is removed and the stranger simultaneously retreats from view. The infant is videotaped for the ensuing minute or two and the tapes are scored by someone unfamiliar with the experiment. By this means it was found that newborn infants' facial expressions were influenced to a significant degree in the direction of the facial expression they had previously observed. A number of startlingly accurate imitations resulted. Prior to these recent studies, the only example of possible imitation in the newborn was the known tendency for all the infants in a nursery to begin crying when one infant starts to cry. This phenomenon could as well be described as the triggering of a behavior with a high likelihood of spontaneous activation, as we observed with startles in Chapter 6.

The possibility exists that the infant is born with a set of preadapted facial responses to specific configurations of visual stimuli, much like reaching and hand opening to an object of a given size. These responses appear not to be modifiable and could be analogous to the newborn reaching response. If this is true, we would expect longitudinal studies to show that this form of imitation disappears in the ensuing weeks, if not actively maintained, and only reappears at 3–4 months when more complex mental functioning has developed. Another point of view holds that these findings show the infant to have more complex capacities than we had previously supposed, that they are able to pick out the relevant portions of the face they are seeing and match this with a mental representation of their own face that they have never seen in a mirror and can only experience by proprioceptive and tactile sensations. They are then supposed to hold these complex concepts in memory storage and finally respond when the pacifier is removed, according to a mental representation of a stimulus configuration that is no longer present. Such complex processes must be postulated to account for the wide range of extremely fine-tuned imitations of novel behaviors that older children and adults can produce, but may not need to be invoked to explain the data on newborns.

Imitation in the newborn is limited to familiar acts that occur spontaneously with considerable frequency, such as tongue protrusion. At 3 months of age, the infant will imitate the mother's cooing vocalization repeatedly but will not give any response to other sounds or gestures. Infants of this age appear to be imitating their own "coos" as readily as their mothers', judging from their timing, for infants of this age will coo repeatedly on their own and even out of phase with their mothers. By 5 months, the infant begins to act *in turn* with the mother or experimenter but without imitating the form of the action. It is as if the action were a spectacle that the infant attempts to set off again and again, by any act of its own that will accomplish this. By 6–7 months, the infant makes approximations of novel stimuli; for example, clicking its tongue in partial imitation of a novel sound. But at this age, these attempts are not modified (shaped) any further with repetition. The third stage finds the infant approaching the configuration of the stimulus by successive approximations. For example, in response to the experimenter blinking his eyes repeatedly, the infant may first open and shut its mouth, then close its eyes tightly, and finally blink its eyes once or twice. Or the infant may rub the experimenter's hand instead of its own hand. During the period from 6 to 18 months, the infant appears to imitate unfamiliar acts sooner if it can use a visible system, its hand and arm, rather than an invisible one such as its facial expressions.

It is not until 15–20 months that immediate and complete imitation of simple novel acts is possible, but the stages preceding the acquisition of this ability give us suggestions as to the processes that go into the development of imitation. In the first step it is actually the mother or experimenter who imitates the infant by using a facial gesture or vocalization they have often seen the infant make on his own. This seems to be a particularly effective stimulus for the elicitation of this familiar act, possibly on a preadapted level, much in the way jarring the infant's crib is particularly likely to elicit a Moro startle response. At this age— less than 5 months—the infant seems unable to distinguish between self- and other-generated stimuli. In the next stage, the infant is learning that a response on its own part will cause a novel stimulus to reappear, much in the way we considered for the head-turning response above. But why is this repeated? Is there something pleasurable about it? The gradual approximation to the novel stimulus gesture is even more problematic, for this seems to occur even in experimental studies designed so that the infant will continue to see the stimulus reappear regardless of whether its act is a close imitation or not; shaping by selective reinforcement is not the answer. In this situation, then, why does the infant modify its response to mimic the experimenter?

Simple forms of imitation occur very early in development and are of great importance to the mother even though they are limited, sporadic, and crude. They are the first examples of reciprocity in the relationship and begin the dancelike synchrony of mother–infant play. In addition, later forms of imitation bring an important shortcut to ordinary learning processes, allowing the infant to bypass a lot of trial-and-error steps in selecting sensory patterns and in modeling action strategies. Imitation is an important early basis for the later psychological process of *identification*, the sense of being like someone else and thus closer to them emotionally as well as cognitively.

THE ACQUISITION OF MIND

Several aspects of the patterns of newborn behavior described in the preceding sections are difficult to conceptualize without resorting to words and ideas we ordinarily associate with the world of the mind— with *psyche* rather than with *soma*. As I stated in the Introduction, it is certainly not the intention of this book to account for mental events in biological terms, but I would like to show how concepts congruent with biological thinking can be used to talk about reasonably complex behaviors. This attempt can serve to pass the reader on to the field of psychological development, and hopefully to illustrate how gradual and intangible that transition really is.

The idea is that within the newborn's capabilities, as described above, lie all the building blocks for the mind as we know it. The sensory plan by which certain information is selected, together with the related action pattern, may be referred to as a *schema*. The human infant begins with some simple preadapted schemas, which I have described. Experiences like those studied in the laboratory experiments of Hein on early visual-motor coordination of kittens, may be supposed to enlarge the number and sharpen the details of such schemas by biological processes similar to those described in previous chapters. The essence of such processes is to form *inner representations* of the outside world and to make "predictions" as to the outcome of actions directed at that world. Both the inner representations and the predicted outcomes are repeatedly modified when discrepancies are detected between the selected schema and the perceived outcome.

At this point in describing the schema, I can bring in some of the unexplained observations from the preceding section of this chapter. Apparently the infant is organized at birth so that when the outcome fits the schema, a contented and attentive state is induced and the sensory-action sequence of the schema is repeated. However, when discrepancy occurs, a state of mild distress is elicited, associated with sensory-orienting behavior and new behavioral patterns or strategies. When these strategies are successful, pleasure and repetition again occur. The number and complexity of such schemas are minimal in the newborn, but the pleasure in matching the schema and the displeasure in discrepancy causes the infant to repeatedly modify them and to create new schemas.

This organization equips the infant to learn not only new behaviors but new concepts without any other conditions being required beside those intrinsically connected to the enactment of the schema itself. This property is probably central to the role of play in early development and can account for the expressions of affect in the learning experiment described and for the continuation of responding after the infant was satiated with milk. It also provides the infant with a set of processes that equip him to grow cognitively, emotionally, and in his relationships with people. For it is the operation of progressively more complex and adaptive schemas that has forced us to use such words as "concept," "intention," "choice," "purpose," and finally "abstract thinking" to describe the complex behavioral capacities of older children and adults.

In the preceding sections we have seen how the infant's first preadapted schema for relating to its mother involves the tactile stimuli of the breast and the strategy of head-turning, rooting, and placing. Within a few days, a highly specific set of olfactory characteristics of the mother is learned and adds considerable selectivity to the evolving schema. Gradually, at 3–4 months, visual recognition and the smile come to form the predominant schema. The studies on imitation showed a stage when the infant did not seem to distinguish between self-generated and mother-generated sounds. Gradually, the rules for making this distinction became part of the schematic repertoire and, after 5 months, successive approximations of maternal expressions began to be made. Bower found that if he arranged a system of mirrors that showed an array of 3 "identical mother" images to 6-month-old infants they would become upset, whereas a month earlier they would happily attempt to interact with each of the 3 images of their mother in turn.

From these sequences of behaviors, we infer that the schema for mother becomes progressively more complex, refined and discriminated over the first 6 months after birth. Still to come is the schema for mother that allows her to be out of sight but not out of mind. Thus, the concept of mother and the differentiation of other from self is gradually formed by the integration of successively formed schemas. Our knowledge about how these schemas are integrated is rudimentary, but in some children the progression is interrupted or delayed so that the infant continues to behave as if it had only relatively primitive schemas. This is one of the hallmarks of some severely disturbed children.

One of the dramatic effects of early deprivation of experience is the failure of development of rules for interpreting and coping with those portions of the real world that were missing in the deprived child's early experience. Thus, social behavior is particularly affected, but advanced problem-solving capacities (intelligence) also suffers. How experimental studies on deprivation can be used to reveal essential steps in the development of complex schemas will be described later in the chapters on parent–infant interaction and the origins of language.

The continuity and the differences between human and other animal minds can also be conceptualized along the lines of the schemas underlying their behavior. Humans have many extremely open, modifiable schemas; frogs, for example, have few and tightly restricted ones. In the frog's sensory schema, food must move, and it will die surrounded by nutritious but dead flies. Similarly, in the goose's motor schema, eggs are returned to the nest with the bill, even if wings or feet might serve much better in many situations, and as a result many embryonic goslings never see the light of day. The human infant also has few schemas and does only certain things and only in certain ways. The rapidity of cognitive growth in the child seems to be limited by certain poorly understood events that must occur before a new level of complexity of cognitive performance develops. These events probably involve an interaction of experience with maturation of underlying higher neural systems, as seemed to be the case for the simple behaviors described above. It should be noted that some schemas of nonhuman animals are extremely open. To take the goose again as an example, it will develop social attachments to unnatural companions, like the experimenter, as the result of a few repetitions of the experience of following him a few hours after emerging from its egg. Thus, we can use animal experiments to learn more about the conditions under which schemas are formed, modified, and disrupted, and about the neural mechanisms that underlie them. In this way we may be able to study the earliest stages of the development of mind in lower animals and have some reason to hope that some of the principles learned may apply also to humans.

One of the characteristics of different species, including the human, is that each one tends to develop certain kinds of sensory processing and motor behaviors with much greater ease and rapidity than others. Like the preadapted sensory and response patterns we have followed through prenatal life into the newborn period, constraints continue to operate throughout development that channel and direct the kinds of schemas formed. What we learn is determined not only by what experiences we have, but also by the neural organization we bring to the experience. (The nature of such interactions, the limits, and the predilections for change will be explored in the next chapters.)

This concept of the schema as a species-specific information-processing system can be used to form a conceptual bridge between relatively simple behaviors understandable in biological terms (e.g., reflex acts, fixed-action patterns, habituation, and facilitation) and more complex behaviors described by such terms as *object constancy*, *psychological conflict*, and *identification*. Finally, the concept of the schema is useful because it can deal with the self-propelled, adaptive, and creative nature of development.

SUMMARY

The infant's experiences while interacting with the environment affect the kinds of stimuli to which it responds and the kinds of behaviors that are likely to be used in subsequent interactions. This process of change is accompanied by affective expressions, indicating the fundamental role of emotion in cognitive development from its earliest stages. The sensory information processing and the strategy for action are apparently revised according to feedback from the results of behavior. The central neural representation for these adaptable programs may be referred to as a *schema*, and such schemas form the basic building blocks for abstract ideas, language, conceptual thought, and such psychological processes as choice, motive, purpose, and emotion. Imitation is another simple and early process for the highly specific molding of behavior, which we understand less well. It is through the early use of learning and imitation that the infant's behavior passes beyond what we can describe and understand according to known biological processes and comes to require the inferring of other processes we call *psychological*. The schema stands at the interface of our current understanding as a bridge between the two academic disciplines that arbitrarily divide the continuum of behavior development into biological and psychological phases.

FURTHER READING

Engel, G. L. *Psychological Development in Health and Disease*. Philadelphia: Saunders, 1962.
Gruber, H. E., and Voneche, J. J. (Eds.) *The Essential Piaget: An Interpretive Reference and Guide*. New York: Basic Books, 1977.
Neisser, U. *Cognition and Reality: Principles and Implications of Cognitive Psychology*. San Francisco: W. H. Freeman and Company, 1976.
Papousek, H. Experimental studies of appetitional behavior in human newborns and infants. In H. W. Stevenson, E. H. Hess, and H. L. Rheingold (Eds.), *Early Behavior: Comparative and Developmental Approaches*. New York: Wiley, 1967. Pp. 249–277.
Yando, R., Seitz, V., and Zigler, E. *Imitation: A Developmental Perspective*. Hillsdale, N.J.: Laurence Erlbaum Associates, 1978.

REFERENCES CITED

1. Johanson, I. B., and Hall, W. G. Appetitive learning in 1-day-old rat pups. *Science*, 205:419–421, 1979.
2. Hein, A., Vital-Durand, F., Salinger, W., and Diamond, R. Eye movements initiate visual-motor development in the cat. *Science*, 204:1321–1322, 1979.
3. Meltzoff, A. N., and Moore, M. K. Imitation of facial and manual gestures by human neonates. *Science*, 198:75–78, 1977.

Part III
INTERACTIONS
AND ENVIRONMENTS

I have outlined the remarkable course of early human behavior development according to a rough chronological progression of stages from its earliest beginnings in the germ cells to the first tentative manifestations of mind in the newborn. The changes that take place during this period are so extensive that they challenge our ability to comprehend them. It has seemed enough just to get the story clearly in mind—and indeed many accounts of very early human development fail to ask how it all comes about.

As the infant matures, it becomes obvious that behavior develops in relation to the environment and all theories of behavior development deal with this interaction in some way, although the importance attributed to the environment as a shaping force varies widely from one theoretical approach to the next. In keeping with this, most accounts of behavior development begin with birth, when interactions between the infant and its environment are prominent. But the story, as I have outlined it above, begins much earlier and ends with the newborn period. How are we to account for the development of behavior throughout this period? And can such an account apply equally well to the postnatal period?

In order to try to answer these questions, we must first recognize that development takes place at different levels of biological organization. During the behavior of the sperm and the egg and the first few cell divisions after fertilization, development is clearly limited to the cellular and subcellular levels. By three weeks of gestational age, a collection of cells has formed the first organ capable of movement—the heart—which begins to function at this age. By 7–8 weeks of gestational age, muscular organs have come under regulation by spinal nerve reflex arcs and an organism is clearly present. But within this

143

organized system, organ, cell, and subcellular levels continue to function and to develop in their own distinctive fashion. One consequence of the fact of the different levels of biological organization is the realization that there are different levels of environment: each cell has its own environment within the organ, as does the adult organism within the world at large. The story of early behavior development involves an enormous expansion of the effective environment, commensurate with the extent of the changes taking place in the developing organism.

Thus, the riddle of behavior development is to be understood as the outcome of very different processes taking place at different levels of biological organization. The unifying theme is the interaction of the biological unit with its own effective environment. The gene interacts with other genes and with the protein molecules within the cell; its function at any given time reflects both its own structural potential and the effect of chemical regulators within the cell that turn it on or off or modify its action. The developing neuronal cell interacts with its fellow cells so that both structure and function in the central nervous system are the outcome of a dynamic interaction between the neuron and its cellular and chemical environment.

Likewise, the organism at a given stage in development has certain characteristics that can only develop further in interaction with its effective environment. For us, this environment gradually slips out of our own control (the egg vesicle fluid), out of our mother's control (the intrauterine environment), and out of our parents' control (the early home environment) until we are free to interact with an environment of our own choosing. In the normal course of events, then, we are exposed to innumerable environmental factors acting on different levels of biological function at different developmental periods. Which of these are crucial to development of a given behavior and exactly how the interaction works are the kinds of questions that need answers. Our knowledge, however, is extremely limited and uneven, with a great deal more known about certain environmental factors and certain behaviors than about others. The approach of this section reflects this situation and describes a number of examples that illustrate some of the more important and best-studied processes that we know about.

If the interaction of the biological unit with its effective environment is seen as the central theme of development, this potentially reduces the perennial gene-environment quandary to a set of more manageable relationships. Any biological unit we choose to consider is the product of a series of interactions. The evidence of gene action is present in the organization of the biological unit at any given stage of development and partially determines how it will interact with the next environmental factor. But the environment has also made its contribution to the organization of the biological unit through the outcome of past interactions.

This progressive interweaving of genetic and environmental influences is difficult to conceptualize at the behavioral level and the problem is compounded by the use of the word "interact" to describe the relationship of gene and environment. Clearly, the gene and the environment do not interact except at the subcellular level, and such an interaction itself cannot produce any behavior. If we speak of genetic and environmental *influences*, we imply that there are two separate entities that interact with each other but remain separable—like wind and current determining the course of a sailboat. Nor is it quite justifiable to substitute the analogy of a chemical reaction for the nautical one: two compounds coming together to create a third compound with wholly different properties and with loss of the individuality of the two components. Many characteristics of behavior development are missing or distorted in these two analogies and yet, without a clear picture of what the gene-environment relationship is like, we become unduly influenced by whatever analogy we may have formed without thinking as a part of our concept of the genesis of behavior. Better than any analogy is a close look at the actual biological processes themselves.

I will begin at the cellular level where we can get a good deal closer to the actual operations of the genes themselves. The biological unit at this level is the neuron. Its interactions with the (cellular) environment are crucial to the specification of the structure and early function of the nervous system. The early (and later) organization of behavior is determined to a major degree by the organization of neural systems that takes place in this phase of our early development. The basic principles of the interaction between a biological unit and its environment are illustrated here, along with some important processes that underlie and shape the development of behavior. In the next chapter I will consider how events in the outside world affect the organization of the brain, the mechanisms of environmental influence on the structure and function of the neural machinery of the brain. These two chapters on biological processes within the brain will be followed by chapters on the two major environments of early development—the intrauterine and parent–infant relationships. The processes and pathways by which the growing individual interacts with these two environments provide the basis for understanding early human life history. Thus, in this section as in the previous one, I will move from the level of the single cell—the neuron—all the way to the level of social relationships between people in order to grasp the nature of the developmental process.

8

The Early History
of the Neuron

The brain does not come into being like a telephone switchboard or the printed circuitry of a computer. Use of the word "blueprint" to describe genetic information conjures up the image of a complicated three-dimensional circuit diagram and suggests that brain development is the gradual laying down of protoplasm along preformed routes, followed by the formation of synapses where indicated on the blueprint. Nothing could be further from the truth.

MIGRATION AND OUTGROWTH

The formation of the brain has much more in common with the colonizing of new territory by a tribe of settlers than it does with the coming to life of a blueprint. Each nerve cell has a journey to make, which is in fact called the phase of *cell migration*. In the course of this migration each cell must begin to move at a certain time and stop at a certain place and in a proper relation to other cell bodies that are also migrating. Neurons probably use supporting (glial) cells as guides in their amoeba-like movement and can alter their course, for example, to dispose themselves radially after an initial longitudinal route. Similar cells aggregate in groups, possibly responding to specific membrane proteins in the mysterious process of *cell recognition*. The biochemical processes responsible for these affinities between neurons and glia and between neurons themselves are not well understood, nor are the mechanisms by which migration is begun and terminated. It is clear, however, that the migrating nerve cell is dependent on its environment and upon cues from neighboring cells in order to reach its proper ultimate destination. If patches of embryonic neural tissue are transplanted to another section of the neural tube, the cells in some cases will migrate to entirely different positions and go on to make different connections.

The next phase in neural development involves the outgrowth of axons, which travel long distances to synapse on particular cell bodies, and of dendrites, which branch many times, making numerous con-

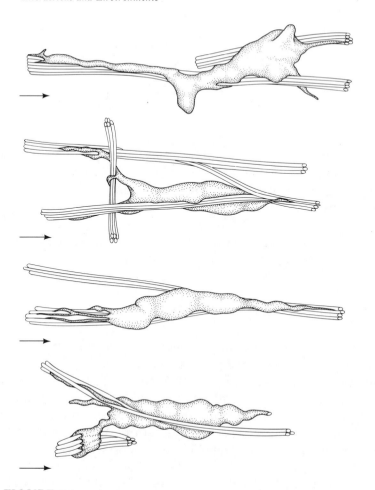

FIGURE 8-1
Reconstructions from serial electron micrographs of migrating neurons from monkey cortex, showing the complex patterns of leading processes associated with radial glia. The neurons are migrating from left to right. (From P. Rakic, L. J. Stensaas, E. P. Sayre, and R. L. Sidman, "Computer-Aided Three-Dimensional Reconstruction and Quantitative Analysis of Cells from Serial Electron Microscopic Montages of Fetal Monkey Brain," *Nature*, 250:31–34, 1974.)

nections with other cells. This phase involves movement again, this time of a "growth cone," the advancing edge of which sends out delicate tubes (filopodia) that attach and then retract, thereby pulling the growth cone forward as a new wave of filopodia extend themselves.

Similar hair-like processes on dendrites form *spines*, the sites for future synapses. In both axon and dendrite outgrowth, the membrane of one cell appears to be able to recognize the membrane of another and the tissue outgrowth behaves accordingly. An axon growth cone may follow another axon, cross it, or make transitory contact with its filopodia, then break off contact and proceed. Physical landmarks are used as guides: axon outgrowth in cell culture will follow scratches in the culture vial glass. Dendrites also appear to send out filopodia that make contact with axons, cell bodies, and other dendrites.

The picture that emerges is one of an active interweaving process, with each cell moving and making connections according to clues in its immediate environment. But where is the plan and how is organization achieved? The cues to which the outgrowths respond are the crucial elements here, and these are thought to be the specific structural configuration of cell membranes, strands of glycoproteins that are embedded in the membrane at one end and protrude from the external surface exposing their specific molecular pattern. The particular configuration of protein molecules is laid out by the gene template within each cell. This allows the cell to specify the nature of its membrane cues and to recognize a particular cell with which it can then interact in a number of different ways; for example, follow, cross, or synapse. The neuron appears to find its way by tactile and chemosensory function of its filopodia "palpating" each structure in its path and proceeding in a trial-and-error fashion (see Figure 8–2).

At this cellular level of organization, the environment of one cell is the structure and behavior of other cells. The usual distinction between gene and environment is called into question at this level of organization, where the genetically determined membrane cues of one cell are the environmental cues to which the next cell responds. In such a world, even the environment seems to be specified by the genes. But because of the nature of the system it is inordinately vulnerable to alterations in the chemical environment originating from sources outside the embryonic tissue itself. For example, drugs ingested by the mother that find their way in minute quantities into the tissue at this stage of organization of the nervous system can cause severe disorders of structure in the nervous system because they supply false cues or interfere with the growing neuron's ability to respond to normal cues. The same drug taken later, after migration and outgrowth processes are complete, may have no effects.

Thus, even at this very early stage in the development of behavior, the neuron begins an interaction with its surroundings that will con-

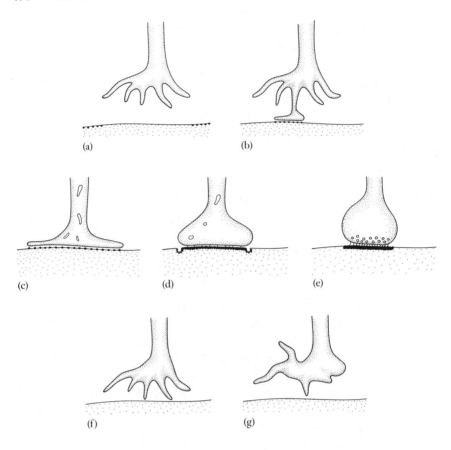

FIGURE 8-2
A growing axon approaching a cell *(a)*, making contact *(b)*, and either forming
a synapse *(c–e)* or failing to establish a contact and moving away *(f–g)*. The
dots on the membrane *(a–c)* signify distribution of receptor molecules. (From
R. D. Lund, *Development and Plasticity of the Brain.* New York: Oxford University Press, 1978.)

tinue throughout its life as the effective environment enlarges from the
nearest tissue sources to the most distant technological extensions of
the adults' sensory processes. It should be clear, however, from all the
foregoing that the neuron is an active participant in these earlier events.
Its interactions with its environment leave it changed, thus modifying
the kinds of interactions possible next. This *epigenetic principle* will be
evident throughout the next sections.

THE ROLE OF FUNCTION IN THE FORMATION OF NERVE NETWORKS

Developing neurons appear to be dependent on making functional connections for their very survival. In the spinal cord and in certain ganglia of the autonomic system, the number of neurons normally decreases by 50 percent at a certain phase in early development. This loss of neurons can be greatly increased by removal of the end organ before innervation occurs. Apparently more neurons are made, and axons sent out than there are terminal sites to innervate. Only those neurons survive that make functional connections. For some types of neurons in the autonomic system, a factor has been isolated *(nerve growth factor)*, that prevents this loss of neurons when present locally. Apparently, it is in making connections with a suitable target organ that growth factor is taken up or made near the tip of the axon and transported back to the cell body. This trophic factor is necessary for the continued life of the neuron. In other experiments, it has been shown that if certain kinds of spinal cord neurons fail to have synapses formed upon them by other cells, they die. These findings describe a means by which inappropriately connected cells can be eliminated, a kind of validation that selects certain patterns of connectivity rather than leaving the whole matter of choice to the membrane recognition mechanisms. It is a mechanism that delegates control of the developing neuron to its functional position rather than to genetic instructions. Muscle also appears to be markedly influenced by its functional innervation. The muscles of the rabbit make a new protein and give a different form of contractile response when they have been innervated by a nerve transplanted from a different muscle or when the stimulation pattern of their own nerve is altered artificially, as described in Chapter 5.

In studies on amphibians and fish, mechanisms have been discovered by which one nerve will suppress the functions of another nerve when dual innervation of a muscle is imposed by experimental surgery (1). A muscle will be driven by an inappropriate nerve if its normal nerve is cut and will produce abnormal limb movement until the normal nerve regenerates. At this point, instead of competition occurring, some studies suggest that the inappropriate nerve synapse may become increasingly ineffective due to a decline in the amount of transmitter released per impulse. The anomalous nerve can still drive the muscle, however, if directly stimulated. Not all muscles have this capacity for suppression and no one knows how function in the "right" synapses exerts the suppressive effect on the "wrong" axon terminals.

The point is that, in this example, organization in the nervous system is defended by a mechanism that depends on functioning. Early in development, abnormal and multiple connections are not prevented simply by specificity of connections. Rather, abnormal and multiple innervations of muscle *do* occur in young organisms but are eliminated or suppressed later in development. In the rat (2) up to 10 days *after* birth, virtually all the fibers in a major leg muscle were found to be innervated by more than one axon. During the next 5 days, almost all these synapses degenerated, thus arriving at the adult complement of one axon per muscle fiber through what appears to be a competitive selection process. The smaller motor units are thought to allow the finely graded contraction and the finer motor coordination character-istic of behavior in 20-day-old rats as compared to 10-day-olds. Cutting the muscle tendon or blocking synaptic transmission delays the elim-ination of synapses so that here, even in the postnatal period, neural organization appears to depend on function, on some signal from mus-cle to nerve.

Another well-known feature of neural organization, the sensory fields of peripheral nerves, also appears to be determined by interac-tion between axons. In salamanders (3) sensory fibers will sprout and innervate a skin area that has had its own nerve cut. If the nerve is not cut, but simply has a drug placed on it that blocks its fast transport mechanisms, its neighbors will encroach as fast as if it had been cut, even though the drug-treated nerve can still carry nerve impulses. This work suggests that the relative spacing of cutaneous nerves may de-pend on materials released by individual axons. Each nerve must de-fend its territory, and the map we have on our skin for each sensory nerve appears to be the result of an early competition and division of the available space.

This theme of organization maintained by competition is also illus-trated in the central nervous system. If certain regions on one side of an embryo rat's brain are destroyed before they have sent out their axonal projections, the axons from the comparable region on the op-posite side will take an abnormal course and grow into the area that had been deprived of its axonal projection. This is true for connections between eye and visual centers, between cerebellum and thalamus, and between sensorimotor cortex and spinal cord. Specificity for con-necting with cells of its own system is maintained, presumably by genetically encoded cell recognition processes, but laterality is maintained by the dynamic interaction of axons growing concurrently.

The positioning and connections of neurons appear to be determined in important ways by their interactions with each other as they send out their long axons and many branched dendrites. Connections appear to be validated and maintained or alternately suppressed by factors produced in functioning. But once established, can a neuron's connections be altered and its biochemical nature changed by interaction with its target cells? Surprisingly, the answer to this question is yes, in certain instances.

INTERACTIONS SHAPING THE NATURE OF THE NEURON

Early experiments in embryology seemed to indicate that neurons relentlessly hunted down target cells that had been preordained for them by their genes. A remarkable finding that seemed to support this point of view was that when skin was transplanted from abdomen to back of a tadpole, the frog that developed acted as if the skin were still on its belly. When sand was dropped on the patch on its back, it wiped at its *abdomen* with its leg. The conclusion was that the skin on the back must have been sought out and innervated by a ventral sensory nerve, thus accounting for the inappropriate *ventral* motor response. Recent work (4) has shown, however, that it is a *dorsal* nerve that innervates the patch and that if the frog is tested soon after transplantation the responses are properly directed to the back. Only with time does the wiping response become directed to the ventrum: apparently the sensorimotor reflex arc becomes reorganized. Together with other data, these new findings have led to the reinterpretation that there is a critical period during which dorsal and ventral sensory neurons become specified, that the information for this specification comes from the peripheral target tissue rather than from the genes within the cell, and that the connections such sensory neurons make with motor cells in the spinal cord are controlled by the interaction of the sensory axon terminal with its target tissue in the periphery rather than by a genetic "wiring diagram" carried in the cells' genes.

The proposition that alterations in the primary input to a developing cell can have marked effects on the central connections established by that cell is supported by findings in the "Boston Siamese" cat where structural abnormalities of the retina lead to altered cortical projection maps (5).

Second, in the development of the autonomic neuron, it has been found that the type of neurotransmitter produced and used by the cell is determined not just by the genes in the cell body but also by the cells with which the axon synapses, by the presence of certain muscle and connective tissue cells, and even by an unknown soluble factor. Neurons taken from a rat even *after* birth, which have all the chemical characteristics of *adrenergic* neurons, will alter their nature to form *cholinergic* synapses on other neurons and skeletal muscles in tissue culture. If purely neural elements are grown, the neurons remain adrenergic. By adjusting the kinds of other cells growing in the medium, pure adrenergic, mixed adrenergic-cholinergic, and pure cholinergic neurons can be produced. That these mechanisms are operative in real life as well as in tissue culture is strongly suggested by transplantation studies in early embryos. Autonomic cells from the upper trunk portion of the neural tube ordinarily send long axons down to innervate the gut and become parasympathetic–cholinergic neurons. If these cells are transplanted to the mid-portion of the neural tube they will travel a shorter path, connect with the adrenal medulla, and form neurons of the sympathetic–adrenergic chain ganglia.

In these experiments the fundamental physiological and neurochemical nature of neurons is specified by the kinds of jobs they are doing and the kinds of tissue they are exposed to.

SUMMARY

What can we learn from these examples of the cellular processes of development of the nervous system? First, that the early cellular environment of a developing neuron can play an essential role in determining the location and connections of a neuron as well as its biochemical nature. Second, that a neuron's functioning can play an essential role in maintenance of its sensory fields, its ability to excite muscle, and even in its survival during critical periods in its life. These two elements—environment and function—continue to play key roles in shaping the fine structure and function of the nervous system throughout life.

The *outside* environment also impinges on the developing nervous system by altering the chemical environment of axons and dendrites in sensory receptors and changing levels and patterns of function in nerve cell networks. Therefore, life experience of the young organism affects those very same cellular mechanisms upon which the developing neuron depends for the determination of its biological nature. Many neurons in the human central nervous system are still going through the phases of differentiation, cell migration, axon and dendrite outgrowth, and neurochemical specifications for a year after birth. Other neurons, particularly in sensorimotor systems vital to life of the newborn, are formed and functioning for months before birth. So that not only is the environment of the human changing enormously during development but so also are the level of function and the stage of development of neurons in different areas of the brain. Thus, the same change in environment will have different effects on different sorts of functions at different times in early development.

From this close look at the process of development, it is clear that evolutionary processes have selected genes that delegate many formative influences in development to the environment, even in the lower forms like amphibians and fish where some of the experimental work has been done. We do not have any reason to believe that human embryological processes are less open to environmental influences. In fact, the trend in mammalian evolution appears to be toward delegating more of the controls of development to the environment, since adaptability to changing conditions seems to have been the trait with the greatest competitive advantage, and adaptability depends on responsiveness to the environment. Thus, we are unlikely to be overestimating the importance of the environment for the development of the human brain in generalizing from experiments on simpler living forms.

The early life history of a neuron appears to contain elements and principles that we can continue to use in trying to understand the early life history of the organism. The difficulty in disentangling genetic from environmental influences is present from the earliest phase of the history of the neuron. The biological unit, from neuron to organism, can express the genetic influence only through interaction with the environment, which then changes the biological unit so that it will have a different interaction in its next encounter with the environment. This epigenetic principle focuses our attention on the biological unit and the processes by which its interacts with its environment at a given point in its development, instead of on the attempt to parcel out overall genetic and environmental contributions.

The distinction between *innate* and *acquired* is particularly difficult to draw when we consider the actual processes of development. Indeed, the closer we look at what is really going on, the less interested we become in such global concepts, and the more interesting questions we can ask about exactly how the various forces work in creating the phenomenon of development.

FURTHER READING

Bunge, R., Johnson, M., and Ross, C. D. Nature and nurture in development of the autonomic neuron. *Science*, 199:1409–1416, 1978.

Changeux, J. P., and Dauchin, A. Selective stabilisation of developing synapses as a mechanism for the specification of neuronal networks. *Nature*, 264:705–712, 1976.

Jacobson, M. *Developmental Neurobiology*. 2nd ed. New York: Plenum Press, 1978.

Lund, R. D. *Development and Plasticity of the Brain*. New York: Oxford University Press, 1978.

REFERENCES CITED

1. Lund, R. D. *Development and Plasticity of the Brain*. New York: Oxford University Press, 1978. Pp. 216–219.
2. Brown, M. C., Jansen, J. K. S., and Van Essen, D. Polyneural innervation of skeletal muscle in new-born rats and its elimination during maturation. *Journal of Physiology*, 261:387–422, 1976.
3. Lund, op. cit., pp. 245–246.
4. Baker, R. E., and Jacobson, M. Development of reflexes from skin grafts in *Rana pipiens:* influence of size and position of grafts. *Developmental Biology*, 22:476–494, 1970.
5. Hubel, D. H., and Wiesel, T. N. Aberrant visual projections in the Siamese cat. *Journal of Physiology* (London), 218:33–62, 1971.

9
Processes Modifying Brain Organization

If we are going to understand how behavior is shaped by early experience, we must conceptualize how an event to which the child responds can make him or her different from that time on. How can an event get inside an organism to produce such a change? If it is by changing the brain, what does this mean? More precisely, how is the developing organization of the brain affected by agents outside of it, and what are those agents? As yet, answers are only available for simplified versions of this basic question, but studies give a useful picture of the kinds of modifications that are possible at the cellular level and point the way toward an understanding of more complex environmental and social effects.

In the previous chapter I outlined some of the ways in which the cells assemble themselves into a structure that can initiate and control behavior. The influence of function was mostly limited to the spontaneous activity of cells and the environment was restricted to the substance of the brain, muscles, and sensory receptors. In this chapter I will ask how outside agents can alter the nature of the organization being laid down by the interaction of neurons in the developing brain.

There are four main categories of influence that I will consider: (1) stimulation of sensory systems, (2) hormones, (3) nutrition, and (4) sensorimotor interaction with the environment.

STIMULATION

One of the most important unanswered questions about stimulation in early development is how to distinguish learning from other effects of stimulation at this age. Alternately, we might ask if that distinction is in fact more in our minds than in the processes of the brain. To give a couple of examples, it is known that exposure of young animals for a number of days in early life to a particular sound, taste, smell, or visual pattern tends to result in that animal growing up with an increased responsiveness to that stimulus, both in terms of threshold and in number of responses. A preference has been acquired. At a cellular level, and over a matter of minutes instead of days, it has been found that a single cell in a kitten's visual cortex will gradually increase its firing rate in response to a stimulus presented repeatedly to one eye (1). Responsiveness of that same cell to stimulation of the other eye is found to be reduced as a consequence of the prior experience, and this change will persist for at least an hour of intermittent stimulation of both eyes. This remarkable effect is present in kittens only during a limited period of their development. Can we say the cell has acquired a preference for stimulation from one eye rather than the other? Certainly there has been a relatively specific increase in response as a result of prior experience, something we usually call "learning." But there has been no associated event and no environmental consequence of the stimulation. What kind of learning is this? Perhaps "conditioning" is a better term, or even a more general term, "plasticity." The important question is how such a change comes about at the level of synaptic function, and this remains a mystery. We may soon discover that it shares certain properties with synaptic changes underlying "true" learning. In any case, this property of sensory systems and individual neurons to become committed to a certain kind of function as the result of their early experience is an extremely important mechanism by which stimulation becomes translated into changed functional organization of the brain, one I will return to soon.

The simplest approach to finding out how sensory stimulation can be related to brain organization is to remove a particular sensory receptor near the time of birth and then look at the brain several weeks later. Experiments of this sort in a wide variety of systems and species have disclosed a close interdependence between the receptor and the relay system within the brain to which it is connected by a series of synapses. The so-called "transsynaptic" effects involve *atrophy* or shrinkage of cells, degeneration of fine structure, and even cell death in the cells of the first central synapse, and lack of branching and spine formation (sites of synapses) on dendrites of more distant neurons. It is of interest that this is a two-way street: all types of sensory receptor cells will degenerate when deprived of their innervation. Even more distant effects occur as in the degeneration of cells of the retina of the eye following destruction of their cortical relay cells in the occipital pole of the brain, at least two synapses away.

What must be realized is that removal of a sensory receptor is not the same thing as removal of sensory stimulation from the environment. Many receptor cells fire intermittently without any sensory input, which provides a background level of stimulation to neurons all

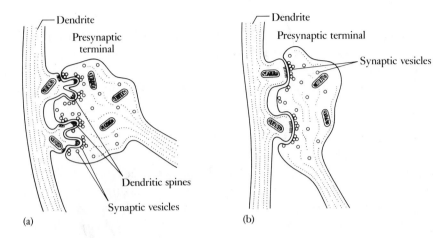

(a)   (b)

FIGURE 9-1
Electron microscopic appearance of dendritic spines in lateral geniculate neurons of dogs. (*a*) Normally, spines of postsynaptic dendrite project into the presynaptic terminal. (*b*) The dark-reared animal has a deficiency of spines. (After J. Hamori, *Recent Developments of Neurobiology in Hungary.* Budapest: Academiae Kiado, 1973.)

along the relay system. It is thought that the neurotransmitter released as a part of this background activity serves somehow to maintain the integrity of the connected neurons. The photoreceptors of the retina are an extreme case in point, since they continuously release transmitter in the dark and *stop* releasing it when light strikes them, thus actually reversing the usual relationship.

During the phases of cell migration, differentiation, and the formation of synapses, the neurons are particularly susceptible to these transsynaptic influences. The organization of the cortex into columns of cells serving a particular sensory function is entirely prevented if receptors are destroyed prior to the formation of these columns but not if receptor destruction occurs later. In the case of the earlier lesions, the cortical cells come to be innervated by projections from receptors adjacent to the area destroyed. When this form of replacement has taken place, the changes in brain organization tend to be irreversible. Destruction of sensory receptors in adults leads to only mild signs of cortical cell degeneration and only after months, whereas widespread cell death often occurs in days after similar lesions in infant animals.

The effects of stimulating or depriving sensory receptors are a great deal more equivocal than what follows destruction of the receptors in most sensory systems. Neurons generally appear to remain intact, migrate, differentiate, and develop some branching and synaptic contacts, despite radical decreases in levels of sensory stimulation. This does not imply that synaptic function and, thus, *functional* organization necessarily remain unaffected, as we shall see in studies on the visual system.

There are certain specifically vulnerable neurons whose integrity is dependent on stimulation. For example, growth of dendritic spines of one group of cells in the visual cortex of mice (2) or dogs is dependent on the normal arrival of visual stimulation with the opening of eyes 2 weeks after birth. If exposure to light is delayed until 30 postnatal days, a permanent deficit of dendritic spines remains (see Figure 9–1). Other cortical visual cells that form dendritic spines before the time of eye opening are structurally unaffected. From a functional standpoint, dark-rearing of a number of species ranging from monkeys to birds sharply and permanently reduces their ability to see clearly, although eyeblink and pupillary reflex remain unaffected. What, then, is going on neurophysiologically?

A series of studies in very young kittens pioneered by Hubel and Wiesel have gone a long way toward defining the cellular basis for the effects of early experience on the functional organization of the brain. Work on this system is most advanced and provides a basis for understanding the specific effects of qualitatively distinct experiences on neuronal function in the developing brain, so it is worth describing in more detail.

Infant kittens and monkeys without visual experience have cortical cells, each of which is predisposed to being a specialist of one sort or another. Some are most easily driven by one eye, some by the other; a few can be driven equally well by both eyes. Some are sensitive to a particular direction of movement or orientation of the stimulus. In the visually naive kitten, the orientation-selective cells are all driven by only one eye, and the binocularly driven cells are not selective to orientation. The major difference in the adult is that the visual cortical cells that are selective to the orientation of a stimulus are selective to the same orientation in both eyes and are binocularly driven. The capacity to compare images arriving at the two eyes is the basis of depth perception and is accounted for by such cells. The cells in the adult have become transformed in their response capabilities by the normal experience of binocular vision.

The effects of various experimental visual experiences on the developing characteristics of visual cortical cells have disclosed several other interesting features. First, marked reduction of patterned visual input to one eye, with a light-diffusing lens from birth to 2 months of age, leads to a marked decrease in the number of binocularly driven cells; but beyond that, to degeneration of cells in the midbrain relay station (the lateral geniculate nucleus) between the retina and the cortex. Thereafter, that eye remains blind even though it is opened to normal visual stimulation after a few weeks. Permanent deficits were produced with monocular deprivation between the third week and the third month of a kitten's life, whereas much longer deprivation in the adult had no effect, and binocular deprivation between 3 weeks and 3 months had much less severe effects. Between 4 and 8 weeks, changing the diffusing lens to the other eye can reverse this ocular dominance and prevent blindness, but not thereafter. The degeneration in the lateral geniculate ganglion is confined to areas of cells subserving binocular function while segments to which the deprived eye projects are structurally unaffected. These findings show that it is the *interaction* between the eyes that is critical for normal neuronal development.

Although the precise mechanisms for the determination of monocular and binocular driving of a given cortical cell are not well understood, two recent findings are of interest. Function can be rapidly restored to the blind eye produced by monocular light diffusion, if the experienced eye is *removed* (not if it is merely deprived of light). Also, a synaptic blocking drug (bicuculline) given intravenously can immediately but transiently restore function in the deprived eye. These findings suggest that the abnormal state is maintained by an inhibitory influence exerted by input from the experienced eye upon input from the early deprived eye, and that the blindness is *potentially* reversible. Furthermore, it has been found that the normal shift from monocular to binocular driving and the abnormal effects of monocular deprivation can be prevented if levels of the catecholamine neurotransmitters are depleted by drugs during the period of the visual experience. Under these conditions, the visual cortical cells remain in the "naive" state of the very young infant. The same drug treatment is ineffective if given *after* the visual experience, so it can prevent the experience from exerting its effect but cannot reverse the effect once it has taken place. In this way, the critical period is extended by such drug treatment, an exciting lead to the biochemical nature of critical or sensitive periods for early experience.

In the normal course of events, an infant is exposed to a vast array of different visual forms—edges, corners, dots, horizontal and vertical lines, and so forth. Furthermore, these stimuli move in different ways. If a human infant has an obstruction to patterned vision in the form of a clouding of the lens or cornea in both eyes and is allowed to grow up before this impediment is removed, we can ask what the person sees immediately after the operation and thus get a rough idea of what role experience may play in our ability to see (3). The fact is that people can see very little at first, even in cases when after the operation the eye is optically perfect. They see nothing but a blur; then they can distinguish objects from background, but cannot see the difference, for example, between an orange and a banana. They must learn to see by experience and training. Having felt the difference between a triangle and a circle with their fingers, they still cannot see the difference right away. In some cases, progress is very slow, but in others, only a few days is required before a clock face can be read, for instance.

The puzzling point is the initial inability to see differences even though the person knows they are there and knows what to look for. Experiments with kittens by Pettigrew and others have led to a clearer understanding of this phenomenon and of the role of patterned stimulation in visual development in infancy. Kittens have been reared from infancy until three months of age in deliberately altered visual worlds by fitting them with goggles that admit, for example, only vertical bars of light, or in a planetarium where the only light source was tiny pinpoints of light. After these sorts of rearing experiences, cats gave evidence of difficulties in perceiving objects that were not made up of vertical bars or dots, depending on their early experience. By recording from cortical cells in these cats it was found that no longer could cells be found that were optimally responsive to other stimuli. Most cells were responsive preferentially to the particular stimuli they had been exposed to during this early period. With special goggles, cats could be produced that responded best to horizontal lines with one eye and vertical lines with the other. Cortical cell response characteristics were appropriate to the visual characteristics of their early experience. These effects were found to persist for many months, although some recovery of function occurred with some cortical cells becoming responsive to other stimuli. Apparently a number of cells remained uncommitted during the early period and were available for modification by new experience even after the early critical period.

Thus, the capacity of the normal adult to detect edges, lines, contrast, and motion is dependent on the establishment of cortical cells, each of which is preferentially responsive to one or another of these qualities of the stimulus. Although such cells in the infant appear to have a predisposition to be responsive to a particular orientation or movement, this is not yet firmly established. Repeated stimulation appears to generate changes in the synaptic function of these cells so that they become firmly fixed in the nature of the visual stimuli to which they will give an optimal response. The usefulness of the early predisposition is obvious since it inclines cells to become specialists in one aspect of the normal highly variable visual world. This predisposition is not a predetermination, however, as is shown by the results of experimental alterations of visual experience. The cell can become sensitive to one eye and blind to the other, or give up its predisposition and become committed to a quite different form of stimulation. This commitment of cells underlies the sensory capacities of the animal and explains the altered function resulting from different early visual experience.

The cortical cells are of course not responding directly to the stimuli, but rather to synaptic input from a hierarchical arrangement of other cortical, midbrain, and retinal cells. The cortical cells that are selectively responsive to the most complex features (for example, a corner or angle) are probably enabled to do so by synaptic connections with other cortical cells responsive to different orientations of edges. These cells, in turn, receive input from a series of diencephalic and retinal ganglion cells responsive to small areas of light–dark contrast, and finally these tap an even larger number of photoreceptors, responsive simply to light. The neural organization of the retina extracts only light–dark contrast information, so that the ability to see objects is dependent on the organization of synaptic connections with cortical cells. These cortical cells must become committed to certain features of the visible world and, when that occurs, the animal or person can detect that feature.

Of course, the experience of seeing is not to be explained on the basis of the firing of a single cell, no matter how many less complex cells may be connected to it. However, these studies do afford a clear view of how the brain acquires the basic tools for vision. That these findings in kittens and monkeys may apply also to people is supported by the adverse long-term effects of ocular defects that remain uncorrected until after infancy. A sensitive period for the development of *human* binocular vision, for example, has been found between 1 and 3 years of age in clinical studies designed on the basis of the research on kittens (4).

In summary, sensory receptors maintain the integrity of their neural relay systems and synaptic connections in their cortical projection areas by a transsynaptic mechanism probably involving the tonic release of neurotransmitters. Stimulation of these receptors may in some cases enhance these effects. The primary action of stimulation of these receptors, at least in the visual system, appears to be to modulate the effectiveness of individual synapses and thus to determine the pattern of functioning connections. An analogy to switches in a complex web of railroad tracks is tempting here, but should not be taken too literally. The principle arising from these studies on visual cortex is that the neurons respond more and more effectively along synaptic pathways that are repeatedly activated. These changes, in turn, tend to inhibit transmission along other synaptic pathways that are not frequently activated. The development of the system thus tends to become canalized along lines determined by the early experience. But the cortical neurons are far from passive in this process. Each one has its own predisposition to become committed in a specific way, so that a very little experience with one kind of stimulation may be enough for a given cell, whereas a great deal of another kind of stimulation may be insufficient. Thus, the characteristics of the biological unit may be at least as important as the experience in determining the final outcome.

These findings give us a clear model for how a nervous system becomes organized in a particular way as the result of specific experience. They provide a way to conceptualize what may be going on in the formation of a "neural substrate for behavior" during development, and for the interaction of predisposition and experience. Finally, these studies describe in concrete terms a model for the processes we infer from our observations on development at the behavioral level. But we must not overextend the implications of this model. Other systems no doubt involve additional or different cellular processes, and we must continue to distinguish between those processes we infer to be going on in the brain and those for which we have evidence. Meanwhile, it is the only area of early experience effects that we understand reasonably well, all the way from the behavioral to the cellular levels.

HORMONES

At first glance, hormones would not appear to belong in this section because they do not originate in the outside environment the way, for example, sound and light do. But during the long period of fetal life, hormones do come from the environment of the fetus, the mother, and the placenta. From the point of view of the brain of the infant, they are as much an outside force shaping its development as are sound and light. Furthermore, one of the ways that the environment communicates with the brain is through hormones, because the level of hormones in the blood that reaches the brain is so responsive to the person's environment. Some hormones are produced in the brain, and most are closely regulated by the central nervous system. The word "hormone" comes from the Greek verb meaning to urge on or excite. In development, hormones act as intermediary agents between the outside environment and the developing brain. That is, the experience of the infant, or of the mother in the case of the fetus, may be translated by the brain into a change in hormone level which then in turn acts on the brain to alter its pattern of growth and development.

Some hormones (e.g., epinephrine, peptide hormones) act primarily at the surface of the cell where they bind to receptors and activate a second messenger (e.g., cyclic AMP) which in turn acts to change intracellular processes. The other major class (e.g., steroid and thyroid) enters the cell and binds directly to the nucleus, activating the synthesis of a different second messenger (RNA), which directs intracellular processes. The peptide hormones, such as growth hormone, do not cross the placenta, but epinephrine, adrenal, sex, and thyroid hormones do. Those that do not cross the placenta can affect it and may act on the fetus by changing placental function or by inducing the release of still a different form of "second messenger" that travels from the placenta to the fetus.

Since many important hormones have been available for several decades we would suppose that we would have a clear picture of precisely how the various hormones affect the development of the brain. But we do not. One of the problems is that they affect too many aspects of growth: cell proliferation and differentiation, dendritic branching, and formation of synapses, to say nothing of the synthesis, release, and uptake of neurotransmitters. The second problem is to distinguish the direct or primary effect of the hormone on brain cells from the indirect, secondary effects of the changes in nutritional and metabolic state of the organism induced by the hormone. Despite these protean effects of hormones, recent studies with tissue culture of specific cells and other techniques promise to bring some clarity to the field.

Thyroid hormone is necessary for normal brain growth after birth in most mammals but plays little role prenatally. Deficiency causes marked reduction in cell numbers and severe functional retardation (cretinism). Excess of this hormone stimulates growth and differentiation in the cerebrum but causes decreased cell branching and cell number in the cerebellum. The schedule of development of the brain is pushed ahead, but the animal then falls short on final levels of performance and in number of cells in certain parts of the brain.

Adrenal glucocorticoids, the hormones that we particularly associate with acute stress, bind to receptors over large portions of the old brain, the limbic system, and glial cells. Excess of this hormone in infancy reduces dendritic spine growth and slows development, but also severely stunts body growth, so that nutritional effects have been impossible to distinguish from direct effects of the hormone on the developing brain. Not nearly enough is known about the early developmental actions of this hormone that could mediate some of the long-term effects of stress during childhood, or during pregnancy, on the development of the fetus.

The roles of the sex hormones on the developing brain are beginning to be clarified. Although we know something about their effects on how menstrual cycles and sexual behavior develop, we do not know exactly how and where they act in the brain to do this. We do not understand the cellular basis for their action. The closest lead we have at present is in the part of the brain that controls menstrual cycles in women. The cycles are due to rhythmic monthly changes in pituitary hormones programmed by the "preoptic" area of the hypothalamus, just adjacent to the pituitary. In the rat, this part of the brain shows a different pattern of synapses in males and females, the only visible brain difference between the sexes found so far (see Figure 9–2). In the female, cell nuclei are larger and there are more synapses on dendritic spines, whereas in the male there are more synapses on the shafts of dendrites. The male synaptic pattern occurs together with an absence of rhythmic changes in pituitary hormone release, a noncycling pattern. But if a male is deprived of the male hormone testosterone by castration at an early age before these two patterns have differentiated, the number of dendritic spine synapses increases and the pituitary will develop a cyclic female pattern at puberty. Conversely, treatment of fetal or early neonatal females with testosterone reduces the number of spine synapses, and menstrual cycles will never develop because the pituitary hormones will be released in the noncycling male pattern. In females, both synaptic pattern and a cycling pituitary will develop without hormone induction and indeed without ovaries. It is not entirely certain how the structural changes in the hypothalamus are related either to the cycling pattern of pituitary function or to behavior later in life. They may simply be associated changes, but they are clear evidence of the formative effect of androgens on the developing brain.

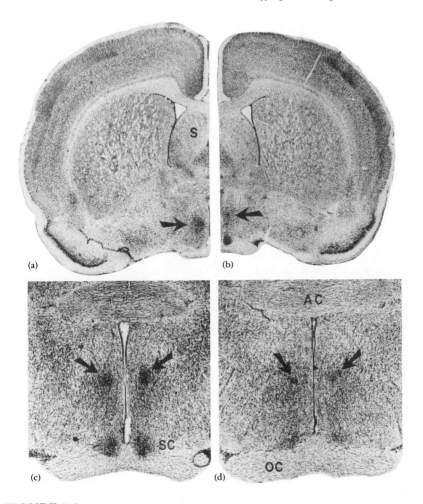

FIGURE 9-2
Visible differences in the brains of male and female rats. Arrows indicate the sexually dimorphic nucleus in the brains of male (*a* and *c*) and female (*b* and *d*) rats. (From R. A. Gorski, "Hormonal Modulation of Neuronal Structure." In F. O. Schmitt and F. G. Worden, Eds., *The Neurosciences: Fourth Study Program.* Cambridge, Mass.: MIT Press, 1979.)

Another aspect of hypothalamic brain cell function is hormone-dependent early in life. In the fetus, both androgens and estrogens are equally well taken up and bound by receptors on nuclei of cells in the hypothalamus. Exposure of these cells to testosterone early in development alters these nuclear receptors so that they preferentially bind testosterone in adulthood, whereas without such early androgen exposure this region of the brain will come to bind estrogen instead. An inductive effect of hormone on brain cell receptors seems to be at work here (5). Such selective hormone uptake by neurons is thought to explain some of the selective effects of hormones produced at the time of puberty and thus may underlie the different physiology and sexual behavior of males and females activated by the hormonal surges beginning at this time of life.

Thus, the hypothalamic area of the brain appears to develop differently, according to whether testosterone is present at a critical period in late fetal life, in monkeys and probably in humans. In experimental animals, when testosterone is not present, as in the normal female fetus, the cells develop larger nuclei, more dendritic spine synapses, and come to bind estrogens preferentially. At puberty, the pituitary will start to cycle rhythmically. Testosterone alters the appearance of the cells of the fetal brain, their preference in taking up hormones, and prevents the development of a cycling pituitary.

The developmental principle for all mammals studied so far is that female characteristics will develop unless certain steroid hormones are present during a critical period early in development. In addition to the brain characteristics described, the form and structure of the male external genitalia are also induced by the same *organizational* effects of hormones in fetal life. In the absence of androgen, the two sides of the genital area fail to fuse and a vagina is formed; the labia are formed on each side instead of the scrotal sacks and the clitoris forms instead of the penis. An interesting twist was introduced to this straightforward story when it was discovered that synthetic estrogen had many of the same effects as androgen. Furthermore, the androgen was found to be converted by a chemical process called *aromatization* into estradiol within the cells of the brain, and it is actually a female-type sex hormone that directs the male-type cellular changes. How then is the female protected against her own and her mother's hormones during the critical period in fetal life? An estrogen binding protein has been discovered in fetal and neonatal blood that prevents circulating estrogen from entering the developing brain. Many synthetic estrogens, however, that may be given to pregnant women, are not bound by this protein and can enter the brain of the fetus and become converted to active estradiol. These estrogens are capable of masculinizing a female fetus. An additional factor protecting the female fetus from estrogen is that the fetal ovary develops its endocrine function slower than the testis and is relatively inactive in fetal life.

These findings on hormonal determination of the structure of certain brain cells, the selective affinity of brain cell hormone receptors, the form of the external genitalia at birth, and the patterns of pituitary function at puberty have led to two different theories of how behavior may be affected by the action of hormones early in life. This topic raises a number of issues that will be dealt with in the next chapter and in Chapter 15. Since the two hypotheses originate from changes found to occur in brain cells, I will outline them at this point. The first theory emphasizes the changes induced by early androgens in the selectivity of uptake of sex hormones by brain cells in regions that have been implicated in sexual behavior (preoptic, hypothalamic, limbic, and mesencephalic). In this view it is the *threshold* for the activation of particular patterns of behavior by hormones produced at puberty that has been influenced by the presence or absence of androgens early in life. The second theory emphasizes the organizational findings on the pattern of synapses (and by analogy, on the tissues of the external genitalia). It is the *organization* of brain cell connections that is supposed to have been affected, according to this theory, so that different neural substrates of behavior are formed in the two sexes. Both theories leave open the question of how subsequent social experience can modify either threshold or organization or other intermediate processes, in the final expression of sexual behavior later in life.

NUTRITION

The third major force influencing the expression of the genetic potential for brain growth and organization is the nutrient supply. The effects that we understand the best are the results of depriving the brain of nutrient. The remarkable fact about this influence, when it occurs in very early life, is not simply that its effects are dramatic, but that they appear to be permanent and irreversible despite a return to optimal diet. In this respect the effect is similar to some of those described for early sensory stimulation and the early action of hormones on the brain. Qualitative effects of diet are not as fully studied yet, but there is some intriguing new information suggesting a role for different variations of a "normal" diet in the biochemical nature of the brain.

The cellular growth of the brain depends on an adequate supply of nutrient, as does the formation of the fatty myelin axon sheaths, and of the glycoproteins necessary for synaptic membranes. The rate of neuron division and of migration, as well as of neuron size and differentiation, is regulated by the supply of nutrients available, as well as by the DNA within the genetic material of the cells themselves.

The early period of development is a crucial one for nutrient effects on the brain because this is the only period of life when malnutrition can exert an effect on cell *number*. Effects exerted at this time of life are permanent because changes in nutrient level do not affect the time at which cell growth stops in the various regions of the brain. For example, dietary deficiency does not prolong the period of cell division. Thus, a return to normal diet after the end of a period of rapid cell growth cannot change the number of neurons in the brain; it can only change cell size. As I have discussed in previous sections, different regions of the central nervous system mature at different periods so that, for example, the spinal cord and brain stem have ceased their period of cell division before the cerebrum and cerebellum have begun theirs. Within these regions, the types of cells have different schedules. The large cells with long axons mature the earliest, followed by the smaller interconnecting neurons and finally the neuroglial cells. In the human, the increase in cell number continues to about the end of the first year after birth, having shown a very rapid rise between 10 and 20 weeks gestational age and a slow progressive increase thereafter.

These facts mean that the effects of short periods of malnutrition may be quite different, depending on their timing within the early development of the child. Certain regions of the brain and certain cell types within that region may thus be selectively affected and particular functions altered as a result. For example, malnutrition during the gestational period will have the most severe permanent effects on the organization of the brain; during the sucking period, fine tuning such as cerebellar function is particularly affected, whereas myelinization and blood supply are permanently affected by later malnutrition. After the first year, malnutrition must be very severe and prolonged for it to have any permanent effects after restoration of a normal diet.

The mechanism for this effect of nutrient on cell division is not well understood, but appears to depend on a diversion of amino acids from DNA synthesis, into RNA synthesis, along with an increase in RNA degradation. Thus, increased RNA turnover is substituted for the normal rates of DNA synthesis necessary for cell division.

It is interesting that this mechanism for nutritional control of cell division is in fact capable of *increasing* the number of neurons in the brain through a *greater* than normal supply of nutrient. These studies on "supernutrition" suggest that normal development is below the genetic potential—at least in terms of the *number* of cells. Such effects can be achieved by reduction of the number of fetuses in the uterus, by supplying extra nutrient to infants after birth, and by giving growth hormone to the pregnant mother. This last treatment results in enlargement of the placenta and probably increases nutrient to the fetuses in that way. There is little evidence, however, that the actual performance of the animals is improved by supernutrition, although this is the exciting possibility raised by our new knowledge of this nutrient regulatory system of brain growth.

Another major effect of early nutrition is on the branching of the dendrites of cells and on the estimated number of synapses. These are strikingly reduced in early malnourished animals. Such effects appear to be permanent if the animal is reared under normal laboratory conditions, even after return to a normal diet. A very stimulating and varied environment will reverse many of the behavioral effects of early malnutrition (6) and in normally nourished rats will increase the dendritic arborization and spine count (see below). These animal findings appear to generalize clearly to humans in a study of malnourished Korean children who were rehabilitated and then raised in different environments (7).

But so far I have discussed only gross deprivation (or excess) of nutrient. Are there not some effects of *qualitative* changes in nutrient on the brain in early development? Does our brain come to reflect what we eat? On this question there is much less information, but the clear implication of recent studies by Wurtman is that shifts in carbohydrate–protein balance and in the amino-acid composition of protein in the diet can control the levels of neurotransmitter in the brain. Here we do not have evidence of structural changes, as can be induced by marked deficiency or excess, but of biochemical changes likely to affect synaptic function. The studies have been carried out in rats past the age of weaning, but we may suppose that the same or greater effects will be found during earlier periods of development.

The amino acids essential for the formation of the three major classes of neurotransmitters are taken up into the brain by a competitive transport system so that the one that has the highest concentration in the blood is taken up preferentially by the brain. Thus, if the amino acid tryptophan, the precursor of the neurotransmitter serotonin, is present in much higher concentration than other amino acids in the nutrient, more of it will be taken up by the brain and this will result in higher brain levels of serotonin. If a high carbohydrate nutrient is given, this will also increase tryptophan blood levels, relative to other amino acids, because the insulin stimulated by the carbohydrate promotes the uptake by body cells of all other amino acids except tryptophan. The brain, where this effect of insulin is absent, is thus induced to take up more tryptophan than other amino acids and to develop higher levels of serotonin than other neurotransmitters. That specific diet-induced biochemical changes may alter brain function is suggested by studies showing that rats fed diets selectively *low* in tryptophan have increased sensitivity to painful stimulation, a behavioral effect known to be produced by depletion of serotonin by drugs or lesions. A similar set of relationships has been found for the catecholamine neurotransmitters, norepinephrine and dopamine as well as for acetylcholine and their amino-acid precursors.

We still need to know how such qualitative alterations of diet in infancy may affect neurotransmitter levels in adulthood, whether the effects are permanent or reversible after return to a normal diet, and to what extent feedback and compensatory neurochemical adaptations tend to nullify the changes produced acutely in adults in these recent experiments. The clinical implications are considerable, for example, in conditions such as hyperactivity in children on high carbohydrate diets: their brains may be exposed to excessive levels of tryptophan and a behavioral disorder may develop as a result of increased serotonin synthesis or as a result of feedback and compensatory adjustment to diet-induced alterations in the serotonin system.

SENSORIMOTOR INTERACTION WITH THE ENVIRONMENT

From very early in fetal life, the infant not only senses and moves, but the two are joined together. In the earliest stages, this is done by the simple reflex arc and in later stages by more complex action patterns elicited both by changes in internal state and by aspects of the environment selected on the basis of previous experience. The kind of environment in which the child develops determines to a large degree the amount of such sensorimotor interaction that takes place. An intuitive understanding of the meaning of this aspect of the environment for development led to the use of words such as "rich" to refer to complex and changing environments and "impoverished" to refer to extremely simple and stable environments. Such word usage could simply reflect value judgments based on cultural biases produced by a materialist society. But experimental studies with animals by Rosenzweig and Bennett have shown a wide range of structural and biochemical changes in the brain to be related to the complexity of the environment in which the animal lives. The animal can not simply be *exposed* to a complex environment for the effects to occur; he must be allowed to respond to it and interact with it. Both social and inanimate features have been found to be important, as is novelty in addition to complexity. These aspects appear to be additive.

In the cases of sensory stimulation, hormones, and nutrition, it has been easy to specify the forces that are shaping the organization of the brain. In the present case, it is more problematic. It is neither the environment itself that exerts the effect nor is it the motor activity itself, because animals given similar or greater amounts of exercise in running wheels do not usually show the same brain effects. Finally, it does not even seem to be the arousal itself of sensory, motor, and emotional systems that is the crucial ingredient. Animals subjected to repeated unavoidable electric shocks show few or none of the effects, nor do animals whose wire mesh cages are placed in the rooms with the interacting animals, even though their cages were subjects of active exploration and they became behaviorally aroused during the same periods of time. The effects may not depend on hormonal mediation, because they occur in animals whose pituitary gland has been removed. Thus, it appears to be the experience of the sensorimotor interaction that is responsible. The behavior of the animals keeps changing with their experience in these changing environments, and it seems likely that learning and memory storage processes are repeatedly activated. In the terms of Chapter 7, "schemas" for sensory processing and motor strategies are being elaborated and laid down. We are still a long way from being able to identify the neural basis for this inferred organizational principle, the schema, but the results of these studies at least indicate what some of the building blocks may be.

Rats were housed singly after weaning in standard bare laboratory cages for an impoverished condition. Others were housed with one or two cagemates of the same sex to study the effects of an opportunity for social interaction. For the complex conditions, 10–12 rats were placed in a 2–3 foot cage into which were placed every day a different set of novel objects (e.g., ladders, ropes, steps, and inclined planes).

Rats were sacrificed after various durations of time spent in the three conditions and a variety of techniques used to study their brains. It was a great surprise for most people, at the time these results were first published about 20 years ago, to find that such gross measures as brain weight and thickness of the cerebral cortex could be affected by the different living conditions: the greater the complexity, the bigger the brain. Subsequent studies have shown that although much of the gross increase is made up by neuroglial cells whose function is obscure, the degree of branching of neuronal dendrites and their spine counts is significantly increased by increasing environmental complexity. The neurons involved are pyramidal and stellate neurons, particularly in the occipital cortex, but increases as great as 25 percent have been reported in the hippocampus, an area of the brain implicated in memory storage. The development of dendrite branching in the human brain is shown in Figure 9–3.

Biochemical evidence for increases in enzymes involved in neurotransmitter metabolism (acetyl-cholinesterase and cholinesterase) have been found and more recently changes in nucleic acid content. The amount of RNA in proportion to DNA is consistently increased by environmental complexity, a result suggesting heightened activity of chemical synthetic processes, possibly involved in memory storage and learning. The lower content of DNA per unit weight is consistent with the interpretation that cell number does not increase substantially, and that there is a much greater increase in the volume of dendrites as a result of interaction with a complex environment.

Since the occipital cortex shows the most marked effects, it seemed possible that visual sensory processes are somehow particularly salient in the interaction with objects and social companions. This possibility now seems unlikely in view of the fact that blinded rats and rats raised in darkened rooms still show the brain changes. The occipital cortex is possibly an important association area for other contingencies being processed during the rats' interactions with complex stimuli and would thus be involved in nonvisual sensorimotor processes.

These brain changes have been easier to document than changes in the *behavior* of the animals with the different early experiences. Generally, the most consistent findings have been a superiority on complex learning and maze problems of the animals raised in complex environments. This is consistent with the notion that schemas useful in the solution of new problems have been elaborated by interaction with a complex early environment.

Some of these brain changes are evident after only 3 or 4 days in the different conditions, for example RNA/DNA ratio and brain size. Furthermore, many of the changes reverse themselves if conditions are changed. Most of the changes cited can be induced in rats of any age from weaning to middle age. However, they take place in less time and are generally more pronounced for a given length of experience, the younger the age at which the experience is begun. In some studies and some areas of the brain, the effects on dendritic branching are only

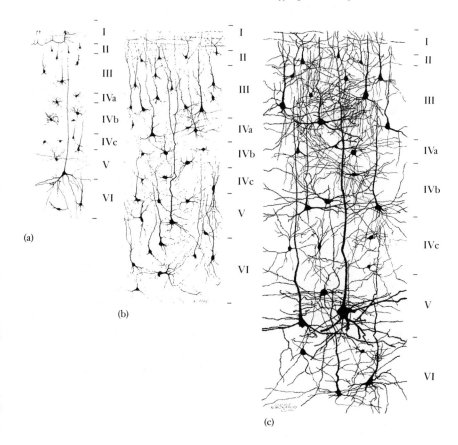

FIGURE 9-3
Development of dendritic arborizations in the human occipital cortex, as revealed by the Golgi stain technique. (*a*) The newborn. (*b*) The 3-month-old. (*c*) The 2-year-old. (Reprinted by permission from J. L. Conel, *The Postnatal Development of the Human Cortex.* Cambridge, Mass.: Harvard University Press. Vol. 1, 1939; Vol. 2, 1947; Vol. 3, 1959.)

evident in rats if enriched just after weaning and do not appear in others given the same experience beginning in young adulthood. Thus, there appears to be a relative sensitive period favoring youth in these effects, but no evidence for critical periods or irreversible effects.

An interesting recent development in this work is the use of a semi-natural environment, instead of the rather contrived complexity created in the laboratory studies (8). In this setting, rats had a 30 × 30 foot area of ground with natural vegetation and they could form networks of burrows. Thirty days in this setting created differences in brain weight and cholinergic enzyme content that were as great, in comparison to *normal* laboratory rearing conditions, as had previously been found between the artificially complex and impoverished laboratory conditions. This impressive effect of a species-typical environment suggests that we still have a good deal to learn about the nature of the complexity and the specific interactions that determine these early changes in brain structure and chemistry.

It has recently been shown that monkeys are at least as sensitive as rats to these environmental influences on brain structure, and the evidence linking enriched environments with increased intelligence quotients in humans is quite extensive. But we need to know more about whether deficits due to prolonged environmental impoverishment early in the life of humans can ever be reversed.

The important point that these experiments make is that whereas some influences on brain organization seem to impose themselves (e.g., visual stimulation, hormones, nutrition) the active participation of the organism in an interaction with its environment can also shape the organization of the brain. Behavior is thus not just a product of the brain, it is an important ingredient in its development. It is this principle that makes the development of behavior so interesting and so complicated.

SUMMARY

There are several known ways by which the environment participates in the development of the connected systems of cells into which the brain is organized. Brain cells connected by synaptic relays to sensory receptors are dependent for their maintenance on the integrity of the receptor and in some instances will degenerate if proper stimulation is not received. Rates of cell division and migration are regulated by hormones such as thyroxine and by the level of nutrient supplied to the brain. The presence of the hormone testosterone early in life can permanently alter the organization of regions of the hypothalamus mediating sexual physiology and behavior into the male pattern. Without testosterone, the female patterns develop.

Levels of sensory stimulation, hormones such as testosterone, nutrient intake, and the individual's own behavioral interaction with a complex environment all act as stimulants for the branching ramification of dendrites necessary for the formation of new synaptic connections between cells. The functional arrangement of these synapses and the effectiveness of neurotransmission across them are the fine structure of the organization of the brain.

The nature of the system of connections established at the cellular level as the result of early experience has only been worked out for visual stimulation in kittens. Evidence here portrays a process of commitment by which individual cells become preferentially responsive along certain synaptic inputs at the expense of others, according to an interaction between their own predisposition and the visual stimulation the young animal receives.

These findings portray how early influences may leave their stamp on the brain by altering the way it becomes organized during early development. These shaping forces are not all inevitably imposed upon us. Many of the processes discussed can be set into motion and at least partially controlled by the individual's own behavior, allowing us to become in this sense the architects of our brains.

FURTHER READING

Hubel, D. H., and Wiesel, T. N. Grass Foundation Lecture. Pp. 9–24 in Society for Neuroscience, Sixth Annual Meeting, 1976, B.I.S. Conference Report No. 45. Los Angeles: Brain Information Service, 1977.

Jacobson, M. *Developmental Neurobiology.* 2nd ed. New York: Plenum Press, 1978. Pp. 219–252.

Kuffler, S. W., and Nicholls, J. G. *From Neuron to Brain.* Sunderland, Mass.: Sinauer Associates, 1976. Pp. 16–61.

Mistretta, C. M., and Bradley, R. M. Effects of early sensory experience on brain and behavioral development. In G. Gottlieb (Ed.), *Studies on the Development of Behavior and the Nervous System.* Vol. 4: *Early Influences.* New York: Academic Press, 1978. Pp. 215–248.

Pettigrew, J. D. The paradox of the critical period for striate cortex. In C. W. Cotman (Ed.), *Neuronal Plasticity.* New York: Raven Press, 1978.

Rosenzweig, M. R., and Bennett, E. L. Experiential influences on brain anatomy and brain chemistry in rodents. In Gottlieb, op. cit., pp. 289–327.

Whitsett, J. M., and Vandenbergh, J. G. Hormonal influences on brain and behavioral development. In Gottlieb, op. cit., pp. 73–107.

Winick, M. *Malnutrition and Brain Development.* New York: Oxford University Press, 1976.

Wurtman, R. J., and Wurtman, J. J. *Nutrition and the Brain.* Vol. 1: *Determinants of the Availability of Nutrients to the Brain.* New York: Raven Press, 1977.

REFERENCES CITED

1. Pettigrew, J., Olson, C., and Barlow, H. B. Kitten visual cortex: short-term, stimulus-induced changes in connectivity. *Science*, 180:1202–1203, 1973.
2. Valverde, F. Apical dendritic spines of the visual cortex and light deprivation in the mouse. *Experimental Brain Research*, 3:337–352, 1967.
3. Gregory, R. L., and Wallace, J. G. Recovery from early blindness: a case study. *Experimental Psychology Society Monograph*, No. 2, Cambridge, 1963.
4. Banks, M. S., Aslin, R. N., and Letson, R. D. Sensitive period for the development of human binocular vision. *Science*, 190:675–677, 1976.
5. Vertes, N., Barnes, A., Lindner, H. R., and King, R. J. B. Studies on androgen and estrogen uptake by rat hypothalamus. *Advances in Experimental Medicine and Biology*, 36:137–173, 1973.
6. Levitsky, D. A., and Barnes, R. H. Nutritional and environmental interactions in the behavioral development of the rat: long-term effects. *Science*, 176:68–71, 1972.
7. Winick, M., Meyer, K. K., and Harris, R. C. Malnutrition and environmental enrichment by early adoption. *Science*, 190:1173–1175, 1975.
8. Rosenzweig, M. R., Bennett, E. L., and Diamond, M. C. Brain changes in response to experience. *Scientific American*, 226:22–29, 1972.

10
The Intrauterine Environment

Humans have always been impressed with the special nature of their earliest environment. The umbilical cord, the enveloping amniotic fluid, and the idea of being inside someone else appear again and again in myth, metaphor, and analogy. Ideas have grown into beliefs that the mother can influence the character of her child by what she does or even thinks during pregnancy. Medieval teaching claimed that there was a direct connection between the mind of the mother and the mind of the unborn baby, and great emphasis was placed on the necessity for elevated thoughts during pregnancy. In the nineteenth century, the fetus was regarded as a skilled voyeur who could be confirmed in evil ways if allowed to witness sexual intercourse. Even today, it is supposed that certain experiences can start the developing fetus on a desired path. Some pregnant mothers go to concerts in the hope of giving their children headstarts as musicians and ski or sail in hopes that this will give them a love and a facility for these sports—or at the least help prevent future motion sickness. These theories have not been entirely disproved and, in fact, new mysteries have been raised by the research that has been done on prenatal influences in the past decade or two.

Modern biological research has ended the old notion that the placenta is an impermeable barrier between mother and infant, and we now know that what a pregnant mother eats, drinks, and breathes has profound influences on her unborn child. But what about her thoughts and feelings, her emotional state—is there any way such events can influence the developing fetus, or is this simply an old wives' tale? It is extremely difficult to test this proposition definitively in the human because the emotional state of the mother tends to persist over time and is even more likely to affect the infant *after* birth, when the two are able to interact behaviorally. There is no way to separate the two possible times of influence without systematic cross-fostering, which of course is feasible only with animals. Even if we look for differences immediately after birth, according to the emotional states of the mothers during pregnancy, we cannot be sure that any relationship found was not simply the result of the mother and the newborn sharing the same genes. The interpretation of well designed animal experiments can be free of this confound. From the results of animal experiments we can learn what to look for and what to measure in the human. If relatively subtle and complex effects such as an influence of the mother's emotional state on fetal development can be demonstrated readily in lower mammals, it seems likely that such higher-level processes will be at least as prominent in the human, if not more so. In fact, prior to research in the past decade, the general prejudice was that no analog of such advanced psychobiological relationships could be found in infrahuman species.

PRENATAL MATERNAL EXPERIENCE

As it turned out, nearly everything that experimenters did to pregnant mother rats and mice affected the behavior of their offspring. Pregnant dams were exposed repeatedly to a box in which they had previously received shocks, they were crowded together in small cages during pregnancy, they were handled for brief periods every day by the experimenter, or were subjected to restraint and bright lights. After birth, the infants were fostered to normal mothers and compared to offspring of mothers randomly selected from the same genetic stock. Major behavioral differences were found as a result of prenatal stress of the mothers, particularly in the areas of emotional and sexual behavior. Learning performance was less severely affected.

Where experiments were more systematic and repeated it was found that the kinds of behaviors affected and the direction of the effects varied widely with the timing, quality, and duration of the disturbance to the mother and with the genetic background of both the mother and the fetus. Within a given genetic stock and a given stress program, results were highly consistent and in some cases dramatic. The offspring of mothers crowded during pregnancy, for example, took two to three times as long to emerge into and explore unfamiliar terrain as their agemates whose mothers were normally housed prior to their birth (1). In other experiments (2) male rats born to mothers stressed during their last trimester of pregnancy by periodic restraint and bright light, failed to develop normal male sexual behavior in the presence of receptive females and assumed female sexual positions when approached by normal experienced males. They were thus both demasculinized and feminized as a result of their mothers' experience during pregnancy. Treatment of the affected animals with testosterone did not fully correct the deficiencies in male sexual behavior and only served to exaggerate the inappropriate female-type behavior. This means that the alteration was in the *neural systems mediating the behavior*, not in the amount of male sex hormone produced in adulthood. Individual animals showed different patterns that were consistent for them. Some were asexual, responding neither to normal females or normal males. Some were bisexual, some only responded with female behavior to males, and some were indistinguishable from normal heterosexual males. Nor was the effect limited to the particular kind of stress used in these experiments, for it has recently been found that females living in overcrowded colonies during pregnancy produce male offspring with the same altered pattern of behavior. The female offspring in all these experiments were entirely normal in their sexual behavior, although their emotional behavior has not been investigated.

How can these results, which seem to confirm our worst superstitions, be explained in terms of known biological processes? Although the full story is far from clear, all the evidence to date favors the idea that maternal hormones, changed in amounts and pattern during stress, act directly on the fetal brain and/or the fetal endocrine glands to modify the characteristics of the neuronal networks being laid down. Later in the life of the offspring, these altered neural networks apparently result in altered patterns of behavior. It has been found, for example, that if hormones released during activity of the autonomic nervous system, such as epinephrine and norepinephrine, are given repeatedly to pregnant mothers, the result is in altered emotional behavior of the offspring, such as the timidity in a new situation referred to above. One of the hormones of the adrenal cortex has likewise been shown to affect emotional behavior of the offspring, but in an opposite direction. Again the dosage and the timing of the altered levels of these hormones seem to be critical to the effect produced, and no overall principles have been worked out. Nothing is known about how these hormones might alter either the fetal brain or the endocrine system to produce the altered behavior in adulthood.

The prenatal effects of sex hormones on the later development of adult sexual behavior are better understood. In a wide variety of mammals, including man, the structure of the internal and external genitalia, the neural programming of the endocrine cycles of sex hormones, and the neural substrates for sexual behavior appear to develop under the regulating influence of their immediate hormonal environment during the prenatal and neonatal period, as described in the previous chapter. Thus, once the gonads have differentiated due to the action of X and Y chromosomes, the male gonad releases a locally acting tissue hormone that induces the development of the male (Wolffian) and suppresses development of the female (Müllerian) embryonic sexual duct systems. Without the substance, the female develops and the male regresses. Once the gonads have developed further and testosterone is produced, the external genitalia, the cyclic organization of the pituitary, and the organization of neural substrates for sexual behavior come under the control of testosterone. If the testis is absent or removed early enough in prenatal life, all these will develop to be female in character, demonstrating that the presence of testosterone is required for male development during this period. Evidence from the occurrence of hormone-secreting tumors and the administration of hormones to humans for other reasons, supports the existence of these relationships for the human. The development of adult human sexual behavior is highly dependent on interactions with caregivers and the social environment so that gender identity and sexual behavior may or may not develop to be congruent with the early hormonal exposure, the genitalia, or the genetic sex.

Since the external genitalia differentiate relatively early in the prenatal period, suppression of testosterone at a later stage could interfere with the full development of male sexual behavior without affecting the external genitalia, as was found in the experiments described above. Since development of female sexual behavior proceeds normally in the absence of testosterone, even in genetic males, the appearance of female behavior is to be expected simply from suppression of testosterone at a critical period in neural differentiation. Preliminary evidence supports this explanation, since a testosterone surge has been found to occur in male rat fetuses (and not in females) at day 18 of the 21-day gestation period, and this surge is not present in fetuses of stressed mothers. Exactly how the mother may suppress the fetal testis remains to be elucidated, but several potential endocrine mechanisms exist.

Neural substrates for male sexual behavior are thought to be facilitated and for female behavior to be suppressed by the action of testosterone. The *potential* for adult behavior is thus influenced by prenatal events. The development of the *expression* of this behavior, however, requires a long series of social interactions throughout postnatal development. For the animal model to resemble the human situation, the organization of adult behavior into characteristic male or female patterns in rats should be influenced by the experiences the young have during this period. Indeed, it has recently been found in rodents (3) that the deficits in adult male copulatory behavior produced by prenatal maternal stress can be ameliorated by 2 weeks of sharing their cage with two prepubertal females. This rehabilitation was ineffective if the prenatally stressed males had been socially isolated from weaning through puberty. Such rehabilitation has also been observed in nonhuman primates.

These examples are the best documented evidence of long-term effects exerted by the behavioral state of the mother during pregnancy upon the behavior of her offspring in adulthood. The endocrine systems of mother and infant supply the connection between the brain of the mother and the brain of the infant in these instances. Our knowledge of the inductive effect of hormones upon the early development of neural systems for behavior is scanty as yet, but is likely to yield interesting new insights.

THE (TRANSUTERINE) INHERITANCE OF ACQUIRED CHARACTERISTICS

Another form of prenatal influence demonstrated by experimental studies on animals appears at first to support the long-abandoned theories of Jean Baptiste Lamarck (1809): that acquired characteristics can be inherited by the next generation. If, for example, female rats of one generation are stressed by shock avoidance conditioning prior to mating and are subsequently made pregnant, their offspring in the next generation will show predictable increases in their emotional behavior when confronted with unfamiliar surroundings (4). If infant rats are separated prematurely from their mothers, they have an increased susceptibility to stomach ulcers under stress as young adults. If the early-weaned females are mated, their offspring also have increased susceptibility to ulcers, even if reared normally (5). The significance of these findings for understanding events during the intrauterine period of life lies in the fact that cross-fostering studies have shown that these effects are transmitted to the next generation during the *prenatal* period rather than by changes in the mother's behavior toward her infants *after* birth.

Results such as these are no longer explained as the genetic transmission of acquired characteristics, because it is recognized that it is not the genetic material but the uterine environment that is the mechanism of inheritance. In our current state of ignorance about early developmental processes, it is hard to think of any way that an experience a female has in infancy can result in her developing a uterine environment in adulthood that tends to induce a behavioral predisposition in her unborn young that is *qualitatively similar* to the behavior induced directly in the mother by the experience. It is reasonable to suppose that this specificity is more apparent than real, the result of finding only those behaviors one looks for. With more studies of this sort and more wide-ranging behavioral tests of the offspring, it seems likely that the alterations in uterine environment produced by experiences the mothers had in early life will be shown to induce a variety of behavioral changes in the offspring, some of which may be opposite to the effects produced directly on the mothers. But this is speculation. What do we know about the uterine environment of the fetus and of the ways the maternal state can affect the unborn infant?

PATHWAYS FROM THE OUTSIDE WORLD: SENSORY INFLUENCES

The placenta is not the only route of communication between fetus and mother, and the hormones described above are certainly not the only substances capable of crossing the placental barrier to influence behavior. We have seen that the sensory receptors of the fetus begin to function as early as the first third of pregnancy when vestibular (balance and motion detectors) and tactile functions are first present. In addition to the fetus' own behavior, the movements of the mother are bound to affect the developing fetal nervous system through these sensory avenues. The levels of such stimulation created by living within an active adult will not be rivaled again after birth until well into the toddler stage. Even during the night, the pregnant mother is restless and active with her leg cramps, heartburn, and frequent trips to the bathroom.

It is well known that maternal movement stimulates fetal movements, so we know that the fetus is at least immediately affected. But what evidence do we have that all this bouncing about actually affects development? Recent studies of infants born prematurely and housed in incubators (6) have added the stimulation of gentle rocking or shaking of the incubator and tactile stimulation of the skin of trunk and limbs for 5–15 minutes of each hour, to replace some of the movements of the intrauterine environment these infants lost prematurely. After 4–6 weeks, the stimulated infants performed better on tests of sensorimotor and visual responsiveness and gained more weight than controls. Observations on their sleep–wake cycles showed more time spent in quiet sleep and less in active wakefulness. Preliminary results of follow-up at one year showed a tendency toward more advanced functioning, particularly in expressive language development. Since prematurely born infants generally lag behind full-terms, some of this lag may be due to loss of the tactile and vestibular stimulation of intrauterine life.

The fetus can probably hear by midgestation, and the common observation of sudden fetal movements following sudden loud noises such as cymbals and pneumatic hammers has led to considerable speculation about the role of this sensory system before birth. There is some evidence that infants after birth are particularly calmed by low-frequency sounds repeated at about the rhythm of the mother's heart beat and that both left- and right-handed mothers in many cultures carry their infants more frequently against their left chest where their heart beat is loudest. These observations suggest that fetuses are conditioned by the sound of their mothers' heart in utero so that after birth it acts as a signal for comfort. However, recordings of sound level in the human uterus (7) have shown that the fetus is exposed, instead, to a constant low-frequency rumble at a remarkably high level or volume, 90–95 decibels. This sound appears to be produced by turbulence in the blood flowing through the uterine arteries. Its level fluctuates in rhythmic peaks, 10 decibels higher than the baseline, each peak occurring three-tenths of a second after the maternal heartbeat, the time required for the surge of blood to reach the uterus. This is the sound we hear throughout our first months of life—like the sound of surf, perhaps. When combined with the 20–30 decibel sound attenuation produced by the abdominal wall, uterine tissues, and amniotic fluid, sounds from the outside environment must be very loud in order to make much of an impression on the fetus, probably more than 110 decibels. Recent systematic recordings within the intact amniotic cavity of sheep, however, indicate that cardiovascular sounds are minimal and with certain placements of the fetal ear, considerable normal environmental sound may get through, especially in the low-frequency range below 1000 cycles per second, in which sound attenuation is minimal.

The uncertainty that we have about auditory influences on the human fetus is challenging, because studies on an accessible animal model of prenatal life have shown a number of subtle and unexpected effects (see Gottlieb). The development of bird embryos in the egg allows much more complete control of the prehatching environment and direct observation through artificial windows in the shell. In duck embryos, the coordinated hatching of a group of eggs is dependent on the individuals hearing each other's prehatching calls. Furthermore, the ability of the duckling to discriminate and follow its own mother's call after hatching is dependent on the embryo hearing its sibling and its own prehatching calls but is not influenced by hearing the maternal call. Gull chicks, on the other hand, approach and snuggle up against a loudspeaker that emits a maternal call they had heard several days before while still in the egg, but show no such response to another type of maternal call they had not yet heard. Here surely is an instance that supports the folklore of prenatal education, at least for birds. Facilitation of behavioral responses to auditory signals can be influenced in a general way in one species of bird and highly specifically in another.

The visual life of the fetus is even more restricted, but the uterus is not a dark place as is commonly supposed. The fetus can be seen to cast a shadow on the wall of the abdomen, and flashing lights applied to the abdominal wall of the pregnant woman will result in changes of fetal heart rate. The retinal structures appear under the microscope to be adequate for function by 5 months of gestation and the eyelids open at 7 months. But all the fetus may see of the outside world are variations in diffuse light, and its view of its own limbs and the intra-uterine wall will be blurred by the refracting effect of the amniotic fluid as it is when we swim underwater in later life. The remarkable results of early postnatal stimulation on organization of the visual system suggest that there is a good deal yet to be learned about possible prenatal visual stimulation in the development of this system.

Taste and olfactory receptors can be readily stimulated by substances present in the amniotic fluid. It is known that infants will increase or decrease their rate of swallowing, as measured by radioisotope techniques, if saccharin or an iodinated dye (used for X-ray contrast) are injected into the amniotic fluid. The opportunity is thus present for taste preference learning with foreign substances, such as drugs that cross the amniotic membranes, although no studies have been made of this possibility as yet.

In summary, the mother reaches and affects the fetus through the early developing fetal sensory receptors for touch, motion, hearing, vision, taste, and smell. Relatively little is known about the short- or long-range developmental effects of such stimulation, although this would appear to be a promising area for study.

THE PLACENTAL ROUTE

The pathway of communication between the outside world and the fetus that has received the most attention is, of course, the placental circulation. Substances diffuse and are actively transported across the membranes that separate the maternal side of the circulation from the fetus'. Oxygen and the protein, fat, and carbohydrate molecules necessary for the fetal metabolic machinery are passed across to the fetus, while carbon dioxide and the metabolic end-product wastes are transferred back to the mother. The fetus is normally more than a degree warmer than the mother, and the placenta acts as a heat exchanger, distributing some of the fetus' metabolic heat to the maternal circulation. When the mother has a fever, the fetus' temperature must be higher, an effect that can markedly alter biochemical growth processes in the fetal brain.

The mother's diet is of obvious importance to fetal tissue growth and can affect brain development as a part of this. Prenatal malnutrition has complex effects on brain and behavior, altering the concentrations of neurotransmitters and even the number of neurons. The long-term behavioral effects of these changes are markedly affected by the levels of postnatal experience. Social isolation and sensory deprivation greatly aggravate the behavioral effects of prenatal malnutrition, while "enriched" environments appear to compensate to a large degree.

But the alterations in maternal diet need not involve frank malnutrition in order to affect the infant's neural development. In a strain of mice with a hereditary balance disturbance (ataxia) due to a genetic abnormality of the inner ear (8), the mother was fed extra supplements of manganese during pregnancy, and her offspring did not develop the ataxia at the expected rate. Neither the mother herself nor other mice treated after birth showed any benefit from supplementary manganese. This study shows how alterations of a specific dietary factor by the mother during pregnancy can determine the expression of the genetic constitution of her offspring and provide a prenatal counterpart for the human disease, phenylketonuria.

It has recently become clear that pregnant mothers can affect the behavioral development of their offspring by excessive alcohol intake, smoking, taking drugs, or by exposure to chemical pollutants during pregnancy. It has been known for a long time that the structural development of most organs can be affected by certain drugs taken during a short period very early in pregnancy when the tissues are dif-

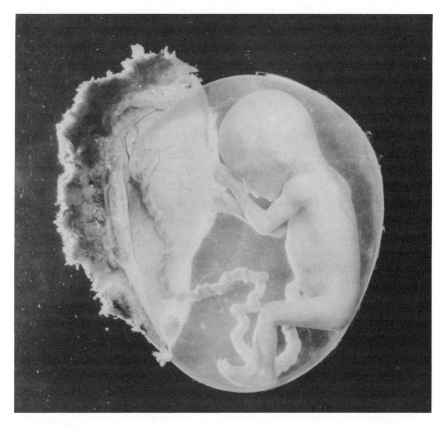

FIGURE 10-1
At 16 weeks gestational age, a 6-inch human fetus is shown floating in the
clear fluid of the amniotic sac, connected to the placenta by the umbilical
cord. (Photograph by Lennart Nilsson.)

ferentiating. The truncated limbs of the thalidomide babies are an
illustration of this. Fortunately, most of these severe abnormalities do
not result in the birth of living "monsters," as they are called, but
rather the fetus dies and there is an early miscarriage. However, the
developing brain continues to be affected by a wide variety of substances throughout the whole period of pregnancy. Functional or ultrastructural abnormalities of brain may be produced by substances
that are not teratogens (not capable of producing structural abnormalities), effects that are usually not lethal but alter the development
of the infant's behavior. In animal experiments where the effects of
one substance at a time can be studied and where postnatal effects can

be prevented by cross-fostering to normal mothers, prenatal exposure to alcohol, methadone, heroin, major tranquilizers, barbiturates, and amphetamines, all have been shown to produce long-term effects on the behavior of offspring when juvenile or adult, weeks and months after the intrauterine period of exposure to these substances. The exact mechanism of action of these substances on fetal brain development is not well understood.

A recent report (9) has shown one way that drugs may influence the brain chemistry of the fetus and its later behavior. Haloperidol, a major antipsychotic medication that blocks access of the neurotransmitter dopamine to its receptors, was given to pregnant rats throughout pregnancy. The infants were fostered to normal mothers at birth and were studied in young adulthood. They were found to have fewer receptors for dopamine in their midbrain tissue and to show less behavioral response to a drug, apomorphine, that acts on these receptors. What makes these effects particularly interesting is that they are opposite to those seen if the drug is given for the same period of time to suckling infants or to adults. At those later ages, an adaptation of receptor function, supersensitivity, develops with increased receptor binding and exaggerated responses to apomorphine, which persists for several weeks after stopping the Haloperidol. Apparently, during the prenatal period, the early development of the receptors for dopamine depends on exposure to that neurotransmitter and when that access is partially blocked by Haloperidol during this period, a significant number of receptors fail to develop. Thus, drugs taken by the pregnant mother may affect the fetus' behavior later in life by interfering with the processes described in the previous chapters by which neurons are shaped according to their chemical environment during early phases of brain development.

In the fetal alcohol syndrome in humans, abnormal migration of neurons, sheets of misplaced supporting (glial) cells, and overall reduced brain size have been found, so that interference with the early phases of the neuronal growth seems to have taken place. Severe mental retardation is the behavioral hallmark of the disorder. However, the limitation of joint movements in many of these infants suggests that the fetus, anesthetized by alcohol much of its early life, failed to perform the vigorous movements necessary to the proper molding of the joint cartilage and muscle tendons.

The babies of mothers in methadone programs experience narcotic withdrawal at birth and must be treated for the resulting irritability, sleeplessness, and seizures. Clinical evidence suggests that these symptoms persist beyond the newborn period but the chaotic postnatal environment of these infants could account for this. Careful animal studies with cross-fostering are just beginning, but suggest that the disturbance of the patterning of sleep and arousal persists into the early adolescent period, and some deficits in performance on complex learning tasks can be detected in adulthood. The search for preventive measures for the 3000 methadone babies born each year in New York City alone can be expedited in such an animal model system. In addition to the possibility of finding biochemical methods for blocking or reversing the central neural effects on the fetus, we may be able to discover social or environmental conditions during the postnatal period by experiments with animals, which will suggest how best to compensate for the behavioral effects of methadone taken by pregnant women.

In addition to maternal diet and drugs, maternal hormones influence the developing fetal brain and lay the groundwork for future behavioral characteristics, as described above for the sex hormones. In addition, both thyroxine and the adrenal cortical hormones cross the placental barrier and are known to affect the *rate* of fetal maturation, with thyroxine generally accelerating rates of growth and differentiation and excess adrenal corticoids retarding development. The hormones of the sympathetic system and the adrenal medulla, norepinephrine and epinephrine, may affect the developing brain directly by influencing the storage, metabolism, and receptors for these neurotransmitters. However, when released excessively by mothers smoking or under stress, they are also known to alter the placental blood supply and affect fetal oxygenation and metabolism.

Finally, the fetus is very sensitive to change in placental blood flow. The fetal circulation cannot compensate for changes in the maternal blood supply to the placenta, since its umbilical vessels and the small branches in close proximity to the exchange membranes have no regulating nerves controlling their diameter. On the maternal side, there is no feedback from the smaller vessels in the placenta to the arteries supplying them, as there is in other organs, so that compensatory changes to local conditions in the placenta are not possible. This places the fetus at the mercy of the physiological systems regulating flow in the mother's uterine arteries. Maternal autonomic nerves and circulating hormones such as norepinephrine can constrict these arteries, leading to decreased oxygen levels and increased levels of metabolic waste products in the fetal circulation. One of the immediate responses of older fetuses to decreased oxygen supply is an increase in diffuse behavioral activity and, consistent with this, periods of maternal emotional distress have been shown to produce extreme increases in objectively recorded fetal movements (10). Little or nothing is known of the long-term consequences of altered fetal metabolic state produced in this way, but it remains an important potential pathway whereby fetal brain development may be influenced during the prenatal period.

SUMMARY

These interactions between the pregnant mother, her outside world, the intrauterine environment, and the fetus are likely to account for some of the influences exerted on the development of behavior during the fetal period. Although the gaps are more impressive than our understanding, we can summarize as follows. Evidence from many sources suggests that the development of human behavior can be influenced by events taking place during the prenatal period. Contrary to initial expectations, animals were found to be susceptible to relatively subtle changes in the experience of their mothers during pregnancy and to alterations of her uterine environment caused by experiences earlier in her life. Study of these effects in animals has led to the discovery of hormonal mechanisms during the prenatal period that strongly influence the potential for emotional and sexual behavior in later life. Some evidence suggests that these findings may generalize to the human. Other possible pathways include the stimulation of tactile, vestibular, auditory, visual, gustatory, and olfactory senses of the fetus, the diet of the mother, her intake of foreign substances such as alcohol, tranquilizers, and opiates, and the control of placental function by the mother's uterine arteries.

FURTHER READING

Clarren, S. K., and Smith, D. W. The fetal alcohol syndrome. *New England Journal of Medicine*, 298:1063–1067, 1978.
Gottlieb, G. (Ed.) *Studies on the Development of Behavior and the Nervous System*. Vol. 4: *Early Influences*. New York: Academic Press, 1978.
Gruenwald, P. (Ed.) *The Placenta and Its Maternal Supply Line*. Baltimore: University Park Press, 1975.
Hutchings, D. E. Behavioral teratology: embryopathic and behavioral effects of drugs during pregnancy. In Gottlieb, op. cit., pp. 7–34.

Impekoven, M., and Gold, P. Pre-natal origins of parent–young interactions in birds: a naturalistic approach. In G. Gottlieb (Ed.), *Studies on the Development of Behavior and the Nervous System*. Vol. 1: *Behavioral Embryology*. New York: Academic Press, 1973. Pp. 325–356.

Joffe, J. M. Hormonal mediation of the effects of prenatal stress on offspring behavior. In Gottlieb, op. cit., Vol. 4, pp. 107–144.

REFERENCES CITED

1. Keeley, K. Prenatal influence on behavior of offspring of crowded mice. *Science*, 135:44–45, 1962.
2. Ward, I. L. Prenatal stress feminizes and demasculinizes the behavior of males. *Science*, 175:82–84, 1972.
   Ward, I. L., and Weisz, J. Maternal stress alters plasma testosterone in fetal males. *Science*, 207:328–329, 1980.
3. Dunlap, J. L., Zadina, J. E., and Gougis, G. Prenatal stress interacts with prepuberal social isolation to reduce male copulatory behavior. *Physiology and Behavior*, 21:873–875, 1978.
4. Wehmer, F., Porter, R. H., and Scales, B. Prenatal stress influences the behavior of subsequent generations. In *Communications in Behavioral Biology*, Part A, 5:001–004, 1970.
5. Skolnick, N. J., Ackerman, S. H., Hofer, M. A., and Weiner, H. Vertical transmission of acquired ulcer susceptibility in the rat. *Science*, 208:1161–1163, 1980.
6. Masi, W. Supplemental stimulation of the premature infant. In T. M. Field (Ed.), *Infants Born at Risk*. New York: Scientific Publications, 1979. Pp. 367–387.
7. Walker, D., Grimwade, J., and Wood, C. Intrauterine noise: a component of the fetal environment. *American Journal of Obstetrics and Gynecology*, 109:91–95, 1971.
8. Erway, L., Hurley, L. S., and Fraser, A. Neurological defect: manganese in phenocopy and prevention of a genetic abnormality of inner ear. *Science*, 152:1766–1767, 1966.
9. Rosengarten, H., and Friedhoff, A. J. Enduring changes in dopamine receptor cells of pups from drug administration to pregnant and nursing rats. *Science*, 203:1133–1135, 1979.
10. Sontag, L. W. Implications of fetal behavior and environment for adult personalities. *Annals of the New York Academy of Sciences*, 134:782–786, 1966.

11

The Parent–Infant Relationship

Birth marks a dramatic shift in the relationship of the baby to its mother, a transition from a biological to a social relationship. It should thus mark the end of an account of the biological origins of human behavior and the beginnings of its social and psychological origins. And in fact, most social and psychological studies, and the theories drawn from them, begin with the child's relationship with its first caretakers. So much of what a parent does with a child seems to be embedded in the fabric of culture and initiated by the feelings that parents experience in this relationship. It appears to be love that holds the relationship together and custom that determines what kind of a relationship it will be. What room is left for biology? Of course, if the mother nurses her infant, this appears to maintain, for a time, a single thread from the rich fabric of biological interactions that existed during the intrauterine period. But even here, in recent custom, the breast has been replaced by the bottle, a victim of cultural evolutionary trends.

Human social relationships are phenomena that exist at an interphase between biological, psychological, and cultural frames of reference. The language and the concepts of these three frames of reference are very different and yet they are brought to bear upon the same phenomena. There is little or no disagreement about the behaviors involved, but few if any ways in which the viewpoints can be said to be congruent. In fact, a great deal of emotion has been aroused by the kinds of disagreements that have followed as different academic divisions struggle for undisputed possession of the territory of the social relationship. To many it has seemed that the humanities have captured the essential nature of human relationship while the sciences are busy attacking each other.

How can we proceed? As a start, when there is this much disagreement and ill-feeling, we should realize that ignorance is probably at the bottom of it. We really do not understand very much about social relationships, despite all that we feel and think we know. If we do not expect to understand too much at once, we may learn something, and if we can break the problem down into smaller units, we may be able to gradually piece some understanding together.

The most troublesome question is the attempt to distinguish, in a social relationship, a biological from a cultural or psychological determinant. For example, is the mother drawn to the baby through the example of societal custom, the feeling of mother love, or the influence of hormones in her blood? Nature, in the form of evolutionary processes, has come to rely on the principle of redundant systems in order to guarantee and protect functions that transmit genes to the next generation. Therefore, we are not likely to find one behavior controlled by a process operating at the level of cultural tradition and another behavior controlled by a biological process. Rather we can expect multiple determinants or "fall-back" systems, operating together in determining and regulating most behaviors. This approach enables us to look for biological *contributions* to the behavior before tackling the more difficult question of determining the relative importance of the several determinants in any given situation.

To return to the first question, where do biological considerations fit into an understanding of the parent–infant relationship? There are three major questions to be considered, the first of which concerns the development of the relationship itself: what determines its initiation, maintenance, and decline? Second, what impact does the relationship have on the development of the young? Third, what processes within the relationship may help to explain that developmental impact? I have divided this chapter into three units, each corresponding to one of these basic questions.

DEVELOPMENT OF THE RELATIONSHIP

Initiation

We might begin by asking why a woman doesn't simply walk away and leave her infant as soon as she has given birth. In fact, sometimes she does; we are not dealing with electromagnetic forces. But generally the recently delivered mother will instead reach out toward the baby, touch its extremities and face, first with her fingertips and then progress to rubbing its trunk with her palms, picking it up, holding it to her breast, and gazing into its eyes. There is an initial hesitancy, particularly with first births, an appearance of two opposing tendencies in the behavior—to approach and to avoid. Often there is a good deal of excitement evident if the mother has not been sedated. Even other people in the birth room tend to be caught up in this mood. These initial responses of new mothers are reasonably consistent across widely different cultures (1) and are thus not likely to be primarily determined by culture as is, for instance, language. But we are hard put to explain this universal maternal response. It seems to be elicited by some aspect(s) of the appearance and behavior of a newborn infant. Often the strength of these eliciting properties is explained by the adult stating, "he wants to be held," meaning "I want to hold him very much." How can we explain the magnetism apparent here? What is the reluctance, the timidity?

It is hard to go any further toward answering these questions without shifting to animal studies where we can do experiments to get beneath the level of the manifest behavior and the statements of the mother as to how she feels and how she believes the baby feels. This is the essence of an analytical biological approach, to attempt to understand the behavior in terms of its underlying sensory, motor, and hormonal mechanisms and in terms of its necessary antecedent events. When we find a set of behaviors occurring in another species in a form that expresses essential properties of the human situation, we have some assurance that very high level cognitive and/or cultural factors are probably not necessary for expression of such behavior. The way is opened for learning more about the kinds of biological processes which are capable of organizing such a behavior. Armed with this knowledge, we will have new ideas of what to look for as the biological contribution to similar behavior in the human.

Studies in domestic pets, rats, and monkeys have shown that species-typical maternal responses to young can be elicited in both sexes starting as early as the juvenile period of development. But in primates, parental behavior is dependent on the test parent's own early experience: if early interactions with mother and siblings are prevented by isolation, maternal responses to infants do not occur. Even in the rat, maternal responses are not automatic and stereotyped, nor do they occur immediately upon exposure to newborns, except directly after parturition.

Rosenblatt (2) found that if the infants are taken from a newly delivered rat for just 3 or 4 days, she will show virtually no maternal behavior toward them when they are returned to her. A virgin female rat requires a period of several days' experience with newborn pups before beginning to show maternal responses. What is there about the pregnancy or delivery that so hastens the onset of maternal behavior? Cross-transfusion of blood from a near-term pregnant mother to a virgin female dramatically reduces the time required for the virgin female to act maternally toward test pups to a matter of minutes, establishing that a hormonal factor is involved. Subsequent studies have shown that the rapid rise in estrogen levels occurring toward the end of pregnancy may be one of the hormonal changes that mediate the rapid onset of intense maternal behavior after birth.

But why the delay in onset of maternal behavior in virgin females? What is it that the hormone has to counteract? After about 24 days of postnatal age, rats start actively to avoid newborn or 1-week-old rat pups. If juveniles are housed with pups for 3–7 days, however, this avoidance suddenly turns into a full display of maternal behavior: nestbuilding, retrieving, licking, and even assuming the nursing position. This period of time can be reduced to less than 24 hours by depriving the rats of their sense of smell, and such anosmic animals show none of the initial avoidance to the young pups. Thus, the inexperienced rat, faced with the complex stimulus array of a newborn is in conflict between the tendency to act maternally and the tendency to avoid the newborn. The tendency to avoid is largely in response to the newborn's odor, and adaptation in this sensory system apparently requires a number of days of proximity. The hormonal changes of late pregnancy counteract this avoidance response, possibly by raising olfactory thresholds, thus allowing the maternal response free expression.

The continuation of maternal behavior in the rat after parturition, however, is not to be attributed to hormonal mechanisms. The cross-transfusion effect disappears within 24 hours after birth, and maternal behavior continues despite removal of the mother's pituitary and ovaries. The experience of interaction with the pups is what normally maintains maternal behavior. A few days' interaction with pups after birth "fixes" maternal behavior so that if they are then removed for 3–4 days, maternal behavior will be immediately available on their return. The hormonally-induced response tendencies do not have this staying power without the subsequent experience of interaction.

How does this picture of the initiation of maternal behavior in the rat help us with our question about the beginnings of human maternal behavior? It suggests that around the time of birth, the mother may be in a uniquely receptive state toward infants because of the hormonal changes of late pregnancy. The way the hormonal changes may work is by reducing the conflict elicited by the first newborn. The mixed feelings all of us have in our first intimate encounter with a newborn infant and the emotional impact of the experience seem to be something we share with many other mammals. The hormonal changes of late pregnancy might reduce the mother's ambivalence in other ways than altering sensory thresholds. That is still an unproven hypothesis, even in the rat. Certainly, alterations of emotional state are very frequent during the postpartum period in women and need to be examined in terms of their effects on the mothers' later behavior toward infants.

Recent studies (3) have shown that when women are removed from their babies for several weeks after premature birth, because the infant must be in an intensive care nursery, the mother–infant relationship is difficult to resume and may continue to present long-term difficulties, including child abuse in some cases. Conversely, when normal infants are given additional time with their mothers right after birth, the relationship appears to become a closer one and evidences of greater attachment can be found as long as a year later. The impetus for these studies came in part from animal work.

Another useful observation in animals is that parental behavior of caretakers other than the newly-delivered mother requires a period of induction and that prolonged experience at close quarters is necessary for this process. It has frequently been observed that male primates of many species take little or no part in the care of infants, and show virtually no "natural inclination" when presented with infants. Many men behave the same way. These observations have been taken by some to indicate an immutable biological law, that men are not meant to care for babies. The finding that male rats (which normally are at least as nonmaternal as rhesus monkeys or some men) could be induced to show a full range of maternal behaviors, led to further experiments with monkeys (4). Rhesus monkey fathers were housed with bottle-fed infants without the mother or other members of the usual social group. Within 5–11 days, the males began to play with the infants; contact and grooming began before this. The relationship blossomed with the males frequently comforting the infant when it was upset and both members showing clear evidence of separation distress when they were apart. Levels of interactive play were even higher than in mother–infant dyads. These findings were impressive, for the experimenter's initial apprehension had been that the male might kill the infant, so a procedure of gradual introduction was used, the infant at first protected by the presence of the mother, then by Plexiglas, and finally by a small cage.

It appears that the capacity for maternal type behaviors may be *latent* in more males than ordinarily show them, so we need to learn much more about the experiences that are helpful to men who want to become infant caretakers.

Maintenance

Once the parent and infant have been brought together and the relationship initiated as described above, what holds them together and what brings them back together again after brief periods of separation? Why does the parent not rapidly tire of the infant and vice versa? What is the biological "glue" that holds the two together?

For a long time the "glue" was thought to be the interconnected needs of the infant to be fed and of the mother to nurse. Both the mother's and the infant's needs were envisioned as building up over a few hours of separation along a hydraulic model exemplified by the progressive engorgement of the ducts of the lactating mother's breasts. In the human case, other needs and pleasures were thought to become enmeshed in a web of mutual dependence, binding the two together. Indeed the word "bond" has long been used to convey the powerful cohesive force in many human relationships. An important difference between humans and other animals was thought to be that animals were held together only insofar as they needed something: if they could get their food elsewhere, for example, they would not stay with their mothers. Only humans were thought capable of long-lasting attachments that came to transcend and outlast their needs for food, warmth, and shelter. This distinguished human love from the baser needs of animals. Experiments with animals have forced a reassessment of our uniqueness in this area and have led to an appreciation of processes that underlie the maintenance of relationships but are not evident on the surface.

Work with young birds, monkeys, and puppies demonstrated that feeding young animals was *not* necessary for attachment to develop. In fact, puppies became attached to experimenters who did not feed them but instead alternately played with them and punished them. Monkeys raised without their mothers clung to soft models in preference to wire models from which they had been fed, and goslings followed for the rest of their lives any object that had merely moved in their field of vision during a certain "critical" period of hours after hatching—even a river barge! A whole new developmental process seemed to have been discovered and the early ethologists called it *imprinting* to distinguish it from ordinary learning. But it was soon found that different conditions and species brought enormous variability in results and led to further inquiry into the process itself.

If the attachment of an infant to its mother is not based primarily on learning from the gratification involved in nursing, what is its basis?

The answer is certainly not yet clear, and there is much to be learned even in the relatively simple case of imprinting in birds. However, some recent experiments have shed new light on the situation (5). It has been found that for each species of inexperienced young bird, certain colors and marking patterns on the moving object are particularly likely to elicit following behavior, and those are the ones closest to its own species. But if the object does not move, little or no attachment develops, so that for the bird, motion is apparently a key feature. In addition, a change in state is involved. Birds are raised in an incubator from hatching until first tested in an unfamiliar test box used for imprinting. Their response to simply being placed in this box is to vocalize at high rates, apparently as a part of their distress in unfamiliar surroundings. These distress vocalizations are immediately reduced by perception of the moving object. Thus, newly hatched birds with little or no experience outside the egg were found to have come into the world with a selective perceptual bias (markings, motion), a predetermined motor response (following), and a predetermined tendency to a change of state (evidenced by reduced vocalization) in response to moving objects within their perceptual bias. These findings are reminiscent of the work on the visual cortical cells of kittens and to the predetermined perceptual and motor schemas of the newborn human infant.

The fact that these crude perceptual and response tendencies are present immediately after hatching makes it very likely that a relationship will be begun with the parent, the most likely creature to fit the predisposition and to be there at the earliest moments. In the laboratory, of course, the predictions of evolution can be altered and moving models substituted. But this only accounts for a response toward a general class of stimuli. What accounts for the highly specific nature of attachment? How does a duckling or a monkey or a human infant become specifically attached to a single individual? The most likely process is one of associative learning: individual variations in appearance, behavior, voice, and odor, being repeatedly paired with the much broader initial perceptual characteristics, come to acquire the nature of a highly specific template or key that uniquely can elicit the behavior of following and thus alleviate distress.

The most perplexing question remaining is how to account for the persistent and compelling nature of attachment, particularly the early attachment of the infant for its parents. The compelling quality with which we are all familiar is the distress experienced on separation from someone to whom we have become attached. Anticipation of this distress is what prevents separation, and the need to reduce it is what reestablishes the relationship after a separation. Separation distress in a very obvious form is evident in the young of many species. If we return to the model in birds, the puzzling nature of the situation can be put quite clearly. When Hoffman allowed ducklings to hatch in the test chamber used for imprinting and to remain alone there for 12 hours, they were not vocalizing at the beginning of the experiment the way they ordinarily did when placed in the chamber after having been raised in the incubator. Now the imprinting object was introduced and moved back and forth for a minute, then withdrawn for a minute. This sequence was repeated a number of times. The duckling followed the imprinting stimulus hesitantly on the first exposure and then with increasing regularity until the behavior stabilized after a few repetitions of the sequence. What happened upon withdrawal of the moving object was interesting. After the object disappeared for the first time, the duckling uttered one or two brief calls. After each subsequent withdrawal of the moving object, the duckling vocalized more and more until it spent as much as half its time vocalizing after the object disappeared. A plateau was reached after 25–30 repetitions. During this remarkable development, little or no vocalization ever occurred in the *presence* of the object. In this experiment, we can witness the gradual acquisition of separation distress during the process of the formation of an attachment. Once this has occurred, but not before, the duckling will work (by key pecking) to bring the moving object back and also to prevent its withdrawal, if the experimenter arranges the mechanical-electronic connections necessary for the duckling to control the moving object.

By discovering what the bird will work to achieve and to avoid, we have gained insight into the new meaning that the moving object has acquired for the duckling as a result of the repeated stimulation. Closeness to the object has become an important goal, the absence of which leads to distress and, in this new goal-corrected system, a variety of behaviors are employed to maintain proximity to the attachment object. The experience of repeated interaction with the object seems to be necessary for the full development of this system. Although we do not know precisely what processes are involved, we may look to the work on early visual stimulation and the alteration of cortical cellular function for ways to conceive of how this may come about. It seems very likely that the brain of the infant of this age is organized in such a way as to predispose to the development of such a system, as is true, for example, in the case of binocular vision. In both cases, stimulation is required for the system to become operative. However, with attachment, a new goal or motive has become established as well as a perceptual preference. It is as if the duckling has "acquired a taste" for the moving object.

In attempting to understand this phenomenon, we are led to infer processes where none are known, to label attachment as an *acquired drive*, and to refer to the stimulation provided by the object as *reinforcing*. (A familiar example of an acquired drive would be addiction to drugs, but the cellular mechanisms for this are not understood either.) To describe the situation without these terms, we can say that certain forms of stimulation leave in their wake a state that is increasingly aversive as the stimulation is repeated. The organism attempts to change this aftermath state and can do so most readily by exposing itself again to the stimulation. If the initial response to the stimulation is to cling and to follow, as is the case with infants and their mothers, a very powerful system for the maintenance of proximity is created and it is this motivational system that forms the biological "glue" for the first social relationship.

The situation in mammals is certainly different than in ducklings, due to the much longer period of immaturity and the more complex forms of interaction that take place between mother and infant in mammalian species. For the duckling, movement and patterned visual stimulation are critical features, and the process takes place in a matter of minutes, or hours at the most. For mammals, the process of attachment appears to take days, weeks, or even months to develop, and it is not known which sensory systems are most important. In kittens as well as primates there appears to be a shift in sensory systems as the infant matures, so that thermal and olfactory stimulation are most important early, then tactile, and finally visual stimuli predominate. Although the *formation* of attachment in mammals may require only relatively simple interactions, the development of the social relationship is a much more complex thing that in turn has implications for the strength and nature of attachment. Studies with ducklings, however, have revealed that the major characteristics of attachment can be produced by relatively simple behavioral interactions. When we understand the nature of the underlying processes we will be in a better position to approach an analysis of the phenomenon in mammals.

The major maturational event that brings this early period for the formation of attachment to a close seems to be the development of fearful avoidance responses to novel objects or persons at about 8 months of age in the human. Obviously, these behaviors are inconsistent with and prevent the interactions necessary for attachment. So far as can be discovered, the development of these first fearful responses is not dependent on any particular experience, although they do not develop normally in young animals or humans grossly deprived of sensory stimulation (see below). Like the development of higher inhibitory systems during the fetal period, the maturation of fearful responses modifies existing behaviors in a permanent fashion. They do not, however, replace or obliterate previously existing systems. A good example of this can be found by returning to Hoffman's ducklings. If the young birds are allowed to grow to 5 days of age they will crouch and then flee when first exposed to a novel moving object instead of following it, as they would have done 3–4 days previously. If allowed to remove themselves from the vicinity of the new object, nothing further will happen. But if they are kept in the same small area with the new moving object, they will gradually show less crouching, come out from the corner where they had fled, and approach the object. An interesting thing happens at this point: they attack the object—they peck with such vigor that they will destroy it if it is made of soft wood or cardboard. With time this second aggressive stage also wanes, as had the fearful stage before. Finally, following begins to appear and the duckling will form a new attachment.

Thus, competing responses of a fearful and aggressive sort available to the older duckling ordinarily prevent the formation of attachments at that age, either by separating the young bird from the new object or by driving the object away. In the rare cases when these outcomes do not occur, such responses wane over a period of hours, unveiling the developmentally older following response and allowing a new attachment to form. An object to which a duckling has previously formed an attachment does not elicit fearful or aggressive behaviors at an older age and these responses in 5-day and older ducklings are thus normally directed outside the "family."

These experiments with young ducklings give us a simple model for conceptualizing the interplay of predisposition, experience, and maturation in the formation of attachment and in the maintenance of a stable and specific early parent–infant relationship. It continues to be a matter of dispute whether imprinting is a form of learning or some different process. We will not have a clear answer until we learn the importance of association and response contingencies and until single cell studies have shown the degree to which simpler forms of plasticity are at work here.

The usefulness of knowing about these behavioral changes in young birds lies at the conceptual level, not as a set of rules to be transplanted and applied unchanged to the human situation or even to rats. What we have learned is that in order to understand attachment in other species as well as our own we should look carefully at the kinds of stimulation provided by the parent, at the responses elicited from the infant by these stimuli, and particularly at evidences for changes in state produced by the interaction. We should expect to find an early period when approach responses are readily elicited by novel stimuli and become more effective and easier to elicit with simple repetition of the same stimulus pattern (the parents' behavior). Later, with increasing maturation, fearful and even aggressive responses may be instead elicited by novel stimuli, thus limiting further attachment and bringing the early optimal period to a close. But these divisive responses can be expected to wane with familiarity (habituation) far more rapidly than approach responses and thus subsequent attachments may be formed, but only if interfering behaviors are rendered ineffective (e.g., by gentle persistence). On the other hand, it would not be sensible to expect that attachment in primates necessarily depends on the visual system, or on one behavior such as following, or that it occurs only during a very limited early period of hours after birth.

The most useful lesson to be learned from the imprinting studies in birds is that enduring and specific social relationships may be created by relatively simple behavioral processes. For the human, more complex psychological processes are superimposed on the simpler biological processes, hiding them from view. These may facilitate or modify behavior, but need not be called upon to explain the most basic attributes of the behavioral system. For example, the addition of cognitive processes such as symbolization, identification, and abstract thought allow the formation of a level of attachment unlikely to be present in the bird or even the monkey. The capacity to form internalized representations of people whom we love may be uniquely human, but it is also likely to be built upon a biological base of simpler processes such as those just described and in previous chapters.

An example of the usefulness of the concept of attachment in animals for understanding human behavior can be found in the light it sheds on the puzzling clinical problem of why children appear to persist in strong attachments to consistently punitive and abusive parents. If infant attachments were dependent on gentleness, nurturance, and the giving of pleasure, then these children should have no problem leaving their parents. But if attachment is the result of repeated stimulation at a stage before avoidance responses develop, then abusive interactions at this stage may actually increase attachment, simply because of the intensification of stimulation, regardless of its quality. In fact, electric shock delivered to the feet of ducklings during standard imprinting experience speeds up and intensifies the attachment formed. In the raising of puppies, they will become more attached to human handlers who alternately pet and punish them than to those who are consistently passive (6). Once attachment is formed to a parent, strong and even painful stimulation by that parent later in development tends to elicit more attachment behavior rather than simply driving the infant away. The same interaction without prior attachment would simply result in avoidance or aggression; but, in the case described, a tension is set up between conflicting response tendencies, the outcome of which will depend on many factors. Due to the lack of habituation inherent in the attachment system and the potentiating effects of stimulation, punishment and abuse do not lead to a decline in attachment unless prolonged for months or years.

Decline

How then does the child's attachment to its parents come to an end? This is an even more complicated problem than the question of how social relationships are held together. Indeed, at the level of emotion and inner experience the relationship tends to remain permanent. One cannot, however, explain the ability of adolescent and young human adults to lead lives away from their parents solely on the basis of the formation of internal mental representations of their parents. For lower animals, unlikely to possess such advanced cognitive abilities, show a similar transition from strong infantile attachment to adolescent independence. The central process appears to be the gradual replacement of interactions with the parents by interactions with the environment outside the original attachment figures and by the formation of new attachments in addition to the original parental figure. These developmental events are made possible by the maturation of motor capacities and of neural systems for appetitive, exploratory, playful, aggressive, sexual, and parental behavior. For the mammalian newborn, the mother *is* the environment; virtually all its interactions are with her. Gradually, the relative role of parental interactions declines and the effective environment increases markedly. The original relationship has not been lost, but has become only one of many. A parallel may be drawn by analogy to the fate of the early prenatal motor behaviors as new physiological capacities mature.

Careful studies in rhesus monkeys by Hinde on the roles of both mother and infant in the gradually changing relationship have shown that initially the mother is responsible for maintaining proximity, but that gradually the infant initiates more interactions (7). This change in the infant's behavior is partly a result of the establishment of strong attachment, partly due to the maturation of motor capacities, and partly in response to changes in the mother's behavior. Gradually she begins to reject their advances and to initiate less of her own. Animals as well as humans treat older children differently from infants. This differential treatment is partly cued by their appearance and partly by their behavior. The development of the parent–infant relationship is a particularly interesting process because of the delicate balance of the shifting forces at work. If the mother rejects the infant too soon, increases in attachment occur as a result of increased separation distress and the absence of alternative ways of changing this state. On the other hand, if the mother continues to encourage the infant's advances and to initiate her own as well, this delays the infant's maturation by restricting the expansion of the infant's effective environment in the maintenance of an exclusive parental attachment. Since infant development can be adversely affected by either of these courses if carried to extremes, the balance becomes an important one for outcome and one that is particularly sensitive to individual differences in both members as well as outside influences.

Parent–infant proximity is thus initiated and maintained by a series of relatively simple behavioral processes that may be understood in biological terms. The interactions made possible by the long proximity of parent and infant are extremely complex and involve many other processes. The relationship itself is formed and characterized by these more complex interactions and consists of a great deal more than the protection and nourishment made possible by continued proximity. The next sections will deal with some of these interactions and with their contribution to the development of the young.

DEVELOPMENTAL IMPACT OF THE RELATIONSHIP

Thus far we have been dealing with one limited aspect of the early parent–infant relationship—the fact that they spend a lot of time near each other. The behavioral processes that have evolved to assure this proximity are powerful and pervasive among higher vertebrates. We may well ask why parent and infant come together and stay together for so long. At first glance, the answer seems obvious: the infant would not otherwise survive. Nutrition, shelter, and protection against predators must be provided for immature organisms and the mother seems to be a natural extension of the egg and the womb. This answer begs the question of why so many infant mammals have such long periods of helpless immaturity. Our best educated guess is that the prolonged immaturity is a strategy of nature that allows a prolonged period of accessibility to environmental influence, which in turn promotes adaptability and favors survival. In humans, development is particularly prolonged and immature features are preserved into adulthood to a greater degree than in any of our primate relatives. This *neoteny*, as it has been termed, may be the most important evolutionary step in our recent ascendance over other forms of life. Thus, an obligatory and prolonged early parent–infant relationship seems to have evolved together with a long period of maximum adaptability. With this in mind, it seems reasonable to suspect that the relationship itself might provide experiences essential for development of the young. This realization has been slow in coming, however. The ancient myths deny the idea of such dependency and boldly assert an ability to succeed without parents. The gods sprang fully armed into the world and human infants such as Romulus and Remus required only a brief sojourn with a lactating wolf before going on to found the Roman civilization.

Feral and Institutional Children

Actual experience since the Middle Ages with children raised by wild animals began to dispel the myth of our early self-sufficiency. In these accounts, the first human observers were shocked and surprised at the "bestial" nature of children raised without human relationships. Naiveté they expected, but with it the capacity for joyous wonderment at the marvels of civilization. In postrevolutionary France, for example, a wild boy captured near Aveyron was found to be "a child . . . destitute of every means of communication, attaching neither expression nor intention to the gestures and motions of his body, passing with rapidity, and without any apparent motive, from a state of profound melancholy, to bursts of the most immoderate laughter; insensible to every species of moral affection, his discernment was never excited but by the stimulus of gluttony; his pleasure, an agreeable sensation of the organs of taste, his intelligence, a susceptibility of producing incoherent ideas, connected with his physical wants; in a word, his whole existence was a life purely animal" (8).

The existing observations on feral children and cases of extreme early isolation are all lacking in details on the degree of deprivation and the nature of the life of the infant up to the time of their discovery. None of these accounts can allay the readers' doubts as to whether the child was normal to start with. Indeed, there is good reason to suppose that some abnormality in very early infancy may have led to the abandonment of such children.

These shortcomings preserved doubt as to exactly how important early human relationships were for later development and the "Wild Boy of Aveyron" was dismissed as a congenital idiot by most learned observers after he failed to acquire the kind of intelligence that they required of him. Nevertheless, there are certain features that were observed in nearly all the carefully described cases of feral children (9), which are of particular interest in the light of the findings in more systematic studies on early isolation in animals. Most feral children walked on all fours and had developed thick callosities on knees and elbows as well as hands and feet. All were mute and most failed to learn a spoken language. They were noted to have remarkably acute senses of smell, which they used to recognize familiar people who were near but out of sight and to explore unfamiliar objects by sniffing. A remarkable insensitivity to cold and pain was a common feature: the children would often not bother to take shelter from the cold and disregarded cuts and burns unless extremely severe. In the emotional area came the most devastating effects. Laughing and smiling were totally absent in wild children and none were observed to make appropriate sexual advances. A preference for the company of animals rather than humans was perhaps the most expectable finding and was quite resistant to change without extraordinary patience on the part of fellow human caretakers.

The view persisted among many people through the first half of this century that early in life the mother is essential to the infant only for the milk she supplies. Institutions for the care of foundlings discovered to their dismay that infants given the best sanitary and nutritional treatment did not thrive unless a close human relationship was also provided. This apparent fact was hard for scientists to accept because relationships are intangible and the whole effect seemed magical. We are just beginning to understand what we mean by "mother love" in terms that allow us to see its connection with physical and behavioral development.

Spitz' dramatic descriptions of developmental retardation, abnormal emotional development, and susceptibility to illness in medically well-cared-for infants in institutions (10) convinced most people that there was something about an infant's interaction with people that was of fundamental biological importance. However, these reports came under strong criticism from academic circles on the grounds that not enough details were given about early care and the names of the institutions were not revealed. Pure sensory deprivation was suggested as the problem rather than anything to do with a relationship.

Experimental Studies with Monkeys

In the 1950s, Harlow separated monkeys from their mothers at birth and raised them artificially in order to study early learning. He found instead that this control procedure resulted in profoundly abnormal young monkeys with marked performance deficits on most motor and learning tasks (11). Their behavior was remarkably similar to the reports of humans reared without adequate human interaction either in the wild, locked in rooms, or cared for in the early foundling institutions. Huddled in the corner with blank and impassive faces, rocking and clasping themselves, the young monkeys showed profound deficits in social behavior, shrinking from social encounters with exaggerated fear or clumsily attacking unfamiliar monkeys or human handlers. Sexual behavior, even after prolonged familiarization, was not attempted or was fragmented and directed without regard for anatomy. Furthermore, if forcibly impregnated, females either disregarded their newborns or brutally repelled their advances. The reproducibility of this effect in several other species of primates and the dramatic similarity of the behavioral deficits to the scanty reports on humans removed disbelief from even the most hardened skeptics. Ironically, studies on monkeys were required to convince us of an important fact of human biology that had been intuitively understood for generations.

What had really been learned from these early experimental studies of maternal deprivation? Certainly it was now clear that the mother supplied something more than milk and protection. Her absence for the first 6–12 months seemed to have produced such profound and wide ranging effects that it was difficult to see how the results could be understood. In fact, we still do not have a comprehensive understanding; the feral children and their laboratory animal counterparts have led to the realization that we have an enormous amount to learn about the first relationship and that we cannot fully understand normal development until we know more about how this relationship works.

The question to be answered first was whether lesser degrees of disruption would leave any traces on the young later in life. This is still a hotly debated issue, particularly in the case of such politically sensitive issues as early day care for infants of working mothers and the alleged need for a single caretaker as an attachment object in the first year of life. The weight of current evidence seems to favor the position that human and monkey infants are capable of forming attachments to more than one caretaker and that a fairly wide range of early rearing systems is consistent with normal development.

Nevertheless, it is also clear that in carefully controlled animal experiments, disruptions of early mothering either by stressing mothers in the postnatal period or by short separations after the relationship has become established, can have demonstrable long-term effects. For example, when one or two separations lasting only 6 days each were carried out with rhesus monkey infants of 4–6 months of age, they grew up to behave differently in response to an unfamiliar situation 2 years later (12). When presented with novel objects in a strange cage, monkeys that had had this early experience showed less exploration, less time playing with companions, and more time sitting and playing alone than controls with uninterrupted early mother–infant relationships. They were slow to begin play and tended to remain with their mothers. This long-term effect bore a close resemblance to the response they had shown as infants after the mother had been removed from the group living cage.

These findings in monkeys, like the earlier results on massive maternal deprivation, bore a striking resemblance to the findings reported in less well-controlled clinical studies on humans. Children normally separate from their parents in a gradual way, but if this event occurs suddenly and earlier than usual—for example, when a mother must enter the hospital—human infants between 6–8 months and 5 years become agitated, vocalize, and attempt to get back to their mothers. As Bowlby has described so well, this immediate response is followed by a phase he characterized as "despair," in which all behavior is reduced, social behavior and play in particular. The infant takes on a sad face, an apathetic posture, and a tendency to weep easily. Gradually, most infants will resume social interactions and play, apparently returning to normal. But if several days go by before the mother's return, the infant will appear detached instead of springing to a joyful reunion. Then, within a few hours of reunion, the infant may become unusually tense and clinging to the mother for several days or weeks. If the mother remains absent and the environment is impoverished, as in some institutions, the depressed state progresses to severe withdrawal and takes on the characteristics of the isolated children described earlier. Even if the mother returns and the environment is reasonably supportive, some studies have demonstrated long-term effects such as an increased susceptibility to depression in humans with histories of early separations. Other studies have shown how resilient most infants are and how they seem to be able to get what they need from their environment unless repeatedly separated and deprived.

The Potential for Recovery

It is clear that early interruptions of the mother–infant relationship have immediate effects. It is also clear that recovery is possible and that the subsequent environment plays an important role in facilitating normal development. Even short and temporary interruptions during the first 1 or 2 postnatal years in the human may have some long-term effects on emotional responsiveness, but it is not clear whether such effects depend on the acute emotional responses to separation, the altered (clinging) relationship that follows reunion, or the withdrawal of some regulating action on development ordinarily provided by the interactions between parent and infant. Furthermore, it should be emphasized that under special circumstances, even the effects of the more severe forms of early deprivation can be at least partially reversed (13). The original abusive and neglectful "motherless mothers" of Harlow's early work were given experience with subsequent pregnancies and infant rearing. By the fourth time they were mothers, they were virtually indistinguishable from normals. Contact with agemates during adolescence also greatly reduced the probability of inadequate maternal care on the first delivery in monkeys raised from birth artificially. Furthermore, if previously isolated juveniles were exposed to much younger infants that were not yet fearful and still had strong indiscriminate tendencies to cling to anything furry, the former isolates could gradually be socially rehabilitated. Such encounters are ordinarily prevented by adults in the social group while the isolated monkey's peers are quickly driven away by the isolate's inappropriate social behavior. The younger monkeys were less specific in their requirements, much less likely to respond aggressively, and provided the interaction necessary to enable socialization of the isolates.

Clearly, social experience can be used at a later date to make up for an earlier deficiency. This reparative effect of social experience should be an encouragement to therapists. However, the evidence shows that severe stress can make the effects of early deprivation manifest where they had been inapparent. And intractable deficits can be produced when an early disruption of the parent–infant relationship is followed by a series of later experiences in which the self-correcting potential is never realized. The original deficit may thus be compounded in different ways at subsequent developmental stages.

Qualitative Differences in Parenting

The next question to be considered is this. If a caretaker is continuously provided but is quite different from a normal mother, does this alteration in the *quality* of the early interaction affect the infant's development? An easy way to ask this question is to foster newborns across species, a laboratory improvement on the wolf child theme of myth, legend, and anecdote. There are limits to this approach, since primates will not accept foster young even of closely related primate species and even if the infants are substituted immediately following parturition. However, rats will readily accept newborn mice, and as a result of the experience the mice will grow up to be quite different from normally reared controls (14). Mice of an aggressive inbred strain that have been reared by rats are markedly less aggressive as a result. The reduction of aggression was traced specifically to the behavioral interaction between rat mother and mouse infant, rather than to some factor in the mother's milk or to visual, auditory, or olfactory stimulation by the presence of the rat mother behind wire mesh in an adjoining cage. These results lead us to believe that qualitative features of the mother–infant interaction can have important developmental effects on behavior but do not suggest precisely how this may come about. Clearly we need to know more about the details of how parent and infant interact.

It has subsequently been found that cross-fostering need not be across species in order for the first social relationship to affect behavior. Experiments with strains of mice and rats having different levels of aggressive behavior demonstrate that the behavior typical of a particular strain may be transmitted by the mother–infant relationship rather than solely by the genetic endowment of the infant (15). Laboratory rats may be bred to produce two strains, one of which attacks and kills mice and another which does not. When infants born to each type of mother were cross-fostered at birth, the offspring developed the characteristics of the foster mother even though they had no opportunity to observe their mothers' behavior toward mice prior to their own testing near the time of puberty. If the offspring were allowed to be present when their mothers killed mice, this enhanced the effect, but the opportunity for observation learning was a minor effect compared to the developmental action of the previous relationship. The mothers somehow shaped the development of their offspring powerfully enough to overcome genetic and prenatal determinants of aggressive behavior. The rats born to the mouse-killing strain and cross-fostered to nonmouse-killing mothers did not attack mice at puberty, but by adulthood their "genes began to show" and a moderate proportion of them killed mice. The early developmental effect of the mouse-killing mother was more persistent, and their foster offspring continued to kill mice as adults, thus persistently behaving contrary to their genetic and prenatal constitution.

How this effect was produced remains a mystery because the differences in maternal behavior between the two strains have not yet been analyzed. It was not a highly specific effect, however, for a variety of behaviors were found to go along with mouse killing. Such animals were found to be irritable and habituate less rapidly to novelty, they consumed more water, fought with each other more intensely, and engaged in more precopulatory activity. Thus, a whole spectrum of behavior was affected by the different mother–infant interaction.

In conclusion, these studies strongly suggest that the interaction between parent and infant has important regulatory effects on development that need to be studied. It is not just the emotional stress of separation or the emotional deprivation of isolation which can alter development of the young. This important concept will be discussed in the next section.

REGULATION OF DEVELOPMENT

In the previous section, I reviewed some of the evidence that participation in the relationship is crucial for normal development. We must now turn to look closely at how involvement in a relationship can affect development of the young. The forces at work between parent and infant in the period between birth and weaning are not confined to the actions of observable behavior. Transactions such as the exchange of heat, the provision of nutrient, and the activation of the infant's vestibular (balance and motion detector) system by the parent, must be considered as well.

The theme that has returned again and again in previous sections has been that development is the result of the interaction between the organism and its environment. For the infant mammal during the long period of time after birth, the mother *is* its environment. The parents, by their continuous closeness and their shutting out the rest of the world, literally become the environment of the infant. The mother's direct biochemical influence is greatly reduced following birth, but continues in the form of the milk supplied. Every sensory characteristic of the parents and everything they do impinges on the infant's sensory systems. In addition, what the infant does changes how the parent acts in return. Thus, timing, contingency, and synchrony are introduced. The regulating action is not simply that of a source of stimulation, however complex, but that of a dance. The elements of rhythm and reciprocity thus add an extraordinarily complicated dimension to the system.

How can we approach such a complex system with any hope of simplifying it for analytic study? First, we need careful naturalistic observations of a few limited categories of interaction such as feeding or play using frame-by-frame film analysis (see below). This kind of work uncovers the nature of the behavioral interactions and suggests how the infant may be affected by them. The second approach is to alter experimentally the sensory interchange through which the relationship must operate on development.

An analysis of the relationship according to sensory interchange involves systems by which mother and infant act upon each other: tactile, olfactory, thermal, vestibular, nutrient-interoceptive, auditory, and visual. The first four dominate the earliest postnatal interactions, while the last two develop later. Activation of the infant's sensory receptor systems is not a simple matter of "on" or "off" and not limited to one system at a time. Even within a single modality, a stimulus can vary in intensity, quality, dynamics (rise and fall time), and duration. The repetition and combination of these elements constitute the patterns and rhythms of parental care. Many of these processes are inapparent to the observer and thus are hidden from our view. It is only by recognizing the constituent elements that we can hope to discover the processes underlying developmental effects such as those described in the previous section.

The contribution of the different sensory systems can be analyzed in two ways—by alterations of the receptor or of the signal. In the first of these, studies are made, for example, of blind infants or of animals. This way, the relationship can be changed in a relatively discrete manner and effects can be looked for in the development of the infant. Developmental outcome may be related to specific aspects of the interaction in this way. The second strategy—to alter the signals—can sometimes be done without otherwise altering the relationship, as when nutrient, thermal, or olfactory properties of the mother can be presented—for example, milk or warmth—to see if this is capable of preventing any of the effects of separation from the mother. The point of these maneuvers is to attempt to relate particular, discrete aspects of the interaction with specific aspects of the infant's behavior and physiology. For if the behavioral interaction regulates development of several systems in the infant, it is likely to do so over several specific pathways.

These approaches are beginning to illuminate the internal workings of the early parent–infant relationship. I will give examples from both human and animal work that reveal some of the processes found to regulate the infant's functioning at the behavioral, physiological, and biochemical levels.

Communicative Behavior

I have described how feral or isolated children and experimentally isolated monkeys show severe impairment in emotional expressiveness. Much of this lack is due to the absence of recognizable facial signals communicating their internal states. It has not been clear whether the emotional states were deranged or simply could not be accurately expressed or both. Certainly, no one could say what particular experience had been missing for these infants. Nor did we have a clear picture of how emotive facial expression normally develops: what interactions and which sensory pathways are crucial.

A clue has come from recognizing the significance of the fact that humans who have been blind from birth show an impairment similar to socially deprived infants in their facial expressiveness. Yet others who have been blind as long, but whose blindness came on after the first year of life, are virtually unimpaired in this important social behavior. Adults blind from birth, but with responsive early parental relationships, develop compensatory means of communicating affects by voice inflection, posture, and hand movement as well as by verbal language, but at first a sighted person feels handicapped in relating to them.

Thus, this experiment of nature allows us to see how interactions with parents involving a single sensory pathway are crucial for the development of a certain set of behaviors. Recall from earlier chapters that the fetus shows a wide range of facial expressions as a part of its spontaneous repertoire of behavior. Also after birth, neonatal smiling develops as an aspect of the REM sleep state. By the first to second month of life, smiles are elicited by the voice of the parent but also by a variety of other stimuli such as being touched or picked up. Frowns, fussiness, and pouting are part of intermediate states in the transition to crying. Up to the second postnatal month, these emotional expressions develop normally in blind infants. After this time, the normal infant smiles predictably to its mother's face, whereas blind children must be bounced and patted as well as talked to in order to elicit smiles. Even then, the results are less certain. By 4–5 months, the blind infant's smile is less complete than normal infants and never shows the exaggerated form of ecstatic smile that evokes such feeling in adults. Furthermore, by this time normal infants have developed stable intermediate expressions linked appropriately with certain states and situations, expressions we might label "attentive," "doubtful," "quizzical," "coy," or "bored." All that can be observed on the face of six-month-old blind infants are occasional variants of smiling and crying, conveying only the simplest dimension of affective state. The wide variety of facial expression that was present in the fetal and neonatal period has all but disappeared, replaced by a blank and immobile countenance that causes an observer to wonder if the child is depressed. No intervention has been found that will sustain the variety of neonatal facial expressions of blind infants into later infancy and shape them to cues and rewards. Blind people who had their sight during this critical first 6 months to 1 year retain normal facial expressiveness for the rest of their lives, despite absent visual input.

What is operating here is a critical period for visual stimulation in the development of expressive facial behavior. What we do not yet understand is the precise nature of the early visual input that is missing. Experience with feral, institutional, and isolated children who have normal visual systems but share this deficit in facial expression suggests that it is not simply the absence of visual stimulation. Rather, something specific to the visual aspects of the parent–infant interaction appears to be necessary. It is not known whether this depends on modeling by imitation of the mother's expression, split-second shaping with responsive visual reward, or simply exposure to specific facial patterning during the first few months.

Unlike socially deprived children, blind children raised by responsive parents have normal emotional development. Fraiberg studied how seeing parents interact with their blind children (16). She found that they attended particularly to hand movements, voice, and postural cues. By attending to these behaviors, the parents recognized and met the moods and needs of blind infants, play could be enjoyed by both parent and infant, and apparently these responsive interactions enabled the child's emotional development to proceed fairly normally. But it is not easy for sighted mothers of blind infants to interact without the signals and rewards of their child's facial expressions. The structure of such complex interactions will be discussed toward the end of this chapter.

Thus it is possible to begin to separate out the processes responsible for the development of facial expressiveness from the processes responsible for the development of emotional regulation. The dependence of the early development of facial behavior upon the visual experience of the relationship with parents may give us a model for learning more about the early development of other behaviors. Sexual and aggressive behaviors, for example, are markedly affected by experimental alterations of the parent–infant relationship and may also depend on specific aspects of this interaction. There is reason to suppose that even maternal behavior in adulthood might be related back to the experience of mothering as a child, but we know too little to be able to specify how that might come about.

Emotional Behavior

Some of the major deficits following social deprivation can be described as *disordered regulation of arousal states*. The excessive fearfulness, the sudden, unexpected, aggressive attacks, the withdrawn self-clasping, the stereotyped repetitive behaviors such as rocking seem in themselves to be evidence of pathological states of arousal and appear to contribute heavily to the fragmentation of sexual and maternal behavior and to the inability to play. The mature emotional states differentiate out of simpler behavioral arousal states present in the fetus and neonate. This differentiation and the normal integration of state and behavior is a major developmental task that seems to require the early parent–infant interaction. We are far from a comprehensive understanding of these events, but certain biological and behavioral processes have become clarified by recent research.

Extreme Sensory Deprivation

Melzack found that when dogs raised from birth in single cages with opaque walls were released into the unfamiliar normal laboratory world, they showed extreme hyperactivity alternating with freezing into immobility if confronted by a new object (17). High levels of excitement failed to habituate, and there was a failure to attend selectively to any one aspect of the environment for more than a few moments. They failed to respond differentially even to sexual or painful stimulation, and they failed to learn simple visual discrimination tasks. These dogs have had some degree of overt sensory deprivation as well as deprivation of interaction with their mother and littermates. Their behavioral abnormalities, however, are quite similar to those described above for socially deprived young animals and humans. Physiological studies of these dogs showed that when they were exposed to an unfamiliar environment there was an overall shift of EEG frequency to the activated high-frequency end of the spectrum and an even more impressive variability: marked shifts in frequency from moment to moment in comparison to the more stable lower frequency records of control dogs. Although there was little difference between isolated and control dogs in their home cage environments, exposure to novelty continued to produce higher frequency and greater variability of EEG frequency as long as 6 months after release from the isolation cages. In addition, cortical-evoked responses to repeated auditory stimulation showed marked variability in wave form and amplitude in the isolation-reared dogs as compared to normally reared controls.

These findings suggest that normal mechanisms for gating and filtering new sensory input are inadequately developed after isolation rearing, that the cortex is flooded with input, and that excessive arousal is induced by ordinary sensory stimulation. Furthermore, excessive variability was evident in neural activation to a consistent form of stimulus and there appeared to be a failure in the development of habituation mechanisms.

Apparently, some form of sensory stimulation supplied by a normal early environment is necessary for the development of neural mechanisms for the modulation and control of central nervous system arousal and for the development of consistent neural responses necessary for the processing of sensory information. These experiments provide some evidence about the nature of the abnormalities of brain function that may underlie the profound emotional impairment of socially deprived human and animal infants.

What they do not help us with is the question of exactly which aspects of the parent–infant interaction normally provide the necessary stimulation, which sensory modalities are primarily involved, and in what form the stimulation is delivered. The next two sections will give examples of how we may begin to answer such questions.

Rocking and the Role of Motion in Space

Motion in space and bodily position in relation to gravity are sensed by the vestibular apparatus of the inner ear and conveyed to the brain stem by a substantial neural pathway. This input is distributed widely to connecting neurons that reach many parts of the brain. It is this system and its widespread connections that make us feel the way we do on rough seas or amusement park rides.

Human neonates and older infants change their states readily in response to vestibular stimulation, a predetermined response long recognized by mothers as they pick up and rock their infants to calm them and to convert crying into sleep. Similarly, monkey infants receive a great deal of vestibular stimulation as they cling to their mothers throughout their active days swinging through trees.

One of the consistent abnormal symptoms of socially deprived human, ape, and monkey infants is self-rocking, a behavior thought to be an expression of affective arousal and distress in the infant. Some have suggested that it reflects a "hunger" for interaction with the parent. In rhesus monkeys raised without mothers but with soft, furry, artificial mother surrogates, this behavior reaches a peak at about 6 months and persists at high levels thereafter. In order to provide vestibular stimulation selectively, Mason and Berkson gave infant monkeys the same surrogate suspended on a wire, so that it could swing when they jumped on it (18). Furthermore, the surrogate was given independent mobility by a motor driven arm that moved it on the end of its wire within the cage at irregular intervals throughout most of the day.

The infants spent the same amount of time clinging to moving and stationary surrogates, but the moving ones *completely* prevented the development of self-rocking. Even after the surrogates were permanently removed at one year of age, no self-rocking appeared in the young monkeys that had been raised on mobile surrogates. In later tests with novel environments and strange intruder animals, the monkeys raised on mobile surrogates reacted with less timidity, distress vocalization, or extremes of locomotor activity and with less self-biting and self-rocking in response to these stresses. At 4–5 years of age, in tests of social and sexual responsiveness, mobile surrogate-reared monkeys showed less extreme emotional behavior, were more responsive to their partners, and benefited more from socializing experience than did controls reared on stationary surrogates. They were still considerably impaired in comparison to normally reared infants in these later tests, and during their early development two other abnormal self-directed behaviors—self-clasping and nonnutritive sucking—were not affected by the mobility of the surrogate.

These studies allow us to understand exactly which aspect of the parent–infant interaction is related to the development of self-rocking in socially deprived monkey infants. Furthermore, they indicate that motion in space, and the vestibular stimulation resulting from it, play a role in the development of the capacity of the infant to modulate and control the arousal of extreme emotional states. The notion that relatively simple sensory stimulation early in life can contribute toward adaptive emotional regulation is a novel one and has exciting implications for further study. It suggests that within the extremely complex interweaving of reciprocal interaction that characterizes the mother–infant interaction, relatively simple sensory processes are hidden that nevertheless have important and far-reaching developmental consequences.

Warmth

We unconsciously recognize the importance of thermal stimulation in the mother–infant interaction when we speak of "warm" or "cold" mothers. In fact, most young mammals do not have fully developed mechanisms for regulating their own temperatures; their body temperature goes up when they are held, fondled, or fed and goes down when the mother is away for a while. Severe and lethal decreases in body temperature can occur quickly in newborns without adequate protection when the mother is absent. Normal rates of development of body and brain are dependent on the mother keeping her infant warm.

Young monkeys and rats as well as human infants who are separated from their mothers show markedly reduced levels of behavior after the initial hyperactivity of their separation distress. They curl up and hardly move at all. Picking them up and placing them in an unfamiliar place, which normally elicits active exploratory behavior, produces only an apathetic response in such infants. For 2-week-old rats, we found that it was not the separation from the mother that was responsible, because separated pups that were kept warm actually showed increased activity. The apathetic responses of the cool infants were unlikely to be simply the result of a cool nervous system and muscles since the heart beat was not slowed in these animals and the motor retardation could be reversed without warming, by administration of the drug amphetamine.

We can infer from these studies that the thermal input regularly provided by the periodic contact of mother and infant mammals serves to maintain behavioral activation as well as determining the rate of biological maturation of body and brain. The physiological mechanisms for these regulatory processes have not yet been established, but they alert us to the importance of assessing the role of thermoregulation in the production of the behavioral effects of early mother–infant separation.

Touching, Holding, and Other Forms
of Tactile Stimulation

In addition to the provision of body heat and of motion in space, can we identify other aspects of the mother–infant interaction that also regulate behavioral arousal? Our studies in 2-week-old rats have been mainly concerned with infants that were separated from their mothers and kept at nest temperature artificially (19). After 8–18 hours of separation from their mothers, if placed in an unfamiliar environment, they became hyperactive like the sensory-deprived puppies studied by Melzack. In addition to increases in locomotion, they did more self-grooming, more rising on their hind legs against the wall, and defecated and urinated more. They took a longer time to quiet down and go to sleep. This heightened behavioral arousal in response to the unfamiliar testing situation was not affected by how much nutrient they received. Furthermore, it did not appear to be a part of the usual "separation distress" that occurs immediately after separation. Rats this age *do* show classical separation distress with agitation and (ultrasonic) vocalization within moments of being separated from mother and littermates in the home cage. But this response abates before the hyperactive response to novelty has developed, at 4–8 hours after separation.

What sort of stimulation could serve to prevent the gradual development of this hyperactive state during the normal mother–infant interaction? Vestibular stimulation by rocking and repeated inversion had no effect; provision of the mother's smell, without any behavioral interaction, had only a small effect. However, tactile stimulation, either through mild electrical current from a grid floor or by very slow rotation in a drum (requiring a position change every 15 seconds) returned the levels of behavior of maternally separated pups to the level and pattern of normally mothered pups.

These results show that when tactile stimulation, which has the immediate effect of eliciting activity, is repeated, it has the cumulative long-term effect of reducing the level of behavioral arousal that will be elicited by unfamiliar surroundings. They suggest that systems mediating behavioral arousal of the infant are regulated in part by the levels of tactile stimulation delivered by the mother as part of her interaction with the infant.

There is some evidence that this process, found originally in rats, may also be at work in early human development. It has been found that repeated tactile, as well as auditory and visual, stimulation, if consistently and regularly presented, has a clear-cut quieting effect on human infants during interfeeding periods away from their mothers (20). Swaddling, which presents widespread and constant tactile stimulation, is particularly effective in reducing human infant arousal, preventing crying, and inducing instead quiet attention or sleep. Nations and cultures differ in how human babies are stimulated, but there appears to be a widespread intuitive understanding of the necessity for regular stimulation of almost any sort to avoid fussiness in infants.

Thus, there may exist a relatively nonspecific process by which levels of repetitive tactile stimulation, as a part of the complex interaction between parent and infant, serves to keep arousal levels within an optimal range. In the absence of these forms of regular stimulation, arousal levels appear to increase in intensity and to lack internal controls over range and variability.

The Mother as a Regulator of Infant Physiology

Physiological development has generally been thought to be unaffected by the child's social environment after birth. The maturation of vital biological control systems such as those regulating growth, maintaining the circulation of the blood, and regulating the onset of puberty would seem best left to genetic programs, heavily buffered from the effects of interaction with the environment. Yet recent evidence suggests that this is not entirely the case. Many of such physiological systems play a role in the organization of the child's behavior through their regulation of the internal environment.

Growth

For many years, pediatricians have recognized a special category of infants among those who fail to thrive—infants who have no discernible illness, who seem to eat reasonably well, but continue to be well below growth norms, even while their feeding is supervised in a hospital. Abnormal growth hormone responses have been found in these infants, but these have been thought to be secondary to the growth failure or to a reduced level of food intake and not a primary cause of the retarded growth. Pediatricians have found that if a nurse is assigned to special duty with such an infant and spends a good deal of time holding him, playing with him, and generally establishing a relationship, the child will grow dramatically. However, when released from the hospital, growth stops again. In these cases, the home environment is often found to be chaotic and the parents withdrawn, alcoholic, or otherwise ineffective. These clinical findings have led to the term *deprivation dwarfism* for this condition.

A discovery was recently made in infant rats that may provide a means for conceptualizing how deprivation dwarfism comes about. It came as the result of experimental detective work by Schanberg, Kuhn, and Butler (21). They were bothered by the fact that infant rats differed markedly in the level of a brain enzyme that regulates synthesis of protein for new brain cells, even when subjects came from the same litter. They found that the level was related to how long the infant had been separated from the mother before the brain enzyme determination was done. Instead of standardizing the interval and stopping there, the investigators went on to do a series of experiments, asking questions about what the mother was doing to influence the level of the brain enzyme in her infants.

What they found was that levels of brain enzyme and growth hormone fell rapidly, within 15 minutes after rat pups were separated from their mothers, and rose equally rapidly again upon reunion. The mother did not seem to be maintaining these levels in her offspring, either by heat or by the milk she provided. Even her presence in the anesthetized state was not sufficient to prevent the decline. But a nonlactating foster mother *did* maintain levels of the brain enzyme, provided she interacted with the infants.

Thus, two physiological regulators of the growth of both body and brain of the infant rat are regulated by the behavioral interaction with the mother. The brain enzyme may be induced by growth hormone or the two may be under separate control. This regulation of brain and body growth processes by active behavioral interaction with the mother in a laboratory animal provides a means to begin to understand the processes that underlie deprivation dwarfism in human infants. We can conclude that an infant's relationship with its mother may provide stimulation used by the infant to determine from minute to minute the level of its physiological growth regulators, enzymes, and hormones.

Cardiovascular Function

The human infant's heart beat varies according to its state, but within a relatively narrow range. Baseline rates and range are different at different postnatal ages, the result of a changing balance between two opposing neural pathways of the autonomic system. Resting heart rates rise after the newborn period to a high plateau during infancy due to high sympathetic tone, then fall slowly throughout the juvenile period as parasympathetic tone increases. These maturational changes account for major differences in resting heart rates between infants, at 140 beats per minute, and adolescents at 70. A similar developmental change is found in rats, although the overall levels are much higher (450–250 beats per minute). Thus the brain controls the heart differently in infancy than in adulthood in these two mammals.

Such changing set points in physiological regulation have been thought most unlikely to be environmentally determined. An accident in our laboratory led to the discovery that the high resting heart rates of the infant rat are maintained by the mother, not by the infant itself. During studies on the developmental course of heart rate regulation, a mother escaped from the cage and could not return to her infants overnight. Resting heart rates of the infants the next morning were almost half their normal level. A number of experiments led to the conclusion that the mother rat ordinarily regulates the heart rates of her infants by the amount of milk she supplies to them (22). She seems to do this through interoceptive stimulation of the infant's stomach and intestinal tract, which conveys a message to the brain resulting in a certain level of sympathetic autonomic tone to the heart; the more milk, the higher the heart rate. In order to reach this conclusion, a number of more probable alternatives first had to be ruled out, among them the notion that milk acted directly on the heart by supplying nutrient for cellular processes necessary to sustain high levels of heart rate. Instead, nutrient appears to act on the brain through internal receptors along the wall of the gastrointestinal tract, providing stimulation that regulates heart rate over autonomic nerve pathways.

These experiments provide a picture of the mother as an external physiological regulatory agent, delicately controlling the heart rate of her infants by the level of milk she provides to their stomachs. These changes in heart rate seem to be only one part of a widespread circulatory adjustment for the processing of large amounts of nutrient in infancy. When nutrient is abundant within the digestive system, the cardiovascular system is wide open with high pumping rates and dilated blood vesssels, carrying absorbed nutrient to rapidly growing tissues all over the body. In the mother's absence, the level of nutrient dwindles, until only low-pumping rates are necessary to distribute blood with little nutrient content to tissues that as a result gradually cease to grow. As growth rates slow later in development and nutrient intake falls as a proportion of body weight, resting heart rate declines and cardiovascular adjustments to food intake become very much reduced.

It is not known whether human infant cardiovascular regulation is similarly influenced by milk provided by the mother, but the similarity in the developmental sequence of autonomic neural influences allows us to suspect other similarities and to know what to look for.

Sexual Maturation

A third example suggests a biological role for parents extending beyond infancy and the juvenile period to the onset of puberty. The research again was done on mice and rats and involves pheromones, or scents produced by specialized cells, which act as airborne messengers perceived by another individual's olfactory system (23). Most humans find such evidence particularly difficult to apply to ourselves, for reasons not entirely rational. But from the point of view of the biologist, the system revealed by the experiments is elegant and not inconsistent with the biology of humans.

The onset of puberty in young female mice is hastened by a continuing relationship with their fathers (or any adult male) and delayed if they interact only with mother and other females. The effects of these social relationships is substantial, amounting to the equivalent of 3–4 years acceleration or delay in the human. The effect is mediated by a chemical substance excreted in the urine of the males or females. The female puberty-delaying pheromone is only produced by females that interact behaviorally in a group for a period of time. The male puberty-accelerating pheromone has recently been found to be a polypeptide, similar to those that occur in the brain and control the pituitary release of luteinizing hormone, one of the pituitary hormones initiating puberty. A speculation is that this pheromone may act within the brain of the young after its absorption by the olfactory membrane.

The idea of applying these principles to the human is made less fanciful by the evidence that young women who live together soon menstruate in synchrony (24). This effect has been found to generalize to the rat and, in the case of that species, to be due to a pheromone. Whether in the human a different, higher cortical process has replaced the simpler biological one can only be answered by further study.

The point remains that the influence of the relationship with parents may extend to a long-term effect on physiological processes for sexual maturation and that chemical communication by scents or pheromones must not be neglected as a possible basis for parent–infant interaction among humans. Through such processes, the early parent–infant relationship can act to influence behavioral events occurring much later in time when the child undergoes the biological changes that initiate adolescence.

From Biological to Psychological Processes

Thus far, I have described a number of relatively simple processes, hidden within the early parent–infant relationship that have definable effects on the development of the young. More complicated processes involving the timing and patterning of interaction create elements of rhythm, synchrony, and reciprocity that give special qualities to a relationship. We use words such as "mutuality" and "sensitiveness" for such qualities and characterize certain mothers as "intrusive," "rejecting," or "seductive" who seem to "mismatch" with the infant. As these words demonstrate, our tendency has been to respond globally to relationships, even when we take the role of observer. But recent studies by Stern using frame-by-frame film analysis have begun to reveal exactly what is going on between parent and infant.

A mother is bottle feeding her three-and-a-half-month-old boy. They are about halfway through. During the first half of the feeding the baby had been sucking away, working seriously and occasionally looking at his mother, sometimes for long stretches (10 to 15 seconds). . . .

Until this point, a normal feeding, not a social interaction, was underway. Then a change began. While talking and looking at me the mother turned her head and gazed at the infant's face. He was gazing at the ceiling, but out of the corner of his eye he saw her head turn toward him and turned to gaze back at her. This had happened before, but now he broke rhythm and stopped sucking. He let go of the nipple and the suction around it broke as he eased into the faintest suggestion of a smile. The mother abruptly stopped talking and, as she watched his face begin to transform, her eyes opened a little wider and her eyebrows raised a bit. His eyes locked on to hers, and together they held motionless for an instant. The infant did not return to sucking and his mother held frozen her slight expression of anticipation. This silent and almost motionless instant continued to hang until the mother suddenly shattered it by saying "Hey!" and simultaneously opening her eyes wider, raising her eyebrows further, and throwing her head up and toward the infant. Almost simultaneously, the baby's eyes widened. His head tilted up and, as his smile broadened, the nipple fell out of his mouth. Now she said, "Well hello! . . . heell'o . . . heeello'ooo!", so that her pitch rose and the "hellos" became longer and more stressed on each successive repetition. With each phrase the baby expressed more pleasure, and his body resonated almost like a balloon being pumped up, filling a little more with each breath. The mother then paused and her face relaxed. They watched each other expectantly for a moment. The shared excitement between them ebbed, but before it faded completely, the baby suddenly took an initiative and intervened to rescue it. His head lurched forward, his hands jerked up, and a fuller smile blossomed. His mother was jolted into motion. She moved forward, mouth open and eyes alight, and said, "Oooooh . . . ya wanna play do ya . . . yeah? . . . I didn't know if you were still hungry . . . no . . . nooooo . . . no I didn't . . ." And off they went.

After some easy exchange the pace and excitement increased to a higher level at which the interaction assumed the form of a repeating game. . . .

During the next four cycles of the renewed and slightly varied game, the mother did pretty much the same, except that on each successive cycle she escalated the level of suspense with her face and voice and timing. . . . During the first cycle the baby stayed captivated by his mother's antics. He smiled broadly and never took his eyes off her face. During the second cycle, he averted his face slightly as she approached, but the smile held. At the beginning of the third sortie by the mother, the baby had still not resumed the full face-to-face position and had his head turned slightly away. As she approached, his face turned even further but still he kept looking at her. At the same time, his smile flattened. The eyebrows and the corners of his mouth flickered back and forth between a smile and a sober expression. As the excitement mounted he seemed to run that narrow path between explosive glee and fright. As the path got narrower, he finally broke gaze with mother, appearing thereby to recompose himself for a second, to deescalate his own level of excitement. Having done so successfully, he returned his gaze to mother and exploded into a big grin. On that cue she began, with gusto, her fourth and most suspenseful cycle, but this one proved too much for him and pushed him across to the other side of the narrow path. He broke gaze immediately, turned away, face averted, and frowned. The mother picked it up immediately. She stopped the game dead in its tracks and said softly, "Oh honey, maybe you're still hungry, huh . . . let's try some milk again." He returned gaze. His face eased and he took the nipple again. The "moment" of social interaction was over. Feeding had resumed. (This whole episode lasted about four minutes.) [Stern, pp. 2–3]

This description is moving but sobering. How many different aspects are there that could influence the child's development? How many ways in which special characteristics of the infant could affect the mother's behavior and thus create by his own actions a different experience for himself? A description of the interrelationship of the behaviors of mother and infant goes beyond biological terms as they are currently used and lays the groundwork for concepts familiar to psychologists and social scientists. Yet there are simpler elements that can be viewed biologically as I have done above. Thus, these 4 minutes in the life of an infant illustrate the transition from biological to psychological and social realms.

One simple process that has been abstracted from the web of these complex interactions involves rhythm. An unexpected correlation has been found between parents' speech rhythms and the rhythm of neonatal limb movements (25). If an awake infant hears human speech, even in a foreign language, the points of change of its limb movements synchronize with sound segments of speech. This effect was obtained as early as 2 days of age and even with the use of tape recordings, so covert behavioral cues were not being used. Nor was it a simple beating of time, since infants did not synchronize their behavior to isolated vowel or tapping sounds. What has been demonstrated is an entrainment of motor patterns of the infant by characteristics of auditory stimulation by the parent. Many such processes probably underlie the early socializing experience, shaping our behavior so that we relate to each other in a common rhythm. Cultural differences and the profound strangeness of feral children may well stem from shaping by unfamiliar early developmental rhythms.

A more complex process that seems to be involved in the segment quoted from Stern is the stimulation and regulation of the infant's arousal during the interaction. It is as if the infant seeks stimulation until its internal state reaches some kind of ceiling, after which further stimulation is avoided. In fact, Stern has found that it is the infant that breaks off eye-to-eye contact with the mother in 94 percent of all instances (26).

These behaviors by the infant appear to modulate an internal arousal state around an optimal level and suggest a mechanism for "emotional homeostasis." It appears reasonable to suppose that this experience plays a very important role in establishing the range and regulation of emotional behavior in later life. An experiment by Papousek supports this notion (27). If a mother leaves an infant after an interaction such as the one described above, and then returns, but this time simply presents an impassive face and remains immobile in front of the infant, an extraordinary sequence takes place. The infant first fixates on the mother's face and then begins a series of smiles, coos, and head bobbings. These escalate in intensity, his limb movements become jerky; finally he turns his face away, becomes motionless, slumps forward, and stares impassively at the floor. Within minutes, the whole temper of the relationship has changed drastically. The infant, for a brief time, gives every appearance of the severely deprived infants described above.

What has happened? The element of reciprocity has been suddenly terminated and this has produced a profound change in the infant's state. The new state bears little similarity to any that is normally observed. Given some time it will dissipate and be replaced by a normal state such as quiet drowsy or sleep. But if this experience is repeated, what effects may this have on social development? The need to infer hypothetical processes is clearly evident here: some element of expectancy appears to have been violated, and some shift in the character of behavior from engaging to disengaging has taken place. It seems necessary to invoke concepts such as the schema (as we did previously, see above) in order to deal with this sort of behavior as well as others such as reactive or defensive emotional states. Our language is forced to shift away from the words we are familiar with in biology and the new concepts can not yet be defined in biological terms. Behaviors like this mark the transition from biological to psychological processes in the early parent–infant relationship.

SUMMARY

The relationship between a newborn and its mother must be formed on new terms after birth and may begin at this point with the father and other caretakers. There is evidence that both the mother and the infant are predisposed toward each other through the operation of biological processes that have been taking place during late gestation. The initial attraction is maintained by the development of attachment, which itself depends on levels of sensory stimulation between the two and upon other simple interactions at the biological level. More complex processes that require inferences at the psychological level contribute to and modify the attachment as the child grows up.

A parent–infant relationship is now known to be essential for the normal development of social and emotional behavior, even if the infant's needs for nutrition and shelter are otherwise met. In fact, the proper integration of most complex sensorimotor responses necessary for higher levels of learning appear to require some interaction with an effective caretaker. We are beginning to learn why this should be so through the study of the many processes hidden within the parent–infant interaction that regulate the behavior and physiology of the developing infant. The instances of recovery from early parental neglect after later social experience of a therapeutic sort attests to the developmental force of these processes. Examples of these processes include visual, tactile, thermal, auditory, vestibular (motion detector), and nutritional modalities acting upon communicative and simple emotional behaviors, growth, and physiological regulation as well as upon complex social behaviors.

The idea that processes at work during parent–infant interaction exert widespread regulatory effects on the developing child has several implications. First, it helps explain the evolutionary survival value of attachment, for if so much of normal development depends on the occurrence of these interactions, a powerful predisposition to maintain proximity is likely to have selective advantage. Second, the growth and maintenance of attachment may be then understood as the result of the sensory stimulation involved in the interaction, operating by neural mechanisms that may be similar to those known to be involved in the commitment of visual cortical cells of the kitten to particular sources of visual stimulation. Third, if interaction with the mother regulates the infant's behavior and physiology, then sudden separation can be viewed as a withdrawal of this regulation and the dramatic responses of very young children (and animals) to maternal separation can be understood as release or escape phenomena, analogous to the withdrawal responses of narcotic addicts after separation from their repeated drug administration.

Thus, the mother appears to regulate the behavioral, neurochemical, autonomic, and hormonal function of her developing young by different aspects of her relationship with them: nutrient, warmth, sensory stimulation, and rhythmic responsiveness. Withdrawing these external regulators leads to new levels of physiological and behavioral function within the infant. The advantage of this view is that it allows us to separate out each developmental effect of separation in relation to its specific mechanism, rather than viewing the phenomenon globally as an emotional stress response.

Finally, the adaptive value of this arrangement is worth considering. If the parent–infant interaction is utilized by evolutionary selection as a powerful regulator of early biological development of the infant, this provides an opportunity for rapid change in the biological characteristics of a species from one generation to the next, according to shifting environmental needs. Events occurring to future parents from their own infancy onward are thus capable of affecting basic physiological and behavioral traits of their offspring through modification of the parents' behavior toward their infants.

FURTHER READING

Bowlby, J. *Attachment and Loss.* Vol. 1: *Attachment.* New York: Basic Books, 1969. Vol. 2: *Separation: Anxiety and Anger.* New York: Basic Books, 1973.

Clarke, A. M., and Clarke, A. D. D. (Eds.) *Early Experience: Myth and Evidence.* New York: Free Press, 1976.

Gubernick, D. J., and Klopfer, P. H. *Parental Care in Mammals.* New York: Plenum Press, 1981.

Hofer, M. A. Hidden regulatory processes in early social relationships. In P. P. G. Bateson and P. H. Klopfer (Eds.), *Perspectives in Ethology.* Vol. 3: *Social Behavior.* New York: Plenum Press, 1978. Pp. 135–166.

Hoffman, H. S. Fear-mediated processes in the context of imprinting. In M. Lewis and L. A. Rosenblum (Eds.), *Origins of Behavior.* Vol. 2: *The Origins of Fear.* New York: Wiley, 1974. Pp. 25–48.

Mason, W. A. Early deprivation in biological perspective. In V. H. Denenberg (Ed.), *Education of the Infant and Young Child.* New York: Academic Press, 1970. Pp. 25–50.

McKinney, Jr., W. T. Primate social isolation. *Archives of General Psychiatry,* 31:422–426, 1974.

Parent–Infant Interaction. Ciba Foundation Symposium No. 33. New York: Elsevier, 1975.

Rajecki, D. W., Lamb, M. E., and Obmascher, P. Toward a general theory of infantile attachment: a comparative review of aspects of the social bond. *Behavioral and Brain Sciences,* 1:417–464, 1978.

Rheingold, H. L., and Eckerman, C. O. The infant separates himself from his mother. *Science,* 168:78–83, 1970.

Schaffer, H. R. *Mothering.* Cambridge, Mass.: Harvard University Press, 1977.

Stern, D. *The First Relationship.* Cambridge, Mass.: Harvard University Press, 1977.

REFERENCES CITED

1. Klaus, M., Trause, M. A., and Kennel, J. H. Does human maternal behavior after delivery show a characteristic pattern? In *Parent–Infant Interaction.* Ciba Foundation Symposium No. 33. New York: Elsevier, 1975. Pp. 69–78.

2. Rosenblatt, J. S. The development of maternal responsiveness in the rat. *American Journal of Orthopsychiatry,* 39:36–56, 1969.
   Rosenblatt, J. S., Pre-partum and post-partum regulation of maternal behavior in the rat. In *Parent–Infant Interaction,* op. cit., pp. 17–30.

3. Kennell, J. H., Trause, M. A., and Klaus, M. H. Evidence for a sensitive period in the human mother. In *Parent–Infant Interaction,* op. cit., pp. 87–95.

4. Redican, W. K., and Mitchell, G. Play between adult male and infant rhesus monkeys. *American Zoologist,* 14:295–302, 1974.

5. Klopfer, P. H. Stimulus preferences and imprinting. *Science,* 156:1394–1396, 1967.

6. Scott, J. P., Stewart, J. M., and deGhett, V. J. Separation in infant dogs.

In J. P. Scott and E. C. Senay (Eds.), *Separation and Depression*. No. 94. Washington, D.C.: American Association for the Advancement of Science, 1973. Pp. 3–32.

7. Hinde, R. A. Mothers' and infants' roles: distinguishing the questions to be asked. In *Parent–Infant Interaction*, op. cit., pp. 5–12. Also Hinde, R. A., and Simpson, J. A. Qualities of mother–infant relationships in monkeys. In *Parent–Infant Interaction*, op. cit., pp. 39–57.

8. Itard, J. On the first developments of the young savage of Aveyron, 1799. Reprinted in L. Malson (Ed.), *Wolf Children and the Problem of Human Nature*. New York: Monthly Review Press, 1972. P. 98.

9. Singh, J. A. L., and Zingg, R. M. *Wolf Children and Feral Man*. Reprinted by Shoe String Press, Hamden, Conn., 1966.
Lane, H. *The Wild Boy of Aveyron*. Cambridge, Mass.: Harvard University Press, 1976.

10. Spitz, R. A. Hospitalism: an inquiry into the genesis of psychiatric conditions in early childhood. *Psychoanalytic Study of the Child*, 1:53–74, 1945.

11. Harlow, H. F. The nature of love. *American Psychologist*, 13:673–685, 1958.

12. Hinde, R. A., and Spencer-Booth, Y. Effects of brief separation from mother on rhesus monkeys. *Science*, 173:111–118, 1971.

13. Ruppenthal, G. C., Arling, G. L., Harlow, H. F., Sackett, G. P., and Suomi, S. J. A 10-year perspective of motherless-mother monkey behavior. *Journal of Abnormal Psychology*, 85:341–349, 1976.
Suomi, S. J., Delizio, R., and Harlow, H. F. Social rehabilitation of separation-induced depressive disorders in monkeys. *American Journal of Psychiatry*, 133:1279–1285, 1976.

14. Denenberg, V. H., Paschke, R., Zarrow, M. X., and Rosenberg, K. M. Mice reared with rats: elimination of odors, vision, and audition as significant stimulus sources. *Developmental Psychobiology*, 2:26–28, 1969.

15. Flandera, V., and Novakova, V. Effect of mother on the development of aggressive behavior in rats. *Developmental Psychobiology*, 8:49–54, 1974.

16. Fraiberg, S. Blind infants and their mothers: an examination of the sign system. In M. Lewis and L. A. Rosenblum (Eds.), *The Effects of the Infant on Its Caregiver*. New York: Wiley, 1974.

17. Melzack, R. The role of early experience in emotional arousal. *Annals of the New York Academy of Sciences*, 159:721–730, 1969.

18. Mason, W. A., and Berkson, G. Effects of maternal mobility on the development of rocking and other behaviors in rhesus monkeys. *Developmental Psychobiology*, 8:197–211, 1974.

19. Hofer, M. A. Studies on how maternal separation produces behavioral change in young rats. *Psychosomatic Medicine*, 37:245–264, 1975.

20. Brackbill, Y. Cumulative effects of continuous stimulation on arousal levels in infants. *Child Development*, 42:17–26, 1971.

21. Kuhn, C. M., Butler, S. R., and Schanberg, S. M. Selective depression of serum growth hormone during maternal deprivation in rat pups. *Science*, 201:1034–1036, 1978.
22. Hofer, M. A., and Weiner, H. Physiological mechanisms for cardiac control by nutritional intake after early maternal separation in the young rat. *Psychosomatic Medicine*, 37:8–24, 1975.
23. Vandenbergh, J. C. Male odor accelerates female sexual maturation in mice. *Endocrinology*, 84:658–660, 1969.
    Drickamer, L. C. Sexual maturation of female house mice: social inhibition. *Developmental Psychobiology*, 7:257–265, 1974.
24. McClintock, M. K. Menstrual synchrony and suppression. *Nature*, 229:244–245, 1971.
    McClintock, M. K. Estrous synchrony and its mediation by airborne chemical communication *(Rattus norvegicus)*. *Hormones and Behavior*, 10:264–276, 1978.
25. Condon, W. S., and Sander, L. W. Neonate movement is synchronized with adult speech: interactional participation and language acquisition. *Science*, 183:99–101, 1974.
26. Stern, D. Mother and infant play: the dyadic interaction involving facial, vocal and gaze behaviors. In M. Lewis and L. A. Rosenblum (Eds.), *The Effects of the Infant on Its Caregiver*. New York: Wiley, 1976. Pp. 187–214.
27. Papousek, H., and Papousek, M. Cognitive aspects of preverbal social interaction between human infants and adults. In *Parent–Infant Interaction*, op. cit., pp. 241–260.

Part IV
THE EMERGENCE
OF THE CHILD

Whereas the newborn does not act at all like an adult, the child of 3 or 4 has a behavioral repertoire that includes all the major classes of adult behavior in clearly recognizable form. Thus, the emergence of the child brings with it the emergence of adult behaviors. This section is concerned with these extremely rapid and important behavioral developments that take place in the first few years after birth. However, the child is *not* a miniature adult and there are further important changes during subsequent years in the form of these behaviors, how they are put together, their application, and their complexity. But their first emergence marks the completion of the early development of our behavior and their story is the last major section of this book.

The process by which these rapid changes take place involves a powerful interaction between three organizational forces: learning, internal states, and the maturation of underlying neural systems. Each component of this triple interaction tends to reinforce the other so that a multiplier effect is generated. Patterns of eating, sleeping, and emotional behavior undergo a series of rapid shifts or discontinuities that involve changes in learning, memory, and concept formation, and make possible the rapid growth in complexity that characterizes the behavior of the child and adult.

Language, play, and the interrelated behaviors of sex, aggression, and parenting are traced in subsequent chapters, as they develop from their beginnings in the fetal and newborn periods. In the early development of these important adult behaviors, the forces of rapid change can be seen to be operating in conjunction with other processes that are specific to these particular behaviors, such as the role of auditory feedback in language development and the role of androgenic hormones in the formation of sexual identity and sex-role behavior.

The early development of these behaviors forms the basis for the establishment of the individual as a unique and special being. The complexity of the interactions involved and the myriad opportunities for experiences different from other infants, combined with the predispositions the infant brings from the fetal and newborn period, create a set of circumstances that make people understandable only in terms of their early history.

12

The Forces
of Rapid Change

The major force behind the sequential changes in fetal behavior is clearly the growth and functional maturation of new neural systems. But even in this early fetal period, and even at the cellular and molecular levels, important environmental interactions and consequences of function have been discovered, so the force of early neurobiological maturation cannot be characterized as an independent process. And in the development of behavior after birth, the influences of the environment and the consequences of the infant's actions on its own subsequent behavior are so prominent that our view of neural maturational processes can easily be eclipsed. Even after close examination, it can be difficult to identify which of the many new behavioral developments of childhood are primarily achieved through maturation of underlying neural systems, the regulating effects of the environment, or learning from the consequences of previous behavior.

The relationship between these variables is a major unsolved problem in developmental theory, and we have yet to find methods for weighing their relative contributions to events in the development of behavior. What is clear is that their interactions continue to take place throughout life and that only through a better understanding of their intimate workings will we gradually come to build a comprehensive theory of development.

The infant responds to its environment with changes in its internal states of arousal, motivation, and emotion, and interacts with its environment according to its growing capacities for learning, memory, and concept formation. Thus, the development of behavior after birth is organized in relation to the changing abilities of the child to process information and to utilize it in relation to its internal states. However, the progressive maturation of underlying neurobiological systems interacts powerfully with these processes and interposes its own schedule of changes on the course of cognitive and emotional development. For instance, maturation of the neuromuscular systems for voluntary walking at 12 months opens up a whole new world of environmental interactions that make new forms of learning and new states of emotion and motivation possible. In the same way, maturation of the neural systems necessary for states of sustained wakefulness and attention at 2 months, provides the impetus for a sudden acceleration of learning from experience.

From previous chapters we know that experience with the environment acts back upon the developing neural networks to speed or slow the multiplication of cells, the growth of dendritic processes, the formation of synaptic connections, and in general to alter the schedule and shape of neural maturation. Thus, there is a strong interaction between learning, behavioral states, and the processes of neurobiological maturation, as shown in Figure 12–1.

These three organizing forces mesh with each other in ways that complement and augment the actions of each one alone. This synergistic action creates a "multiplier" effect, which moves development forward rapidly and in many different areas of behavior organization simultaneously. For example, the capacity to retrieve objects by reach at 5 months—in combination with state characteristics of arousal, attention, and together with new associative learning capacities—leads to a quantum jump in the formation of new concepts and motivation states in the ensuing weeks. For different events in development and for different behavioral systems, some arrows in Figure 12–1 would have to be drawn very heavily and others very lightly, to signify that some directions in this interaction are relatively more important than others in different situations. The task of developmental research, in fact, is the working out of such a pattern of arrows for each behavioral event.

This triple interaction may be likened to an engine driving behavior development forward from infancy to childhood. But the components of this engine are different from machines, because they are themselves changing and changed by the interaction. Thus, the characteristics of early learning and early memory formation are different from those processes as we know them in adulthood. Similarly, states of arousal, motivation, and emotion become increasingly differentiated and take on many new properties in the course of these early months.

In this chapter I will discuss some of the special properties of learning, memory, and internal states during early development and show how they change in relation to underlying processes of neural maturation. The resulting uneven course of early development, with its surges, plateaus, shifts, and discontinuities will be the topic of the final section.

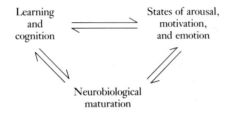

FIGURE 12-1
Interaction between organizing forces
of rapid change in infancy and childhood.

EARLY LEARNING AND COGNITION

Of the three components discussed above, learning is the one that offers the greatest capacity for adaptive change. Learning provides us with our most specific and sophisticated forms of behavior organization, contributes to the formation of our cognitive abilities, and provides the variety and range of our inner experience.

If learning is defined as a change in behavior brought about through experience, then most of the formative developmental interactions described in the previous chapters must be considered to be forms of learning. But we do not ordinarily use that word to describe those processes. Instead, learning is generally reserved for changes in behavior based on *associations* between cues and events. In ordinary language, the word *learning* refers to knowledge or information gained through experience. In infants and animals this new knowledge is revealed through behavior instead of words.

We are usually speaking of rapid changes of behavior in relation to specific aspects of the environment when we use the word learning, although the concept is fuzzy at the edges. For example, habituation and sensitization (see Chapter 3) are sometimes classed as simple forms of learning and at other times as physiological adaptations. More complex processes involving associations between cues and events were described for the infant as forming the transition from biology to psychology (Chapter 7). In fact, it is the establishing of associations through learned behavior that is thought to underlie the acquisition of mental representations and the formation of concepts. The storage and recall of such mental representations is a function of memory and their manipulation is thought.

These transitions from sensory experience and motor behavior to concept formation in infants and young children were proposed as the origin of intelligence by Piaget in 1936. It is interesting to realize that his theory may well have had its roots in his early career as a biologist when he discovered that a species of deepwater shellfish (*Limnea stagnalis*) dredged up from the depths of the Lake of Geneva changed their characteristic shell shape and markings in subsequent generations, when raised by him from larvae in shallow water aquaria without the deep mud of the lake bottom (1). The structural characteristics that had previously been thought to represent differences between species were thus shown to be the product of interactions of the young with their early environment. For in shallow, turbulent water, Piaget found that the snail's foot increased its activity and repeatedly changed shape with the alternate contraction and relaxation that enabled it to maintain its position against the water currents. This activity of the foot resulted in widening and shortening of the shell so that this new generation of adults more closely resembled the shallow-water species than their deep-water ancestors. Piaget went on to study the development of cognition in children and proposed a series of psychological processes based on this biological model, by which the structure of knowledge is acquired through a functional adaptation within preexisting biological structures, based on the child's encounters with its environment. Imitation and other complex forms of learning are clearly necessary for the formation of such higher cognitive structures but are probably influenced by biologically determined predispositions.

There are several interesting characteristics of early learning in the human, which are also found in young animals and which suggest the operation of hitherto unsuspected biological forces in the development of learning and memory. One might expect, for example, that habituation and sensitization, which we think of as primitive forms of learning (see Chapter 3), might develop before classical (Pavlovian) conditioning, and that operant or instrumental learning would be the last of the four to appear, since it underlies the higher forms of adaptive behavior. However, this notion does not seem to be clearly supported by the facts, and our judgments regarding "primitive" and "advanced" forms of learning may have to be modified accordingly. First of all, different sensory and response systems mature at different rates and thus become amenable to learning at different times. This means that the cues and responses involved in locating a nipple and beginning to suck can be utilized for learning much earlier than a tone signaling a pinprick to the bottom of the foot.

Thus, as investigators have begun to look in the "right" sensory and motor systems of infants, they have found all forms of learning taking place earlier and earlier in development. With this in mind, the current notion that instrumental learning of behavior is possible at birth, while classical conditioning cannot take place until 4 weeks later in the human, must be taken with considerable reserve. The disparity does not seem to be based on an inability of the newborn to form associative connections between stimuli, since classical conditioning in some physiological systems is present at birth. By the third month of life, quite complex forms of behavior can be rapidly learned by a combination of classical and instrumental techniques in a feeding situation. What takes time to develop are complex associations, discrimination, abstraction, and memory, which require new cognitive strategies that must be built up over time.

The simpler forms of learning—habituation and sensitization—are present at birth in the human and even during fetal life, but seem to be weak and unstable for the first month or two of life. For reasons of discomfort, repeated trains of stimuli cannot be tested easily with human infants, and the strong stimuli required for sensitization can never be studied experimentally, although they occur frequently enough in natural life to be of great interest. Therefore, we should turn to animal studies to find out more about the early development of these fundamental forms of behavior plasticity.

Studies by Campbell in young rats allow us to gain a better understanding of changes in the properties of habituation and sensitization during early development. Habituation of a limb withdrawal response to rapidly repeated painful stimuli takes place at the same rate from 3 days of postnatal age onward. No changes occur in sensory threshold for this response over time, indicating very early development of this system and stability during a period of rapid change in many other systems. General responses to the stimulus, such as vocalization and movement of other limbs, habituate along with the specific limb withdrawal movement. Changing the site of stimulation restores all responses, suggesting that the process of habituation takes place in sensory rather than motor pathways, as if the animal were becoming progressively less perceptive of a specific stimulus. There seems to be a developmental shift in the neural mechanisms for this process, since central nervous system cuts isolating the cerebrum from midbrain and lower centers abolishes habituation in 15-day or older animals but has no effect on 5- or 10-day-olds. The locus for this simple form of learning seems to have shifted upward in the brain, a pattern I have described before in the control of other behaviors (see Chapter 5).

Sensitization (increased responsiveness after one or more powerful stimuli) has a different developmental course. The very young infant rat in the first week of life shows marked short-term sensitization, with diffuse and disorganized behavior, that lasts a number of minutes immediately following stimulation. During the second week of life the pattern of response becomes confined to a single discrete and coordinated withdrawal from the stimulus. Transition from the diffuse to the localized response to strong stimulation can clearly be observed in human infants during the first 2 months of life.

Whereas habituation in these young animals was found to be "forgotten" quite rapidly at all ages, and 1-week-olds no longer showed increased responsiveness to shock 18 hours after the original experience, 2-week-olds showed long-term sensitization. This age difference in the capacity for long-term sensitization coincides with the disappearance of the short-term sensitization described above.

This alteration of strategies of simple learning would appear to be related to underlying events in the development of infants' central nervous systems. The neural mechanism for the appearance of long-term sensitization is not yet clear, but its predecessor, short-term sensitization, appears to be localized to the spinal cord. In this simple model system, we may be able to learn how maturational events in the central nervous system interact with the neural substrates for these simple forms of learning to produce rapid changes in behavioral potential. In the case of habituation, there is little or no change in the behavior, despite shifts in the neural substrates mediating it; whereas in the case of sensitization, the behavior undergoes marked changes over the same time period.

We cannot conclude from the slow development of sensitization in limb withdrawal that more complex forms of associative and instrumental learning are impossible in younger animals, however. Other behavioral systems, such as those mediating ingestive behavior, appear to be capable of both associative and instrumental learning as early as 2 days after birth in rats (see review by Blass, Hall, and Teicher). Learning capacities clearly mature at different rates in different systems, so that the schedule of development for learning is heterogeneous within each individual. These results demonstrate that the level of sophistication of the answer that an infant can give depends in part on how you ask the question.

INFANTILE AMNESIA AND THE CONSTRUCTION OF MEMORIES

> In my opinion we take the fact of infantile amnesia—the loss, that is, of the memories of the first years of our life—much too easily; and we fail to look upon it as a strange riddle. We forget how high are the intellectual achievements and how complicated the emotional impulses of which a child of some four years is capable, and we ought to be positively astonished that the memory of later years has as a rule preserved so little of these mental processes, especially as we have every reason to suppose that these same forgotten childhood achievements have not, as might be thought, slipped away without leaving their mark on the subject's development, but have exercised a determining influence for the whole of his later life. And in spite of this unique efficacy they have been forgotten! This suggests that there are conditions for remembering (in the sense of conscious reproducing) of a quite special kind, which have evaded recognition by us up to now. [Sigmund Freud, 1901] (2)

The paradoxical situation wherein an early experience may produce long-term developmental effects without leaving a clear memory trace was beautifully described by Freud at the turn of the century. The biological processes responsible for long-term effects of early experiences on brain and behavior have been described in previous chapters. But why does an adult not remember an experience that occurred at 3 or 4 years of age, whereas if it occurred at 8 or 9 it will never be forgotten? Through free-association techniques and from the analysis of dreams, Freud surmised that memories of childhood are not lost, but simply *overlaid*. Piaget has been able to demonstrate just such a process (3). Children from 3 to 6 years of age were shown a pattern of sticks arranged in descending order by height (see Figure 12–2). One week later, when asked to reproduce the pattern from memory by choosing sticks from a large supply of varying sizes, the responses were different, according to the ages of the children, as illustrated. Six months later, when again asked to reconstruct the original array from memory, all the children said they remembered it, but their memories seemed to have changed. The youngest produced what the middle group had produced 6 months earlier, and the oldest group now reproduced exactly what they had originally seen. In these short-term experiments, we are not dealing with loss of memory; in fact, the children's memories became more accurate in the case of the oldest

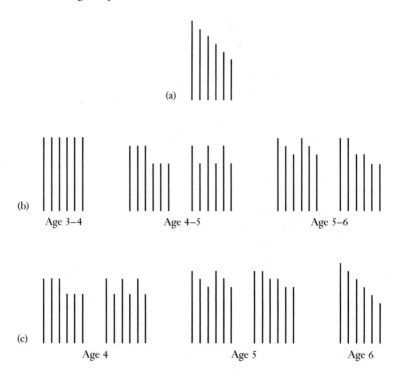

FIGURE 12-2
(a) Patterns of sticks shown by Piaget to young children of different ages.
(b) One week later the children drew what they remembered. *(c)* Six months
later the same children recalled different patterns.

group. What is demonstrated, in the 6-month recall tests, is the existence of an extensive reordering and reconstruction of what had been
remembered within a week of the experience. Apparently, major
changes in cognitive processes during this period of development can
overlay and otherwise alter recall of the original pattern. Clearly, memories are not stored and recalled like photographs in an album. Periods
of extensive reorganization during development may alter memories
beyond recall.

Freud became convinced that the reorganizing process responsible
for infantile amnesia was directed at the motivations, states, and experiences of infantile sexuality, which had to be altered to suit the
requirements of society as the child grew up. This explanation, based
on the inferred psychologic process of repression, is widely accepted
by clinicians. But it requires the operation of very high order cognitive
processes and the existence of uniquely human attributes such as cul-

tural taboos. The recent discovery of evidence for infantile amnesia in monkeys, dogs, and even in young rats forces us to ask whether we need to rely entirely on higher order processes in order to understand infantile amnesia in humans. Possibly there are simpler processes operating in the human case, of which we are entirely unaware. Understanding the processes involved in animals such as the rat may thus suggest what to look for in the human.

Three-week-old rat pups soon forget cues associated with either painful stimulation or food, while 5-week-old or adult rats, with carefully equated learning experience, remember the cues for many months thereafter. It is particularly surprising that juvenile rats that are shocked in a black box and rapidly learn to avoid such places, will show no signs of having had any such experience when retested 2 weeks later. One might have expected that such an experience would make an indelible impression; it does for an older animal. It was soon discovered that the tendency to forget was markedly alleviated by "reminders" of the original experience (as reviewed in Spear and Campbell). Single brief reexperiencing of the cue–shock association at weekly intervals was found to maintain the avoidance response, while such brief experiences produced no learning in control groups that had not been conditioned at 20 days. Subsequently it has been found that brief experience with the cues alone—or more effective yet, the shock alone at weekly intervals—will also reinstate the learned behavior. Most interesting, perhaps, is that hormones such as ACTH or epinephrine, which were released during the original conditioning, are capable of acting as reinstating agents when given at weekly intervals without either the environmental cues or the electric shock. This is a highly specific matter, for the artificial stimulants, amphetamine or strychnine, are ineffective in reinstating the previously learned behavior.

It might be supposed that some event in neural maturation, occurring at a particular interval after the original learning, could serve to overlay, reorganize, or inhibit the memory trace. But when reminders in the form of a single associative event were given at different intervals (5, 10 and 15 days) after the original learning, they were all equally effective in reinstating the learned behavior. Most recently it has been found that exposure to shock or to other stressful experiences a day or two *before* the learning experience at 3 weeks also tended to promote retention of the fear response, without exerting any effect on the learning of the behavior.

What these studies are beginning to tell us is that although young animals are capable of learning rapidly from new experiences, they are also predisposed to soon forget what they have learned unless the experience recurs again. Such an arrangement would appear to have survival value in that only those contingencies that had some probability of occurring repeatedly would be carried in memory into adulthood. Otherwise, infants might learn to avoid or to approach too many different cues in their environment. Memories are apparently retained in a form available for recall by some process of reactivation that requires only part of the experience in order to promote recall of associated cues and relationships. These studies point the way toward an understanding of why certain major traumatic experiences we have in our childhood continue to govern our behavior quite specifically while others exert only more general "characterologic" effects or seem to have been almost completely overcome.

STATES OF AROUSAL, MOTIVATION, AND EMOTION

These concepts are not easy to deal with even in the adult because of the degree of inference required and because state concepts encourage sloppy thinking, such as the fallacious use of instinct or drive concepts. Therefore, it is not surprising that in the rapidly developing infant when sensory, motor, and integrative organization is changing rapidly according to schedules we do not yet understand, inferences about states of motivation or emotion become enormously difficult to sort out from changes in other aspects of behavior organization. For example, does an infant lose interest in nursing from its mother's breast or a bottle because of a change in motivation, changes in sensory capacities, changes in the mother's behavior that produce learning, or the maturation of higher centers inhibiting early reflex systems for sucking? What basic emotional states does the infant come equipped with at birth, and which are acquired during later development? If the potential for an emotional state requires specific experiences for its full development, what might these experiences be?

Although beginnings have been made in answering some of these questions, as described in previous chapters, the topic of motivational and emotional development is the area of our greatest ignorance about our origins, despite its crucial role in learning, social interaction, and in the very survival of the infant.

The place to begin is with states of arousal. The major categories here—wakefulness and the two stages of sleep—are reasonably easy to define. By a combination of physiological and behavioral criteria, these states can be identified reasonably clearly. The relative time spent in the three states during the 24-hour day, and the pattern of alteration between periods in each state, can be mapped from infancy to adulthood. Much of this data has been described in previous chapters.

The first 2 months of life after birth bring two major changes: the marked increase in the total amount of time spent awake (from less than 6 hours to more than 8 hours per day) and the shift of sleep toward the hours of darkness, which begins at 6–8 weeks. The decline in the relative proportions of active, rapid-eye-movement (REM) sleep in relation to quiet, slow-wave sleep (SWS) continues steadily throughout the first few years of life. Although we still have no clear idea of why infants spend so much time in the REM state, much recent evidence favors the view that this state may be necessary for some form of information-processing related to the interactions experienced during the day. One particularly dramatic experiment involved the effects of short daily periods of social interaction on mice which were isolated from weaning to adulthood (4). If the mice were sleep-deprived during the hour after their socialization experience, they grew up to act in the same hyperaggressive way that totally isolated mice did. However, if the period of sleep deprivation took place before the social interaction, and sleep was possible immediately afterward, the mice showed the effects of the socialization by acquiring nearly normal patterns of adult interaction, without any abnormal aggressiveness. Other data (5) on the neurochemistry of REM sleep show that this state is characterized by high levels of activity in biochemical systems thought to mediate the consolidation of memory. Furthermore, REM sleep percentage is increased following complex training tasks.

Thus, we have some evidence to support the notion that REM sleep is a state during which traces of the day's activities are reprocessed and integrated into the developing systems for the organization of behavior. Other than this hypothesis, we have little to suggest why young children spend so much time asleep. If deprived, they tend to make up the loss in subsequent nights. It is easy to suppose that all this time is put to some essential purpose, but almost no evidence exists to suggest what precisely the need for sleep may be.

There are other needs or motivational states, such as hunger, which are somewhat better understood, at least for adults. But in the young, we become acutely aware of how our inferences about motivation are based on implicit assumptions about the systems regulating performance of the consummatory act. For example, we might assume that human infants nursing at the breast stop sucking, come off the nipple, and go to sleep when their need for milk is satisfied. But it has been found that 90 percent of the total milk is taken in the first 4 minutes of a breast feeding (6) and all subsequent sucking is nonnutritive. The question of why they stop sucking becomes a question of why they go on and on. The solution has been to suppose that sucking in infants is a fixed-action pattern, released by the stimulus of a nipple in the mouth. Therefore, it continues regardless of milk, so long as the nipple is in the mouth.

At this point, evidence from animal experiments (7) is of use, because competing theories can be tested by experiments that would be unconscionable in humans. Prolonged separation from the mother rat has been shown to increase rates of sucking, even on a nipple that produces no milk, and to elicit a pattern of sucking that normally occurs following milk delivery (8). If milk is provided by a fine tube while the infant rat sucks on the mother's teat, the infant will continue to ingest milk until it literally chokes to death, rather than stop sucking, come off the nipple, and go to sleep. Finally, young rats will learn to solve a maze in order to obtain the experience of sucking on a dry nipple. These findings have led us to ask whether sucking may not have its own motivational system in infancy which is independent of hunger and even in defiance of internal signals for satiety.

While the systems for the regulation of sucking seem to have priority over metabolic requirements in the infant and even over internal danger signals such as stomach distention and regurgitation, a system for the regulation of nutrient intake according to need clearly exists. If a rat pup is given milk while away from its mother by placing it near a puddle of milk on the floor or giving milk through a mouth tube, the infant will take increased amounts only if there has been a previous period of nutrient deprivation. So it has a neural system to regulate nutrient intake according to nutrient requirements (an appetitive motivational system) but this system is overridden by other behavioral control systems early in development. A week or two later, with increased maturity, the regulation of milk intake is the same, whether the consummatory act is nursing or solid food ingestion.

We can conclude that the infant may regulate its behavior according to set points that are quite different from adults, and may experience motivational states whose existence we do not even suspect. These special motivational states may take precedence over the more familiar states of hunger and pain. Thus, we should not infer states in children without gaining more knowledge about what form of sensory input is being regulated, by what acts the state is terminated, and how to differentiate one motivational state from another. This shift in attention toward the study of how behaviors are regulated has resulted in the discovery of how differently the infant perceives, evaluates, and responds to its environment.

Emotions serve both motivational and communicative functions. They may be considered to be a form of motivational state that has to do with the individual's external environment, particularly its social environment, and are generally inferred from the so-called affective behaviors, like crying and smiling, which we observe and emotionally respond to ourselves. From the very beginning, learning and the development of cognitive structures are dependent on states of pleasure and displeasure arising from stimuli and acts that go beyond the provision of bodily need. This phenomenon was described in Chapter 7 and forms a basis for curiosity, play, and creativity.

Research by Ekman has revealed that six emotions are recognized across a wide range of human cultures: happiness, surprise, fear, sadness, anger, and disgust. We can presume that these states are recognized as different because identifying them allows us to predict the behaviors that will result when we attempt to interact with someone who is "wearing" such an expression. The newborn does not have the capacity to organize these facial expressions or to coordinate such a variety of predictable behavioral repertoires. (The influence of visual interaction on the development of facial expression of affect is described above in Chapter 11.)

By the end of their first year after birth, however, infants show a panoply of facial expressions (9) and often can be precipitated into states that appear to fluctuate between surprise, fear, and happiness; for example, when a parent puts on a novel hat or a stranger bends down over the infant. The state that predominates will be determined by the context (10), the age of the infant, and the infant's previous experience, as well as by the special features and behavior of the stimulus itself. Thus, cognitive factors play an important role in determining emotional states. For example, the ability of the child to recognize its familiar mother within the novel stimulus array of a strange hat or mask depends on the child's cognitive capacities; that is, the flexibility and accuracy of its schema for mother. Discrepancy between expectation and outcome appears to underlie positive affects such as smiling or laughter, as well as the negative affect of fear. The degree of discrepancy determines which of the two will occur; the more severe the discrepancy, the more likely it will elicit fear. These affectively expressed states are organized so that in the one, behaviors of approach will predominate and in the other situation, the infant will tend to withdraw or try to escape.

Tobach has proposed that the emotions develop from two basic predispositions: approach and avoidance. These basic response tendencies exist in the simplest organisms, even single-celled creatures (see Chapter 3). States in which one or the other tendency is very likely to occur become differentiated into the major positive or negative emotional states, as the goals of the associated behaviors become increasingly circumscribed and defined in the course of development. One of the major principles in the course of this development, in human and animal alike, is that fear and avoidance responses to novel situations are not present at birth but emerge in late infancy. We can easily imagine that the survival value of such a schedule might be that it would allow time for the formation of attachment to parents. The appearance of fear is a dramatic developmental event that alters the child's interactions from that point forward for the rest of his or her life and marks one of the discontinuities in development. People have long argued whether the development of fear is a response to a hostile world or a basic biological response tendency that would appear no matter how the infant is treated. Present evidence leans toward the latter point of view. The interaction of forces and events that surround the emergence of fear of the unfamiliar at about 7–9 months is one of the topics of the last section in this chapter.

NEUROBIOLOGICAL MATURATION

Hidden though its events may be from ordinary observation, the force of neural maturation makes itself evident in the changing nature and special properties of early learning, memory, and internal states, as described above. In addition, the neurobiological processes involved guide and constrain the nature of the behaviors likely to emerge from the interaction of the forces of rapid change. This concept of an underlying strategy of development is implicit in the regularities of the development of behavior and is perhaps most clearly shown in the embryology of anatomical structures. Waddington (11) represented these progressive constraints in his "epigenetic landscape." The ball in Figure 12–3, representing the embryologic tissue, at first is free to roll

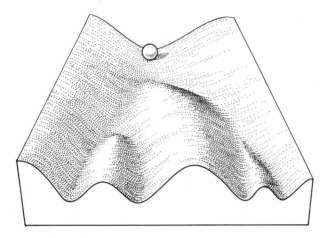

FIGURE 12-3
Waddington's "epigenetic landscape." The ball represents some tissue or behavior at an early stage in ontogeny. Development is represented by the ball descending through the landscape. The mechanisms regulating development are represented by the position and shape of the valleys. (From C. H. Waddington, *The Strategy of the Genes*. London: Allen and Unwin, 1957.)

along a variety of different trajectories. But as time goes on, the ball becomes more and more restricted in its possibilities of lateral movement so that certain alternatives are no longer open. In addition, the number of possible outcomes is limited. The landscape can represent the developmental pathways for behavior as well as for embryological tissue and gives a visual analogy for the processes by which behavior develops into a very definite pattern for each species.

The position and shapes of the valleys in the landscape are built in to the organization of behavior by the processes described in Chapters 8 and 9 on the early history of neurons and the formation of the brain. Cells and neural pathways become committed or *canalized* into one or another of several alternative structures and functions. These are then expressed in the perceptual and motor predispositions of the newborn and later in the ways the child is predisposed to process information and to behave. These predispositions account for the characteristics of behavior that are similar for all mammals, such as attachment between mother and infant, and for all humans, such as the development of language. These predispositions clearly influence the course of learning, memory, and even concept formation, since certain things are much more readily learned, remembered, and conceived by humans than other animals. Furthermore, individuals each show their own special predispositions from an early age.

However, the processes represented in the epigenetic landscape are not limited to those taking place at the level of neurons and their connections. Some contours represent properties of organized systems like learning and complex states, and thus are intimately involved in the child's ongoing experience with its environment. There is a place in this analogy, then, for the interactions emphasized above.

The valleys in Figure 12–3, with their inclined troughs, also represent the self-stabilizing nature of the underlying strategy of development. That is, an obstacle in one of the valleys results in a temporary deviation in the ball's path, followed by an eventual return to the groove. Examples of such a self-correcting property have been given in Chapter 11 in relation to recovery from early maternal deprivation, but the principle involved in this capacity has broad applicability in development. The implication that there is more than one route to a final outcome is amply borne out in the history of behavior development, for example, in the emotional development of blind children, as described in Chapter 11.

As mentioned in the beginning of this chapter, neurobiological maturation becomes less and less obvious as a force in behavior development during the months after birth. It is hard to follow because its important events are hidden from ordinary observation. It is possible to correlate studies of the maturation of neural structures, using autopsy material, with the development of new behaviors in normal infants. And from these studies, we become directly aware of the importance of neurobiological maturation for the appearance of the major advances in behavioral organization. This structure–function correlation approach has been particularly useful in the case of changes in reflexes and posture. However, our knowledge about the brain structures underlying more complex behaviors is too minimal for this approach to be very productive as yet. Furthermore, one really needs to make correlations between neural and behavioral maturation *within* the same individual because there are enormous differences in the rates of maturation and times of onset of behaviors in different individuals.

A useful approach has been recording brain waves (EEG), heart rate, and other electrophysiological measures as an index of the maturation of neural systems underlying behavior. Changes in these measures can then be correlated with the appearance of learning capacities, cognition, and affective states in an effort to explore the timing and interrelationship between the three components of the "engine" described at the beginning of this chapter.

One of the most far reaching of these studies has been the work of Emde, who found two major nodal points or *biobehavioral shifts*, as he called them, during the first year after birth. Table 12–1 outlines his findings according to the EEG, electrophysiology, and heart rate measures he used as indices of shifts in neurobiological maturation.

TABLE 12–1 Synopsis of changes in electrophysiological indices of neurobiological maturation, together with changes in emotional states, perception, learning, and social communication at two ages found by Emde to involve rapid shifts in many systems ("biobehavioral shifts").

	2–3 Months	*7–9 Months*
EEG	Onset EEG sleep spindles	Onset K-complexes
Electrophysiology	Day–Night Differentiation Sleep Onset: REM→ NonREM 1st Wakefulness Plateau	2nd Wakefulness Plateau
Heart rate	Heart rate response to tone shifts from + to −	Heart rate response to visual cliff and stranger shifts from − to +
Affect state	Onset of social smile Offset of unexplained crying	Onset of stranger anxiety
Perceptual	Increase scanning directed at eyes or face	
Learning	Onset of habituation Rapid increased conditionability— particularly associative type	Increase in attentiveness begins Rapid increases in memory (e.g., object permanence)
Parent's response	"A human, at last"	"A special relationship with me, at last"

There was clear evidence of a general clustering of changes in the areas of cognition, affect, and biological maturation at two points, 2–3 months and 7–9 months postnatal age, which were reflected in new responses of the parents to the babies. However, as he studied the relationship of these changes to each other more closely, Emde found that shifts in cognitive, emotional and electrophysiological development often did not occur in a fixed relationship to each other. For example, it had been thought that the emergence of the emotional state of "stranger anxiety" at 7–8 months of age was dependent on the prior achievement of a certain stage in cognitive development in which an infant is capable of internalized expectation, that is when "out of sight" is no longer "out of mind." According to this line of reasoning, the infant *expects* an approaching person to be the mother, and when the stranger's face is perceived the resultant discrepancy produces distress. The cognitive capacity (*object permanence*) can be independently assessed by standardized tests involving a favorite toy and cloth screens. The capacity for object permanence is fully achieved when the infants push aside the screen to grab the toy they saw the tester hide there. When infants were tested repeatedly for the emergence of both behaviors, more than half of them developed stranger anxiety *before* the stage of object permanence was achieved, as defined by such cognitive testing. This was not an isolated finding representing some inappropriateness of the particular testing procedure, for Emde found that "Again and again . . . in virtually all sequences we could imagine . . . of emergence of EEG phenomena, cognitive phenomena and affect expressions . . . one or more variables could be found grossly out of sequence in individual cases" (12).

This pattern of clustering without invariant sequence is an example of how schedules of development in different systems may synchronize roughly with each other to initiate a new series of interactions based on new capacities in several major systems emerging simultaneously. The inference here is that processes of neural maturation underlying affective state organization, learning, and cognition have their own intrinsic timetables that are coordinated but not dependent on each other. These simultaneous shifts are an alternative mode of development to the processes described above in which, for instance, a sudden spurt of new cognitive growth cannot occur until maturation of neural substrates for reaching and retrieving objects has been completed.

STAGES, DISCONTINUITIES, AND CONSTRAINTS

Shifts in the organization of behavior form the basis for dividing the course of development into *stages*, each of which is characterized by the operation of certain fairly predictable principles of cognitive, affective, and perceptual-motor function. The time of the stable periods (or stages) and the periods of rapid change (often called *surges, discontinuities*, or *biobehavioral shifts*) depend on the perspective of the viewer to a considerable extent. For example, a person interested in sleep state organization, as in the previous example, will see different stages and transitions than another who is interested in the organization of ingestive behavior. Theorists such as Freud, Piaget, Spitz, and Erikson differ significantly from each other and from those more biologically inclined, such as Hughlings Jackson and Heinz Werner, on the nature and timing of the important stages of development. They also disagree on whether to attribute the timing of stage shifts to timetables of neural maturation or to the time necessary for completion of behavioral interaction processes at the previous stage. The recent research findings described in previous chapters have shown the extent to which neurobiological development is *itself* strongly affected by interactions with the environment. As we slowly gather more evidence and are less dependent on inductions from powerful theories for the definition of stages and shifts, more agreement should be possible. It appears likely that each separate behavioral system may well have its own characteristic schedule influenced by events in other systems only to a limited degree. This would be consistent with current concepts on *heterochrony* in the development of organ systems as discussed in Chapter 1.

"Discontinuity" is a relative term. It is used to convey the sense that, whereas during some long periods development appears to progress slowly and steadily, at other short periods there are changes so rapid they give the appearance of totally new forms of behavior. These sudden changes raise questions of how we are to trace a given behavior across such shifts that may involve a complete reversal in the relationship of one function to another (for example, see Table 12–1).

The significance of these periods of rapid change lies not only in the challenge they present for developmental theory but also in the relevance they may have for the impact of environmental events. If a child is forced to adapt to a new situation while in the midst of one of these periods, it may have a greater or more prolonged disorganizing effect than if he or she confronts a new situation during a stable phase. Second, those rapid shifts involve affective and cognitive capacities that have great meaning for parents. With the new emergence, it is like a rebirth for the parent, eliciting a whole new set of responses and ushering in a new, qualitatively different interaction. The feedback effects of the new ways in which adults and older children respond to the infant exert a multiplier action, thus increasing the extent of such sudden surges in development.

There are, however, powerful constraints on the extent and outcome of these rapid shifts in behavioral development. The sources of these constraints are many, and include the predictable responses of a stable environment, the persistence of memories and of learned habits, and the organizing function of internal states as well as the intrinsic schedules and patterning of neurobiological maturation.

Considering the many influences toward stability, it is remarkable how much children change in basic characteristics of their behavior from one year to the next. Thomas and Chess' classic study on behavioral measures of temperament (e.g., activity level, persistence) found no significant correlations from one year to the next in one-third of their measures during the first 5 years of life and only one of nine measures (threshold of responsiveness) showed statistically significant continuity over the 4-year period from age 1 to 5, and that at a very low level of correlation. These figures for the entire sample of 100 children do not express the fact that some children *did* show consistency in a number of behavioral traits over the entire study period from infancy to midadolescence and that others showed consistency in some aspects during one period of several years and in other aspects during another period. Thus, not only were there remarkable temperamental differences between individual infants from 3 months of age onward, but there were marked differences in the stability of these behavioral characteristics over the period of childhood.

The discontinuous nature of development poses a challenge to simple notions based either on nature or nurture. And the examples of continuity make it impossible to take the position that the course of development is controlled by random events. We are left with an uneasy situation for which we lack a simple unifying theory. Considering these facts, it seems most profitable for the present to focus our attention on trying to understand the workings of the interactions that take place during the different periods of life, until we learn enough about the processes involved to formulate a general theory of development.

SUMMARY

The rapid changes that occur in the infant's behavior during the first few years after birth are the result of a powerful interweaving of three organizational forces: learning, internal states, and the maturation of underlying neural systems.

The capacity for different forms of learning at a given age depends on maturational events in the neural substrates for the behaviors required, and this may help explain why learning capacities develop at different rates and sequences in different behavioral systems. Piaget has taught us how concepts may be built up through early learning experiences involving simple sensorimotor behavior. In this process, reconstruction of concepts and memories is continually taking place. It may be that the rapidity and extent of this internal reorganization during the 3–4 years of infancy accounts for the phenomenon of infantile amnesia, whereby so many experiences of our first years are lost to later recall. But recent exploration of early memory in animals such as the rat suggest that unsuspected neurobiological events may underlie infantile amnesia.

The force of underlying maturational events is clearly shown in the development of the states of arousal, motivation, and emotion. The role of sleep states in information processing and memory consolidation, the interplay of motivational systems involved in sucking and early ingestive behavior, and the late emergence of states of fear are briefly discussed as examples.

Neurobiological processes serve to "canalize" development along a limited number of alternative paths, which are reflected in the perceptual, cognitive, and affective predispositions of the infant. Studies using physiological measures have begun to trace the progress of neurobiological maturation and to uncover the basis for "biobehavioral shifts" in development, which involve rapid alternations in the organization of internal states, learning, and memory.

The interaction of the forces of rapid change produce discontinuities in development that punctuate the transitions between stages. And although the timing and character of stages may vary according to the perspective and theoretical orientation of the observer, the fact is that most children are not very consistent in their behavior from one year to the next, even in basic traits of temperament. Such discontinuity challenges conventional concepts of development and points out how much more we need to know about the interactions and processes described in this chapter.

FURTHER READING

Blass, E. M., Hall, W. G., and Teicher, M. H. The ontogeny of suckling and ingestive behaviors. In J. Sprague and A. Epstein (Eds.), *Progress in Psychobiology and Physiological Psychology*. Vol. 8. New York: Academic Press, 1979. Pp. 243–299.

Bolles, R. C. *Learning Theory*. 2nd ed. New York: Holt, Rinehart and Winston, 1979.

Ekman, P., and Friesen, W. *Unmasking the Face*. Englewood Cliffs, N.J.: Prentice-Hall, 1975.

Emde, R. N., Gaensbauer, T. J., and Harmon, R. J. *Emotional Expression in Infancy. Psychological Issues*, Vol. 10, Monograph 37. New York: International Universities Press, 1976.

Kagan, J. The form of early development: continuity and discontinuity in emergent competences. *Archives of General Psychiatry*, 36:1047–1054, 1979.

Lewis, M., and Rosenblum, L. A. (Eds.) *The Origins of Fear*. New York: Wiley, 1974.

Piaget, J. The first year of life of the child (1927). The origins of intelligence in children (1936). The construction of reality in the child (1937). In H. E. Gruber and J. J. Voneche (Eds.), *The Essential Piaget: An Interpretive Reference and Guide*. New York: Basic Books, 1977. Pp. 197–296.

Plutchik, R. *Emotion: A Psychoevolutionary Synthesis*. New York: Harper & Row, 1980.

Spear, N. E., and Campbell, B. A. (Eds.) *The Ontogeny of Learning and Memory*. Hillsdale, N.J.: Laurence Erlbaum Associates, 1979.

Thomas, A., and Chess, S. *Temperament and Development*. New York: Brunner/Mazel, 1977.

Tobach, E. Some guidelines to the study of the evolution and development of emotion. In L. R. Aronson, E. Tobach, D. S. Lehrman, and J. S. Rosenblatt (Eds.) *Development and Evolution of Behavior*. San Francisco: W. H. Freeman and Company, 1970. Pp. 238–253.

REFERENCES CITED

1. Piaget, J. Notes on the biology of deepwater limnea. In H. E. Gruber and J. J. Vaneche (Eds.), *The Essential Piaget: An Interpretive Reference and Guide*. New York: Basic Books, 1977. Pp. 14–18.

2. Freud, S. *Psychopathology of Everyday Life* (1901). In J. Strachey (Ed.), Standard Edition, Vol. 6. London: Hogarth Press, 1960. P. 46.

3. Piaget, J., and Inhelder, B. *Memory and Intelligence*. New York: Basic Books, 1973.

4. Watson, F. M. C., and Henry, J. P. Loss of socialized patterns of behavior in mouse colonies following daily sleep disturbance and maturation. *Physiology and Behavior*, 18:119–123, 1977.

5. Pearlman, C. A. REM sleep and information processing: evidence from animal studies. *Neuroscience and Biobehavioral Review*, 3:57–68, 1979.

6. Lucas, A., Lucas, P. J., and Baum, J. D. Pattern of milk flow in breast-fed infants. *Lancet*, 2:57–58, 1979.

7. Blass, E. M., Hall, W. G., and Teicher, M. H. The ontogeny of suckling and ingestive behaviors. In J. Sprague and A. Epstein (Eds.), *Progress in Psychobiology and Physiological Psychology*. Vol. 8. New York: Academic Press, 1979. Pp. 243–299.

8. Brake, S. C., Wolfson, V., and Hofer, M. A. Electromyographic patterns associated with nonnutritive sucking in 11–13-day-old rat pups. *Journal of Comparative Physiology and Psychology*, 93:760–770, 1979.

9. Young, G., and Decarie, T. G. An ethology-based catalogue of facial/vocal behaviour in infancy. *Animal Behaviour*, 25:95–107, 1977.

10. Sroufe, A., Waters, E., and Matas, L. Contextual determinants of infant affective response. In Lewis and Rosenblum, op. cit., pp. 49–72.

11. Waddington, C. H. *The Strategy of the Genes*. London: Allen and Unwin, 1957.

12. Emde, et al., op. cit., pp. 152–153.

13

The Origins
of Language

When the wild boy, Victor, was discovered near the village of Aveyron, France, in 1797, his teacher Itard hoped that study of his special case would "determine what he is and deduce from what he lacks, the hitherto uncalculated sum of knowledge and ideas which man owes to his education" (1). By that time, anecdotal accounts of a number of wild children had dispelled myths such as "Romulus and Remus" and ended the Medieval debate over whether a child allowed to grow up without human contact would speak Hebrew or Ancient Greek. Humans who do not hear language do not speak. But the men of the French Enlightenment wanted to know what "innate ideas" a person had before being touched by the prevailing culture. When it proved virtually impossible to teach Victor to speak, attention was turned to the mystery of language acquisition and to the more prevalent problems of the deaf mute.

We share with these men of nearly two centuries ago a frustrated curiosity about how we learn to speak and what our experience would be like without language. We even have our modern-day Victor in the form of Washoe and other chimpanzees being taught American Sign Language (Ameslan), used by deaf humans. To complete the tie with the past, the origins of Ameslan can be traced to Itard himself and to the School for Deaf Mutes in Paris where Victor was studied during the same years that the first deaf people were successfully taught a complex gestural language. Our first language is learned long before we arrive at school and we do not understand very well how it is acquired. We would like to know why Victor and other early isolated children have such great difficulty learning to talk and exactly what kinds of experience we *do* need in order to speak.

To begin to answer such questions, I will review evidence for the biological origins of language in three main areas: (1) the early stages of vocalization and speech processing in humans, (2) the critical periods for language acquisition and for neuroanatomical localization of language function, and (3) findings on the neurobiology and development of song in birds that suggest how the human findings may be understood.

FROM SOUNDS TO SPEECH

Human infants cry in the womb if air is substituted for amniotic fluid in order to do special X rays, and the newborn cry seems to be part of its repertoire of spontaneous behaviors as well as a communication of the infant's state in at least two modes. By a month or two of age, other sounds begin to make their appearance, and gradually "cooing" becomes more and more frequent up to about three months. Cooing occurs in a different state than crying, frequently when the infant is alone rather than in a social situation. During the third to fifth month, the infant introduces changes in pitch and articulation until full scale babbling begins at about 5 months. This babbling phase lasts for 4–6 more months and is a most interesting and puzzling behavior. To start with, it defies description and quantification. Observers have said that every sound of every human language is present in babbling; while this may not be strictly true, the variability is bewildering. The order in which new sounds appear is, however, quite consistent. Beginning with vowels formed in the middle of the mouth, the progression is both forward and backward in tongue position. Then consonants in their own predictable progression and finally clusters of vowel and consonant-like sounds make their appearance. Interestingly, babbling occurs most often when the infant is alone, and a hidden observer will also find the infant at times moving mouth and tongue without making sounds. These vocalizations become progressively dissociated from postural and behavioral movements over the 5–9-month span, while the length of utterances becomes progressively longer. Between 9 and 12 months, the length of utterances contracts again to the length of the first words produced.

After 12 months, babbling and its vast variety of phonetic forms disappears, leaving a small but rapidly expanding repertoire of sounds directly related to the phonological structure of language. These early words are increasingly used in the presence of familiar adults, first as single words to denote objects (or people) and then in two-word combinations with action words. The third phase is the addition of a questioning word. These words are put together according to rules that are not those of adult speech and are not simply a gradual convergence. Early rules are soon abandoned and new ones taken up for a time. An example of such structure in early language might be the sudden emergence of the phrase, "Harry wented!" Here the child is clearly using (although misapplying) a rule and clearly not simply imitating its parents. All these events and sequences in early language development are given in some detail because they are common to all children no matter what culture or language they grow up with. Even in adults, evidence of *deep structure* can be found to underlie all languages, although the common basis has not been clearly identified. The implication is that development imposes a form on the acquisition of language that determines when and how and what will be learned. But how can that be? What kinds of processes could possibly impose such a form on language, one of our most flexible functions?

In order to answer this question we should first look at the development of the *perception* of speech. In a previous chapter I described how newborns appear to be preadapted to respond selectively to speech sounds instead of other noises and that the right ear (and left cerebral hemisphere) discriminates between speech sounds better than the opposite side of the brain. Another capacity of the adult especially suited to the processing of speech—categorical perception—has been found to be present in infants as young as 1 month of age (2). If a graded series of synthetic speech sounds is presented to adults or newborns, they will have great difficulty in telling apart sounds that differ slightly in the characteristic of voice onset time. (The newborn tells us it can distinguish two sounds by responding to the second one with a change in heart rate when it has habituated to the first sound.) Along the continuum for voice onset durations, there is only *one* point across which small differences can easily be discriminated. All durations larger than this are perceived by the adult as "Pa" and all smaller values as "Ba." This strong tendency to categorize sounds into a few perceptually distinct groups is of obvious advantage for the acquisition of language, and it is striking that such perceptual processing is present in newborns. It suggests one process by which form is imposed on language acquisition from its beginnings in the newborn period.

CRITICAL PERIODS AND THE ROLE
OF EXPERIENCE

Another constraint in language acquisition is in timing: whereas a second language is acquired before puberty by steps similar to those for the first language and without formal instruction, after puberty the steps are different and formal training is almost always required. Foreign accents and full competency in syntax and semantics are rarely acquired after puberty but easily acquired before it. What events occur at this time of life that make language acquisition thereafter so different? Now that we realize the existence of such a critical period we have another explanation than idiocy for the wild boy Victor's disappointing inability to acquire speech, for he was just entering puberty at the time of his capture.

The critical period is evident also in our knowledge about the neurological substrates for language. Adults with extensive injuries to the left cerebral hemisphere lose and never can regain their capacity to speak or understand language, but if the same injury occurs before the age of 5, language can be relearned reasonably well. The percentage of cases of permanent aphasia in children over 5 is about the same as it is in adults.

Thus, the left hemisphere appears to become committed to language processing by age 5. By that time the other hemisphere apparently cannot take over that function, although at an earlier age it seems to be able to do so readily. The processes determining these characteristics of the neuroanatomical substrate for language are completely unknown, but we can get some hints as to the possible cellular basis for them by examining the early commitment of neurons in the visual system (Chapter 9).

These are the stages and the constraints on the timing of the experience necessary for the development of language. But what role does experience play in the early stages of the development of vocalization? Must an infant hear others in order to move through the early stages? Must he be able to hear himself?

Our clearest evidence comes from the world of the deaf, where hearing infants are raised in homes without spoken language and deaf infants grow up with speaking parents (3). Infants in both situations show the normal stages in development of vocalization through the first 3–6 months of life. Their crying is normal, with the same rhythms and variability; cooing develops normally and with the same duration and pattern. Even fussing is normal despite the fact that hearing parents respond much more frequently than the deaf to the fussing of their infants. By 6 months, babbling develops on schedule in deaf children, but is described as more monotonous than in hearing children. However, babbling is normal in the hearing children of deaf parents, who go on to learn two language systems, a sign language which they use with their parents, and normal spoken language which they use with visitors. Deaf children, on the other hand, fail to show the normal increase in variability of phonetic units normally found in the later stages of babbling. Instead they babble less and less frequently until they are mute, except for crying when distressed. If hearing aids are provided for both ears at this point, babbling will resume again, run a normal course, and the child will go on to learn spoken language. Tactile or visual stimulation cannot take the place of the auditory sense in providing what is necessary to maintain this precursor of language, babbling.

We may conclude that language develops into the stage of babbling without requiring sounds to imitate or consequences to follow vocal behavior. This does not mean that the level of vocalization over this first-month period is independent of the environment. Infants raised in institutions between birth and 6 months have lower levels of both crying and noncrying vocalization and of both vowel and consonant sound types than children raised in families. Apparently some non-auditory aspects of the early interaction with parents are important to the early development of vocalization, during the period when deaf and hearing children develop identically.

The earliest evidences for the role of specific experience in language development are during the period of babbling. Social reinforcement can increase the relative frequency of a given sound but does not alter the sequence of development and does not account for the appearance of new sounds. By 6–8 months, sound spectrographic analysis begins to show differences between Japanese and American infants and between American infants raised in Argentina and in the United States. Differences in intonation and stress have been found during this period between Russian and U.S. infants. Some of the characteristics of the adult language are apparently being picked up by the infant for the first time.

In summary, fully developed adult language shares a number of linguistic features across widely divergent and independent cultures, yet there are even more obvious differences specific to individual culture groups. Even within cultural groups, dialects sometimes separate regions to such a degree that their inhabitants cannot understand each other. The early stages of vocalization are surprisingly uniform, however, in their timing, sequence, and even fine structure, and there is growing evidence that speech sounds are selectively and specially processed starting virtually at birth. Despite these specialized sensory capacities that may underlie the constancies in the organization of language, vocalization develops normally up to six months without the benefit of hearing. The right hemisphere loses the capacity to organize language by the age of 5 years and the process of primary language acquisition is impossible after puberty.

It is puzzling that the hearing child in the silent household of deaf parents has a normal progression in babbling while the deaf child does not. And why the monotonous character of deaf babbling? Studies have shown that if vowel sounds are presented repeatedly to a normal babbling infant, the relative frequency of vowels will decrease in its utterances; or if consonants are presented, they in turn will start to drop out of its repertoire. This finding argues that the variability of babbling may be the result of infants producing sounds that are different from what they hear. If they hear nothing because they are deaf, they would not produce different kinds of sounds. On the other hand, evidence from somewhat older children at 1½–2 years of age, indicates that they are not attending to feedback from their own vocalizations and are oblivious to inaccuracies in their own speech that they readily perceive if the same inaccuracy is produced by another. This would suggest that babbling may be maintained by kinesthetic rather than vocal feedback and that the speech sounds of others are the major element in the progressive changes that take place. A decision between these views cannot be made at present.

Another puzzle that remains unsolved is why perceptual capacities for processing speech develop months before language, when we know that deafness occurring in adults has little effect on speech. What might the differences in perceptual and motor organization be at the two stages? Exactly what sort of vocalizations develop if one is deprived of listening to one's own species? Is there any mechanism in nature by which sounds perceived a long time before speech begins can influence complex vocalizations produced much later in life? The findings on early language acquisition in humans outlined above suggest a number of ideas about the biological basis for language, but do not tell a coherent story. They can be integrated into any one of several current theories, but such theories require the assumption of processes that may not exist anywhere in nature. An animal model can be very useful at this stage in our understanding to lend an empirical base for the existence of the inferred processes, to allow testing and clarification of theories, to generate new ideas as to how the phenomenon may be better studied in the human, and to allow work to proceed on the underlying neural mechanisms. The development of song in birds provides such a model.

SONG DEVELOPMENT IN BIRDS AS A MODEL

Recent studies by Marler on a variety of species of birds have provided examples of most of the characteristics outlined above for the acquisition of speech in humans. Songbirds have an early stage of food-begging vocalization, a later stage of "subsong" that has many parallels with human babbling and finally, a complex adult song that in a number of species has local regional variations or dialects. These age differences allow social distinctions to be made in breeding and in territorial defense. Information regarding sex, age, and the emotional state of the signaller are transmitted by distinctive variations in intonation, pitch, and amplitude. Furthermore, there is strong evidence of lateral specialization of the left hemisphere and left nerve to the larynx; cortical and subcortical structures and pathways mediating song have been clearly defined.

If male white-crowned sparrows do not hear song between 10 and 50 days of age, they develop only a few of the major components of their song, even if raised normally after this early critical period. If birds are deafened at various points in their acquisition of song, the contribution of specific experience in hearing themselves and others can be discovered. If sparrows or canaries are allowed to hear during the stage of food begging but are then deafened prior to the beginning of subsong next spring, they will begin to sing at the normal time but produce only scratchy, buzzy vocalizations with components that change suddenly and without a consistent pattern. If they are deafened somewhat later, during the period of subsong but before a stable adult song pattern has been acquired, their newly acquired song structure will deteriorate and only a few elements of typical song will ever be produced. Finally, deafening even later, after song has "crystallized," will not affect the quality or song repertoire at all in these species.

Clearly, hearing their own or other vocalizations during the transition from subsong to full song is of vital importance to songbirds. But what about the timing of experience with the specific song of their species?

Recorded songs can be played to otherwise isolated birds at different stages of their development to test for what kinds of auditory experience are necessary at what phase in the acquisition of song. It has been found that if swamp sparrows hear their own species' song *only* during the first two months of life, they will show normal subsong and adult song structure despite the continued isolation. They will also show normal adult song if both their own and another sparrow species' song is played to them during this period. But if *only* the other species' song is provided, their song later develops as if they had been isolated throughout. The song sparrow is a little different. It will acquire either its own or swamp sparrow syllables, depending on which it is exposed to in the early critical period; if isolated throughout, it will produce a song that is again very different from wild birds.

Recent findings suggest that the extreme specificity of the swamp sparrow's requirement for early experience with song is due to selective early sensory processing. What can we make of these studies on sparrows? First, that the period for acquisition of specific characteristics of song is separate from and much earlier than the period during which the actual singing begins. Secondly, that the young bird during the early period can be very selective in which characteristics of the song it will acquire. Putting this together with the findings on isolation and deafening, we can be reasonably certain that during the period of transition from subsong to adult song the bird is comparing the sound of its own vocalizations with a memory trace or species-specific template established much earlier in its life, and is adjusting its song progressively to that template.

These findings give us a picture of how early sensory processing, occurring at a critical period, combines with a developmental program of stages in vocalization and a process of feedback modification to produce species-specific song in birds. It is a reasonably clear story and we can be fairly sure about the major points. We cannot say that this explains the early stages of human speech acquisition, but it does give us a way to conceptualize how it could work and how the information we have can be put together.

The model also gives us an opportunity to learn about neural mechanisms that underlie some of the early stages in language acquisition and may be common to both birds and humans. Parallels have already been found in the early development of laterality of the neuroanatomical substrate for bird song. Nottebohm has shown that if an adult male canary's left hypoglossal nerve is cut, its song is devastated and does not recover. If the left hemisphere is lesioned in one of its vocal areas, there follows a severe breakdown of the structure of song so that it is unstable and monotonous. Comparable cuts and lesions on the right side produce comparatively minor changes. If, on the other hand, the left hypoglossal nerve is cut during the first two months of life, the bird develops normal song which is then found to be entirely dependent on the right hypoglossal nerve. Lesions of the right hemisphere in these birds when adult cause severe deterioration of song similar to lesions of the left hemisphere in normal birds.

These experiments demonstrate clearly what is suggested by the few clinical examples available in the human: that there is a critical period during which cortical regions become committed to functions such as speech in the human and song in the bird; that although the left side ordinarily serves this function, the right can do so if given experience at the proper time. Combined with what was learned about the nature of this experience and the characteristics required for it to be effective, we can begin to see how lateral cortical localization of substrates for language may become established.

Before we leave the bird model, it should be mentioned that different species of birds have very different degrees of participation of early sensory and feedback mechanisms. Some, like the Ring Dove, develop a full adult repertoire despite isolation and deafening at the time of hatching, whereas others like the cardinal and the canary, even after song is fully established, lose their song entirely when deafened. These species differences provide many models for understanding the different processes that may be involved in the acquisition of human speech.

It should also be noted that there are clear-cut sex differences in song birds. The female white-crowned sparrow, for instance, does not sing—unless she is given testosterone. Only then can we be sure that she also forms a specific template early in her life. Under normal conditions this sensory template is not used for song acquisition but rather for discrimination of the proper mate, by giving her the information necessary to recognize him by his song. The variety of processes evident in studies on birds can enrich our hypotheses for the human, but at the same time caution us against simple generalizations from song to speech.

Although the development and anatomical basis for song in birds shares a number of features with human speech, its use as a model is *not* that of a precise replica of the human system. This is quickly apparent in the effects of social isolation that prevent the development of human language but do not prevent complex bird song except in a few species and then only if it occurs very early. Studies on birds have given us a relatively unambiguous picture of how a complex vocal repertoire may be acquired. The ideas of a perceptual template and of the process of auditory feedback and matching to this template can not only be tested for the human but can also be analyzed further in birds. As new mechanisms and processes are revealed in the study of birds, they can be looked for in humans.

In fact, a recent report has shown that 2-month-old infants of a Bantu tribe whose language uses sounds that are not present in English, have a perceptual category between two positions on the voice onset time gradient that American infants and adults fail to discriminate (4). These Bantu infants also discriminate across the *p–b* position, which does not actually occur in their language. This finding suggests that for the human infant, certain aspects of auditory processing can be acquired by early experience with local language characteristics, whereas others are predetermined. The parallel to swamp and song sparrows is intriguing.

Ideas are the most important result of any research and we will clearly have to be willing to modify and adapt them in our efforts to explore the human case. They have the most potential for helping us understand the *early* stages of language acquisition in humans, which in the past have been the least studied. Further knowledge about these early stages could be of most benefit to the training of congenitally deaf children, which continues to pose great difficulty by current methods.

SUMMARY

Language is an essential human quality, one which provides the foundation for our uniqueness among species, for the creation of abstract thought, and even for the degree of civilization we have been able to attain. The early stages of its development involve a number of biological predispositions: the spontaneous crying, cooing, and babbling; the selective perception of speech sounds by the right ear (and left cerebral hemisphere); and the characteristics of speech processing specially tuned to make important distinctions between human speech sounds months before the child is capable of any language reception.

The acquisition of language depends on experience in some surprising ways. Vocalization develops normally for the first 3–6 months in deaf children, well into the babbling stage, but then dies out. If a hearing aid is provided, babbling will resume, demonstrating the role of feedback in the maintenance of this stage in language development. By 6–8 months, specific aspects of different spoken languages to which the infant is exposed begin to appear in its speech.

At the end of the first year, babbling declines and the period of rapid specific language acquisition begins. Here again there is evidence for an imposed structure in the form of syntactical rules by which the infant seems to organize the sounds that he or she is initiating and learning. The left or sometimes the right hemisphere of the brain becomes committed to language before the age of 5; if not learned by then, language is virtually impossible to acquire. A perfect accent and the ability to speak a language "like a native" can rarely be acquired after 12.

Many of these features have also been found to be present in the acquisition of song by some species of birds: lateralization, critical periods, predispositions, selective processing, subsong (an analogy of babbling), the requirements for feedback from their own early vocal efforts, and even the production of dialects that distinguish flocks inhabiting adjacent valleys. The developmental processes and their neuroanatomical substrates can be clarified by experiments in these avian model systems and are yielding important new concepts and hypotheses for a further understanding of early language acquisition in the human.

FURTHER READING

Hinde, R. A. (Ed.) *Bird Vocalizations: Their Relations to Current Problems in Biology and Psychology.* London: Cambridge University Press, 1969.

Krashen, S. D. The critical period for language acquisition and its possible bases. *Annals of the New York Academy of Sciences*, 263:211–224, 1975.

Lane, H. L. *The Wild Boy of Aveyron.* Cambridge, Mass.: Harvard University Press, 1976.

Lenneberg, E. H., and Lenneberg, E. (Eds.) *Foundations of Language Development: A Multidisciplinary Approach.* New York: Academic Press, 1975.

Marler, P. Sensory templates, vocal perception, and development: a comparative view. In M. Lewis and L. A. Rosenblum (Eds.), *Interaction, Conversation, and the Development of Language.* New York: Wiley, 1977. Pp. 95–114.

Nakazima, S. Phonemicization and symbolization in language development. In Lenneberg and Lenneberg, op. cit., pp. 181–187.

Nottebohm, F. Asymmetries in neural control of vocalization in the canary. In S. Harnad, R. W. Doty, L. Goldstein, J. Jaynes, and G. Krauthamer (Eds.), *Lateralization in the Nervous System.* New York: Academic Press, 1977. Pp. 23–44.

REFERENCES CITED

1. Itard, J. M. G. On the education of a man of the wild (1801). Quoted in Lane, op. cit., p. 101.
2. Eimas, P., Siqueland, E. R., Jusczyk, P., and Vigorito, J. Speech perception in infants. *Science*, 171:303–306, 1971.

3. Fry, D. B. The development of the phonological system in the normal and the deaf child. In F. Smith and G. A. Miller (Eds.), *The Genesis of Language: A Psycholinguistic Approach*. Cambridge, Mass.: MIT Press, 1966. Pp. 187–206.

4. Streeter, L. A. Language perception of 2-month-old infants shows effects of both innate mechanisms and experience. *Nature*, 259:39–41, 1976.

14

Play: The Cradle
of Adult Behavior

By most definitions, play should not be taken seriously. It is what children are told to do when adults are tired of having them underfoot. Nothing seems to be accomplished by it except that it seems to be entertaining and relaxing; something to be done when no other needs are pressing. In the past, only a few scientists gave the topic serious thought, and for the most part this has been for its role in the development of cognition and in the creative process.

Recently, biologists have become aware that play occurs with great frequency in the early development of a wide variety of mammals, particularly those having long periods of parental dependency and complex social behaviors similar to the human. Its clear presence has demanded some understanding. The problem that play presents to a biologist is that it lacks a biologically significant goal such as protection or reproduction and indeed does not appear to have any adaptive function. Since biological thinking about behavior is usually organized around its role in adaptation, this has posed conceptual problems. Furthermore, play appears to be composed of elements from other behaviors, rather than to have a distinctive pattern of its own, making the category difficult to deal with even at a purely descriptive level.

With all these difficulties, why bother with it? The answer is that play occupies the major part of the wakeful behavior of higher mammals during the transition from infancy to adulthood and that it provides the first expression of the behaviors we characterize in adults as exploratory, aggressive, sexual, affiliative, and parental. In addition, it provides early developmental precursors of motor and sensory skills, language, abstract intelligence, and humor. That is, if you trace any of these adult activities back to its earliest crude approximations in early development, you will find it occurs during play.

SPECIAL CHARACTERISTICS

The very fact that play behavior is uncoupled from consequences gives it some of its identifying character. It is often repetitious and seems to lead nowhere. In fact, if an actual sequence is carefully studied, it resembles adult adaptive behavior except that the elements are scrambled. For instance, a young mammal at play may begin with a pounce on some object or other animal and then run about chasing it. In addition, the behavior itself is exaggerated, first by the extent of movements, second by repetition, and third by prolongation of certain phases of movements. These quantitative modifications are very easy for an adult or older child to recognize and allow the proper distinction from "serious" (goal-directed) behavior. This is necessary so that the sexual or aggressive nature of some play behaviors are not misinterpreted. Apparently, as an additional safeguard of this sort, play signals have evolved: facial expressions or bodily movements that make clear what is about to follow is "just a game." These latter features make it possible for play behaviors to become more and more similar to adult goal-directed behaviors in a gradual shading off process, which extends into adulthood and even old age in many mammals. Under the protection of play signals, movements become more and more economical, sequences become purposefully ordered, and extraneous frills are eliminated. But, if properly signaled, it is still responded to playfully by other animals.

Thus, although play behavior resembles many other behaviors, it has distinctive features that allow it to be differentiated. It occurs in a wide range of mammals during the juvenile period, so that it is not a creation of human cultural evolution. Rather, it appears to be a general fact about behavior development, a universal stage in the maturation of social animals. But why does it occur? What is its survival value? What benefits does it provide for evolutionary fitness? This last question is particularly challenging because of the nonadaptive character of play behavior.

ROLE IN DEVELOPMENT

In trying to understand the developmental significance of play behavior, we are in the same position as when we confronted early fetal behavior. The behavior seems to anticipate the need. The same kinds of guesses recur in the history of theories about early play: that it is just a discharge of surplus nervous energy, that it is vestigial, left over from some past evolutionary stage and now separated from its original adaptational role; or that it is a necessary form of "practice," leaving open exactly what that may mean by that word. You will recall that in the case of prenatal behavior we are just beginning to learn about a number of processes within the early history of nerve and muscle cell development, which depend upon movement and sensory stimulation for their sustenance and direction.

Our ignorance about juvenile play is greater, but it seems very likely that there are processes in the development of adult behavior made possible by play. Prenatal and some neonatal behavior is made up of small units that do not last very long—just fractions of a second—and involve only a few muscles at a time. By the time of birth, some of these units which have the longest history of functioning are assembled into the simple goal-directed sequence of nursing. But this involves only a part of the body and is relatively crude, repetitive, and stereotyped. Early play behavior involves larger units of behavior; that is, more muscle groups acting in a coordinated fashion over longer periods of time in a relatively consistent pattern. The movements are formed into short sequences and involve coordination of changing sensory patterns and motor output. A good illustration of early infant play behavior with the mother is given in the last part of Chapter 11.

Although the units of play behavior are longer and more complex than in the prenatal period, they are still shorter than adult behavior. The sequences are put together in a highly variable order and are not organized toward a common goal. Behaviors tend to be either exaggerated or perfunctory and occur in unpredictable order. Gradually, sequences become more ordered, movements more economical, and the sequences cluster together into predictable categories.

Thus, it would appear that the sequences of behavior found in juvenile play may be a later counterpart of the individual movements found in the prenatal period. Their role may also be in promoting neurobiological development, but not the development of neurons, sensory receptors, muscles, and joints, for they are completed by this stage. Rather, play may act to promote the neural *integration* of behavior, the formation of neural systems capable of complex, goal-directed sequences that allow adaptation to the social and inanimate environment.

The evidence for such a role of play in development is not compelling as yet because no way has been found to deprive a young animal of play in a way that would allow all other experience. Young monkeys raised without mothers but with other young monkeys of the same age are improved over isolated monkeys in social behaviors as adults. It is not clear from this, however, whether their peers are providing surrogate mothering or whether play behavior is essential for the effect. Rhesus infants raised with mothers but without opportunities for play with peers showed deficits in both affectional and aggressive behavior. But here again, under these conditions the relationship with the mother was prolonged and likely to have become abnormal. Furthermore, play in primates can occur with mothers and other adults as well as with peers, making selective deprivation impossible to achieve.

In the rat there is much less play between adults and young but a period of vigorous social play with peers occurs from the second postnatal week to just before puberty. Fragments of sexual, aggressive, predatory, and parental behavior can be identified in these playful interactions. If male rats are allowed normal mothering until two weeks after birth and then some of them are housed alone, some in a group, and some alone but across a wire mesh from the group, then only the males raised in a group develop normal mating behavior when presented with a receptive female (1). A group of males is as effective as a heterosexual group, so that prior experience with females is not involved. Isolated males show aberrant responses such as climbing under and over, appear hyperexcitable, and direct their mounting and clasping approaches in a fragmented way toward flanks, shoulders, and heads of the females, as well as toward posterior regions. Even when the female is approached from the rear, clasping, mounting, and thrusting are not combined into an effective sequence allowing intromission and ejaculation.

The control condition allowing proximity but preventing actual interaction by a wire mesh wall, helps to isolate *behavioral* interaction as the essential element of experience. These males maintained sensory contact with the others through smell, hearing, and sight; they were aware of the groups' interactions and were not subjected to gross sensory deprivation. Yet their sexual performance in adulthood was not significantly improved over isolated rats.

The results of this study leave us with the conclusion that without play (or huddling, grooming, or some other behavioral interaction in the juvenile period) the sexual behavior of the male rat develops only in a fragmented, misdirected, and uncoordinated form. By the present evidence, play can not be positively identified as the crucial experience, but it is certainly a prime suspect. Huddling and grooming may also contribute their part. Only more careful studies with discrete experiences will be able to parcel out the relative contributions.

How might play act to promote the sensorimotor integration that is so lacking in experimental animals raised without social interaction after the early mother–infant period? A clue may be found in the now classic experiments of Held and Hein on kittens (2). Raised normally from birth to about 10 weeks of age, except for the absence of light, kittens were then given specially arranged experience during 3-hour daily periods in the light. One member of each pair was free to move around a circular apparatus with striped walls. He was harnessed, however, through a series of levers and bars to a small enclosed box in which the other kitten stood with its head protruding. All the movements of the first kitten were transmitted to the second kitten so that it moved in the environment just like the first one, the difference being that the first kitten experienced the environment actively, the second, passively. At the end of each 3-hour period, both kittens were returned to their mother and siblings in the dark. After 10 days of this experience, the kittens were tested. The active member of each pair showed normal behavior on visually guided tasks: it blinked at an approaching object, it put out its paw to ward off collision, and it avoided the deep side of a visual cliff illusion. The passive members failed to show any of these behaviors.

This experiment demonstrates that it is the repeated correlation of visual stimulation with motor patterns that is necessary for the development of visual control of behavior. The passive kitten could move its limbs and could see the environment; in fact, it perceived as many different movements and changes in perspective as the active kitten. But its limb movements were not connected in a lawful way with its changing visual experience. Neurophysiologists have found a pathway between motor systems of the brain and sensory systems such that volleys of neural excitation reach the sensory system in time with each movement. This "reafference" appears to be a characteristic of brain organization that underlies the coordination of sensory and motor systems. Presumably, synaptic changes take place as a result that build integrated substrates for complex organized behavior.

Play provides a multitude of settings in which rapidly changing sensory stimulation is repeatedly correlated in time with newly developed patterns of behavior. Early social play—such as the rough and tumble variety that characterizes so many mammals, including humans—presents the sensory patterns of another similar body, together with segments of its own motor behavior. The reafference resulting from these repeated correlations may provide a necessary organizing process for the establishment of sensory-guided social behavior that is appropriate, integrated, and efficient later in life.

By this conception, the young organism need only have crude approximations of segments of adult behavior to start with, like those we have described above in the newborn. These segments would then be released in play and would gradually acquire the sensory guidance and the integration of sequences characteristic of adult adaptive behavior. Without the experience of play and other social interactions, these behaviors would continue to be elicited only in fragments, unintegrated with each other and lacking directed sensory coordination—the very characteristics described for monkeys and rat pups deprived of peers.

The neural process entailed in sensorimotor feedback and its role in the development of sensory-guided behavior is a form of plasticity that may be related to learning in terms of its cellular mechanisms, but is different from learning in that the resulting behavior is not identical to that which is experienced. Young rats do not gradually learn sexual behavior patterns during rough and tumble play; rather, they acquire the *potential* for the full expression of sexual behavior through the performance of other behaviors, in the same way that the active kittens in Held and Hein's experiments acquired the ability to perform visually-guided tasks in situations they had never experienced before.

Obviously play, particularly in humans, provides many opportunities for ordinary learning, and much of the most successful educational approaches are built on that principle. Social learning certainly takes place and plays an important role in the fine tuning of every kind of social behavior. But the groundwork of sensorimotor coordination and behavioral sequence integration may take place at a more elementary level of plasticity, which allows undirected fragments of behavior to become synthesized into the species-typical sequences of sexual, aggressive, and parental behavior. This may well be how we seem to "know what to do" (more or less) on our very first try at these roles in adulthood. The behavior just seems to be there, without having to be learned. This quality has led us to label these behaviors as "instinctive" or "innate," but experiments with animals have shown that they are far from innate and depend upon experiences occurring a long time after birth. We are beginning to unravel the nature of these crucial experiences and how they may come to facilitate normal development.

REGULATION

When does play begin and what sustains it? In previous chapters we have caught its beginnings in the smile, which is evoked during play with the mother, and even during a simple learning situation when people are absent. Smiles and laughter are evidences of the relaxed state during which play takes place; a sick or bewildered child does not either smile or play. The smile is evidence of the pleasure a child takes in play and occurs in situations when tension is evoked by some incongruity and then released with recognition; that is, when an expectation is only partially met (for example, the mother appears in a strange hat). The distortion is not too great to be frightening and the expected features are sufficient to permit matching against the sensory schema. The matching of expectation with perception, despite new elements, appears to be pleasurable, to evoke a smile and to elicit behavior likely to repeat the experience, as described in Chapter 7. Familiarity heightens expectation, novelty heightens tension; thus, play is recreated and sustained with both familiar and novel objects and with people until habituation brings each episode to a close.

Therefore, the smile is a clue to the self-rewarding nature of play behavior. The kinds of behavior that occur during play are an end in themselves. Their ultimate purpose appears to be their contribution to the development of behavior and cognition, but their immediate goal—that sustains them in the short term of the individual's life— seems to be the pleasure in performance. From this perspective, play does not seem so purposeless; it has both immediate and ultimate goals, and on this basis can be considered highly adaptive.

The developmental course of play behavior is a complex and rich area for study, one which goes far beyond the scope of this book. We have traced its earliest origins in the newborn period where it seems to begin both with objects and with the mother. The distinction between animate and inanimate objects for play is probably an artificial one from the very beginning, except that living creatures usually provide the most complex and variable sources for playful interaction. But because of these properties, infants begin to play with unfamiliar objects before playing with unfamiliar people. By 18 months there begins a shift from solitary to social play with other infants, but this is a slow transition marked by a long period of "parallel play," with each infant playing alone near other infants. Encounters between infants of 2–3 are likely to turn quickly into struggles and screaming. Apparently, signals are misinterpreted, and behavior is erratic. Too much novelty and tension, too much incongruity, and not enough predictability in their behavior make infants of this age incapable of sustaining a play interaction. Instead, a state change in one or both parties terminates a bout soon after it begins. The next phase, rough and tumble play, begins at about 4–5 years of age in the human, when elements of aggressive, sexual, and parental behavior are mixed in with a profusion of gymnastic maneuvers.

This progression of stages is of particular interest to the biologist, because it is virtually identical in young primates and not too distant from the phases seen in puppies, kittens, and rodents such as squirrels and rats. Play in the human continues on to more elaborate play with objects, play with language, play with social roles, and finally, play with rules (e.g., chess, football). At least some of these forms of play are continued into adult life by most humans. An appealing case can be made that most of the creative achievements of civilization have been made possible by this extension of an early juvenile behavior into adulthood.

SUMMARY

We are beginning to realize that play is not simply a trivial childish amusement, but occurs consistently during certain stages in the development of social mammals and may provide important developmental experience. The characteristics of repetition, exaggeration, reversed sequence, fragmentation, and the absence of consequences identify play as distinct from ordinary adaptive behaviors.

The role of play in development is not yet firmly established, but experiments with kittens and rat pups suggest that play may facilitate the organization and synthesis of the complex behavior sequences necessary for adult social behaviors. The motivational basis for play seems to lie in the same matching of expectation and perception we have previously described during early learning (Chapter 7) and the development of cognition (Chapter 12).

Play develops in a series of stages: with parents, solitary, parallel, and "rough and tumble" with agemates. Similar sequences in the development of nonhuman primates and even in less closely-related animals suggests a long evolutionary history and an important biological role for play behavior in early development. Humans, more than other species, retain elements of play into adulthood and the ability to be playful seems to be one of the essential ingredients of serious creativity as well as of recreation.

FURTHER READING

Bruner, J. S., Jolly, A., and Sylva, K. *Play: Its Role in Development and Evolution.* New York: Basic Books, 1976.
Garvey, C. *Play.* Cambridge, Mass.: Harvard University Press, 1977.

Loizos, C. Play behaviour in higher primates: a review. In D. Morris (Ed.), *Primate Ethology*. Chicago: Aldine Publishing, 1967. Pp. 176–218.

Poole, T. B., and Fish, J. An investigation of playful behaviour in *Rattus norvegicus* and *Mus musculus* (Mammalia). *Journal of Zoology* (London), 175:61–71, 1975.

REFERENCES CITED

1. Gerall, H. D., Ward, I. L., and Gerall, A. A. Disruption of the male rat's sexual behaviour induced by social isolation. *Animal Behaviour*, 15:54–58, 1967.
2. Held, R., and Hein, A. Movement-produced stimulation in the development of visually guided behavior. *Journal of Comparative and Physiological Psychology*, 56:872–876, 1963.

15

Early Sexual, Aggressive, and Parenting Behavior

Although children's play raises some puzzling developmental questions, as discussed in the previous chapter, we take its occurrence for granted and welcome it. Aggressive behavior is also recognized in children and has continuity with early affective behavior of infants in the first months after birth. Parental behavior, when it occurs in children, is generally considered to be playful, although it may not have the characteristics we generally require for that label. Indeed, a 3–4-year-old often seems quite serious while caring for her baby brother under the parent's watchful eye. But when it comes to childhood sexuality, we look the other way. Described as the "last frontier of sex research" (1) the topic raises almost as many eyebrows today as it did when Freud shocked turn-of-the-century Vienna with his observations on its existence and his brilliant ideas, many of which are not fully appreciated, even today.

Recent research on animals has led us to take another look at ourselves, for young animals of a wide range of species show parental and sexual behaviors long before their reproductive organs have matured sufficiently to allow fertilization or child bearing. And the appearance of these behaviors in young animals with extremely limited imitative capacities, such as the rat, suggest that their appearance in human children is not simply an example of superficial mimicry, but may well represent early instances of the same motivated behaviors we recognize clearly after puberty.

Years of clinical experience with humans and a great deal of anthropological data on other cultures also strongly suggest that this may be so. The developmental importance of experiences involving these behaviors in the long period before adolescence then becomes evident. For our capacity to express these behaviors fully in later life will be shaped by the nature and outcome of these early experiences, despite our reluctance to acknowledge them. Clearly, it is worthwhile to open our eyes.

INCOMPLETE DIFFERENTIATION
OF THE CATEGORIES

We have seen that in rough-and-tumble play of many mammals, elements of the three behaviors are expressed, often in rapid succession, often out of sequence, sometimes exaggerated or embellished, but recognizable nevertheless by anyone familiar with the fully developed adult form in that species. At this stage in development, these behaviors are rarely distinct, either in terms of the situations that elicit them or in the way the elements are clustered together in time.

Even as adults, one of the causes of our difficulty in dealing with these behaviors stems from the fact that they never become entirely differentiated from each other. As students of behavior, we have had to recognize that these categories are artificial and do not fit natural situations, particularly in primates. In a given encounter—for example, an adult human sexual interaction—elements of parental and/or aggressive behavior are usually interspersed and may even outweigh the time spent in "purely" sexual behavior. Similarly, if we listen to the words spoken by two lovers, their language is rich in expressions of parental and aggressive emotions, in addition to those of sex. Humans have a need to keep these categories of feelings and behaviors distinct from each other in their minds. This differentiation is not maintained just for the purposes of clarity in our thinking about behavior. We have to know what to expect from another person and do so by categorizing the basic theme of the encounter along certain lines that have predictive value. This may well have been the origin of the words that we use for the different behaviors (sexual, aggressive, and parental)—words that predict what the probable consequences of an encounter are likely to be. In thinking about behavior, we can classify it according to its form, or to the situation that elicits it, or to its consequences (see Chapter 3). But many social encounters in addition to play are difficult to categorize by any of these criteria.

PRECURSORS OF ADULT BEHAVIORS

There are no reliable systematic observational studies on the development of these three behaviors in human infants. However, most parents have observed their children behaving aggressively, sexually, and parentally well before 3 years of age. In Chapters 6 and 7, the early prototypes of negative affect were described and, between 3 and

6 months, clear-cut infantile "tantrums" begin to occur in response to frustration. These involve striking, kicking, and classical facial expressions of anger; they appear in form, in eliciting condition, and in consequences to be identical to some forms of aggressive behavior in older children and adults. Parenting responses begin as affectional holding and physical attachment behaviors elicited by stuffed animals, dolls, and younger siblings. More specific parental behaviors such as rocking, feeding, caressing, play sequences, and baby talk are added as the child becomes capable of these. Usually thought to be mere imitation or dismissed as a form of play, these early precursors may well be important events in the formation of adult patterns. Elements of aggression and sexual behavior may be mixed in with the parental behavior toward dolls—and toward babies when this is allowed.

The first evidences of sexual behavior begin in the form of masturbation at about 6 months of age. It is argued whether this is simply a form of exploratory behavior at first and that the penis or vulva is no different from any other object to the infant of this age. But by the end of the first year, the behavior begins to occur in settings of social isolation and emotional upset, which suggest it is being used for soothing and tension-relieving purposes—a setting congruent with adult masturbation. By 2–3 years of age, infants with their parents or peers show pelvic thrusting, rub their pelvic regions against their parents, attempt to touch their parents' sexual organs, and act generally in ways easily recognizable as flirtatious or seductive. These behaviors tend to be more often directed at the parent of the opposite sex and occur in settings of intimacy and relaxation such as coming into the parental bed on Sunday morning. Again, the form and the elicitation of the behavior closely resemble that of adult sexual behavior. The consequences of this behavior in children are highly variable. Most adults clearly discourage these advances because they make the adults uncomfortable. A very few parents or other adults encourage them too much and become sexually aroused themselves in the process. Clinical experience strongly suggests that this is "overstimulating" for the child and leads to sexual difficulties in later life. Indeed, most people feel an abhorrence for sexual activity by adults with children or infants because of the severe exploitation inherent in the adults' overpowering position in the relationship.

The question of whether childhood and particularly infantile sexual behavior is really a form of exploration, a mere imitation of adults, or instead a behavior continuous with adult sexual behavior, is difficult to settle definitively. However, clinical experience with hormone-producing tumors of the pituitary gland in children demonstrates that childhood sexual behaviors are markedly facilitated by the same hormones that later facilitate the sexual activity of adolescence. Indeed, girls as young as 5 years of age have become pregnant under these conditions. Furthermore, Kinsey, Pomeroy, and Martin, in their monumental 1948 survey, were able to collect observations by adults on 317 preadolescent males who were observed in self-masturbation or who were observed in contacts with other boys or other adults in sexual activity that proceeded to the point of orgasm. Orgasm was reported in boys of every age from 5 months to adolescence. Orgasms occurred in 9 of 28 infants observed under the age of 1 year, and in 11 of 22 infants between 1 and 2 years. The percent of cases observed to have orgasm increased with age to 80 percent of 115 preadolescent boys. Orgastic behaviors observed in infants involved:

> . . . a series of gradual physiologic changes, increasing rhythmic body movements, distinct pelvic thrusts, a final tension of abdominal, hip, and back muscles, and a sudden release of this tension with convulsions, including rhythmic anal contractions. . . . after climax the child loses erection quickly and subsides into the calm that typically follows adult orgasm. It may be some time before erection can be induced again after such an experience. There are observations of 16 males up to 11 months of age with such typical orgasm reached in 7 cases (2).

The question of the continuity of such infantile behaviors with "real" orgasm later in life is answered by:

> . . . observations over periods of months or years, until the individuals were old enough to make it certain that true orgasm was involved, and in all cases the later reactions were so similar to the earlier behavior that there could be no doubt of the orgastic nature of the first experience (2).

The only feature of adult orgasm lacking in preadolescent males is ejaculation, which cannot take place until prostate gland and seminal vesicles mature under the influence of the testosterone surge at puberty. Similar observational data were obtained for females and reported by the same authors in 1952. First-hand observations of orgasm in infant girls were reported in the same behavioral and physiological detail, in four cases under the age of 1 year and in 23 cases in girls 3 years of age or younger, usually during masturbation.

Thus, there is considerable evidence to support the existence of infantile and childhood sexual behaviors continuous with adult sexuality in terms of eliciting conditions, the detailed patterns and sequences of the behaviors, including orgasm, the selective facilitation of these behaviors by hormones, and direct observation of continuity in individual characteristics of the behaviors from the first experience in early childhood to the full expression of sexuality in adulthood.

However, as in other behavior categories, there are important developmental differences between early and adult expressions of the behaviors. Sexual behavior first appears in a very loose relationship to eliciting stimuli and does not usually proceed to the consequences of adult life such as orgasm. In Chapter 6, for example, I described male penile erections making their first appearance as a sleep phenomenon (as does the smile). In the first few months of life, erections occur frequently in response to almost any stimuli. This generalized nature of the sexual response in early development is further supported in descriptions provided by older preadolescents, demonstrating that erections can be stimulated at age 8–12 by such diverse physical stimuli as skiing and sitting in church; such diverse emotional stimuli as being late to school, watching a fire, and hearing band music; as well as by seeing pictures of nude females or hearing a sex joke. In early preadolescence, almost any emotional response may be accompanied by an erection; by the late teens, males rarely respond in this way to anything except specifically sexual situations.

The diffuse character of eliciting conditions for the sexual response in early development is an important feature that complicates our recognition of the behavior as sexual and raises questions about its meaning at an early age. Indeed, early sexual activity is usually referred to as sex *play*. According to Kinsey's interviews with young children and their parents, 8–14 percent of males and 6 percent of females begin genital sexual play with other children by the age of 5. The extent to which this may be exploratory and not primarily sexual behavior would depend on one's definition; for example, the extent of specific physiological and behavioral responses required for such behaviors to be classified as sexual. Although there are no systematic longitudinal studies on this question, it is reasonable to suppose that play is important in the development of adult sexuality, as described in the previous chapter. But this does not mean that all early sexual behavior is a form of play: childhood sexual behavior can clearly be as serious as childhood aggressive behavior.

Studies in animals confirm these observations on childhood sexuality in humans that by themselves could be challenged as not having been conducted by objective, trained observers, as subject to strong subjective reporting biases, and as not having been confirmed and replicated by other studies. For example, it has recently been discovered that 50 percent of infant rats as young as six days of age will show a complete female sexual response of lordosis and head bobbing in response to flank pressure by brushes, similar to stimulation provided in adults by the mounting male (3). If female hormones are administered, 100 percent will show this response. Parental behavior in rat pups begins a little later, but still before the pups are themselves fully weaned from nursing their own mothers, at 3 weeks of age (4). About 50 percent of pups of this age will retrieve and huddle with a pile of 1-week-old pups, will lick the younger pups, and will build nests for them in a pattern closely resembling the lactating adult female rat. Interestingly, rat pups require less experience with the newborns before showing maternal behavior than similarly inexperienced young adult females. And at this juvenile period, males show the maternal response as readily as females.

These examples of very early sexual and parental behaviors in nursing rats extend into an even earlier developmental period, the data of anthropologists and zoologists on early sexual behaviors in nonhuman primates and primitive human cultures, reported in Ford and Beach's classic book in 1951. The behaviors are quite distinct from the fragmentary, exaggerated, and unsequenced components of sexual, aggressive, and parental behavior occurring during rough-and-tumble play in 3-week-old rats. And they are highly unlikely to be imitations of adult behaviors. Taken together, the evidence is convincing that major components of sexual and parental behavior develop during infancy in most mammals including humans. The beginnings of these important behaviors in infancy need much more systematic, longitudinal study in order to answer obvious questions about the consequences that early experience with these behaviors may have for the expression of sexuality and parenting in adulthood.

BEHAVIORAL DIFFERENCES BETWEEN THE SEXES

The only way parents can tell a newborn boy from a girl is by inspection of its genitals. This fact has been hard for some people to accept and there are many myths about differences in behavior detectable even before birth—by the way the fetus moves or how the mother feels. A number of studies have attempted to find reliable differences in behavior between male and female newborns, and although some have found differences (e.g., boys are somewhat more active and girls slightly more sensitive to light touch), others have failed to find the same thing in other groups of neonates. The exhaustive recent review of Maccoby and Jacklin concludes that most probably boys and girls show few if any behavioral differences at birth.

Experience with Parents

The difference between the sexes at birth occurs in how they are treated by adults and what is expected of them. Here again, a number of stereotypes and myths do not hold up across studies, but several findings turn up consistently. Male infants are handled more roughly by both parents, there is more vigorous tickling and rubbing, more tossing in the air and more jumbling about of boy than girl babies from the very beginning. Later on, there is more encouragement of rough-and-tumble play, first with the parents and then with peers. Since there is no clear difference in overall activity level during the newborn period, the difference appears to originate in the parent and not be a response to different behavior on the part of the child. Parents punish and praise boys more; in general they act as if boys' behavior was more interesting or attention-provoking than girls'. Finally, parents act more to prevent sex-inappropriate behavior in boys than in girls.

These significant differences in parents' behavior show a good deal of consistency across cultures. Furthermore, monkey mothers also differentiate between male and female infants, embracing and clasping females more than males and restraining them more from exploration and interaction with peers. Thus, the differential treatment of infants of the two sexes in the human case is unlikely to be purely cultural, but to have biological roots. Monkeys show a great deal of interest in the genitals of newborn infants, and all the adults in the group will huddle around to inspect the newborn. Male infants' genitalia arouse much more attention than females', according to several studies, regardless of the sex or relationship of the adult animal.

It is interesting to speculate why these differential behaviors of parents have evolved. Apparently they are related to the early development of one of the few consistent behavioral differences between the sexes outside of the category of sexual behavior, namely aggression. Consistently across studies, across cultures, and across mammalian species, males show more aggressive behavior. This difference is true as early as the first rough-and-tumble play and includes mock aggression, verbal aggression, and inner fantasies as well as outright fights. Another consistent difference between the sexes is their vulnerability. In the first month after birth, 25 percent more boys than girls die. Despite their greater size (except during the years 10–13), boys continue to have more severe disease, both psychological and medical, and a higher death rate. It is tempting to view the parents' differential stimulation of rough, major motor behavior as producing the differences between the sexes on aggression. Similarly the parents' increased attention toward boys' behavior might be the result of boys' increased susceptibility to illness and accident. Finally, it is possible to relate parents' greater pressure against sex-inappropriate behavior in boys to the greater biological difficulty of becoming a successfully procreative male than a female, as will be described below. But these are speculations and must be taken with a healthy dose of skepticism.

The other major area of differential parental response to boy and girl infants involves a more complex process. Each parent treats the child of the opposite sex differently than the other parent does. For example, fathers are more tolerant of aggression from a daughter than from a son while mothers are more tolerant of the son's aggression. Mothers are more tolerant of dependency behavior in sons and fathers in daughters. Finally, and perhaps most clear and important, when infants direct sexual behavior toward a parent, the response depends on their own sex and the sex of the parent. The parent normally turns the interaction into an imitative or competitive mode with the same-sex child, whereas it becomes complementary or reciprocal if the child is of the opposite sex. We have only the most fragmentary understanding of exactly how parents respond to the more explicit sexual advances of their children. We do know that there is enormous variability in how individual parents respond, and clinical experience tells us that these interactions may be of great importance for the development of sexual behavior with peers later in life.

What evidence do we have that the behavior of parents toward their infants early in life makes an important difference, considering the biological influence of the genes and the early hormonal effects on the anatomy of the genitalia, the physiology of the pituitary, and the neural substrates for behavior? If for any reason one attempts to change the sex assignment of an infant, it must be done in the first 1½–2 years.

After this, clinical experience tells us the person predictably has great difficulty in changing his or her sense of their own sexual identity or their sexual role behavior. This period coincides with the period for primary language development, early concept formation, and a number of other essential early psychological developments, so that it is not clear exactly which of these several processes are crucial for the formation of sexual identity and role behavior. It is not even clear that the problem is primarily within the child. It may be too difficult for parents and others to change their ways of interacting with the child after a year or two have passed.

The power of early sex assignment, and the experiences that follow, to overcome the combined influences of chromosomal sex, early hormonal status, and later human treatment, is well illustrated by John Money's clinical case reports. There are a number of cases in which chromosomal males and females have been assigned to the opposite sex at birth because their external genitalia were misinterpreted due to structural developmental defects. If rearing was consistent for the first 3–4 years, it was impossible for these people to change their sexual identity or sex role later in life. However, the early fetal hormonal influence on many of these cases was uncertain or unstudied.

Androgens and Experience

The influence of the concept of sexual neutrality at birth and belief in the overwhelming importance of the sex-rearing experience for humans has been challenged by a recent study on children with a rare enzyme deficiency. These new observations show that if there is fetal exposure to the androgen testosterone and pubertal exposure to the normal increase in levels of testosterone at that age, the effects of sex assignment and early rearing can be overcome.

The study involved 23 interrelated families spanning four generations in three rural villages in the Dominican Republic (5). Infants with this defect are exposed to normal levels of the androgen testosterone during the fetal period but due to an enzyme deficiency in the skin fail to convert the testosterone to the locally active product, dihydrotestosterone, which controls the early development of external genitalia. As a result, they are born with female-appearing genitalia, including a vaginal pouch, and are thus raised as girls despite being chromosomal males and having been exposed in utero to the organizational action of testosterone on the brain. At puberty, when the testosterone surge of adolescence occurs, their clitoris-like penis enlarges greatly, the testes descend into the divided, labia-like scrotal sacs, their voices deepen, and their hair and muscle development becomes that of normal pubertal males. They have erections but ejaculate through an opening at the base of their penises and are thus not usually fertile. The villagers who are familiar with the condition refer to them as "machihembra" or "first woman, then man."

In this study, the influence of sex rearing as a female came into direct conflict with the organizational influence of testosterone on the brain in fetal life and the activating influence of increased testosterone at puberty. The 18 subjects who were adequately studied began to realize they were different from the other girls in the village between 7 and 12 years of age, when they did not develop breasts and when their bodies began to change in a masculine direction. But, unexpectedly, 17 of the 18 began to evolve a male gender identity over the next several years. Sixteen of the 18 went on to develop full male sex-roles and 15 to living with women in common-law marriages. This result is at variance with Money's previous conclusions and suggests an important role for testosterone in establishing sex-role behavior and sexual identity in the male. However, other factors may have also made important contributions in this study. The cultural environment was an accepting one for sex-role change, by our standards, and the slight ambiguity of the external genitalia at birth may have led to ambiguities in rearing and parental expectancy, which made later change easier. Furthermore, testosterone may have exerted its effects primarily through its actions at puberty by enlarging what was thought to be a clitoris into what was clearly a penis and by bringing about the muscular, hair, and voice changes of male puberty.

Thus, although this study contradicts the idea that sexual identity is imprinted irreversibly during the first 3 years by the experiences that follow sex assignment at birth, it leaves open the question of how important the androgens are at the different stages of development and how they act to influence the final outcome of sexual identity and role in adult life. Such interactions will be discussed further below.

The behavior differentiation of males and females, the so-called *sexually dimorphic* behaviors, begin to make their appearance a number of months after birth. The first of these begins at about 18 months of age, when male infants become consistently rougher than females in their play, both with objects and other people. This difference enlarges into various other aspects of aggressive behavior. It is tempting to explain this first difference between the sexes simply on the basis of the consistently different behaviors of the parents toward boys, as described above. But things are more complicated than that—the androgenic hormone testosterone, both prenatally and neonatally, acts to increase rough-and-tumble play. Girl babies who have had abnormal adrenal glands that secrete excessive androgens during the prenatal period show this effect, as do girls born of mothers who are treated during pregnancy with hormones that have androgenic effects. Boys, similarly affected, show increases in precursors of aggressive behavior in later infancy. Testosterone given to 6-month-old female monkeys resulted in marked increases in aggressive behavior and reversal of the former dominance of the like-aged males in the group. Thus, the tendency for parents to treat boy babies differently from birth onward is complemented by an independent tendency of boys to engage in the very behavior the parents tend to elicit. This synchrony and dovetailing of experience and biological predisposition is typical of developmental processes.

The first clear differences in infantile sexual behavior between boys and girls are not known. We know that there are differences in the expectancies of the parents and how they say they respond to the two sexes of children. We also know that the presence of testosterone in the prenatal period predisposes to the eventual development of male sexual behavior. But this is only a predisposition and can be overridden in the human by the early experiences following sex reassignment, as described above. Furthermore, in animal studies, the effects of the low levels of testosterone in normal male infants do not seem to be evident in sexual behavior until levels rise at puberty. In the sexual play of young animals, both sexes play equally at being mounted as well as mounting. The difference produced by prenatal testosterone treatment is primarily in the precursors of *aggression* in play, not of sex.

At puberty, the pituitary influences the gonad to increase its production of hormone specific to the genetic sex of the young person; the predominant hormone is clearly different in boys (testosterone) and in girls (estrogen). However, both sexes produce some of both hormones and there are some women who produce more testosterone than men. From animal studies and some human clinical situations, we know that the two different hormones do not in themselves determine the kind of sexual behavior the individual shows. For the sensitivity of the brain to the two hormones is determined by the presence or absence of testosterone prenatally. Thus, the prenatal hormonal influence is one determinant while the hormone produced at puberty is another. Even in animals, the prior relationship with the mother and with peers is a third determinant. With humans, these early behavior interactions are even more important than in other animals.

Considering these multiple determinants, it is small wonder that sexual behavior exists in such variety. One may wonder instead that procreation of the species is left to such a vague and imprecise conglomeration of developmental processes. Of course, we must remember that most of the time it works in a very straightforward manner, and the processes tend to overlap and support each other. The presence or absence of testosterone prenatally determines whether the brain will respond preferentially to testosterone or estrogen at puberty. If testosterone is absent prenatally, animals respond to estrogen at puberty with female sexual behavior toward an experienced male and with little or no sexual behavior toward other females. Testosterone given at puberty produces only defective and inconsistent male behavior either in normal females or in genetic males deprived of prenatal testosterone. If, on the other hand, testosterone was present prenatally in either genetic males or females, then testosterone is selectively responded to at puberty with male type sexual behavior toward females. More mounting and/or presenting to the same sex is found in males treated with additional testosterone at puberty. Estrogens at puberty fail to produce normal female behavior in such animals. It is the surge of pubertal hormones that activates the latent behavior potential, and in fact can do so before the time of puberty. If testosterone or estrogen is given to infant animals or humans, a great deal more sexual precursor behaviors are elicited and may become persistent and explicit.

It is from the less extreme perturbations of these sequences that we can learn more about the biological processes involved in sexual development. For example, we would like to know whether the neural substrate for sexual behavior is like the genitals—a single system, which can be male, intermediate, or female according to its exposure to prenatal testosterone. Or are there two independent systems, one for male and one for female behaviors, thus allowing coincident male and female behavior? Some of the evidence favors the last view. If female animals are exposed to testosterone during the prenatal period, there are two classes of effects that can be distinguished: masculinization and defeminization. Conversely, male fetuses deprived of androgen prenatally may be demasculinized, feminized, or both. The readiness with which the animal will behave in patterns opposite to its genetic sex is separable from the readiness with which it shows behavior typical of its sex.

An example of a naturally occurring change in sex-related behavior can be found in animals with multiple births such as the mouse (6). Females whose uterine position was between two males show slight modification of their genitals in the male direction, are more aggressive, do more urinary marking of their cages (a male trait), and are less attractive to males than their littermates with uterine positions between two females. The implication is that the proximity to males in utero, and some sharing of their placental circulation, resulted in their being exposed to somewhat more testosterone during the prenatal period. However, it was found that those masculinized females were not defeminized. They were no different in their responses to estrogen, and they were as capable of all female reproductive functions, including maternal behavior and the raising of young, as their female littermates who had been together in the uterus. Thus, with different amounts and timing of exposure to testosterone in male animals, behavior may be feminized without being demasculinized. If the exposure to testosterone is either totally absent or involves large amounts over a long period of time, as described previously, defeminization of females and demasculinization of males takes place as well as masculinization of females and feminization of males.

These findings lead us to infer that for adult humans, a number of sex-related behaviors may depend to a certain extent on the presence of testosterone in early development, that both genetic males and genetic females possess the potential for both masculine and feminine behavior traits, and that traits of the opposite sex may be increased or decreased without necessarily impairing the behaviors related to the genetic sex.

Interactions with Peers

By now, many of the interactions should be evident between hormones and experience in the production of behavioral differences between the sexes. The dovetailing of parental treatment of males and the behavioral actions of testosterone on rough-and-tumble play have been outlined. Boy babies are born bigger and from the age of 1 they have measurably less subcutaneous fat. By the age of 6, girls begin to show a preferential distribution of this fat around hips and buttocks while boys develop broader shoulders and chests. Although muscle mass is similar at this age, muscular capacity is 10 percent greater in boys on the average. These physical differences can be produced by administration of low doses of testosterone or estrogen respectively. But the sex-role typing and the different toys and different forms of play interactions of boys and girls provide experiences that are likely to work in the same direction as the hormones.

One of the experiences most likely to work together with hormones toward sexual differentiation is the strong tendency of young children to choose playmates of the same sex. This has been found to begin as early as 2 years of age and continues throughout childhood and into adolescence, until stable heterosexual pairs become established. The tendency is strongest among boys and fits neatly with the fact that boys' aggressive behavior is directed selectively toward other boys. By the age of 6 or 7, many boys have as little as possible to do with girls at school despite the efforts of schoolteachers in coeducational schools to integrate activities. If given a choice, girls are less exclusive. To what extent is this selectivity determined by parental expectation and approval? The evidence is that adult pressures are not nearly as strong as the children's response in this case, suggesting that a predisposition may exist. Certainly, similar patterns are evident in some other species of primates indicating an independence from human cultural forces. We do not know whether testosterone, either prenatally or concurrently, predisposes boys to associate selectively with other boys, but by its effect on rough-and-tumble play should lead boys in this direction. Thus, there is some reason to think that here again we have a synchrony between biological and experiential forces in the shaping of differences between the sexes.

The developmental effects of the self-segregation of the sexes from age 6 on is likely to be enormous, although we have no way of testing this speculation. For the likelihood that the two sexes will acquire different behavior patterns and cognitive styles by learning, imitation, and identification are maximized by such segregation. It seems possible that this developmental process functions together wth other determinants to ensure enough differentiation of behavior so that procreation of the species will be guaranteed.

SUMMARY

It is not sufficiently recognized that sexual and parental behaviors, as well as aggression, begin in childhood and even in infancy. The fact that these behaviors can be evoked years before they are needed for their biological roles in reproduction and defense raises many questions about the developmental role of early experiences that elicit these behaviors. We need to know much more about the processes underlying the early origins of individual adult characteristics in the areas of sex, aggression, and parenting.

Elements of these three behaviors tend to occur together or in alternation much of the time, particularly in childhood, but can occur in relatively "pure" sequences under certain conditions. Direct observations of children reveal the occurrence of masturbatory and other sexual activity, including typical orgasms, well before the age of 3 and at less than a year in some instances. Many of the components of parental behavior can be elicited in young children of both sexes. The occurrence of a nearly full range of maternal behaviors in nursing infants of animal species, such as the rat, strongly suggests that their occurrence in the human is not mere imitation. The activation of the early sexual behaviors by appropriate sex hormones suggests that they involve the same neurohumoral brain circuitry as underlies adult sexual behavior. However, early sexual behavior at first may be elicited by a wide variety of stimuli and does not frequently progress to the adult consequences of intercourse and orgasm. Early aggression and parenting require quite specific eliciting stimuli, but are often incompletely integrated and rarely fully expressed.

Behavioral differences develop between the sexes in aggression, parenting, and other areas, as well as in specific sexual behaviors. Differences between the sexes at birth are minimal, but differences between the way parents and other adults treat boy and girl babies are clearcut from the first hours after birth onward. This difference is not simply an aspect of human cultures, because monkey parents show the same tendencies. Boy babies are generally stimulated more roughly, punished and praised more, restrained less from exploration, and prevented more often from sex-inappropriate behavior than girls, who are clasped, held, and talked to more. In addition, fathers treat sons differently than mothers do, and the same is true for daughters. These subtle interactional differences create a powerful matrix of experiences that result in the establishment of either a male or a female sense of sexual identity and a set of male or female sex-role behaviors.

The different treatment that follows sex assignment at birth is complemented by different behavioral predispositions between male and female infants that may have been caused by the organizational effects of testosterone during the fetal period of the males. The predisposition toward male roughness of play is enhanced by levels of androgenic hormones during childhood. The relative importance of androgens and of rearing experiences following sex assignment at birth, for the formation of sexual identity and sex role behavior in humans, is widely debated. Clinical case material exists which demonstrates that early rearing experience can irreversibly override chromosomal and hormonal determinants; other recent studies show the opposite can occur. Clearly, there is an important interaction and meshing of experiential and hormonal determinants in the forging of a sense of sexual identity and of sex-role behaviors in the course of human development. The tendency of young children aged 6–12 to choose playmates of the same sex is an important facilitator of sexual differentiation, for these self-segregated groups will tend to develop independently different forms of play, behavior patterns, and cognitive styles.

Thus, the establishment of individual patterns of sexual, aggressive, and parenting behavior is a complex process involving interactions between the brain and its hormonal environment during the fetal period, interactions between the infant and its parents, and between the child and its peers. All of these are intermeshed with continuing predispositions and activating effects produced by the sex hormones on these categories of behavior. The fact that most people's psychological difficulties lie predominantly with these three behaviors attests to their central position as a meeting ground for a wide variety of developmental processes and to the conflict that has been built in to the organization of each of them during evolution. This inherent conflict is the source of our extraordinary adaptability and subtlety as well as the reason for so much of our distress.

FURTHER READING

Beach, F. A. (Ed.) *Human Sexuality in Four Perspectives*. Baltimore: Johns Hopkins University Press, 1977.

Ford, C. S., and Beach, F. A. *Patterns of Sexual Behavior*. New York: Harper, 1951.

Freud, S. Infantile sexuality [1905]. In J. Strachey (Ed.), Standard Edition, Vol. 7. London: Hogarth Press, 1962. Pp. 173–206.

Hinde, R. A. *Biological Bases of Human Social Behavior*. New York: McGraw-Hill, 1974.

Kinsey, A. C., Pomeroy, W. B., and Martin, C. E. *Sexual Behavior in the Human Female*. Philadelphia: Saunders, 1953.

Kinsey, A. C., Pomeroy, W. B., and Martin, C. E. *Sexual Behavior in the Human Male*. Philadelphia: Saunders, 1948.

Maccoby, E. E., and Jacklin, C. N. *The Psychology of Sex Differences.* Vol.
1/Text. Stanford: Stanford University Press, 1974.
Money, J., and Ehrhardt, A. A. *Man and Woman, Boy and Girl.* Baltimore:
Johns Hopkins University Press, 1972.

REFERENCES CITED

1. Money, J. Childhood: the last frontier in sex research. In *The Sciences.* New
   York Academy of Science, 16:12–15, 27. 1976.
2. Kinsey, et al., op. cit., 1948, p. 177.
3. Williams, C. The ontogeny of steroid-facilitated lordosis and ear-wiggling
   in infant rats. Paper presented at Annual Meeting of the International
   Society for Developmental Psychobiology, 1979.
4. Mayer, A. D., and Rosenblatt, J. S. Ontogeny of maternal behavior in
   the laboratory rat: early origins in 18- to 27-day-old young. *Developmental
   Psychobiology*, 12:407–424, 1979.
5. Imperato-McGinley, J., Peterson, R. E., Gautier, T., and Sturla, E. Androgens and the evolution of male gender identity among male pseudo-
   hermaphrodites with 5-α-reductase deficiency. *New England Journal of Medicine*, 300:1233–1237, 1979.
6. Vom Saal, F. S., and Bronson, F. H. In utero proximity of female mouse
   fetuses to males: effect on reproductive performance during later life. *Biology of Reproduction*, 19:842–853, 1978.

Summary
and Perspective

In this concluding chapter, I will summarize the main lines of thought that run through this book, embedded within the context of the many events and interactions of our early development. Since the major points of each phase of the story are presented in the individual chapter summaries, I have not repeated them below, but instead have reviewed the themes of the book, extracting these from the narrative of observations, experiments, and inferences that constitute the body of the preceding chapters. Finally, I have carried some of these ideas and approaches further in their implications for an understanding of the development of mind from simple biological forms in early development.

BASIC QUESTIONS AND A FRAMEWORK
FOR ANSWERING THEM

This book has been concerned with the origins of human behavior and has confronted a set of related problems in thinking about this subject by focusing on early development. The story of human development from the germ cells to the young child poses basic questions about human nature with compelling simplicity. What is the relationship between the behavior of the sperm and that of the child? How does the one develop into the other? In particular, what role do the genes play, how does behavior act to shape its own development, and how do early experiences exert an effect on the kind of child that emerges? What are the early biological influences on behavior development? If the early processes are biological, at what point do psychological processes become involved? How does this transition take place, and what does it tell us about the relationship between the two frames of reference? Finally, the simple nature of our early behaviors and the characteristics of our nervous systems that we share with all animals raise the question of how our behavior is related to that of other living creatures.

Thus, the questions raised by considering our early development involve four interrelated conceptual relationships: between a cellular event and a complex behavior, between gene and environment, between biology and psychology, and between animal and human.

I have attempted to find a way toward answering these difficult questions, which are essential to understanding the roots of our behavior, by using certain approaches and lines of thinking. I have employed an historical approach based on the two great forces of biological change, evolution and development. Out of a consideration of the conservative nature of these two processes, it has become clear that more complex biological systems are built up out of simpler (or more primitive) mechanisms rather than being new designs. Looking closely at early stages and simpler animals can reveal principles that are likely to be at work in the more complex and advanced organisms.

One of the most valuable principles for understanding behavior is that it has evolved because it was useful to the organism. The goal-directed or purposeful character of behavior is a key to the nature of its organization. With these points in mind, the relationship between early and advanced developmental forms of behavior and between simpler animals and humans can be understood on the basis of the degree and kind of organization involved in their functioning. Thus, the idea of *levels* of organization is central to an understanding of the development of human behavior. In the beginning, at the germ-cell stage, the behavior of the spermatozoon is organized only at the cellular level, where the relationship between gene, behavior, and environment is presented in its simplest form. But the interaction between these three elements can be traced at later stages of development; for example, in the formation of the neural networks of the brain, in the responsiveness of the brain to stimulation or hormones, and in the interaction of the child with its parents.

No analogy does justice to the process of developmental interaction, and it must be traced in its various forms at different levels of organization from that between cells in the early formation of the brain to that between the organism and its environment, the driving force of behavioral development. It is only in the details of these various levels of interaction that the relationship becomes clear between the gene, the behavior, and the environment in the shaping of developmental outcome.

As the processes of development bring the organism to new levels of organization, new properties of behavior emerge. Built up out of behavioral processes present in previous stages, these emergent properties can be understood in terms of the interaction between simpler processes. By applying these principles, we can begin to see how we get all the way from the swimming of a spermatozoon to the spoken language of the child. The transition from biology to psychology can be traced, according to our definitions of these two words, in the development of new kinds of behavioral organization. Psychology begins when the processes inferred to underlie the behavior can no longer be expressed in biological terms. Although the dividing line is bound to be an arguable one and is certainly a creation of humans and not of nature, the emergent property of consciousness remains virtually entirely within the psychological realm.

Thus, the framework for answering basic questions about the roots of our behavior consists of:

1. An historical approach, both in terms of the two processes—evolution and development—and also in the telling of the story of our early development, event by event.
2. The approach of trying to understand behavior in terms of its organization, emphasizing the goal-directed basis of behavior and the concept of new properties emerging at new levels of behavior organization.
3. The detailed analysis of the processes of developmental interaction as a key to understanding the many transitions and immense changes wrought by development.
4. The experimental analysis of simpler systems in other animals in order to discern basic principles of behavior organization and basic developmental processes that are likely to be shared by human beings.

MAJOR THEMES

One of the major themes of this book has been the new research that shows how biological development is profoundly influenced by experiences the young have during the early periods of their lives. These kinds of effects have usually been associated with psychology rather than biology, but the study of early development is beginning to generate principles that serve to bring the fields of biology and psychology closer together. By limiting the kinds of observations they make and the kinds of questions they ask, embryologists, evolutionary biologists, and neurophysiologists ordinarily manage to stay out of contact with developmental and experimental psychologists and psychoanalysts. This isolation of disciplines is made easier by the enormous complexity of child and adult behavior; there is enough for everybody to do without getting in each other's way. But as one begins to look at earlier and earlier stages of our behavior development, the distinctions between the different disciplines become less clear, the available observations become more limited, and the questions to be asked become fewer and clearer. Also, as the cases become simpler, so do the theories needed to account for them, and the commonality between the theoretical frameworks becomes more evident. It is the meeting of the two realms of biology and psychology in early development that makes this such an important stage for us to understand. Knowledge about this period can then serve as a foundation for moving on into any one of the various approaches to the study and treatment of children and adults.

Another major aim of this book has been to present a clear alternative to the nature–nurture or gene–environment controversy that has fueled argument in political and ideological camps as well as in the sheltered halls of universities. New information on the role of the environment at the chemical and cellular levels of organization begins to clarify the many steps between the biochemical template of the gene and the patterned movements of the infant. The changing interaction of the organism with its environment is the key to understanding the process of development; in this interaction, the gene and its environment have already become inextricably linked. One of the most recent manifestations of our old difficulties with nature and nurture is the current sociobiology controversy. Greater knowledge about the detailed processes of development helps put sociobiology in perspective by casting the genes as conveyors of human potential rather than as modern-day equivalents of the Fates.

Current views on the evolution of behavior are extending our appreciation of the place of human beings in the natural world, by clarifying the continuity that exists between species in the goal-directed and adaptive character of behavior. The extension of evolutionary selection mechanisms to social behavior through kin selection theory has provided new understanding of the origins of altruism and of other complex social interaction strategies involving aggressive and reproductive behaviors. An appreciation of the evolution of the brain along a hierarchical plan, retaining the neural systems of more primitive mammals and reptiles at its base, allows new approaches to discovering how the nervous system initiates and regulates behavior. And finally, the discovery of genes that regulate the timing of development in different organ systems has provided a basis for neoteny and other alterations in schedules of development. These have profound implications for understanding how we diverged so rapidly from other primates, as well as for the apparent analogies between evolution and development.

Whereas the biological processes of cell function and of gene action within the cell are discoveries of the last generation, it has only been in the last few years that the relationship of cellular function to behaviors has begun to be understood. New knowledge has opened the way to a view of behavior as a basic phenomenon of life, retaining a common set of principles that can be observed in the behavior of a bacterium as well as of a person. Simple animals have been found to show surprisingly complicated behaviors and to have simple versions of characteristics once thought to be essentially human, such as memory, choice, and discrimination. Realization of this continuity in the nature of behavior allows us to use experiments on animals to point toward new ways of viewing and studying the development of human behavior.

Indeed, observations on animals have led us to pay much more attention to early social relationships as regulators of development, have led to the concept of attachment as a vital early motivational system, have attracted our attention to play as an essential and poorly understood phase in the development of our behavior, have laid out the processes by which sexual behavior potential is formed in fetal life, and have given us a model for the lateralized acquisition of language during childhood.

The continuity of principles in behavior development across species and the new knowledge about elementary behavior allow the construction of a general view of the biological organization of behavior, which was presented in Part I of this book. This synthesis presents an integrated view of the biology of behavior that serves to define terms and to lay out a conceptual approach for the consideration of behavior development in the ensuing chapters.

One of the most important facts about our early development is how soon we begin to behave in interesting ways. The rapid growth and variety of fetal behaviors between the seventh and seventeenth weeks of gestation clearly have been neglected by behavioral researchers and may be studied with little risk by new techniques such as ultrasound imaging. The behavior of the spermatozoon and the genetic selection capacity of the female reproductive tract is another area that seems to have great potential. Perhaps we have been limiting ourselves by focusing on behavior after birth. The importance of these early behavioral developments is suggested by new data showing the unexpected precocity of the human newborn. By the time of birth and possibly earlier, infants have been found to process visual and auditory information in ways that predispose them to attend selectively to their mother's face, to distinguish categories in human speech, and to respond selectively to its cadences. Imitation, specific recognition of the mother by olfactory cues, and a radar-like capacity have been recently found in newborns. The presence of these remarkable capacities at the time of birth makes it clear that the period *prior* to birth is when these advanced behaviors are being laid down and shaped by interactions we need to understand far better than we do at this time.

The view of the infant that emerges from recent developmental work is that of a surprisingly competent creature, preadapted to have considerable power to interact with its environment and to manipulate its caretaker by its behavior. It is able to affect its mother even during sleep by smiling and sucking and evokes a whole system of parental behavior in its caretaker through the features and rhythms of its behavior as well as through its special physical characteristics.

The parent–infant relationship is revealed in recent research as a complex environment as crucial to adequate behavioral development as the environment of the womb. We are used to thinking of development being made possible by the protective cocoon of the amniotic fluid and the uterine membranes and being regulated by the flow of blood through the umbilical cord. Now we are beginning to see that the parent–infant relationship after birth is also a powerful regulator of development, controlling such biological functions as the levels of cardiac rate and of brain enzymes as well as the development of emotionally communicative facial expressions or providing the experiences necessary for sexual, aggressive, and parenting behavior to occur normally later in life.

The way in which early experience affects the developing young to alter their behavior later in life is gradually becoming clear from research at the level of cells, hormones, and neurotransmitter molecules. The effects of the levels of stimulation imposed on the young, or gained as a result of behavior, and the impact of the discrete, contingent, and associative stimulation involved in learning are being tracked down to the cellular level where evidence suggests these three forms of stimulation may share common cellular mechanisms. Perhaps they are on a continuum and will be united by a theory based on the specification of events at synapses within the neural networks subserving behavior.

The emergence of the child comes about through periods of rapid change that produce discontinuities in development. The first of these discontinuities occurs as early as 17 weeks of gestation, when behaviors all but disappear, only to emerge in new combinations and sequences. This is understood as the result of the maturation of new neural systems, at higher levels of the neuraxis. Thus, the presence of discontinuities is not new to development in the months after birth, but it is more complicated during this period because of the interaction between neural maturation, the organizational force of learning, and the states of arousal, motivation, and emotion, which become so prominent during this period. These three organizational forces interact powerfully with each other as they drive behavior development forward in a series of rapid changes toward the emergence of a child that possesses all the major classes of adult behavior.

The development of language is a good model to illustrate the interweaving of many of the phenomena described in this book:

1. The presence of an early prototype behavior—babbling— which occurs well in advance of actual talking, but which plays an important role in the later development of language through a feedback mechanism.
2. The presence of powerful predispositions on both the motor side (to make sounds) and on the perceptual side (categorical perception of voice onset time).
3. The presence of critical periods for the effects of experience.
4. The localization of a neural substrate on one side of the brain.
5. The interweaving of predisposition, neural maturation, non-specific experience effects, specific learning and states of motivation and emotion.
6. Finally, in language development, as in so many other areas, we have learned many useful concepts from the study of an animal model, the development of bird song.

The presence of play and of early sexual, aggressive, and parenting behavior in infancy and early childhood again illustrates the occurrence of important behaviors before they have an obvious adaptive function. The frequency and complexity of these behaviors in early childhood raise the same question posed by the presence of early fetal behavior: what are they there for? In particular, we would like to know how the consequences of their expression affect later development. Clinical knowledge suggests that early experience with these behaviors may be very important in the development of a full and happy adult life, and indeed patients' most serious difficulties tend to center in the areas of sex, aggression, and parenting. An appreciation of the nature of the earliest forms of these behaviors is thus an important emphasis of the last two chapters of this book.

In addition, there is a general perspective or approach (on which this book is based) that I would like to make more explicit: namely, that we are *participants* in the very phenomenon we are trying to understand and not simply observers. I have emphasized our reluctance to accept the evidence on the evolution of behavior, our great difficulties with the concept of interaction in development, our emotional preoccupation with the newborn, our neglect of the fetus, our ignorance of the sperm's behavior, our prejudices about children's early sexuality, and against using data from animals to help understand our own nature. These are not simply intellectual problems but represent the force of our emotional needs as participants interfering with an objective assessment of human nature, as observers.

But this role as participant is not simply a liability, standing in the way of appreciating our real nature. It is also a source of intuitive hunches, new ideas, and the ability to put ourselves in somebody else's place, to reach a small way into their minds. It is a crucial part of being a good investigator as well as a good clinician. Thus, we need to cultivate both modes of functions, to realize the assets and liabilities of each, and above all to realize when we are functioning in one mode or the other.

The roles of participant and observer and the subject of our mental perspective on human nature lead to the question of what implications all this work on early behavior may have for the development of mind.

A DEVELOPMENTAL PERSPECTIVE ON MIND

Since this is a book about our origins, it crosses great distances in time and great differences in form. It is very difficult to comprehend the relationship between the behavior of a spermatozoon swimming upstream and that of a 4-year-old child playing with a doll. No matter how well we understand the sperm, the principles learned will not be sufficient to understand the child. But if this is so, what do we make of the continuity between them? This question is related to another difficult one: what are the essential differences between a human, and a monkey or a rat, or a bacterium?

The answer to these questions seems to lie in the concept of organization and in the presence in nature of a hierarchical structure of levels of organization. Behavior is a central element in all organized systems and we recognize this by using the word freely in our ordinary speech to apply to the actions of molecules (and even of subatomic particles) as well as of adult humans. This is not just a metaphorical use of the term, because several of the features of behavior as we know it in animals are present in chemical reactions. Here again, what differentiates the levels of behavior is the complexity of its organization. The structures mediating behavior become increasingly complex as we move from single-celled to multi-celled organisms and on to human beings. But it is at first hard to accept that an increase in complexity of organization can make all the difference between a human being in the spermatozoon stage and one in the adult stage. Even the phrase "human being in the spermatozoon stage" has an odd ring to it. In the same way, something inside us insists that there is an *essential* difference between a human being and a rat.

The key to the nature of differences produced by ascending levels of organization is the concept of emergent properties. To take an example from physics, the property of electrical conductivity in a copper wire emerges from the organization of the copper crystal lattice of the metal and the electrons moving within it. The property is not possessed by the copper atoms of which the wire is composed. This concept, as applied to the organization of behavior, is one of the central threads running through this book. Sleep–wake states, adaptive behavior, long-term memory, and language are examples of such emergent properties of progressive organization in human development. New behavioral properties emerge as the organization of the growing fetus becomes more complex. These new behaviors are made possible by progress in organization of the neural structures and the neurohumoral connections that gradually become functional during development. But the equipment is shaped by its function and by the interaction of the behaving organism with the environment. Thus, the increasingly complex organization that makes possible the emergent properties of the child's behavior is forged through an immensely complex set of interactions that occur throughout development at all levels of organization.

Studies of bacteria are useful because they are simple enough for us to see how the property of memory can emerge from an organization of chemical reactions. At another level, studies on young birds are useful because they are simple enough for us to begin to see how social attachment emerges out of repeated perceptual-motor interactions. These examples are not replicas of human memory or love, but they are conceptual models to be used in attempting to understand how the more complex organizations of human memory and love may be put together. Because evolution and development build up more complex organizations out of earlier structures, these simpler processes are not abandoned, but rather are used as building blocks.

Thus, the strategy of this book has been to try to understand human behavior by working from the simple and the early toward the more complex functions of later development. The usefulness of the strategy is based on the fact that the simpler processes, being building blocks, continue to operate in the more complex behavioral organizations of later life and thus provide a conceptual grip on at least part of what goes on in the most complex behaviors.

The search for simple instances of emergent properties leads to the use of words such as "purposeful," "anticipatory," or "discriminating" to refer to the behavior of very simple organisms and simple stages in our own development. Such words suggest to us the presence of some conscious, subjective self, because when we behave in similar ways, we have this inner experience. Likewise, inferring certain motivational or emotional states in very young infants or in lower animals, by using such words as "hunger" or "fear" seems unjustified if we imply, by them, the presence of inner experience similar to our own. In order to avoid such connotations, we may substitute such words as "goal-directed" for "purposeful," "precursor" for "anticipatory," and "behavioral predispositions" for "motives" and "emotions." What we gain in clarity of thinking, we lose in perspective. For it is the relationship of the simple behaviors to our own complicated situation that gives us our chance to understand ourselves through an understanding of our evolutionary and developmental roots.

The inner experiences of purpose, anticipation, hunger, and fear are themselves emergent properties, although we have as yet no model for understanding how they derive from the network of cells that make up our brains. They add an element to human behavior that may or may not be unique. Certainly the capacity to describe them in abstract language seems to be unique. But having this property does *not* mean that our behavior isn't made up of the simpler building blocks present in fetal life. Thus, although our mind's inner awareness has emerged like foliage on a tree, our roots are still firmly in the ground of simpler biological processes.

One of the most useful clarifications in thinking about the nature of mind was made by the philosopher Gilbert Ryle 30 years ago. He argued persuasively that we often make a "category mistake" when we speak of mind and matter as alternative or cooperative causes of behavior. He described this as an implicit metaphor of "a ghost harnessed to a machine." Instead, according to Ryle, mind is a different logical type from matter. He used a number of analogies to illustrate this point, one of them being that of the foreign visitor to Oxford or Cambridge who was shown the libraries, dormitories, playing fields, laboratories, and administrative offices. The visitor then asks, "but where is the university?" Ryle pointed out that too often we think of minds as extra centers of causal processes, the way the foreign visitor expected to find an extra building called the university. Instead, the mind is in a different logical category from the neural structures of the brain, the way the university is in a different logical category from its buildings. What then is this other logical category to which mind belongs? Ryle did not attempt a complete answer to this question, but in terms of the ideas used in this book the answer may lie in an appreciation of mind as inherent in the organization of behavior, much the way the concept of a university depends on the organization of the buildings and their occupants.

Thus, the mind of one animal or human is different from the mind of another insofar as the organization of their behaviors is different. Increasing levels of organization of behavior from the single-celled bacterium or spermatozoon to the human child brings with it certain emergent properties at each level. The rapid development of these properties of behavior organization constitutes the emergence of the child as described in Part IV, with the appearance of advanced cognitive capacities and states, verbal language, play, and the complex motivated behaviors of sex, aggression, and parenting. The gradual attainment of a full range of consciousness with inner awareness of the mind's workings as well as of the outside world is an integral part of the emergence of the child's level of behavior organization and eventually will be understood in this context.

FURTHER READING

Pribram, K. H., and Gill, M. M. *Freud's "Project" Re-assessed.* New York: Basic Books, 1976.
Ryle, G. *The Concept of Mind.* New York: Barnes and Noble, 1950.
Sinnott, E. W. *Cell and Psyche: The Biology of Purpose.* New York: Harper, 1950.

Glossary

Action Potential (Spike Potential, Nerve Impulse) The electrochemical signal conducted along nerve axons to their terminals. It is a sudden, localized wave of reversal in the usual electrical potential difference across the cell membrane. When it reaches the terminal region of the axon, it initiates the process of synaptic transmission.

Active Sleep See *REM Sleep*.

Activity The property of originating action. The movement may be of ions, as in the nerve impulse, or of the whole organism, through activity of individual muscles.

Adrenalin See *Epinephrine*.

Adrenergic Usually applied to a synapse, neuron, or group of neurons that characteristically release noradrenalin or adrenalin as neurotransmitters.

Affective Behavior A form of communicative behavior that conveys information on the individual's emotional state and *affects* the emotional states of others. Facial expression, posture, tone of voice, and certain gestures express subtle aspects of inner feeling in humans as well as basic needs, wishes, and fears.

Afferent Direction of flow of nerve impulses *toward* a center of reference, usually the central nervous system. Opposite direction from *efferent*.

Altruistic Behavior A sequence or pattern of actions that have the immediate consequence of benefiting another individual or group, even at considerable immediate cost or risk to the initiator. The long-term consequences of altruistic behavior can be to increase the survival and reproductive capacity of individuals who share the same genes, thus spreading genes for altruism in the community. This evolutionary mechanism is one of the foundations of social behavior.

Amphetamine A drug that affects behavior by its action at adrenergic synapses to produce a hyperalert state. In high doses it produces a temporary psychosis.

Androgens   The term for a class of steroid hormones characteristically produced by cells in the testes of males. Testosterone and dihydro-testosterone are two androgens of major importance mentioned in this book.

Arousal   A process by which a system of nerve cells is brought into a state of increased responsiveness and/or an organism is brought into a state of increased wakefulness, vigilance, and excitability. Arousal states range from the stages of sleep to maximum irritability. The concept must be applied carefully, for organisms are not homogeneous in this dimension and certain systems may be highly aroused while others are relatively quiescent.

Associative Learning (Classical or *Pavlovian Conditioning)*   A type of learning that takes place when two stimuli repeatedly occur in close temporal contiguity. Classically, one stimulus is relatively neutral, serving as a signal, and the other is a powerful physiological event (e.g., food or painful stimulation); the organism comes to respond to the signal alone as if it were the event. This process tends to take place to some extent between any two repeatedly paired stimuli.

Atrophy   A wasting away due to imperfect nerve, hormone, or nutrient supply.

Axon   The extension of the nerve cell that carries the nerve impulse. Structurally, an axon usually is much longer, more slowly tapering, and has fewer branches than a dendrite. Sometimes called a *nerve fiber.*

Behavior   A course of action. Primarily applied to living organisms to denote observable processes by which an animal responds to its environment or changes its internal state. Elementary behavior consists of simple units such as reflex acts and fixed-action patterns. Complex behaviors consist of more extended and highly organized sequences or "programs." Secondarily applied to the units from which organisms are made, e.g., the *behavior* of organs and cells, molecules and atomic particles.

Cholinergic   Usually applied to a synapse, neuron, or group of neurons that characteristically release acetylcholine as a neurotransmitter.

Chromosomal Sex   The determination of the sex of an individual according to whether the sex chromosome pair within cells sampled from the body contain two identical X chromosomes (female) or two chromosomes with different appearances, an X and a Y chromosome (male).

Circadian Rhythm   A cycle of waxing and waning in the frequency, intensity, or level of a physiological function or behavior that recurs about every 24 hours. The timing is often imprecise and can be set or entrained by naturally occurring daily events such as sunrise.

Classical Conditioning   See *Associative Learning.*

Consciousness   The awareness of thoughts, memories, feelings, and perceptions. A private, inner experience that fluctuates over a wide range of intensity and quality both within and between individuals.

Consummatory Act or *Behavior*   The termination of a behavioral sequence or pattern, usually stereotyped in form and involving the achievement of a biological goal.

Consummatory Stimuli   The last stimuli encountered in a complex behavior pattern. They serve as cues eliciting and guiding the terminal or consummatory act.

Demasculinize   With reference to hormones and behavior, to prevent the formation of neural substrates for male sexual behavior by elimination of testosterone, or blocking its effects, in the late fetal period. Feminization is probably an additional distinct effect.

Dendrites   Extensions of nerve cells that serve as the major receptive area. Rapidly branching and tapering, the dendrites form a pattern similar to the branches of a tree, extending out from the body of the nerve cell. Known collectively as *dendritic arborization.*

Dendritic Spines   Very short, twiglike extensions protruding at right angles from the branches of dendrites. They serve to expand the receptive area and allow for more synaptic connections.

Depolarize   To decrease the electrical potential difference between two points, usually across the membrane of a nerve cell. With increasing depolarization, the membrane becomes more sensitive as the threshold for triggering an action potential is approached.

Deprivation Dwarfism   A clinical term for infants and children from disturbed families who are far behind their age group in height and weight, who have endocrine abnormalities such as low levels of growth hormone, and who respond with rapid growth, not simply to enhanced nutrition, but particularly to a close relationship with a caretaker.

Efferent   See *Afferent.*

Endocrine System   A regulatory control system consisting of glands that secrete hormones into the bloodstream, thus affecting distant organs and functions, including the brain and behavior.

Endogenous Smile A stereotyped facial expression of the newborn period arising out of a substate of REM sleep during which the eyes are open. Not a response to the environment, but one of the spontaneous events characteristic of REM sleep during this stage of development.

Enthalpy Energy in the form of heat that can be either released or stored by chemical reactions. Spontaneous chemical reactions usually result in states of decreased enthalpy, through the release of heat energy.

Entropy The degree of disorder in any system. Spontaneous chemical reactions always result in states of increased entropy because of the fragmentation of molecular structures involved.

Epigenetic Applied to the stepwise nature of development whereby new characteristics are brought into being serially as the result of the repeated interactions of the organism with its environment. This principle of development is to be contrasted with early *preformationist* theories, which held that all future characteristics were present in the germ cells and that development consisted merely in their unfolding.

Epinephrine (Adrenalin) A hormone produced by the central portion of the adrenal gland, and a neurotransmitter of some adrenergic synapses in the brain and throughout the body.

Equilibrium A state of balance between forces. In chemical reactions, equilibrium exists when forward and reverse reactions are equally rapid and no net change occurs in reactants or products.

Estrogens One of two major classes of hormones characteristically produced by the ovaries and consisting primarily of estradiol, estrone, and estriol. The other class produced by the ovaries are the progestogens, primarily progesterone.

Excitation The release of potential energy built into a system leading to a change in state. An excitatory neuron is one that tends to trigger an action potential in the neuron with which it synapses. In the whole organism, the change in state is toward arousal. Excitation of an inhibitory system within the brain can lead to immobility.

Facilitation The process by which a response to stimulation is promoted or made easier. At the synapse, facilitation involves membrane changes that do not in themselves transmit nerve impulses, but allow passage of impulses that would ordinarily fail to cross the junction. At the behavioral level, sometimes used synonymously with *sensitization*.

Feedback One of the results of an ongoing event that is capable of influencing the further course of the event. In behavior, sensory stimulation resulting from a movement that is used to guide or control further movement.

Feminize With reference to hormones and behavior, to increase the readiness of the individual to respond with normal female sexual behavior in the presence of an active male. In males, depends in part on the elimination of fetal testosterone effects, but probably is an additional distinct effect.

Fixed-Action Pattern A relatively stereotyped pattern of action that is often characteristic for individual species. Composed of elementary components termed *fixed acts* and involving an assemblage of motor neurons that fire in a sequence related to the program of motor cell function rather than to characteristics of the sensory input. (The word "fixed" is not to be taken too literally since the pattern is capable of some modification as a result of experience.)

Follicle A sac of cells surrounding and contributing to the function of the specialized structure within (e.g., ovarian or hair follicles). In the ovary it is associated with nourishment of the egg and secretion of female sex hormones.

Free Running Rhythm A cycle of waxing and waning in the frequency, intensity, or level of physiological function or behavior that occurs when entraining stimuli are no longer present (e.g., during constant light or darkness). Free running cycle lengths are regular and usually longer or shorter than 24 hours.

Gender Identity; Gender Role See *Sexual Identity; Sex-Role Behavior.*

Gene A discrete region on a chromosome responsible for a specific cellular product that determines one or more hereditary traits. The basic unit of heredity.

Gustatory Applied to the sense of taste and the sensory systems involved in perception in this modality.

Habituation The process by which a response to a specific stimulus is gradually attenuated and reduced as a result of repetition of the same stimulus without affecting responses to other stimuli.

Haploid Having a chromosome complement consisting of one copy of each chromosome. In animals, the only cells that are haploid usually derive from the germinal cells of either males or females and are the units of reproduction (gametes), the sperm and the egg.

Heterochrony In developmental schedules, this means that rates of development of organs are not synchronized within each individual but are capable of separate variation. Particularly, the rate of development of a feature in descendants may be either accelerated or retarded in comparison to its schedule in ancestors (e.g., recapitulation and neoteny).

Hierarchy   A principle of organization by which certain functions or systems are subordinated to others in a ranking system, one above another in order or preference, likelihood of occurrence, or locus of control. In the organization of nervous systems, the function of lower structures such as the spinal cord and brain stem are subordinated to the control of higher centers such as the limbic system and neocortex; thus a *neural hierarchy*. In a given state of the organism, certain behaviors take preference over others while still others cannot be elicited at all; thus a *behavioral hierarchy*.

Hormone   A substance produced in one part of the body and transported to another part (usually via the bloodstream), where it exerts a specific effect on the functioning of a discrete group of cells.

Hyperpolarize   To increase the electrical potential difference between two points, usually across the membrane of a nerve cell. With increasing hyperpolarization, the membrane becomes progressively more refractory as the stimulus required to trigger an action potential becomes greater.

Identification   A complex psychological process by which a person takes on certain characteristics of another, more or less permanently and usually without self-awareness. Based on concepts of inner representation and intrapsychic conflict, identification can involve perception and emotion as well as behavior.

Imitation   The performance of specific actions that are modeled on those performed by another individual.

Imprinting   The rapid acquisition of a long-lasting response, characteristically occurring only in early postnatal development and not requiring any obvious rewards to maintain the response. Usually applied to the tendency of young ducklings, geese, and sheep to follow the first moving object they encounter during a period of hours after birth and to continue to maintain a strong social attachment to that particular object for many months or even years thereafter.

Inhibition   The suppression of one activity by another, leading to a change in state. An inhibitory neuron is one that tends to prevent action potentials in the neuron with which it synapses. In the whole organism, the change in state is toward immobility. Inhibition of an inhibitory system within the brain can lead to arousal.

Instrumental Learning (Operant Conditioning) A type of learning that takes place when an action is instrumental in producing a rewarding effect. The contingency is between an action and the reward that follows. The organism comes to produce more frequently the action that results in reward *(reinforcement)*.

Integration The process of putting parts together to make a whole. In terms of brain and behavior, the coordination of part processes (e.g., sensory and motor systems) into a function that has properties of flexibility and is suited to the situation in which it occurs. Integration is the basis for the adaptive character of behavior.

Interneuron A nerve cell that connects two other nerve cells rather than being sensory or motor in function.

Ion An atom with electrons added or removed, giving it a negative or positive electrical charge.

Ion Channel A passageway through the cell membrane for the transport of ions and small molecules.

Kin Selection An evolutionary selection process by which genes are increased in a population due to behavior of individuals that favors (or limits) the survival and reproduction of relatives who possess the same genes by common descent.

Learning The modification of behavioral responses through experience with certain patterns of environmental cues and with the relationships between actions and their results. *Habituation* and *sensitization* are relatively simple forms, while *associative learning* and *instrumental learning* are more complex. *Imprinting* is another form of learning characteristic of special situations.

Limbic System A set of interconnected structures lying at the base of the highest integrative centers of the brain, the neocortex. This system is thought to organize emotional and complex motivational states involved with sexual and aggressive behavior.

Membrane of Cell The outer envelope of the cell composed of lipids and proteins and containing the molecular machinery by which cells communicate with one another. The outer surface is studded with elongated molecular chains (glycoproteins and glycolipids) protruding like antennae into the intercellular space. Those molecules provide specific recognition sites and act as receptors for certain hormones. The inner component of the membrane, facing the cell cytoplasm, is made up of mixed lipids and contains many kinds of specialized molecular machinery (e.g., pumps and receptors). Membranes are not static structures; lipid and protein molecules can move rapidly throughout, and the components are being constantly renewed.

Mind   The system of functions that is responsible for the integration of behavior with the environment and with the internal state of the individual; it provides organization for the inner events of consciousness.

Moro Reflex (Neonatal Startle Response)   A stereotyped behavior of the newborn period consisting of a sudden outward and forward reaching of both arms, accompanied by extension of the fingers. Occurs both spontaneously and in response to startling stimulation.

Mosaic Evolution   The concept that evolutionary pressures can act separately on different organ systems, shaping them individually through alterations of their particular developmental schedules. See also *Heterochrony*.

Motivation   The changing tendency of an individual to behave in a selective, organized way. *Motivational states* are generally involved in regulation of the internal environment, such as hunger and thirst.

Myogenic Response   A muscle contraction occurring prior to innervation or in muscles deprived of all neural connections and structures; a spontaneous chemical reaction, as occurs in the "pacemaker" area of heart muscle.

Neocortex   The most recent of the major brain areas in evolutionary terms, forming the outer and topmost layers; site of the highest integrative functions.

Neonatal   Newborn; a designation that covers the first month after birth.

Neonatal Startle Response   See *Moro Reflex*.

Neoteny   The retention of formerly juvenile characters by adult descendants; produced by retardation of development. Also known as *paedomorphosis*.

Nerve Impulse   See *Action Potential*.

Neuron   A nerve cell; the basic unit of the nervous system in all animals. A form of cell with long, branching processes, specialized to generate electrochemical signals that pass to other neurons or effector cells.

Neurotransmitters   Small molecules, such as acetylcholine, norepinephrine, dopamine, and serotonin, that are secreted by the axon terminal of one nerve and then bound by the receptors of another nerve, thus transmitting a signal across the synaptic cleft.

Norepinephrine (Noradrenalin) The major neurotransmitter of the sympathetic autonomic nervous system throughout the body and of adrenergic nerve cells in the brain.

Olfactory Applied to the sense of smell and the sensory systems involved in perception in this modality.

Operant Conditioning See *Instrumental Learning.*

Oscillator A cell or system of cells that functions in a regularly recurring fashion so as to produce a predictable alternation in states, as in the generation of respiratory movements.

Paedomorphosis See *Neoteny.*

Pavlovian Conditioning See *Associative Learning.*

Phasic Brief and transitory. A term for the relative duration of an effect, one that is contrasted with more sustained, *tonic* effects.

Placing Reflex Part of the behavioral sequence of nursing in the newborn: opening and closing of the mouth to grasp a stimulus touching the lips, normally the nipple.

Preformationist See *Epigenetic.*

Presynaptic Terminal A specialized region at the tip of an axon that contacts the receptive surface of other cells transmitting the nerve impulses by chemical (or electrical) means.

Progestogens See *Estrogens.*

Psyche From the Greek word for breath; denotes that which gives life, soul, or spirit to the body (*soma*). Hence its use to refer to mind and to processes (e.g., *psych*ological) that are inferred in order to deal with behavior and inner experience that cannot be understood in terms of known biological events.

Reafference The provision of a source of neural input directly from active motor pathways to sensory relay centers over special pathways within the central nervous system. Provides a more direct and faster feedback than the usual pathway from muscle and tendon spindles and from the sensory consequences of actions. It is not yet clear how extensive reafferent activity may be within the brain.

Recapitulation The repetition of formerly adult stages in the juvenile stages of descendants; produced by acceleration of development.

Receptivity   The property of being able to convert information from the environment into a form that is available for integration with neural activity into some form of coordinated behavior.

Receptor   A specialized structure that selectively takes in certain features of its immediate environment and converts this event into a change in its state. Membrane receptors bind hormones and neurotransmitter molecules leading to changes in membrane and cellular function. In nerve cells and cell systems, receptors convert environmental stimulation into nerve impulses.

Redundancy   Information in excess of that necessary to convey an intended meaning. In neurophysiology, redundant systems are assemblages of neurons that are involved in mediating a certain behavioral response, but are in excess of the minimal equipment necessary. These systems serve confirmatory sensory functions and provide relief or backup motor capability that gives the organism a functional reserve—in effect a guarantee that essential behaviors will be carried out.

Reflex Act   The simplest unit of behavior, denoting a graded response to sensory stimulation. Requires, as a minimum, only a sensory and a motor neuron. More complex, *reflex patterns* are made up of elementary reflex acts. The form and duration of the response are related to the amplitude and pattern of sensory input, rather than to the program of motor cell function as in the fixed-action pattern.

Regulatory Gene   A gene that turns on or off the action of other genes (structural genes), controlling the synthesis of protein for building parts of the body. In this way, regulatory genes are thought to play a role in regulating developmental schedules.

Reinforcement   In learning theory, any event following a response that increases the probability of the response being made again in the same setting.

REM Sleep (Rapid Eye Movement or Active Sleep)   One of the two major sleep states, characterized by flurries of eye movements; fast, low-amplitude brain waves (EEG); and low or absent muscle tone (EMG). Irregular respiration, frequent muscular twitches, and flurries of change in visceral function controlled by the autonomic nervous system earn this stage of sleep the seemingly paradoxical term, *active sleep*. This state is associated with particularly vivid dreams, and can be distinguished from the awake state by the unresponsiveness of the individual to its environment and the very low muscle tone.

Rhythm   In biological terminology, a recurrent pattern in the frequency, intensity, or level of a physiological function or behavior.

Ribosome   A structure within the cytoplasm of a cell that is the site of protein synthesis.

RNA (Ribonucleic Acid)   A constituent of the nucleus of a cell used in the copying of genetic information from the genes and in the translation of this information into the protein structure synthesized by the cells. *Messenger RNA* is a disposable copy of one of the strands of DNA, and *transfer RNA* accepts specific, activated amino acids and adds them to a growing polypeptide chain for the eventual construction of complex protein molecules.

Rooting Reflex   Part of the behavioral sequence of nursing in the newborn: a turning of the head and nosing into a source of stimulation on the cheek or side of the face.

Schema   A modifiable plan or form of organization within sensory and motor systems that allows an organism to select certain information from its environment (*sensory schema*) and to have available a suitable plan of action with which to respond (*motor schema*). "Schema" is a term at the interface of biological and psychological terminology. It refers to a functional arrangement of neurons that embodies a neural representation of the past experience of the species and of the individual. This neural plan results in certain sensory and motor predispositions that can be built up into strategies or programs of more complex behaviors, and finally into what we call knowledge and abstract thought. (The Latin plural form *schemata* is replaced by the simpler form, *schemas*, in this book.)

Sensitization   The process by which responsiveness is increased as a result of prior stimulation. Sometimes used synonymously with *facilitation*.

Sex Assignment   The designation of a newborn baby as either male or female, usually on the basis of the external genitalia. More complex criteria, such as chromosomal typing, are increasingly being used in those few cases that are ambiguous.

Sex-Role Behavior (Gender Role)   Behavior that characteristically differentiates the two sexes in a given social group or culture. It generally is congruent with chromosomal sex and sex assignment at birth, but may be at variance with these, in rare instances.

Sexual Identity (Gender Identity)   An inner conviction of belonging to one or the other sex, arising from a complex developmental interaction, usually but not necessarily corresponding to chromosomal sex, sex assignment at birth, and sex-role behavior. Any of these may, in rare instances, be at variance with the person's inner experience of sexual identity.

Slow-Wave Sleep   One of the two major sleep states, characterized by slow, high-amplitude brain waves (EEG); muscle tone (EMG) sufficient to maintain posture against gravity; regular respiration; and absence of flurries of eye movements seen in REM sleep. Partially organized movements, such as changes in posture, occur intermittently. Dreams in this state tend to be less elaborate and detailed. Sleep-walking and night terrors originate from this state.

Sociobiology   The study of animal societies, particularly the evolutionary origins of social behavior.

Soma   From the Greek word for body; denotes the body of an organism in contrast to the germ cells, which have a different number of chromosomes (see *Haploid*). Also used in contrast to *psyche* to refer to bodily (*somatic*) functions, which can be understood in terms of known biological events.

Spike Potential   See *Action Potential*.

Startle Response, Neonatal   See *"Moro" Reflex*.

State   A temporary configuration of internal conditions within the individual that predispose to certain patterns of behavior and perception.

Stato-Kinetic Response   The repeated stepping reflex elicited by pressure on the bottom of the foot in the newborn that forms the basis for walking at this age.

Synapse   The site of nerve-cell interaction. A functional connection established by contact or near contact of membranes and differentiation of special membrane properties on both sides of the junction (e.g., terminal, vesicles, receptors).

Synaptic Cleft   A space or potential space forming a functional connection between two nerves (or between nerve cells and muscle or specialized receptors). Chemical transmission of the nerve impulse is accomplished by the action of a neurotransmitter across this cleft.

Synaptic Depression   The process by which nerve-impulse traffic across a synapse is impeded or prevented. For example, the cellular mechanism for habituation may involve either a decrease in neurotransmitter release, a decrease in sensitivity of the postsynaptic receptors, or both.

Synaptic Transmission   The process by which the nerve impulse is passed from one nerve to the next across the synaptic cleft. The action potential in one nerve triggers the release of neurotransmitter molecules into the synaptic cleft, which are then bound by receptors on the next nerve membrane and initiate an action potential in that nerve.

Tonic   Sustained and continuous functioning. A term for the relative duration of an effect, one that is contrasted with more transitory, *phasic* effects.

Tonic Neck Reflex   A postural reflex of early infancy elicited by turning of the head and neck to either side. A persistent extension of the arm and leg occurs on the side toward which the head turns, and flexion of the limbs on the opposite side.

Transcription   The process whereby genetic information contained in the chemical structure of DNA is used to arrange RNA molecules so that they can in turn carry the specific information necessary for the assembly of particular proteins by the cells.

Transduction   The action of changing one form of energy into another. Elements of the nervous system, such as specialized sensory receptors, convert energy from the environment into patterns of nerve impulses. The brain as a whole converts information from the environment into behavior and physiological adjustments.

Trophic Factor   A growth-maintaining or -promoting substance (released, for example, during nerve-cell activity) that can act to maintain the integrity of receptors and other nerve cells with which the cell is connected.

Vestibular   Applied to the sensory system that maintains balance and by which motion of the individual in space is detected.

Voluntary   Usually applied to behavior that is initiated by an individual on the basis of higher integrative functioning, involving prior experience and the weighing of predicted outcomes, rather than on the basis of the immediate demands of the current situation. Voluntary behavior gives the appearance of being spontaneous and may involve the inner experience of being willful, as distinct from reflex or involuntary responses, which depend to a far greater extent on the properties of immediate sensory stimulation.

Index

Acetylcholinesterase, 82, 174
Action potentials, 26–35 *passim*, 58, 67, 95–96
Active sleep: *See* Rapid-eye-movement sleep
Activity, 25–31, 46
Adaptive behavior, 19, 41, 57, 60–67, 302, 305
of fetuses, 107
of infants, 116–117, 127, 134–136, 239, 240
and integration, 34–38, 63, 66–67
and play, 272, 273
Adrenal corticoids, 165, 166, 190
Adrenergic neurons, 154
Adult behaviors, 235, 272–279, 282–286
Affective behaviors, 123–125, 249–250
See also Crying; Facial expressions
Aggressive behavior, 202, 247, 281–283, 290–291, 305–306
Alcohol, 95, 189
Altruistic behavior, 19–22, 302
Amnesia, infantile, 243–246
Amphetamine, 245
Amphibians, 93, 94, 100, 140, 151, 153
Androgens, 166, 167, 168, 169, 289–293
See also Testosterone
Anoxia, 99
Anticipation, 26, 93–94, 101, 199–200
Aplysia (sea snail), 46–47, 49–51, 58
Approach, 124, 125, 199–203 *passim*, 250
Arborization, dendritic, 147–148, 171, 174–175
Aromatization, 167
Arousal, 55–56, 58–59, 216–221, 228, 246–250
See also Rapid-eye-movement sleep; Slow-wave sleep
Associative learning, 67, 199, 239, 240, 241, 242
Ataxia, 187
Atrophy, 158
Attachment, 141, 198–204, 303, 307–308
Auditory system, 32, 96, 119, 185–186, 304
and language, 119, 227–228, 260–269 *passim*, 304
Avoidance, 124, 125, 200–204 *passim*, 250
Axons, 147–150, 152–153, 154

Babbling, 261, 263–265, 305
Bacteria, 42–45, 52, 53, 67, 307
Bantus, 268
BARCROFT, J., 99
BEACH, F. A., 286
Bees, 21
Behavioral sequences, 47–49, 56
BELL, R. Q., 128
BENNETT, E. L., 172
BERKSON, G., 218
BINDRA, D., 66
Biobehavioral shifts: *See* Discontinuities
Biological determinism, 19
Birds, 94–95, 140, 141, 185–186
attachment among, 141, 198–199, 200–202, 203, 204, 307–308
auditory systems of, 185–186, 266, 267, 268–269
song development of, 265–269, 305
Birth, 110–111, 193, 194–195, 286–287, 304
Blindness, 119, 121, 161, 174, 214–216
Blood flow, 190–191
Bones, fetal, 95, 105–106
BOWER, T. G. R., 119, 120, 140
BOWLBY, J., 209
Brain, 5, 12–14, 106–107, 147, 157–177, 300, 302
and anoxia, 99
birth and, 110–111
and blood flow, 190–191
and breathing, 62, 63, 64
drugs and, 161, 188–190
and epigenetic landscape, 251–254
hemispheric differences of, 69–71, 263, 266, 267
hierarchy in, 52–53, 302
hormones and, 38, 164–169, 181, 190, 222–223
and learning, 52, 157–158, 174, 241–242
and neoteny, 15
and social relationships, 200–201, 217, 218, 222–223
and states, 63–64, 103, 217, 218
Breathing, 60–64, 92–93, 102, 103–104
BUFFON, G. L., 7
BUTLER, S. R., 222

CAMPBELL, B. A., 241
Canaries, 266, 267, 268
Cardinals, 268
Cats, 51–52, 100, 153–154
    fur color of, 10
    and play, 275–276, 277, 279
    and social relationships, 201
    visual system of, 135, 158, 160–161, 162, 163, 276, 277
Cell level (general), 3, 10–11, 25–28 *passim*, 143–144, 300, 304
    See also Neurons
Cell membranes, 29–30, 31–32, 35, 58, 67, 149
Cell migration, 147–150
Cell recognition, 147
Chemical reactions, 26–28, 29, 30, 31, 45, 307
CHESS, S., 256
Chicks, 94–95
Childhood, 235–296, 305, 309
    See also Infants
Chimpanzees, 14, 15–16, 69, 260
Cholinergic systems, 82, 154, 174, 176
Chromosomal sex, 79–81, 82, 181–182
Circadian rhythm, 29
Circulatory system, 37–38, 111, 187
Classical conditioning: *See* Associative learning
COHEN, J., 83
Comparative method, 7, 14
Consciousness, 2, 8, 67–72, 301, 309
Constraints, developmental, 250–252, 256, 263
Consummatory behavior, 58–59, 65–66, 247–248
Consummatory stimuli, 59
Cooing, 261, 263
Coordination, of activity, 30–31
Cost–benefit ratio, and altruism, 20–21
CRAIN, S. M., 93
Crying, 102, 115, 123–124, 261, 263

DARWIN, C., 9, 11, 17, 87
DAWKINS, R., 21
Deafness, 260, 263–265, 266, 267, 268, 269
Defenses, psychological, 59
Demasculinization, 180–182, 292–293
Dendrites, 147–150, 160, 166, 168, 171, 174–175
Dendritic arborization, 147–148, 171, 174–175
Depolarization, 35
Deprivation dwarfism, 222–223
Developmental constraints, 250–252, 256, 263
Dihydrotestosterone, 289
Diploid organisms, 77

Discontinuities, 97–100, 235, 253, 255–256, 305
DNA, 10, 35, 170, 174
Dogs, 100
    amnesia in, 245
    brain development of, 160
    and play, 279
    and social relationships, 198, 204, 217
Dopamine, 189
Doves, 268
Drives, 25, 54–55, 201
Drugs, 149, 161, 187–190
Ducks, 186, 200–201, 202, 204
Dwarfism, deprivation, 222–223

Ears: *See* Auditory system
Eating behavior, 65–66
Echoes, 119
Efferent nerves, 64–65
Eggs, 42, 77–79, 83, 84
Ejaculation, 284
EKMAN, P., 249
Electrophysiology, 58, 94, 102–104, 252–254
Embryology, 6, 75, 87, 90, 153, 250–251
Embryos, 87–90, 94
    See also Fetuses
EMDE, R. N., 124, 253–254
Emotional states, 57, 59–60, 123–125, 179–180, 181, 246–250, 254
    and brain hemispheres, 70
    and social relationships, 197, 216–221, 228
    See also Affective behaviors
Endocrine system, 38, 181, 183
Endogenous smiles, 124–125
Enthalpy, 26–27
Entropy, 26–27
Environment, 4–5, 26, 28, 143–230, 237–238, 300
    birth and, 111
    fetuses and, 107, 179–191
    vs. genes (controversy), 10–12, 17–19, 81–82, 144–145, 149, 302
    infants and, 114, 115, 116, 123, 125
    and integration, 38
    and receptivity, 31–32
    See also Learning
Enzymes, 67, 87
    and brain development, 174
    and integration, 35
    and receptivity, 31
    and rhythms, 29–30
    and sexuality, 289
    and social relationships, 222–223
Epigenetic development, 97, 150, 250–254
Epinephrine, 165, 181, 190, 245
Equilibrium, 27, 29, 57
Erections, penile, 112–113, 285

ERIKSON, E., 2.
Estradiol, 168
Estrogens:
  and brain devel   167–168
  and maternal bel   96
  and sexual behavi   292, 293, 294
  and sperm transpc
Evolution, 4–23 *passi,*   1, 87, 206,
  302–303
Excitation, 37, 100
Eyeblink response, 118
  See also Rapid-eye-mov   leep;
    Visual system

Facial expressions:
  of fetuses, 92, 99, 102, 105, 215
  of infants, 112, 114, 123, 124–125,
    136–138, 140, 214–216, 249–250,
    277–278
  and social relationships, 214–216
Facilitation, 49, 99, 135
  See also Sensitization
FANTZ, R. L., 118
Fear, 201–202, 203, 250
Feedback, 29, 30, 38, 64–65, 135, 256
Feminization, 180–182, 292–293
Feral children, 206–207, 208–209, 214,
  260, 263
Fetuses, 6, 52–53, 75, 87–108, 143–144,
  179–191, 237, 303
  and brain development, 52–53, 99,
    164–165, 167–168, 170–171, 188–191
  breathing by, 60, 93, 103–104
  crying by, 261
  and epigenetic landscape, 250–251
  and states, 54, 100–105, 179–180
Fish, 100, 151
Fixed-action patterns, 5–6, 31, 41, 46–47,
  63–64
  and hierarchy, 52–53, 63
  sucking and, 248
Follicles, 77
FORD, C. S., 286
FRAIBERG, S., 216
Free running rhythms, 56
FREUD, S., 4, 16, 243, 244, 255, 281
Frogs, 140, 153
Function, 151–153, 157, 158, 160

Game theory, 22
GAZZANIGA, M. S., 69
Geese, 140, 141, 198
Genes, 4–5, 77–79, 81
  and altruism, 20–22
  vs. environment (controversy), 10–12,
    17–19, 81–82, 144–145, 149, 302
  female-tract selection of, 81–82, 83–84,
    303
  regulatory, 11, 15–17, 87, 302–303

Genitalia, 168, 182, 286–287, 289, 290
GESELL, A., 105
GINSBERG, B. E., 11, 18
Goal-directedness, 47, 57, 64, 300, 301
  evolution and, 17–19, 22, 41, 302
  integration and, 35
  in nursing, 126, 274
  play and, 273, 274
  of single-celled organisms, 42–43
GOULD, S. J., 16, 87
Grasping reflex, 52, 92, 105, 120–121
Growth, 38, 166, 222–223
Growth cone, 148–149
Guinea pigs, 90
Gulls, 186
GUNTHER, M., 127

Habits, 9, 11
Habituation, 49–52, 107, 132–133, 217,
  239, 240–242
HALDANE, J. B. S., 20
Haloperidol, 189
HAMILTON, W. D., 20
Haploid organisms, 77, 82
HARLOW, H. F., 208, 210
Heart beat, 88–89, 143, 223–224
HEIN, A., 135, 139, 275–276, 277
HELD, R., 275–276, 277
Hemispheres, brain, 69–71, 263, 266, 267
Heterochrony, 16–17, 255
Hierarchy, 52–53, 63–64, 107, 302, 307
HINDE, R. A., 205
Histamine, 83
Histoire Naturelle de L'Homme (Buffon), 7
Historical approach, 4–5, 19, 301
HOFFMAN, H. S., 200, 202
HOOKER, D., 90–91
Hormones, 304
  and brain development, 38, 164–169,
    181, 190, 222–223
  and integration, 37–38
  and memory, 245
  and social relationships, 196–197, 222,
    225
  See also Sex hormones
HUBEL, D. H., 160
HUMPHREY, T., 90–91
Hunger, 66, 114–115, 124, 247–248
  See also Nutrition
Hyperactivity, 172
Hyperpolarization, 35

Identification, 138
Imitation, 136–138, 140, 304
Imprinting, 141, 198–204, 303, 307–308
Individuality, 11, 17–18, 127–128
Infantile amnesia, 243–246
Infants, 52, 53, 75–76, 101–102, 110–142,
  143, 304

Infants *(continued)*
  and aggressive behavior, 282–283,
    290–291, 305–306
  and brain development, 157–158,
    160–163, 166
  breathing by, 60–61, 93, 102
  and language, 119, 227–228, 261–269 *pas-*
    sim, 304, 305
  learning by, 124, 132–136, 140, 157–158,
    198–199, 237–256 *passim*
  and parenting behavior, 283, 286,
    305–306
  play by, 277–278, 290–291
  and sexual behavior, 282, 283–285, 286,
    305–306
  and social relationships, 123–125, 138,
    193–230, 287–289, 290–291, 304
Inhibition, 106, 135
  in breathing, 62
  and discontinuities, 97–100
  and hierarchy, 53
  and integration, 35, 37
  and reaching, 121
  and statokinetic reflex, 122
Instincts, 9, 17, 54, 277
Institutionalization, 207–208, 210, 264
Instrumental learning, 67, 240, 241, 242
Insulin, 171–172
Integration, 34–38, 46, 63, 66–67
  in fetuses, 105–107
  in infants, 140
  play and, 274
Intensity, of emotion, 125
Interactions, 143–230, 235–238, 300, 301,
  305
  See also Environment
Ion channels, 35
Ions, 29, 31, 35
Isolation, 206–209, 210, 214, 217, 275
  and language, 260, 263, 264, 268
  and sleep deprivation, 247

Jacklin, C. N., 287
Jackson, H., 255
Joints, fetal, 94–95, 189
Jung, C. G., 16

Kandel, E. R., 46–47, 49–50
Kin selection, 20–21, 302
Kinsey, A. C., 284, 285
Koshland, D. E., 42–44, 67
Kuhn, C. M., 222

Lactose, 35
Lamarck, J. B., 183
Language, 260–270, 303, 305
  brain hemispheres and, 70
  chimpanzees and, 69

infants and, 119, 227–228, 261–269 *pas-*
  sim, 304, 305
Learning, 9, 11, 17, 49–52, 67, 174
  by infants, 124, 132–136, 140, 157–158,
    198–199, 237–256 *passim*
  and play, 277
  and prenatal stress, 180
  by single-celled organisms, 43–44, 45, 307
Leeches, 30–31
Leshner, A., 38
Limbic system, 12, 13
Lipsitt, L. P., 127
Lobsters, 10

Maccoby, E. E., 287
MacFarlane, A., 119
MacLean, P. D., 13
Marler, P., 265
Martin, C. E., 284
Mason, W. A., 218
Masturbation, 283, 284
Maternal behavior, 194–197, 281, 286
Measurements, physiological, 57–58, 94,
  100, 102–104, 252–254
Melzack, R., 217, 220
Membranes, cell, 29–30, 31–32, 35, 58, 67,
  149
Memory, 49, 51, 67, 135, 239
  and amnesia, 243–246
  and epigenetic landscape, 251–252
  of single-celled organisms, 43–44, 307
  and sleep, 247
Menstrual cycles, 77–79, 166
Messenger RNA, 10, 35, 165
Methadone, 189–190
Mice, 11, 18, 95, 180
  brain development of, 160
  and prenatal nutrition, 187
  and sexuality, 293
  and sleep, 247
  and social relationships, 211–212, 225,
    247
Mind, 2, 138–141, 239, 306–309
Molecule level (general), 3, 10–11,
  25–28 *passim*, 143–144, 304
Money, J., 289, 290
Monkeys:
  amnesia in, 245
  and brain development, 160–161, 163,
    168, 176
  and sexual behavior, 287, 291
  social relationships of, 195, 197, 198,
    205–220 *passim*, 274–275
Moro startle response, 112, 113, 114, 115,
  118
Mosaic evolution, 16–17, 255
Motivation, 54–55, 56–57, 59–60, 66,
  246–250

Motor schemas, 66–67, 140, 141, 173, 174, 199
Mouthing:
  by fetuses, 91, 95
  by newborns, 112, 113
Multiplier effect, 238
Muscles, 25–26, 28–29, 90–106 *passim*, 151–152, 224
Myogenic response, 90

Natural selection, 12, 17
Neocortex, 12
Neonatal experience: *See* Newborns
Neoteny, 14–17, 206, 303
Nerve cells: *See* Neurons
Nerve fibers (axons), 147–150, 152–153, 154
Nerve growth factor, 151
Nerve impulses, 26–35 *passim*, 58, 67, 95–96
Neural regeneration, 67
Neurons, 5, 25–35 *passim*, 58, 95–96, 105, 144–177 *passim*
  in epigenetic landscape, 251–252
  and fixed-action pattern, 46
  and habituation, 51–52
  and integration, 35–37, 67
  and sensitization, 51–52
Neurotransmitters, 154, 304
  and brain development, 159, 161, 164, 171–172, 174, 190
  and integration, 35–37
  and sperm, 82, 83
Newborns, 52, 53, 75–76, 93, 110–129, 304
  and language, 119, 261, 262, 304
  sex assignment to, 286–287
  and social relationships, 193, 194–197, 304
Newspaper chemistry, 26–27
Norepinephrine, 181, 190
NOTTEBOHM, F., 267
Nursing, of infants, 125–127, 193, 198, 248, 274
Nutrition, 65–66, 114–115, 169–172, 187, 224, 248

Object permanence, 254
Olfaction, 119–120, 139–140, 186, 196, 224–225, 304
Olfactory bulb, 12
Operant conditioning, 67, 240, 241, 242
Orangutans, 14
Organism level (general), 3, 25, 28, 143–144
Organization:
  behavioral, 6, 41–73, 107, 112–117, 139, 300–309 *passim*

biological, 2–4, 7–8, 25, 28, 143–144, 300, 307, 309
  neural, 52–53, 64, 107, 147–177, 302, 307
Organ level (general), 3, 25, 28, 41, 143–144
Orgasms, 284
Origin of Species (Darwin), 9
Oscillators, 46
Oxytocin, 83

Paedomorphosis, 14–17, 206, 303
Palate, fetal, 95
PAPOUSEK, H., 132, 228
Parent–child relationships, 123–125, 138, 193–230, 287–289, 290–291, 304
Parenting behavior, 194–197, 281–282, 283, 286, 305–306
Pavlovian conditioning: *See* Associative learning
Penile erections, 112–113, 285
Peptide hormones, 165
Perception, of speech, 119, 227, 262, 304
  See also Auditory system; Visual system
PETTIGREW, J. D., 162
Phenylketonuria, 187
Pheromones, 224–225
Physiological measurements, 57–58, 94, 100, 102–104, 252–254
PIAGET, J., 4, 240, 243, 255
Placing reflex, 124, 126
Plasticity, 67, 101, 135, 158, 241, 277
Play, 272–279, 281, 282, 290–291, 303, 305–306
  affective behavior and, 123
  imitation and, 138
  schemas and, 139
  sexual behavior and, 275, 277, 282, 285, 294
POMEROY, W. B., 284
Postures, 104–106
POWERS, W. T., 66
Presynaptic terminal, 35, 51
Primates, nonhuman, 14, 195, 197, 201, 211, 279
  See also Chimpanzees; Monkeys
Problem solving, 132–136, 140
  See also Learning
Progesterone, 83
Programs (sequences of behavior), 47–49
Prostaglandins, 83
Psyche, 1–2, 4, 138–141, 225–229, 306–309
Psychological defenses, 59
Puberty, 77
  hormones and, 166, 168, 169, 289–290, 291–292
  and language, 262–263

Puberty *(continued)*
    and social relationships, 225
Purposefulness: *See* Goal-directedness

Quiet sleep: *See* Slow-wave sleep

Rabbits, 96
Rapid-eye-movement (REM) sleep, 55, 247
    fetuses and, 101, 102, 103–104
    infants and, 101, 112, 114, 116–117,
        124–125, 215, 247
Rats, 152, 154, 180–181, 183
    amnesia in, 245
    and brain development, 166, 171, 172,
        173–176, 189
    and learning, 17, 132, 241–242, 277
    and play, 275, 277
    sexual behavior of, 180–181, 182, 275,
        277, 286
    social relationships of, 195–196, 197,
        211–212, 219–220, 222–223, 225, 275
    and sucking, 248
Reaching, 52, 120–121, 238
Reafference, 276
Recapitulation, 16, 87
Receptivity, 31–33, 35, 46
Receptors, 31–32
    in bacteria, 42, 45
    and brain development, 158–164,
        167–168
    for breathing, 62–63, 64
    for eating, 66
    and efferent nerves, 64–65
    of fetuses, 53, 96, 184, 186, 189
    for hormones, 38
    of infants, 53, 213–214
    and integration, 35, 37–38
    See also individual sensory systems
Reciprocal altruism, 21
Reflex acts, 3, 5–6, 41, 46–47, 63–64
    in fetuses, 52–53
    of infants, 52, 92, 104–105, 112–127 *pas-
        sim*
    of snails, 50
Regulatory genes, 11, 15–17, 87, 302–303
Reinforcement, 201
REM: *See* Rapid-eye-movement sleep
Reptiles, 12
Respiration, 60–64, 92–93, 102, 103–104
Rhythms, 28–30, 53, 56, 66
    of fetuses, 100–105
    of infants, 112–113, 123–124, 126–127,
        227–228
Ribosomes, 10
RNA, 10, 35, 165, 170, 174
Rocking, 124, 184, 218–219
Rodents, 90, 96, 182–183, 279
    See also Mice; Rats
ROFFWARG, H., 103

Rooting reflex, 52, 124, 126
ROSENBLATT, J. S., 195
ROSENZWEIG, M. R., 172
RYLE, G., 308–309

Salamanders, 152
SCHANBERG, S. M., 222
Schemas, 66–67, 135, 139–141, 249
    and brain organization, 173, 174
    and social relationships, 199, 228–229
Sea snail *Aplysia*, 46–47, 49–51, 58
Selfish behaviors, 21–22
Sensitization, 49–52, 107, 239, 240,
    241–242
Sensory schemas, 66–67, 135, 141, 173,
    174, 199
Separation distress, 199–200, 219–220
Serotonin, 171–172
Sex assignment, 286–287, 289–290
Sex hormones, 83–84, 165, 166–169,
    180–183, 283–284, 286
    See also Androgens; Estrogens
Sex-role behavior, 287–291, 294
Sexual behavior, 180–183, 244, 281–296,
    303, 305–306
    and brain organization, 169
    hormones and, 38, 169, 180–183,
        283–284, 286, 289–293, 294
    and play, 275, 277, 282, 285, 294
Sexual identity, 289–290
Sheep, 93, 99, 103–104, 185
Shellfish, 10, 46–47, 49–51, 58, 240
Single-celled organisms, 29, 250
    See also Bacteria; Eggs; Sperm
Sleep: *See* Rapid-eye-movement sleep;
    Slow-wave sleep
Slow-wave sleep, 55, 112, 114, 115, 116,
    247
Smiling, 112, 114, 124–125, 140, 215,
    277–278
Snail, sea *(Aplysia)*, 46–47, 49–51, 58
Social relationships, 123–125, 139–140,
    193–230, 247, 304
    altruistic, 19–22, 302
    and attachment, 141, 198–204, 303,
        307–308
    imitation and, 138
    and play, 123, 138, 139, 274–275, 282,
        294, 303
    and sexual behavior, 275, 282, 287–289,
        290–291, 293–294
Sociobiology, 7, 9, 20, 302
Soma, 1–2
Sparrows, 266–267, 268
Sperm, 42–43, 44–45, 75, 79–84, 300, 303
SPERRY, R. W., 69, 70, 71
Spindle organs, 64
Spines, dendritic, 149, 160, 166, 168, 171
SPITZ, R. A., 208, 255

Stages, of development (general), 97, 255–256, 263
Startles, 112, 113, 114, 115, 118
States, 54–60, 63–64, 66
  fetuses and, 54, 100–105, 179–180
  and infants, 112–117, 123–125, 126, 215, 216–221, 228–229, 237–238, 246–250, 254
  and social relationships, 197, 199, 201, 215, 216–221, 228–229
Statokinetic reflex, 122
STENT, G. S., 30
STERN, D., 226–227, 228
Stranger anxiety, 254
Stress, 166, 180–181, 182–183
Strychnine, 100, 245
Sucking, 52, 53, 113, 124, 125–127, 248
Surges: *See* Discontinuities
Swaddling, 124, 221
Synapses, 3, 152, 158–171 *passim*
  and integration, 35–37
  and learning, 51, 135
  and reafference, 276
  and reflex acts, 46

Tactile sense, 50, 120, 139, 184–185, 220–221
Taste, 186
Tendons, fetal, 105–106
Testosterone:
  and aggressive behavior, 291
  and bird song, 268
  and brain development, 166, 167–168
  and sexual behavior, 180–182, 284, 289–293, 294
Thermostats, 66, 134–135
THOMAS, A., 256
THOMPSON, R. F., 51
Thyroid hormone, 37–38, 165–166, 190
Timing, developmental, 255
  and language, 262–265
  and nutrition, 170

and states, 54, 55–56
  See also Rhythms
TOBACH, E., 250
Tonic neck reflex, 104–105
Transcription, 10
Transduction, 32
Transfer RNA, 10
Transsynaptic effects, 158–159, 164
Trophic factors, 95–96, 151
Tryptophan, 171–172
TURKEWITZ, G., 119
Typhoid bacillus, 42–44, 67

Ulcers, 183
Unity, of nature, 5

Vestibular sense, 96, 113, 124, 184–185, 218–219
Visual system, 135, 140, 276
  and brain development, 159, 160–163, 174
  of fetuses, 96, 105, 186
  of newborns, 116, 117–119, 121, 304
  and social relationships, 200–201, 214–216
  See also Rapid-eye-movement sleep
Vocalizations:
  by birds, 199, 265–269, 305
  by infants, 102, 115, 123–124, 137–138, 261, 263–265, 305
Voluntary behavior, 64, 123
Vulnerability, sex differences and, 288

WADDINGTON, C. H., 250–251
Waking REM states, 124–125
Walking, 52, 120, 122–123, 237–238
Warmth, 124, 219–220
WERNER, H., 255
WIESEL, T. N., 160
WOLFF, P. H., 113

ZELAZO, P. R., 122